D0546637

THE JOB TRAINING
CHARADE

THE
JOB TRAINING
CHARADE

Gordon Lafer

CORNELL UNIVERSITY PRESS

ITHACA AND LONDON

The bibliography for this book appears at the website
www.cornellpress.cornell.edu/cornellpress/cup3_go.taf?t=3785.

First published 2002 by Cornell University Press

Printed in the United States of America

Library of Congress Cataloging-in-Publication Data
Lafer, Gordon.
  The job training charade / Gordon Lafer.
    p. cm.
Includes bibliographical references and index.
  ISBN 0-8014-3964-7 (cloth : alk. paper)
  1. Occupational training—Government policy—United
States—Evaluation. I. Title.
  HD5715.2 .L33 2002
  331.25'92'0973—dc21   2001008387

Cornell University Press strives to use environmentally
responsible suppliers and materials to the fullest extent
possible in the publishing of its books. Such materials
include vegetable-based, low-VOC inks and acid-free papers
that are recycled, totally chlorine-free, or partly composed
of nonwood fibers. For further information, visit our website
at www.cornellpress.cornell.edu.

Cloth printing   10 9 8 7 6 5 4 3 2 1

For my parents,
Fred and Barbara Lafer

Proceeds from the sale of this book will go to the Federation of University Employees Strike Fund, HERE, Yale University, and the Royal Lahaina Hotel Strike Fund, ILWU Local 142, Maui, Hawai'i.

CONTENTS

ACKNOWLEDGMENTS

My research on job training began while I was a Ph.D. candidate in the Yale University political science department. I am indebted to Adolph Reed and Rogers Smith, both formerly of that department. They not only provided important guidance early in the project, but also, each in his own way, provided a role model proving that it is possible to be an academic and still act with integrity and relevance in the world.

This book is largely about power. More than anything I read in archives, I learned about power from the labor unions at Yale University. While I was researching and writing this book, we were on strike five different times. Throughout these struggles, the union members at Yale opened my eyes to a true understanding of how power functions, and showed me the meaning of courage and of honor. I will always be grateful to Local 34 and Local 35 of the Hotel Employees and Restaurant Employees International Union, and particularly to Lucille Dickess, Laura Smith, Tommy Gaudioso, and especially Bobby Proto, for the chance to work together in such a worthwhile cause.

Above all, my graduate education was shaped by my fellow organizers in the Graduate Employees and Students Organization at Yale, which one day will be legally recognized as the union of Yale graduate teachers. I will always be grateful to them for showing me how to make intellectual life matter in the real world, and for the gift of comradeship which overcame the ugliness we all had to endure from the Yale administration. The strikes at Yale changed many of us, and one of the most fortunate changes was to forge bonds that I believe will last as long as we do. I'm particularly thankful to the GESO staff organizers I was privileged to work with: Eve Weinbaum, Nikhil Singh, Ivana Krajcinovic, Kathy

Newman, Traci Ardren, Michele Janette, Tamara Joseph, Corey Robin, Robin Brown, Wendi Walsh, and David Sanders.

I must also thank the International Longshore and Warehouse Union, and particularly ILWU Local 142 president Bo Lapenia, for the opportunity to be part of the fight for justice for Hawai'i hotel workers. My work with the ILWU would not have been possible or worthwhile without the support and friendship of Maui Division Mobilizer Leonard Nakoa.

During the course of writing this book, I have benefited from the unending support, insightful discussion, and lifegiving friendship of Hillary Kunins, Michael Berkowitz, Joel Westheimer, Barbara Leckie, Noah Efron, Eve Weinbaum, Jonathan Stein, Greg Grandin, Pete Hallward, Diana Paton, K. G. Bina, Andy Spitz, Derek Spitz, Reuven Kleinman, Don Rauf, Rachelle Abrahami, Eric Wittstein, Delia Rickard, and Alisa Klein.

At the University of Oregon, I have found a remarkable home in the Labor Education and Research Center. I am grateful to my colleagues—Bob Bussel, Barbara Byrd, Steven Deutsch, Lynn Feekin, Steve Hecker, and Marcus Widenor, and particularly former LERC Director Margaret Hallock—for the support that enabled me to complete this project. I have also benefited from the insight of colleagues in the broader University of Oregon community, especially Sandi Morgen and Gerry Berk.

Pamela Burdman provided crucial editing assistance, and Philip Palaveev provided valuable research assistance. I am indebted to Gordon Fisher of the U.S. Department of Health and Human Services for sharing his unpublished writings on the history of the poverty line, and to numerous economists at the Bureau of Labor Statistics for their generous response to a long list of queries.

Research for this book was supported in part by grants from the Economic Policy Institute and the University of Oregon's Wayne Morse Center for Law and Politics. In addition, I wrote several chapters while a fellow in residence at the Westheimer Center for Excellence in Higher Education.

At Cornell University Press, Fran Benson was a dream editor. Her enthusiasm and commitment were instrumental to making the book possible, and her critiques have greatly improved the finished product.

This book is dedicated to my parents, Fred and Barbara Lafer, who not only provided constant support and encouragement, but who also instilled in me the most basic values of fairness and equality, and who taught me the importance of community service and social action through the examples of their own lives.

Finally, I thank Rachel Kirtner, not only for her contributions to this book but also for all the pleasures of going through life with her: her intelligence and humor, her courage and generosity, her comradeship in the heat of battle. Her fury at injustice burns as bright as anyone I know, and she has the talent to do something about it. I look forward to her coming adventures as much as the bosses must dread them, if only they knew.

THE JOB TRAINING CHARADE

Introduction

Training without job opportunities for those trained is a con game. . . .
Manpower reform that does not include job creation is not manpower
reform at all. It serves no real purpose other than to fool the public and
frustrate the unemployed.

—AFL-CIO spokesperson Kenneth Young[1]

It is ironic that . . . so many educators . . . are seeking new methods to
instill middle class values in Negro youth. . . . It was precisely when
young Negroes threw off their middle class values that they made an
historic social contribution . . . when they put careers and wealth in a
secondary role . . . [and] cheerfully became jailbirds and troublemakers.

—Martin Luther King, Jr.[2]

For the past twenty years, one of the most popular prescriptions of
economic policy makers has been the call for American workers to improve the
skills and education they bring to the labor market. As manufacturing employees compete with low-wage workers abroad, as the nation's older cities confront
seemingly intractable poverty rates, and as families across the country contend
with layoffs and downsizing, politicians of both parties have increasingly focused
on job training as the path to renewed prosperity.

This book provides the first comprehensive critique of the history, track
record, and economic assumptions underlying this policy. Ultimately, the book
focuses on two questions: How was job training catapulted from being a minor
backwater of federal employment policy to becoming the government's primary
labor market policy for improving the employment and earnings of low-income
Americans? And why has job training retained such broad political popularity
despite widespread evidence of its economic failure?

The promotion of job training as a central response to unemployment and
poverty is a relatively new phenomenon. In the 1960s and 1970s, training

constituted a small component of federal employment policy, with far greater effort devoted to creating new jobs. With the passage of the Job Training Partnership Act (JTPA) in 1982, however, the administration of President Ronald Reagan explicitly replaced job *creation* with job *training* as the focus of federal employment policy. In the years that followed, Republicans and Democrats have argued over the size of the training budget and the appropriate content of training programs; however, the general focus on training as the government's primary labor market policy has enjoyed wide bipartisan support.

The consensus behind training as a solution to economic distress is captured in a *New York Times* editorial issued as a call to action during the 1992 presidential campaign. After noting the dramatic increase in income inequality over the course of the 1980s, the *Times* offered the following analysis:

> Economists are increasingly persuaded that this rising inequality cannot be explained by something as simple as greed [or] politics. . . . They look to something more deeply ingrained in modern industrialized economies—call it technology for short. The days when high school dropouts could earn high wages in manufacturing are gone. Modern economies more than ever require educated, skilled labor. . . . The modern industrial economy is calling out for skilled, educated workers. . . . The right way for Congress to respond is to promote the education of sophisticated workers. That means massive new commitments to . . . training high school dropouts and welfare mothers.[3]

The *Times*'s analysis embodies three fundamental assumptions that have underlain job training policy for the past twenty years. First, that there is an ample supply of decently paying jobs in the economy, if only everyone were adequately trained to fill them. Second, that the wages workers earn are primarily determined by the skills they bring to a job. And third, that both the cause of poverty and its solution are fundamentally nonpolitical: the root of income inequality lies in the impersonal progress of technology, a dynamic neither created by nor responsive to political argument.

It is this apolitical status which above all sets job training apart from other employment policies. If poverty stems from inadequate wages or race discrimination, for instance, its solution will inevitably entail a political conflict between the interests of workers and those of employers. However, if poverty stems from a "mismatch" in which workers are unemployed because they lack skills and firms are understaffed because they lack skilled workers, then there is a technocratic solution to poverty which serves everyone's interests. The focus on job training, therefore, embodies the unlikely hope that poverty can be ended without conflict.

This book challenges all of these assumptions. The chapters that follow address both the empirical economic claims of job training advocates and the political dynamics that, I believe, account for the enduring popularity of job training policy in the face of its apparent failure.

Are There Enough Jobs?

In chapter 1, I examine the relationship between labor supply and demand. The assumption that jobs are available for everyone who needs them—if only everyone were sufficiently skilled—lies at the heart of training policy. Beginning with President Reagan, federal officials have consistently asserted that much or all of the unemployment problem reflects a skills mismatch rather than a shortage of jobs. In fact, however, all available evidence points to the opposite conclusion. For interesting historical reasons, the U.S. Department of Labor has long avoided collecting the type of statistics which would make it easy to compare the number of job openings available with the number of people in need of work. As a result, economists have been forced to rely on a series of indirect and proxy measurements in order to estimate the relationship between the supply and demand for jobs.

For the first time in the course of the mismatch debate, this book introduces a new methodology that moves beyond proxy measures to directly compare the number of Americans in need of decently paying jobs with the number of such jobs available. The results of this comparison are dramatic and disturbing. Over the period 1984 to 1996—throughout the height of the presumed skills shortage—the number of people in need of work exceeded the total number of job openings by an average of five to one. In 1996, for example, the country would have needed 14.4 million jobs in order for all low-income people to work their way out of poverty. However, there were at most 2.4 million job openings available to meet this need; of these, only 1 million were in full-time, non-managerial positions.

Since I believe the official federal definitions of poverty are unrealistically low, I have developed alternative poverty thresholds which more accurately identify the level of income needed to maintain a minimally decent standard of living. In 1996, this alternative threshold equaled $27,632 for a family of four. When defined as the number of jobs needed for all Americans to work their way up to this standard of living, the jobs gap is wider still. In 1996, the number of jobs needed to achieve this standard totaled 25.9 million. By contrast, there were a maximum of 2.1 million openings in such jobs; demand for decently paying jobs outstripped supply in that year by more than twelve to one.

Thus, one of the central assumptions of training policy for the past two decades turns out to be mistaken. The data presented in chapter 1 show incontrovertibly that there simply are not enough decently paying jobs for the number of people who need them—no matter how well trained they are—and thus suggest that training programs cannot hope to address more than a small fraction of the poverty problem.

The Relationship between Education and Earnings

In chapter 2 I assess the extent to which training is the appropriate policy even for those sections of the economy where job openings are available. While the data in chapter 1 indicate that there are only enough jobs for a fraction of those in need, this fraction may still represent several million people. If training is the right policy for this population, it would still constitute an important government initiative. For this to be true, it must be the case that skills and training are the key determinants of wages for entry-level workers. However, this second claim of training advocates is not substantiated by economic evidence.

Even allowing for every possible variation in the definition of "skill," there is no measure of human capital that convincingly accounts for the falling wages and growing income inequality of the past three decades. Instead, the evidence suggests that, while education and skills play a role in the determination of wages, their effect is quite limited, accounting for less than a third of the overall distribution of wages.

The most commonly cited evidence for the skills mismatch thesis is the dramatic rise in the "college premium." Many researchers have pointed to the growing gap between the wages of college-educated workers and those with only a high school diploma as evidence of the increased demand for education in the labor market. However, while the college premium points to a disturbing trend in inequality, it is irrelevant to training policy. No economist predicts that the total demand for college-educated workers will exceed 25% to 30% of the labor force at any point in the foreseeable future. Thus it is appropriate for every parent to hope that their child becomes a professional; but it is not appropriate for federal policy makers to hope that every American becomes one. Furthermore, these are not, in fact, the jobs which public training programs aim at. The relevant question for training policy is not whether poor people can become yuppies, but simply whether they can attain a modest middle-class salary. In the two-thirds of the labor market where college degrees are not required, the relationship between education and wages is extremely weak. Instead, the earnings of nonprofessional workers appear to be primarily determined by legal, institutional, and political factors such as gender, race, unionization, wage laws, and regulations governing international trade. Thus, even where jobs do exist, there is no reason to believe that training offers an effective stepping-stone out of poverty for low-income Americans.

The bottom line in assessing the demand for skills is the evidence from direct surveys of private employers. Unfortunately, while many employers complain of a shortage of skilled workers, there is little evidence that a more highly trained workforce would generate either more jobs or higher wages. When asked exactly which skills their workers lack, only an extremely small number of firms mention the type of technological competencies imagined by mismatch theorists. A larger number, but still a distinct minority, emphasize basic English and mathematic skills. By far the most common complaint of employers focuses not on any traditionally defined skill at all, but rather on workers' discipline, punctuality, loyalty, and "work ethic." However, it is unclear that punctuality and discipline can accurately be termed "skills": they may constitute acquired habits, but they are also in large part commitments which one chooses to offer or withhold on the basis of the wages and conditions provided. To the extent that employers are simply paying too little to get the work commitment they desire, this is a mismatch of a different sort—and the project of solving this dilemma by "training" people to work hard at low wages seems an inappropriate agenda for federal employment policy. Moreover, the fact that millions of Americans work full-time and year-round and yet remain below the poverty line indicates that even the demonstration of a satisfactory work ethic does not guarantee one a living wage. Taken together with the evidence from economic studies of wage determinants, employer survey data suggest that even a well-designed training policy cannot hope to have more than a marginal impact on poverty; and that an anti-poverty strategy which focuses on job training is fundamentally misguided.

The Track Record of Training

Chapter 3 addresses the actual track record of JTPA and similar training programs. Given the evidence presented in chapters 1 and 2, it is unsurprising that JTPA has failed to significantly improve the employment and earnings of its participants. The primary evaluation of the program, a massive study mandated by the Department of Labor, tracked 20,000 people over a four-year period. The study examined multiple demographic groups and types of training services, comparing the employment and wages of JTPA participants with those of a control group of similar workers who were excluded from the program. For the majority of participants, the program had no statistically significant effects. For those aged sixteen to twenty-one, the program actually had negative effects, with JTPA trainees earning less than the control group. The largest earnings gains were realized by adult women. Yet even this most successful group achieved extremely modest improvements compared with the program's goals. Measured against the official poverty line for a family of three, the control group of women who were excluded from JTPA earned 46.9% of the poverty line; yet the program's participants earned only 54% of the poverty line.[4] These results are in keeping with studies of similar programs, which have generally reported small or insignificant effects. It is unsurprising, then, that the program completely failed in its goal of reducing welfare dependency: compared with the level of income needed to earn one's way out of poverty, even the most successful group of trainees experienced negligible increases in earnings.

It might be argued that the failures of JTPA and other training programs reflect the inevitable incompetence or inefficiency of government-run programs. However, federal training programs are not operated primarily by public agencies, but rather by a network of contractors including private for-profit organizations. Moreover, there is no evidence that the proprietary training schools which operate wholly outside the federal training system have achieved greater improvements in the employment and wages of low-income workers. There are of course better- and worse-run programs. But the shortcomings reported in the Department of Labor study, combining results from multiple sites across the country and tracing outcomes over a four-year period, do not stem from administrative shortcomings. Rather, they reflect structural economic barriers which limit the effectiveness of even the best-run training program. Indeed, results from a wide range of training programs serving teenagers, dislocated workers, and welfare recipients all point to the same conclusion as the JTPA study, namely that programs have at best a modest effect on earnings and virtually no impact on poverty.

Training for High Performance

In chapter 4 I examine working conditions in a range of manufacturing and service industries, in order to gauge the true demand for skills through firsthand accounts of working life. As layoffs, relocation, and downsizing have come to impact a broader swath of the economy, job training has been promoted for a growing share of middle-income workers who have lost jobs to foreign trade, technological change, or corporate restructuring. Unlike welfare recipients, these workers generally possess long histories of regular work; thus training policy does not focus on equipping them with the "skills" of punctuality or discipline.

However, no less than for entry-level workers, training providers are unable to point to any specific technical skills for which there is significant excess demand or to identify any specific occupations which promise large numbers of well-paying jobs for the recently laid off. Instead, training for more experienced workers has focused increasingly on the "soft skills" of teamwork, cooperation, and flexibility. Many scholars have characterized the emerging growth industries as harbingers of an "information" or "knowledge" economy in which general "thinking skills" are increasingly demanded of all workers. Both public sector policy analysts and private sector management gurus have touted the concept of "total quality" or "high performance" firms in which every worker's input is essential to the production process. In this view, training has become more important than ever, in two ways. First, employers now demand a qualitatively higher order of skills—not only manual or technical skills, but also the foresight to anticipate bottlenecks, the confidence to suggest more efficient work methods, and the creativity to design product innovations that help the company maintain its competitive edge. Second, because successful companies need the input of every worker, competition is forcing employers to become less hierarchical and more democratic. In this view, well-trained workers can now look forward not only to high wages but also to a hitherto unimaginable degree of freedom and self-actualization on the job. Thus, at exactly the point when downward mobility threatens a broader range of workers, and when traditional skills-training strategies seem to have reached a dead end, a new type of training is being promoted which promises even greater rewards than its predecessors.

By analyzing worksite reports across several sectors of the economy, I assess the claims of "empowerment" boosters, finding scant evidence of a more emancipated work life even at those companies touted as "high performance" models. With few exceptions, reengineered corporations have provided neither the incomes nor the autonomy their champions promise. On the contrary, new developments in technology and organization have often been used to lay off workers, limit wages among the remaining labor force, and exert heightened control over employees' daily activities. Most important, the evidence suggests that firms may successfully meet the goals of "total quality" and "flexible production" without requiring significantly increased skills or granting workers increased freedom. Indeed, many successful firms appear to have used the "empowerment" process to encourage greater work effort and expanded responsibilities without corresponding wage increases; in this sense, the strategy has served to weaken rather than strengthen the link between workers' abilities and earnings. Thus the "high performance" thesis—the most ambitious formulation of the skills mismatch argument—appears incapable of providing a new rationale for training policy. Despite the millennial rhetoric, it remains the case that for the vast majority of the labor market, skills are critical neither for the expansion of firms nor for the earnings of workers.

Why Training? The Political Logic of JTPA

If training represents neither an urgent need of business nor an effective strategy for poor people, why has the policy enjoyed such widespread and long-lasting support? The answer to this question is the subject of chapter 5. I argue that the legislative history of JTPA indicates that the program was adopted for political rather than economic reasons. Its continued support reflects the fact that it has remained politically functional even when it has proved economically impotent.

JTPA was not simply the product of reasoned, if conservative policy analysis. Rather, it was the product of a compromise between the radical free-market orientation of the early Reagan administration and its political need to fashion some response to the unemployment crisis of the early 1980s. When President Reagan first took office, neither his administration nor the Democratic leadership in Congress held job training to be a legislative priority. As the Comprehensive Employment and Training Administration (CETA) approached its expiration date in 1982, the administration initially planned to let the program expire, without substituting any alternative effort whatsoever. By mid-year, however, national unemployment rates had topped 10%, their highest level since the Great Depression, and it became politically impossible for the government to sit back and do nothing in the face of rising joblessness.

As a response to unemployment, JTPA marked a radical break from the policies which preceded it. While there was a training component in CETA, the bulk of the program's funding was dedicated to public service employment. CETA was based on the assumption that people were out of work because there weren't enough jobs, and therefore established the government as employer of last resort. Moreover, since CETA viewed the unemployment of poor and middle-class people as stemming from essentially similar causes, the program was initially open to participants across a relatively wide portion of the economy. By contrast, JTPA was based on the conviction that the unemployment of the poor and that of the middle class were fundamentally different phenomena, and that neither required public jobs. As administration officials explained to Congress, middle-class workers were unemployed due to cyclical fluctuations in the economy; once the president's supply-side stimulants took effect, there would be plenty of jobs for them in the private sector. The problem for poor people, by contrast, was not a lack of jobs but a lack of skills. And since government jobs, according to the Republicans, sapped participants' work ethic without teaching them the real skills needed by private employers, public service jobs ended up rendering people less rather than more employable. Thus JTPA was designed as a program of short-term training, targeted strictly to welfare recipients and the long-term poor, and banning any form of public job creation.

Beyond the agenda of reconfiguring employment policy, JTPA also served important political goals for the new administration. CETA programs had been operated primarily at the municipal level, and the funds they provided were an important source of support for big-city Democratic regimes. Under JTPA, however, primary budgetary authority was placed in the hands of governors, a far more conservative and Republican-dominated level of government. In addition, while community-based organizations played a central role in CETA operations, JTPA guidelines—for the first time in the history of anti-poverty programs—established private sector business councils which were granted primary authority over local planning. Thus, many of the very organizations which had historically rallied poor communities in pursuit of progressive economic demands were now statutorily subordinated to private employers, and were forced to market themselves to business representatives in order to obtain program funds.

In this sense, job training policy has served to demobilize poor communities in both ideological and political terms. Rhetorically, the focus on training demoralized potential agitators by suggesting that the causes of their poverty lay in themselves rather than in any potential object of protest. Rather than focusing on the government's failure to provide public employment, for instance, depressed communities were encouraged to channel economic frustration into conservative self-help initiatives concentrating on "self-inflicted" causes of poverty such as teenage childbearing, drug use, and neighborhood crime. Yet while these dynamics may represent serious social problems, they do not constitute the fundamental causes of unemployment, and solving these problems without addressing the failures of the labor market will not appreciably alleviate urban poverty. To encourage people whose job opportunities are in fact restricted by external economic factors to instead understand their suffering as the result of internal social pathologies is to undermine the moral and ideological basis for political mobilization. Simultaneously, the reconfiguration of funding and authority made it more difficult for any community organization to serve as an effective vehicle for challenging a conservative business agenda. Finally, the assertion that poor people's unemployment was qualitatively different from that of working-class Americans, and the embodiment of this assertion in program guidelines and eligibility criteria, cut poor communities off from potential allies in working- and middle-class organizations—most significantly, labor unions.

As a political agenda, training appears to have been quite successful. One of the remarkable political facts of the past twenty years is that elected officials have been able to enact substantial cuts in social welfare benefits without generating any significant social upheaval. Of course, many factors contributed to this situation, and job training policy is not the most central. But by defining poverty in terms which required minimal budgetary commitments and which focused attention on the actions of poor people rather than on those of their government, training policy has played an important role in allowing officials to enact Dickensian cuts while insulating them from political backlash.

An examination of the record of congressional hearings on JTPA suggests that the legislation was driven more by these political goals than by the program's purported economic aims. Indeed, throughout the 1980s, Republican social policy was marked by a continuing contradiction between words and deeds. While administration officials declared education and training to be a central requirement for both alleviating poverty and improving the nation's international competitiveness, the programs addressing these needs were poorly designed and severely underfunded. Support for higher education was so reduced in the Reagan and Bush years that by the late 1980s the college-bound share of the population had declined for the first time in the country's history. Similarly, funding for JTPA itself belies the supposed importance of this policy. At the end of the Reagan presidency, the federal government spent $2.5 billion on JTPA, slightly less than was allocated in its first year of operation in 1984; as a result, the program ended the decade serving 100,000 fewer people than when it started, or roughly 5% of the eligible population.[5] Furthermore, the administration often appeared to be complacent in the face of evidence that the program was failing. In 1986, it was reported that the average wage for JTPA trainees placed into jobs was insufficient to raise a family of four above the poverty line. In 1989, the Senate Labor Committee reported that JTPA operators regularly "creamed" the eligible population, that 60% of JTPA on-the-job training contracts were wasted, and that one-third of the program's participants received no training whatsoever. Yet the possibility of program failure was not a cause for concern: for the first five years of JTPA's operation, the Labor Department refused to collect the follow-up data needed to determine which training models were most effective, and most program administrators had no way of knowing how many graduates were back on the unemployment line within months of completing training.[6]

Under the Clinton and George W. Bush administrations, job training has remained one of the only social policies that regularly enjoys bipartisan support, despite continuing reports of the program's anemic results. As corporate downsizing and globalization forced layoffs on middle-class employees, a growing share of training resources was earmarked for this population. While training was trumpeted as the response to a wide range of economic problems, initiatives for both welfare recipients and laid-off manufacturing employees remained severely underfunded, and the programs reported universally disappointing outcomes. Moreover, repeated reports of the program's failure seem to have had little impact on its political popularity. In the year 2000, JTPA was succeeded by the Workforce Investment Act (WIA) which, while touted by Labor Secretary Elaine Chao as "a new roadmap . . . to help us prepare the 21st century workforce," largely repeats the same strategies found to have failed under JTPA.[7]

This, then, is the character of job training policy: the crisis of underemployment has largely been met by a series of symbolic and token policies—failed programs that no one tries to reform, highly publicized initiatives which serve less than 5% of the population in need, and an endless series of "demonstration" and "pilot" programs that never turn into systemic policies.

It is clear that job training policy has met important ideological and political goals for Republican lawmakers. Yet training has also been enthusiastically endorsed by Democratic officials, at both the national and local levels. Over the past two decades, congressional Democrats consistently argued for longer-term training, increased childcare and transportation assistance, and above all, expanded funding for JTPA. Early in the debate, the Democrats seem to have conceded the basic preference for training rather than public jobs, and spent the next twenty years arguing for more and better programs within that paradigm. As it was framed in the early 1980s, the debate over employment and poverty boiled down to a disagreement as to exactly which traits of poor workers made them unemployable. Conservatives asserted that the poor suffered primarily from motivational problems, which could be cured by cutting the social benefits that undermined the work incentive. Liberals argued that poor people already wanted to work, but needed skills training before this noble desire could be realized. Thus, for many Democrats, training was promoted as the preferred option to more drastic cutbacks. The rhetoric of job training suggested a way of thinking about poverty which allowed public officials to maintain political credibility while operating within increasingly draconian budget constraints. If joblessness were defined simply as a lack of jobs, and if the government were held responsible as an employer of last resort, the poverty rates of the past twenty years would likely have toppled a host of elected officials. By promoting a view of poverty as complex and intractable, in which schools, families, drugs, crime, bigotry, lazy mothers, and absent fathers all reinforce each other in a hopelessly intertwined web of complicity, training advocates helped to radically lower the public's expectations of government. Thus it was possible for officials to portray "demonstration" programs serving less than 5% of the population in need as good-faith efforts to address a legitimately difficult problem. For different reasons, then, Democrats no less than Republicans have found job training politically functional even when it has proven economically useless.

Job Training as Political Diversion

For both public and corporate officials, job training appears to have had greater value as political symbolism than as economic policy. In the private sector, the duplicity with which corporate spokespeople sometimes deploy the skills mismatch rhetoric confirms how instrumental this notion can be in defining the poverty debate in terms which minimize corporate responsibility. At times, the use of training programs to divert attention away from corporate restructuring is crystallized within the actions of a single company. For example, shortly after defense manufacturer Pratt & Whitney announced the layoff of up to 10,000 workers, the company unveiled a Small Business Administration program to train unemployed workers to become entrepreneurs.[8] When Green Giant closed its California cannery in favor of relocation to Mexico, management offered laid-off workers training in résumé writing and language skills.[9] In 1996, while Yale University officials provoked a strike over the demand for steep wage and benefit cuts for campus dining hall workers, the school simultaneously championed its support for the "New Haven is Cooking" program, which trained welfare recipients for jobs in the food service industry.[10] Perhaps the most Orwellian such instance belongs to Chrysler, which, while laying off tens of thousands of auto workers, announced the establishment of a "robotics training program." The local media celebrated the opening in an editorial titled "Retraining Crucial to County's Hope"—despite the fact that the express purpose of robotics is to make more and more workers redundant.[11]

The use of training policy to focus political attention in benign directions is at least as important for public officials as for private employers. A year after the 1992 riots in Los Angeles, the Rebuild L.A. task force couldn't point to any new jobs created through its efforts, but could and did point to two job training programs—one of which was funded by IBM, which had recently announced plans to lay off 100,000 workers across the country.[12] Even the city of Flint, Michigan, testified on behalf of JTPA, touting the success of a program that trained teenagers in "basic 'coping' skills necessary to deal with the world of employment."[13] Given the devastation of this city (as depicted in Michael Moore's *Roger and Me*), it is hard to imagine what "coping skills" might mean in Flint, if not Valium. Yet the ability to spotlight even such a meager program as this allows elected officials to suggest that they are doing *something* to tackle the thorny problems of poverty and relieves them of responsibility for failing to take on GM or provide alternative public jobs, by implying that the intractability of poverty has more to do with the job-readiness of the population than the disappearance of their jobs.

The case of Flint illustrates the ways in which job training may function as a form of political diversion without being driven by any conscious efforts at conspiracy. I do not believe that the Flint city managers sat down to concoct a plan for misleading the public. On the contrary, I assume that many of them were genuinely moved by the plight of individuals whose lives were ruined by the GM layoffs. However, given the scarcity of resources and the need to maintain political legitimacy, training appeared as the preferred option even for those who, in their heart of hearts, might have preferred more progressive policies. In this sense, job training has emerged as something like the path of least political resistance, on which Republicans and Democrats, mayors and governors, big business and local community organizations can all come to agreement. The source of this agreement, however, lies precisely in the program's marginality and ineffectiveness: training is popular not because it meets a critical need of any constituency, but because it makes minimal demands on those in power and has little effect on reshaping the labor market.

The Strange Evolution and Enduring Utility of Job Training Policy

The evolution of job training policy over the past twenty years points to both the ultimate bankruptcy and the surprising resilience of the skills mismatch thesis. In the years since 1980, the fundamental assumptions underlying job training policy have undergone a series of metamorphoses, in which researchers disprove one version of the thesis only to find it resurrected, Hydra-like, in a new guise. The clearest instance of such revisionism concerns the central question of whether or not there is a shortage of skilled labor, and if so, how it may be observed.

In 1982, President Reagan declared that there was an immediate labor shortage, and that anyone could see it by looking at the want ads. However, as it became clear that the total number of want ads represented only a small fraction of the number of people in need of work, this argument was modified. In the mid-1980s, training advocates explained that, while labor shortages were widespread, they were not always visible, since many employers had become discouraged and stopped actively recruiting for new positions. By the late 1980s, mismatch theorists gave up declaring that a labor shortage existed at all, but they insisted that a shortage was imminent in the immediate future. As these predictions failed to materialize over the next few years, advocates moved away from projecting definite labor shortages at any point in time and asserted simply that there *would* be a shortage if employers converted to "high performance" modes of production. Finally, in the mid-1990s, as evidence mounted that relatively few firms were moving in this direction, the existence of a critical skills shortage was transformed into a strictly normative claim: that firms *should* convert to "high performance" along lines that *should* require widespread skill increases and therefore *should* lead to skills shortages. At this point, however, the only evidence for the likelihood of a significant skills shortage is the extent to which we trust that romantic economists know better than CEOs what firms' hiring practices should be. Thus training advocates have responded to contradictory evidence not by questioning their initial assumptions but by reformulating their assertions in terms that are less and less susceptible to empirical verification.

Similarly, the question of exactly which skills are in demand has undergone a radical transformation in the years since JTPA was first adopted. When the legislation was originally enacted, analysts focused on the need for training in specific technical occupations such as programming, tool and die making, or air conditioner repair. It soon became clear, however, that the excess demand for these occupations amounted to only a small fraction of the unemployed population. In the years that followed, both the scholarly work of mismatch theorists and the curricula of JTPA programs were reconstructed to de-emphasize occupation-specific skills and to focus instead on basic English and math. Finally, as employer surveys showed that few firms were overly concerned with even these academic skills, training advocates have increasingly defined the critical traits in demand as amorphous attitudinal "skills" such as punctuality, loyalty, and discipline. Whether a worker possesses discipline or a good attitude is, of course, impossible to measure in any objective way. It is even less feasible to calculate the distribution of these "skills" in the population at large, or to determine whether workers with these attributes get better jobs or higher wages than others. Thus, as in the debate concerning the evidence for skills shortages, mismatch theorists have continually reformulated the definition of skill in directions that are increasingly untestable by social science.

Finally, the question of what defines success in job training programs has been subjected to repeated revision, such that it is now often impossible to determine whether a program has attained its goals. The original intent of JTPA was clear: to increase the employment and earnings of participants. Funding would be evaluated on the basis of how well programs met those goals. However, the reality of the labor market is such that training programs had difficulty placing graduates into secure or well-paying jobs. In response, the criteria for determining success or failure were gradually reconfigured. Over time, participants came to be deemed successful as long as they landed some job at the end of the program—regardless of its duration or wages—or even if they simply went on to further training without finding a job at all.

Job Training and Welfare Reform

This evolutionary process has reached its apogee in the welfare-to-work programs enacted in the wake of the 1996 Personal Responsibility and Work Opportunity Reconciliation Act (PRWORA).[14] Chapter 6 discusses the transformations in welfare training programs effected by the abolition of the Aid to Families with Dependent Children (AFDC) program and its replacement by the stingier Temporary Assistance for Needy Families (TANF) program. For the most part, welfare-to-work programs have abandoned all pretense of training participants in any identifiable skill whatsoever. Instead, the programs assume that participants will benefit—in unspecified and unmeasured ways—from simply being required to show up on time and perform whatever menial tasks they are assigned. As one conservative scholar suggests: "We need to provide the means for [poor people] to gain the skills of employability. . . . And those skills don't have to do with rocket science; they have to do with being able to take orders and be polite to customers."[15] The flip side of a definition of training unrelated to skills is a definition of success unrelated to income. Many welfare-to-work programs have avoided establishing any meaningful criteria against which their success or failure can be measured. Rather than demanding concrete improvements in employment or earnings, for instance, welfare reform boosters increasingly insist that work is its own reward—that there is no need for program justification beyond the enhanced self-esteem workfare participants are presumed to enjoy and the improved role models they are imagined to offer their children. In this way, the success of workfare is declared by ideological fiat rather than measured by empirical testing.

On one hand, this history of constant revision points to the ultimate bankruptcy of job training ideology. At each stage of the argument, when researchers probe the claims of training policy, they find a remarkable lack of supporting evidence. Moreover, training advocates themselves have engaged repeatedly in the intellectual equivalent of a strategic retreat—abandoning previously held positions only to regroup around newer, if somewhat less plausible, means for justifying the same ends. At the same time, however, the continual reinvention of the mismatch thesis attests to the remarkable depth of its proponents' conviction that, somehow, the attributes of workers must be to blame for falling wages or rising inequality. This, indeed, is the enduring core of job training ideology. Over the past two decades, each of the key assumptions framing job training policy has been abandoned or transformed beyond recognition. Nevertheless, there is a common bond that has held together all the myriad reincarnations of mismatch theory. At the heart of this thesis—the one constant in a series of arguments that has otherwise proved almost infinitely malleable—is the conviction that poverty and unemployment must ultimately be blamed on shortcomings in American workers themselves, and that the hope of renewed prosperity lies primarily in self-improvement.

It is this core of job training ideology which also links the training programs for welfare recipients with those for more experienced workers. At first glance, these two branches of training policy appear to be fundamentally separate. Where programs for entry-level workers focus primarily on discipline, those for experienced workers stress the "higher-order thinking skills" associated with high-technology or highly participatory workplaces. In fact, however, both streams of training originate in the failure of the original JTPA conception. In the early 1980s, training boosters promoted occupation-specific skill training for both low-income and middle-income workers. As the failure of this project became evident, training curricula split into two distinct streams: discipline for the poor, and empowerment or teamwork for more experienced workers. Yet these two schools of training share something more than their common origin in a failed strategy. While the content of different types of training programs may at first seem incompatible, training for both sets of workers revolves around this central conviction of job training: that workers must look inside themselves—rather than to the government or corporations—for the solution to economic difficulties.

Power and Quiescence: The Political Function of Job Training Ideology

Over the past twenty-five years, nonprofessional workers have witnessed a slow but steady decline in real wages and benefits.[16] The same period has been marked by periodic spasms of widespread layoffs, plant closings, or corporate restructuring. Indeed, the combination of strong growth and low inflation that characterized the late-1990s boom in part reflected a profound insecurity among workers who had been conditioned to settle for flat wages even when times were good. While corporate leaders may find this anxiety useful in labor negotiations, they must be concerned about its contribution to the broader political discourse. In 1996, 30% of Americans thought that corporations bore "a lot" of the blame for layoffs; only 21% thought a lot of the fault lay with workers themselves. In households already hard hit by layoffs, fully 47% blamed corporate practices, and only 17% thought that workers had themselves to blame.[17] It is this context that lends political urgency to the mismatch debate. Training advocates speak to this same popular anxiety, but urge the opposite conclusion. Workers are encouraged not to blame corporate profits, the export of jobs abroad, or eroding wage standards—that is, anything they can *fight*—but rather to look inward for the source of their misfortune and the seeds of their resurrection.[18]

At its core, job training ideology revolves around an argument about power. The rationale for training is based in the belief that economic competition has changed such that the interests of employers and workers have come into alignment. If it is true that the selfish interest of profit-maximizing firms is served by training low-income workers for high-skill, high-wage jobs, then political power has become irrelevant to workers' economic advancement. If, on the other hand—contrary to the *New York Times*'s analysis quoted above—it remains true that "rising inequality [can] be explained by . . . greed [or] politics," then the exercise of power both in Congress and in the workplace remains critical.

I argue that the suggestion that workers can safely eschew political mobilization, trusting in the enlightened self-interest of employers as the surest path to prosperity, is fundamentally mistaken. Despite frequent assertions that the economy has entered a stage of development in which conflict has been rendered anachronistic, the evidence from economic studies, employer surveys, and workplace ethnographies alike points to continued conflicts of interest between employers, workers, and those outside the labor market hoping to get in.

Contrary to the contention that power has become irrelevant, the recent history of federal employment policy attests to the enduring centrality of political power. The structure of JTPA was crafted not by the urgent labor demands of employers, nor by the studied consensus of impartial analysts, but by the cross-currents of conflicting political interests. The details of the legislation read less like a blueprint for economic policy than a record of the wins and losses produced by the balance of political forces in effect in the early 1980s. Indeed, the history of employment legislation over the past three decades seems to have been driven primarily by shifts in power among Republicans and Democrats, and business, labor, and community groups. In 1996, a triumphant Republican Congress ushered in radical reforms in welfare and employment policy. However, the central tenets of Newt Gingrich's Contract with America and George W. Bush's "compassionate conservatism"—defederalism, privatization, block grants, vouchers, and workfare—were virtually identical to those voiced by President Reagan in the early 1980s and President Nixon a decade earlier. That the latest generation of Republican leadership achieved more of these goals than its predecessors is not due to the originality of their proposals. Rather, the steady advance of conservative policy, from CETA to JTPA to TANF and WIA, primarily reflects the weakened condition of its opponents in the liberal wing of the Democratic Party and in labor and community organizations. Thus, JTPA's legislative history not only refutes the notion of training as representing the convergence of universal interest but shows training policy to be the product of processes which are almost entirely dominated by the struggle of conflicting interests.

In this sense, the narrative thread of this book proceeds through an analysis in which job training starts out looking like a policy issue and ends up looking like a political strategy. The past twenty-five years have brought a gradual but steady decline in the real earnings of nonmanagerial workers, with a growing share of the population afflicted by economic anxiety. In this context, job training has functioned as a form of political diversion. On the simplest level, training policy has encouraged workers to channel their aspirations into educational initiatives rather than unionization drives, demands for minimum wage laws, or other collective demands for governmental action or corporate reform. On a deeper level, the assumptions underlying training policy have encouraged a popular view of the economy in which the political mobilization of workers is irrelevant at best and self-destructive at worst.

The evidence presented in the chapters that follow suggests that job training cannot possibly deliver on the promise of its proponents. If there is a hope of steering policy in a more productive direction, it must begin by contesting the assumption that political power has become irrelevant and by refocusing the debate away from training and back toward the more fundamental, if more contested, roots of poverty and unemployment.

CHAPTER ONE

How Many Jobs Are There? Labor Demand and the Limits of Training Policy

The program that we have for job training is based on something I called attention to one day. . . . I looked in the Sunday paper at the help-wanted ads . . . you count as many as 65 pages. . . . And you say, Wait a minute, you know, 9.8 percent unemployment, but here are the employers. . . . These newspaper ads convinced us that there are jobs waiting and people not trained for those jobs.

—President Ronald Reagan[1]

We're used to thinking of unemployment as a case of too many people and too few jobs. . . . In the 1990s, into the next century, our problem, our nation's problem, will be just the opposite: more than enough jobs and too few people qualified to fill them. . . . Think about it: For every child growing up today—black or white and, yes, urban or rural—there will be a job waiting. The question, our challenge, is whether they'll have the education and the skills that they need to seize that opportunity.

—President George H. W. Bush[2]

This is the story of how a sheet of classified ads has dictated federal employment policy for more than twenty years. During this time, the government has spent more than $85 billion on job training and placement programs for hundreds of thousands of low-income and unemployed workers, despite the absence of any data suggesting that jobs existed for these people. At the same time, programs that provided public jobs for nearly one million Americans have been eliminated on the assumption that they were unneeded, despite the lack of any evidence that private employers were ready to hire those displaced.

The notion that jobs are available for anyone truly ready to work, symbolized by President Reagan's want ads, became an article of faith during much of the 1980s and 1990s. But remarkably, when the president first made this point in 1982, the ads were not merely the administration's primary anecdote about employment policy: they were its data. Neither in 1982 nor at any point since has the government performed a systematic calculation comparing the number of Americans in need of jobs with the number of jobs available. Instead, policy debates for the past twenty years have been driven largely by anecdote, assumption, and ideology.

Making Sense of Unemployment

In the absence of any hard data about job availability, scholars and policy makers have largely relied on the unemployment rate to assess the relationship between the supply and the demand for jobs. It is unclear, however, what meaning should be attributed to unemployment figures. From 1980 through 1999, a period spanning two cycles of recession and expansion, the number of people unemployed at any given time has averaged 7.6 million, and the number of people living in poverty has averaged over 34 million.[3] Yet the question of how to interpret these data has been a subject of deep disagreement.

Joblessness is traditionally divided into three types: "frictional" unemployment caused by the normal activity of people moving between jobs or moving in and out of the labor force; "structural" unemployment caused by a mismatch between the needs of employers and the characteristics of the workforce; and "deficient-demand" unemployment caused by a simple shortage of jobs. The effort to determine what share of unemployment is accounted for by each of these dynamics constitutes one of the major projects of macroeconomics, and the answer to this question has critical implications for employment policy. Frictional unemployment is normal and requires no policy intervention; it is the natural rate of unemployment which cannot be lowered except through hyper-inflationary measures. Structural unemployment mandates improvements in workers' skills or in the geographic matching of workers and jobs. Deficient demand is the most serious form of joblessness and requires either macro-economic stimulation or direct job creation by the federal government.

Throughout much of the 1960s and 1970s, federal policy reflected a conviction that Americans struggling to escape poverty faced both structural and deficient-demand problems. As a result, training and education policies were combined with significant public employment initiatives. The election of President Reagan in 1980, however, marked a profound shift in federal policy. The new administration insisted that there was no problem of deficient demand—that, with the exception of temporary cyclical downturns, there were enough jobs in the economy for everyone who needed them. If some people experienced long-term unemployment, it was not because jobs were unavailable but because they lacked the skills or motivation to make themselves employable. Even during the recession of 1981–82, when national unemployment rates reached their highest level since the Great Depression, administration officials insisted that jobs were available for those with the talent and tenacity to work their way up.[4]

On the basis of this contention, the Reagan administration abolished virtually all forms of public employment. At its height in 1978, the Comprehensive Employment and Training Administration (CETA) had provided nearly three-quarters of a million full-time jobs for adults and an additional million summer jobs for teenagers. By 1982, the number of summer jobs had been cut in half, and the adult employment program had been eliminated entirely.[5] In place of CETA, the Reagan administration authorized the Job Training Partnership Act (JTPA), which provided short-term training for the poor and unemployed. Over and over again, Reagan justified the switch from job creation to job training by insisting that there already were enough jobs for those prepared to take them. Shortly after signing JTPA into law, he was asked "what . . . a training program [could] do to reduce unemployment when there are so few jobs available." In response, the president offered an anecdote which was to become the hallmark of his administration's labor policy:

> Well . . . maybe there are more jobs available than we realize. . . . Take a look on any given Sunday to a metropolitan newspaper. . . . Just a couple of weeks ago, the Washington paper had 34 full pages of help wanted ads, and the Los Angeles paper had 52 such pages. This is true in most metropolitan areas on any given Sunday. Now . . . the reason those jobs are open is because there aren't people with the training or experience to fill those jobs.[6]

A "Labor Shortage" Economy?

As the decade progressed, the unemployment rate improved dramatically. If the president's early declarations were greeted with some skepticism, this was quickly replaced by a widespread consensus that the country's biggest employment problem was not a job shortage but a *labor* shortage. Throughout the decade, popular magazines, academic journals, and government publications alike increasingly attributed high poverty rates to the shortcomings of poor people themselves rather than to the lack of employment opportunities. Indeed, by the late 1980s, many analysts warned that the shortage of qualified labor was becoming so severe as to threaten the country's international competitiveness.[7]

Both in the late 1980s and again in the mid-1990s, pundits, journalists, and scholars alike declared not only that jobs were plentiful but that employers were growing increasingly desperate in their quest to find even minimally qualified workers. In a 1986 article entitled "A Maddening Labor Mismatch," *Time* magazine explained that "more than ever, the U.S. is suffering from a mismatch between the new jobs that are flooding the labor market and the people who are available to fill them."[8] In 1988 *The Economist* bemoaned "the miseries of full employment," noting that throughout the United States, "jobs are going begging. . . . Employers are desperate for workers, from trained secretaries to nurses, from bank clerks to hamburger cooks and technicians."[9] And in a landmark 1987 study conducted for the Department of Labor, the Hudson Institute forecast a growing economy whose expanding employment was limited only by the capacities of its workforce:

> If every child who reaches the age of seventeen between now and the year 2000 could read sophisticated materials, write clearly, speak articulately, and solve complex problems . . . the American economy could easily approach or exceed [a] . . . boom scenario. Unconstrained by shortages of competent, well-educated workers . . . U.S.-based companies would reassert historic American leadership in old and new industries, and American workers would enjoy the rising standards of living they enjoyed in the 1950s and 1960s.[10]

The expansion of the late 1990s brought similar accounts of tight labor markets and desperate employers. "Sign of the Times: Help Wanted," proclaimed *Business Week* in 1997. "All across the U.S.," the magazine declared, "employers are strapped for workers."[11] In the late 1990s the unemployment rate fell to its lowest level in thirty years, and employer associations in industries from agriculture to high-tech sought permission to import foreign workers for jobs they reported could not be filled by the domestic labor force. In the past, noted Deputy Secretary of Labor Kitty Higgins, people wondered where the jobs were. "Now we've got the jobs," insisted Higgins. "Where are the workers?"[12]

Finally, nearly twenty years after President Reagan first pointed to the want ads as justification for national employment policy, incoming Labor Secretary Elaine Chao reenacted his demonstration before the Senate Labor Committee. The "greatest challenge faced by the Department of Labor" under the George W. Bush administration, she explained, "is represented by what I am holding in my hand . . . a recently-published listing of unfilled high-tech positions."[13] The new labor secretary declared that the country faced "a current skills gap and a long-term worker shortage" and stressed the new administration's commitment to "bridge the gap between these high-skilled positions that need qualified workers, and the millions of Americans who need additional training to be able to fill them."[14]

The assertion that employment opportunities are plentiful—if only workers were qualified to fill them—has been a central tenet of federal policy for twenty years. But is it true? Interestingly, the federal government has long avoided any systematic collection of data on job vacancies. Thus, the shift from job creation to job training policies was carried out without any reliable information regarding the relationship between the supply and demand for jobs. Instead, the primary unit of argument in employment policy debates has been the anecdote.

Stories about individual employers' hiring woes are only meaningful if they are representative of some broader national trend. Yet overwhelmingly, both journalists and government officials have used labor-shortage anecdotes as substitutes for—rather than illustrations of—scientific data. If they had consulted statistical studies, analysts would have found that every major study to date has reached the opposite conclusion of that suggested by labor-shortage anecdotes. Rather than documenting a shortage of qualified workers, virtually all the available evidence shows that at any given time there are far more unemployed people than there are job openings.

In what follows, I will focus on employment data from 1984 to 1996; however, I believe that the analysis holds true for the present economy as well. Starting with the first year of JTPA's operation, the 1984 to 1996 period covers two cycles of recession and expansion and three presidential administrations. By including periods of expansion, I aim to test the extent to which problems of job supply may reflect long-term structural rather than short-term cyclical dynamics. The period in question marks the height of public proclamations regarding a shortage of skilled labor. It also includes several of the most important decisions that shaped federal employment policy, from the implementation of JTPA to the passage of NAFTA and radical welfare reform. By documenting labor market conditions during the time that these decisions were taken, I hope to shed light on the economic background that framed the politics of employment policy. Finally, while the expansion of the late 1990s brought record-low unemployment rates, the overall rate of job growth in these years was well within the range of the 1984 to 1996 period.[15] Thus, I believe that the economic picture that emerges from this study remains accurate for the early twenty-first century as well.

In the data presented below, I show that throughout the height of the putative "labor shortage" economy, the number of people in need of decently paying jobs consistently exceeded the supply of such jobs by a wide margin. To do this, I have developed a new methodology which, for the first time in the history of the mismatch debate, provides a direct and systematic comparison between the supply and the demand for jobs in the United States. This comparison shows that throughout the period 1984 to 1996, the number of decently paying jobs was—at best—enough for a quarter of the people who needed them. Moreover, this conclusion is based on the most optimistic possible set of assumptions. If we make more realistic assumptions about the economy, it is clear that the number of good jobs was sufficient for less than one-twentieth of the population in need.

These facts are in keeping with the conclusions of earlier studies, but go beyond them in several important ways. A series of small pilot studies examined labor supply and demand in the 1980s, and following the 1996 welfare reforms a number of studies compared the supply of jobs with the number of people scheduled to move from welfare to work. Because of the limitations in the type of data collected by the federal government, each of these studies was forced to rely on incomplete or proxy measures—using local data to estimate national trends, focusing on one set of jobs as a proxy for the labor market as a whole, or using the track record of employed low-skill workers to guess at the job prospects of those leaving the welfare rolls. I have developed a new methodology for measuring the job gap precisely because each of these proxy methods leaves important questions unanswered about the national labor market. However, the results of previous studies are significant in two ways. First, it is useful to have a context of comparative findings against which to judge the facts I present below. Second, it is instructive to know what type of data was available when public officials were mandating the switch from job creation to job training policy. For these reasons, I first make a brief detour to present an overview of the data that has been available to policy makers in past years, before going on to discuss the conclusions reached using my own methodology.

Earlier Studies of Job Availability

While the government has never collected information on job vacancies for the country as a whole, it has occasionally experimented with collecting this information in specific locations, and until now these experiments provided the best insights on the relationship between supply and demand for jobs. The most comprehensive data come from pilot studies done in six states between 1964 and 1980. The results were analyzed by Katharine Abraham, a prominent authority on vacancy rates who was later appointed commissioner of labor statistics in the first Clinton administration. Over the course of this fifteen-year period, the number of unemployed people was found to consistently exceed the number of job openings; the problem grew worse as the unemployment rate increased over time. The combined results from all six studies showed that, at an unemployment rate of 5%, there were between three and four unemployed people for every vacancy.[16] The same trend was shown in a second set of pilot studies conducted in the late 1970s and early 1980s, when unemployment rates were higher. This time, when the unemployment rate was at 7%, there were 4.6 unemployed people for every available job.[17] Thus, the limited vacancy data that have been available suggest exactly the opposite of President Reagan's assertion: not a shortage of workers but a shortage of jobs.

While these findings are instructive, they are lacking in two respects. First, the vacancy rate measures openings in all occupations, without distinguishing between high-wage and low-wage or full-time and part-time jobs. Yet one of the most important debates in recent years concerns the *quality* of the jobs being created. In order to get at this dimension of the problem, we must combine vacancy data with information on the wages and hours offered by various occupations.

Second and most important, these studies restricted their scope to those people considered officially unemployed by government standards—that is, someone who is not working but who has actively looked for a job within the past month. Over the past two decades, however, federal policy has come to treat a much broader segment of the population as if they should be working, even if they are not currently seeking employment. This was the express intention of JTPA: to institute a "training program for the drop-out youth who are not prepared for employment, for welfare recipients who need training to escape from dependency, for the economically disadvantaged who cannot compete in the labor market without help."[18] And this is the goal of the 1996 welfare reform legislation, mandating work requirements and strict time limits for public assistance recipients.[19] Thus the number of job vacancies is critical not only for the officially unemployed but also for those low-income Americans who are currently out of the labor market. In order to test the extent to which training can provide a way out of poverty for this population, we must compare the total number of job openings not with the number of people who are officially unemployed but with the entire population which federal policy currently assumes is in need of decently paying jobs, that is, the entire working-age, nondisabled population which is currently below the poverty line.

The most recent information on labor supply and demand has come in the wake of the 1996 welfare reforms, as analysts across the country have sought to assess the employment prospects of those being removed from public assistance. In 1997, scholars surveyed six midwestern states, all of which combined strong economic growth with aggressive welfare-to-work policies. Across this region, they found that the number of people in need of low-skill jobs outnumbered total openings by four to one. When they restricted their focus to those jobs that paid above-poverty wages, the ratio grew to 22:1; when they considered only those jobs paying a "livable wage," it became 97:1.[20] Similarly, nearly every city that has attempted to compare supply and demand for entry-level jobs predicted that it would not be able to employ the number of welfare recipients poised to hit the streets. In a 1997 study, the U.S. Conference of Mayors reported that 92% of cities surveyed "will not have a sufficient number of low-skill jobs to allow compliance with the welfare law's work participation requirements."[21] While the long-term expansion of the late 1990s provided greater job opportunities than these analysts expected, the anticipated paucity of living-wage jobs has proven frighteningly accurate.[22]

These studies have never been challenged by anything other than anecdotes or casual observance of unemployment trends.[23] However, as with the pilot studies of vacancies, the research on jobs for welfare recipients leaves important questions unanswered. First, by focusing on the employment experience of low-skilled workers, or by restricting the analysis to the supply of low-skill jobs, these analyses leave unanswered the central question of training policy: Could welfare recipients find decently paying jobs if they had better skills? If there is a shortage of low-skill jobs but a surfeit of higher-skilled jobs, then there is no true "job gap," but simply a skills gap. To document a definitive job shortage, it is necessary to measure job openings across the entire economy, rather than solely in the low-skill market. Second, job gaps identified in particular geographic areas—particularly in central cities—may have less to do with an absolute job gap than a geographic mismatch between urban workers and suburban jobs. To the extent that poverty can be alleviated through regional transportation improvements, or by emigration from one part of the country to another, this may not be properly characterized as a problem of employment policy.

Thus, while each of the major studies done to date points in the same direction, each is limited in its own way: the vacancy studies concern only the officially unemployed, and the welfare data are restricted to low-skill workers or to specific cities and states. In order to definitively assess the potential for low-income Americans to work their way out of poverty, it is necessary to compare the number of people in need of decently paying jobs with the total supply of such jobs—at any level of skill and in any part of the country. It is this comparison which I have undertaken to measure.

In the sections that follow, I develop a definition of "decently paying" jobs which serves as an alternative to the official poverty thresholds; calculate the number of jobs needed to provide all Americans with this minimum standard of living; and estimate a highest-possible measure of job openings available for this population. The data reveal that over the course of the period 1984 to 1996 the number of people in need of decently paying jobs consistently exceeded the supply of such jobs by a wide margin.

A New Measure of Labor Supply and Demand

Determining the relationship between the number of openings in decently paying jobs and the number of people who need them involves three steps: defining what income level is "decently paying"; identifying the number of annual job openings in occupations which pay at or above this level; and determining the number of would-be workers who are either not employed or employed at less than "decent" wages. Each of these steps involves a fairly complex series of procedures, and I will discuss each before presenting and analyzing the data as a whole. A more detailed outline of methodology is in Appendix A.

Defining "Decently Paying" Jobs

The simplest definition of "decently paying" jobs is the federal poverty threshold. This is the official definition of need, used as the eligibility criterion for participation in JTPA and other social welfare programs. The methodology used to calculate the official poverty thresholds, however, contains several fundamental flaws which render the thresholds unrealistically low. I have calculated alternative poverty thresholds for the 1984 to 1996 period and will use these to define a "decently paying" job.

One of the fundamental questions about measuring poverty is whether the poverty line is a relative or an absolute standard. On the one hand, a completely relative definition of poverty—say, that people are poor if their income is less than 50% of the country's median—works as a measure of inequality but may fail as a measure of deprivation. In an affluent country, a relative standard of poverty might define people as poor who in fact face no pressing difficulties. On the other hand, a strictly absolute standard of poverty quickly becomes meaningless as standards of living change over time. Some poor people in the United States have possessions that would be envied by medieval noblemen, yet to define the U.S. poor as aristocrats obviously misses the point of having a poverty line. No absolute standard of need remains consistent over time, except perhaps that of starvation—yet the idea of the poverty line is not to identify people who are dying, but rather people who are living in unacceptable conditions. To be meaningful, then, a definition of poverty must combine both absolute and relative notions: what we want to get at is the amount of money which allows people to lead minimally acceptable lives in a particular society at a particular time.

The official poverty line developed by the federal government attempts to measure just such a combination of absolute and relative need. The poverty line we now use was first developed in the early 1960s by Mollie Orshansky, an analyst with the Social Security Administration.[24] Orshansky began by studying the Department of Agriculture's food budgets for families of various sizes. Of the four food plans then published, Orshansky took the lowest (the "economy food plan") as her definition of the minimum amount needed to keep a family from falling into malnutrition. The Department of Agriculture had determined that food made up about a third of the average family's expenditures.[25] Multiplying the food budget by three produced the poverty threshold for each family size.

Orshansky's measure is thus both absolute and relative. By starting with the amount of money needed to keep a family fed, it is grounded in the concrete need for physical survival. By indexing this amount to the average family budget, however, the poverty line is then also tied to the particular standards of living of that time. As Fisher explains, Orshansky's concept of poverty began by "considering a hypothetical average (middle income) family, spending one-third of its income on food, which was faced with a need to cut back on its expenditures. She made the assumption that the family would be able to cut back its food expenditures and its nonfood expenditures by the same proportion."[26] The resulting thresholds reflected a commonsense notion of poverty. As Schwarz and Volgy explain, "people were impoverished, even if they were not starving or destitute, when they had incomes beneath the amount required to purchase basic necessities at the most frugal standard of an ordinary family."[27]

What's Wrong with the Official Poverty Thresholds? Although Orshansky's original method provided a reasonable definition of poverty, there are at least three serious flaws in the official poverty line, all of which serve to keep the thresholds artificially low. First, the food budgets on which the thresholds are based are unrealistically stingy. The Department of Agriculture's "economy food plan" was intended as a temporary budget for short-term emergencies.[28] For a family to get by on this budget, not only must they never eat out and never buy an ice cream cone for their children or a stick of gum for themselves, but every cent must be spent exactly nutritionally correctly, with all food perfectly prepared and nothing wasted. As Levitan noted, "this regimen requires sophisticated nutritional planning, adequate refrigerator space, equipment, and low-cost markets—resources frequently unavailable to the poor."[29] In fact, a Department of Agriculture survey revealed that families who spent the amount allowed under the economy food plan had only a 10% chance of obtaining nutritionally adequate diets.[30]

Second, the poverty line calculations ignore the effect of taxation. While the poverty thresholds measure net income needs, the determination of one's poverty status is based on gross (before tax) income. This discrepancy was less problematic when the poverty line was first established in the early 1960s, since most poor people then paid little or no income taxes. In the past forty years, however, the tax rate on low-income earners has increased substantially, so that the failure to account for taxes in poverty calculations now represents a significant distortion in the thresholds.[31]

Finally, the most important flaw in the current poverty thresholds is that they have not been adjusted for changes in the share of average family budgets devoted to food; rather, thresholds for the past forty years have been updated only by the rate of inflation. Orshansky's original one-third ratio was based on household consumption patterns in 1955. However, the proportion of income spent on food has been falling steadily since the beginning of industrialization, as the national economy grows more complex and daily life becomes structured around a growing number of nonfood needs. Orshansky's ratio was already significantly lower than that of the average family at the turn of the century, which spent 46% of its income on food; by 1996 this percentage had fallen to 17.5%.[32] This decline in the percent of income spent on food, or food share, represents not merely increased consumption of luxury goods but rather the fact that people now require new types of equipment or technology in order to function in daily economic interactions. A car and a telephone may have been considered luxuries in 1955, but half a century later, they are necessities for most people.[33] There are now far more single-parent families, and two-parent families in which both parents work, than there were in 1955, so that childcare expenses require a greater share of family budgets. Similarly, washing machines, indoor plumbing, and improved medical procedures are all part of a current family's standard needs, but are not fully represented in the 1955 budgets. Finally, many costs have risen faster than those for food, including housing and medical bills. Thus the official poverty line—understood as the inflation-adjusted ability to secure what constituted a minimally decent standard of living in 1955—has become disconnected from any meaningful notion of economic privation. As the data for Orshansky's original calculations fade further into the past, the discrepancy between official and actual poverty grows wider. Since the 1950s, the Gallup poll has asked survey participants to estimate "the smallest amount of money a family of four needs to get along in your community." While respondents have almost always cited a figure higher than the official poverty line, the gap between commonsense and official poverty has grown significantly. In 1950 the median response to the Gallup question was just 102% of the official threshold; by 1989 the figure had risen to 172%.[34]

What Does a Family Need to Live On? In order to determine how many "decently paying" jobs are available, we must identify some threshold that represents a minimally adequate standard of living for American families. While the official poverty line remains the standard for most means-tested government programs, it no longer works as a commonsense measure of "getting by." Thus I have calculated alternative thresholds using the same basic concepts of Orshansky's original methodology. For the 1984 to 1996 period, I have calculated the alternative threshold based on the Department of Agriculture's Thrifty Food Plan and the current food share of average family budgets as recorded in the Consumer Price Index.[35] In 1996, for instance, the Thrifty Food Plan budgeted $4,830 for a family of four, and the average family spent 17.5% of its income on food. Calculating the income level for which 17.5% equals $4,893 produces an adjusted poverty line of $27,632. This is the exact same method used to calculate the original poverty line, except that the food share of family budgets is updated to reflect the current facts—an adjustment urged by Orshansky herself.[36] The results, shown in table 1.1, range from 152% to 175%

Table 1.1 Alternative Poverty Thresholds for a Family of Four, Based on Original Orshansky Method, 1984 to 1996

	1984	1986	1988	1990	1992	1994	1996
Original Orshansky (alternative) poverty threshold, family of four	$16,106	$18,503	$20,365	$23,317	$24,618	$25,905	$27,632
Offical poverty threshold, family of four	$10,609	$11,203	$12,092	$13,359	$14,343	$15,141	$16,036
Ratio of alternative to official threshold	152%	165%	168%	175%	172%	171%	172%
Thrifty Food Plan, family of four	$3,189	$3,298	$3,608	$4,129	$4,283	$4,510	$4,830
Food share of average family budget	19.8%	17.8%	17.7%	17.7%	17.4%	17.4%	17.5%

Sources: Monthy Thrifty Food Plans provided by U.S. Department of Agriculture. (Food plan figures are for a family of four, composed of a couple 20–50 years old, with two children aged 6–8 and 9–11. This is the family type used to define Food Stamp eligibility.) Family budget shares are from U.S. Department of Labor, Bureau of Labor Statistics, Consumer Price Index Detailed Report, 1984–1996. Shares are drawn from the consumer price index for urban areas, covering approximately 80% of U.S. consumers.

of the official poverty line. This is where the official poverty line would stand were it properly updated. Since this method replicates the calculation of the original poverty line, I refer to these as the Original Orshansky thresholds.

Some might argue that a 1996 poverty threshold of $27,632 for a family of four is overly generous, that people living at this income cannot be called truly poor. I believe, however, that these thresholds do capture the commonsense notion of a line which divides those who are "getting by" from those who face severe and chronic economic hardship; indeed, families at this level lead lives of extreme austerity. One researcher recorded the lifestyle of a family of four living on 155% of the official threshold. On this budget, families

> never go out to eat . . . never go out to a movie, concert or ball game or indeed to any . . . establishment that charges admission . . . have no cable television . . . never purchase alcohol or cigarettes; never take a vacation or holiday that involves any motel or hotel or, again, any meals out; never hire a baby-sitter or have any other paid child care; never give an allowance or other spending money to the children; never purchase any lessons or home-learning tools for the children; never buy books or records for the adults or children, or any toys . . . never pay for a haircut; never buy a magazine; have no money for the feeding or veterinary care of any pets . . . never spend any money for preschool for the children, or educational trips for them away from home, or any summer camp or other activity with a fee. . . . The budget allots no money either for any

absence from work because of illness or to pay for emergencies or other unanticipated major expenses; no money to help other persons, such as an ill or elderly parent, or to pay life insurance or to pay interest on consumer-credit borrowing except for car financing; and no money for savings for college for the children or to support a pension for retirement other than Social Security.[37]

Scholars who have examined the lifestyle that is possible at various levels of income have virtually all concluded that the official thresholds are impossibly low. Thus, the income levels defined here as "decently paying" fall squarely within the accepted range of alternative thresholds.[38]

In the analysis presented below, I compare the number of job openings with the number of people in need of work using both the official poverty line and the Original Orshansky thresholds. Since eligibility both for job training programs and for a variety of social welfare benefits is currently tied to the official poverty line, a comparison of labor supply and demand at this income level is instructive for measuring the potential for job training to provide a means of upward mobility for that part of the population which federal policy defines as officially poor. However, in order to test the broader claims of job training advocates—that training can provide a stepping-stone to economic security for the general population of unemployed and underemployed—it is necessary to measure the supply of jobs that realistically allow a family to become self-supporting. For these purposes, it is the Original Orshansky thresholds, and not the official line, which allows a meaningful comparison between the supply of "decently paying" jobs and the number of people who need them.

How Many People Need Jobs?

In keeping with the trends in federal policy discussed above, I have defined the number of people in need of decently paying jobs as all those whose family incomes fall below the poverty threshold, with the exception of the elderly and those disabled people who are unable to work. Table 1.2 shows the number of poor families in the years 1984 to 1996, according to both the Original Orshansky definitions and the official measure.

Yet simply knowing the number of poor families does not immediately tell us how many jobs are needed to support these families, or what wages these jobs must pay. A single-parent family obviously needs one job which provides the full income needed to support that family. In families where two adults are present, however, I have assumed that both are available to work; in these cases, neither adult needs to earn the full poverty threshold, as long as both their incomes combine to attain this level. Where neither of the adults is currently working, I assumed that each one needs a job that pays a salary equal to at least 50% of the poverty threshold. Where one of the adults is already working, I

Table 1.2 Number of Families in Poverty, 1984 to 1996

Year	At Original Orshansky thresholds	At official poverty thresholds
1984	24,865,840	14,141,450
1986	26,918,049	14,162,990
1988	28,065,396	14,200,971
1990	30,282,335	14,881,024
1992	32,351,103	16,319,050
1994	32,994,000	16,657,000
1996	33,272,000	16,434,000

Source: Author's calculations based on U.S. Department of Commerce, Census Bureau, "Current Population Survey: Annual Demographic File" (Washington, D.C.: U.S. Department of Commerce, 1984–1996), unpublished tabulations. Numbers include unrelated individuals and unrelated subfamilies.

assumed that the second needs to earn only enough to cover the difference between the poverty threshold and the first adult's income.[39]

In 1996, there were 33.3 million poor families, based on the Original Orshansky thresholds. To raise this population above the poverty line would require 25.9 million additional jobs, at annual wages ranging from $7,700 to $55,100. The official poverty population represents a much smaller number of families, but its employment needs are still daunting; simply lifting this population out of poverty would require 14.4 million new jobs paying between $5,100 and $32,000.

How Many Jobs Are There?

Job training advocates assert that the economy of the 1980s and 1990s was characterized by high levels of structural unemployment. A large number of job vacancies went unfilled even while poverty rates remained high, they say, because poor people either had the wrong skills or were in the wrong place to take advantage of these opportunities. Without the detailed vacancy data which the federal government has to date refused to collect, it is impossible to know exactly how many jobs might have been available for graduates of training programs. Thus we cannot evaluate the claims of training advocates with complete accuracy. However, it is possible to calculate the maximum number of vacancies that might possibly have been available in any given year. Using best-case assumptions, we can test the extent to which—under the most optimistic conditions—job training might possibly offer a solution to poverty.

Discouraged Vacancies For job training policy, the most important question about the labor market is not the rate of job growth, or even the number of annual job openings, but rather the number of jobs that *would have been* created if all poor people were well trained. Obviously, the natural functioning of the labor market creates millions of job openings every year, and in most years the total number of jobs increases by a million or more, in keeping with the country's overall population growth and economic expansion. Yet it is equally clear that this growth by itself has not been sufficient to eradicate poverty. In every year from 1984 to 1996—a period including the longest peacetime expansion in U.S. history—there were 25 million or more families living below the Original Orshansky thresholds (or 14 to 16 million families below the official poverty line).

To determine the extent to which the private economy might have absorbed this population, we must develop a means for estimating the number of "discouraged vacancies"—jobs that were never filled (and therefore do not show up as "new job creation" in any of the national employment data) but that would have been created had qualified labor been available. For job training advocates to be right, the total number of discouraged vacancies must be so great as to provide enough jobs for the entire poverty population, or 25.9 million in 1996. The available evidence is not encouraging on this count. The only direct measure of "discouraged vacancies" to date is a study conducted by the Bureau of Labor Statistics in 1979–80, which asked employers in Florida and Texas to list positions for which they had given up recruiting. Adding these jobs to the total number of vacancies increased the overall vacancy rate by only 3% and 6%, respectively.[40] For 1996, this would make the number of discouraged vacancies somewhere between 150,000 and 300,000, or less than 2% of the jobs needed by the poverty population.[41]

While the data from Florida and Texas are dramatic, they provide only a partial and indirect measure. Therefore I have developed a more direct method for calculating the number of discouraged vacancies, using actual national employment data for the years 1984 to 1996. As a proxy for the unmet excess demand for workers, I make the extremely optimistic assumption that firms' unmet hiring needs in each year were such that, had they been met, overall employment would have expanded at a rate equal to its fastest postwar growth rate. Actual annual employment growth in the 1984 to 1996 period ranged from 1.4% to 2.6% (with the exception of 1990–91, during which employment fell by 0.8%).[42] The fastest rate of employment growth since World War II was 4.6% in 1945–46. Therefore I have assumed that, if the labor force were perfectly trained, employment would have grown by 4.6% in every year during the period in question. I have treated the difference between 4.6% and the actual growth rates as discouraged vacancies due to excess demand for workers.[43] Again, I have used wage data to select only those vacancies which are in "decently paying" occupations.

This methodology almost certainly overstates the extent of discouraged vacancies. The 1946 growth rate was realized under conditions of unparalleled economic expansion, including hundreds of thousands of soldiers returning home, complete U.S. domination of world trade, and the outpouring of massive consumer demand pent up during the years of wartime rationing. There is no evidence—either from statistical studies or from employer surveys—to believe that firms' unmet desire for expansion could have pushed employment up by such a large factor during the 1980s or 1990s. The Bureau of Labor Statistics projects that in the years 1996 to 2006 employment will grow by only 1.3% per year.[44] Nor have job training advocates asserted that even a fully trained workforce could grow by as much as 4.6% per year. For instance, the Hudson Institute's *Workforce 2000* report, which served as the premier statement of the 1980s skills mismatch thesis, provided low, moderate, and high-growth projections of employment demand for the 1987 to 2000 period. Even the "boom" scenario in this report, which assumed "high rates of investment in . . . human capital, coupled with rapid productivity growth in services," predicted annual employment growth of only 1.8%.[45] Thus the projections made here are two and a half times more optimistic than even the rosiest forecast of the leading job training advocates. Nevertheless, I have used these figures as proxies for the highest possible level of excess demand.

Using this method, the total number of possible openings due to discouraged vacancies ranged from 1.5 million to 3.2 million over the period 1984 to 1996 (see table 1.3). These numbers are almost certainly overestimates—the 1996 figure is three times higher than the highest level of vacancies projected by Abraham's findings. Yet even this volume of vacancies represents only a small fraction of what would be needed for poor Americans to earn their way out of poverty.

Conclusions: A Dramatic Job Gap

As shown in table 1.3, throughout the 1984 to 1996 period, the total number of possible discouraged vacancies in decently paying occupations was never more than one-seventh the number of people who needed jobs, and the gap between jobs needed and jobs available was never less than 16 million. The job gap numbers are not strictly comparable from one year to the next, and therefore cannot be read as a trend over time; rather, they provide a series of snapshots comparing the supply and demand for jobs in any given year.[46] The figures show that even in those years when the United States was widely characterized as having a "labor shortage" economy, there was a dramatic gap between the number of jobs needed and those available. In 1996, when the economy was expanding rapidly and actual employment grew by 2.2%, the total (optimistic) number of possible discouraged vacancies was just over 2.1 million. At the same time, there were 25.9 million people in need of decently paying jobs. Thus the total of potential openings was sufficient to employ only one-twelfth the number of people who needed work, and the gap between jobs needed and jobs available stood at 23.7 million.

Even these figures may overstate the true level of employment opportunity for poor Americans. The total number of job openings reported in table 1.3 includes part-time work and self-employed positions. However, it is not clear that part-time jobs or self-employed ventures represent viable avenues to independence for impoverished workers. The majority of part-time jobs offer no health insurance and thus are unlikely vehicles for supporting a family. So, too, Abraham doubts that "self-employment vacancy is . . . a meaningful concept," since individuals who quit self-employment leave no obvious position to fill.[47] It is conceivable but seems unlikely that low-income workers would identify a market niche or innovative service that had gone unnoticed by the millions of middle-class Americans who try their hand at entrepreneurial ventures each year. It is even less likely that impoverished workers would possess the resources necessary to keep a new venture afloat through the turbulence and cash-flow volatility characteristic of start-up businesses. By separating out part-time and self-employment, it is possible to compare the number of jobs needed with both the total number of vacancies and the more limited number of vacancies in full-time jobs.

Finally, the ratio of jobs needed to potential vacancies may be further refined by subtracting out the vacancies in managerial and professional occupations. There are two reasons to believe that this may yield a more realistic picture of the labor market. First, it is unlikely that positions with the highest educational and experiential requirements will be filled by low-income workers. If demand for more workers in these occupations exists, it is most likely to benefit the more affluent and educated segments of the population which may be drawn into the labor force by these opportunities. Second, these are not, in fact, the positions for which job training aims to prepare people. No training program aspires to make workers currently below the poverty line into managers or professionals. The functional question for training policy is not whether poor people can become professionals but simply whether they can become self-sufficient. Thus it is probably more realistic to exclude these jobs from the total number of vacancies available to the poverty population.

By ignoring vacancies in part-time, self-employed, managerial, and professional positions, we can focus on the most realistic framework for assessing the potential effectiveness of training programs: a comparison between the number of jobs needed by the population in poverty and the number of openings available in full-time, nonmanagerial positions (see table 1.3). This is the real labor market in which poor Americans must pursue the means to support their families, and in which job placement officers must seek to place the graduates of training programs. Within these boundaries, the relationship between supply

Table 1.3 Jobs Needed and Potential Job Openings, 1984 to 1996 (in thousands)

	1984	1986	1988	1990	1992	1994	1996
At Original Orshansky poverty thresholds							
Jobs needed	18,986	20,124	20,877	22,676	24,435	25,985	25,903
Total openings	2,291	1,567	2,424	1,660	3,195	3,013	2,130
Jobs gap	16,695	18,557	18,453	21,016	21,240	22,972	23,773
Ratio of jobs needed to openings	8.3	12.8	8.6	13.7	7.6	8.6	12.2
Full-time openings	1,915	1,314	2,091	1,384	2,654	2,122	1,519
Full-time jobs gap	17,071	18,810	18,786	21,292	21,781	23,863	24,384
Ratio of jobs needed to full-time openings	9.9	15.3	10.0	16.4	9.2	12.2	17.1
Managerial/professional openings	610	427	609	477	955	914	690
Nonmanagerial openings	1,681	1,140	1,815	1,183	2,240	2,099	1,440
Nonmanagerial jobs gap	17,305	18,984	19,062	21,493	22,195	23,886	24,463
Ratio of jobs needed to nonmanagerial openings	11.3	17.7	11.5	19.2	10.9	12.4	18.0
Full-time openings in nonmanagerial positions	1,440	978	1,569	1,012	1,913	1,346	1,014
Full-time, nonmanagerial jobs gap	17,546	19,146	19,308	21,664	22,522	24,639	24,889
Ratio of jobs needed to full-time, nonmanagerial openings	13.2	20.6	13.3	22.4	12.8	19.3	25.5

	1984	1986	1988	1990	1992	1994	1996
At official poverty thresholds							
Jobs needed	11,907	11,527	11,634	12,129	13,449	14,089	14,426
Total openings	2,518	1,552	2,620	1,805	3,671	3,747	2,376
Jobs gap	9,389	9,975	9,014	10,324	9,778	10,342	12,050
Ratio of jobs needed to openings	4.7	7.0	4.4	6.7	3.7	3.8	6.1
Full-time job openings	1,919	1,316	2,095	1,386	2,658	2,122	1,520
Full-time jobs gap	9,988	10,311	9,539	10,743	10,791	11,967	12,906
Ratio of jobs needed to full-time openings	6.2	8.8	5.6	8.8	5.1	6.6	9.5
Managerial/professional openings	611	428	694	477	955	914	690
Nonmanagerial jobs gap	10,000	10,403	9,708	10,801	10,733	11,256	12,740
Ratio of jobs needed to nonmanagerial openings	6.2	9.5	6.0	9.1	5.0	5.0	8.6
Openings in full-time, nonmanagerial positions	1,444	980	1,543	1,014	1,917	1,346	1,015
Full-time, nonmanagerial jobs gap	10,463	10,647	10,091	11,115	11,532	12,743	13,411
Ratio of jobs needed to full-time, nonmanagerial positions	8.2	11.9	7.5	12.0	7.0	10.5	14.2

Sources: For jobs needed: author's calculations based on U.S. Department of Commerce, Census Bureau, "Current Population Survey: Annual Demographic File" (Washington, D.C.: U.S. Department of Commerce, 1984–96). For calculations of job openings, see appendix A.

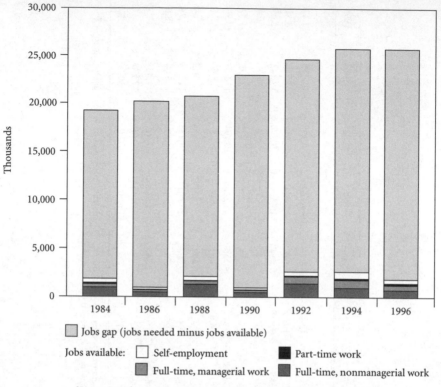

Jobs gap (jobs needed minus jobs available)

Jobs available: ☐ Self-employment   ■ Part-time work
                 ■ Full-time, managerial work   ■ Full-time, nonmanagerial work

Sources: For jobs needed: author's calculations based on U.S. Department of Commerce, Census Bureau, "Current Population Survey: Annual Demographic File" (Washington D.C.: U.S. Department of Commerce, 1984–96). For calculations of job openings, see appendix A.

Figure 1.1 Jobs Needed to Eliminate Poverty Compared with Jobs Available, 1984 to 1996, at Original Orshansky Thresholds

and demand is starkly inadequate. Even at official poverty thresholds, the ratio of jobs needed to available openings ranged from 7:1 to 14:1 in the 1984 to 1996 period, and the job shortfall was never less than 10 million. When measured by the more realistic definitions of the Original Orshansky thresholds, the ratio of jobs needed to vacancies ranged from 12:1 to 25:1, and the number of additional jobs needed to provide all Americans a minimally decent standard of living ranged from 17.5 million to 24.8 million (see figures 1.1, 1.2, and 1.3).

This, then, marks the limits of job training policies. Even in the most optimistic scenario, job training can provide a minimally decent standard of living for only one out of seven poor people, leaving the rest with no means for working their way out of poverty. In 1996, the year in which the entitlement to cash welfare was eliminated on the assumption that poor people could find work if they truly wanted to, there were, at best, just over one million job openings

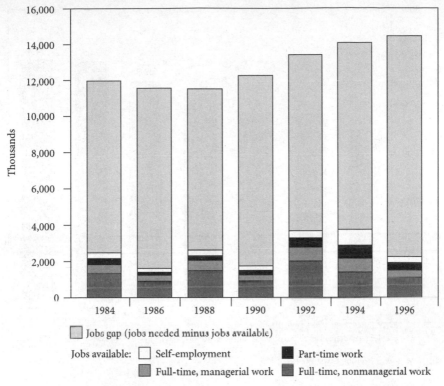

□ Jobs gap (jobs needed minus jobs available)

Jobs available: □ Self-employment   ■ Part-time work

           ■ Full-time, managerial work   ■ Full-time, nonmanagerial work

Sources: For jobs needed: author's calculations based on U.S. Department of Commerce, Census Bureau, "Current Population Survey: Annual Demographic File" (Washington D.C.: U.S. Department of Commerce, 1984–96). For calculation of job openings, see appendix A.

Figure 1.2 Jobs Needed to Eliminate Poverty Compared with Jobs Available, 1984 to 1996, at Official Poverty Thresholds

that paid salaries above the Original Orshansky thresholds, compared with 25.9 million people in need. Thus the amount of poverty and unemployment which might be said to result from a structural skills mismatch represents a very minor share of the overall problem. Far more important is the failure of the private economy to generate a sufficient number of jobs at living wages.

The supply-demand ratios presented in this analysis are offered as rough estimates, with significant room for variation depending on the assumptions one makes at multiple points in the process. Nevertheless, the overall pattern presents a clear challenge to the notion that education and training can substantially solve the problem of poverty. Of the fifty-six different ratios of jobs needed to potential vacancies calculated in table 1.3, only two project that available jobs will be sufficient for more than one-quarter of the population in need of work. And in order for this ratio to be true, it is necessary to believe the most extreme

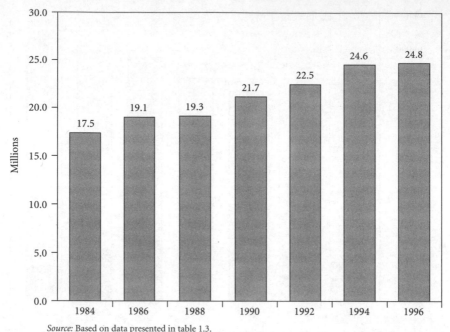

Source: Based on data presented in table 1.3.
Note: Jobs gap defined as unmet need for full-time, nonmanagerial jobs at Original Orshansky Thresholds.

Figure 1.3 The Jobs Gap, 1984 to 1996

version of every assumption: that the official poverty thresholds are realistic; that it costs nothing to relocate from one part of the country to another; that part-time jobs are as good as full-time jobs; that self-employment "vacancies" represent real opportunities; that managerial and professional jobs are accessible to the working poor; and that firms' desire for expansion is great enough to generate growth rates equal to the most expansive year of the postwar era.

Even if the only change we make to these hyper-optimistic premises is to assume that a worker must work full-time in order to escape from poverty, and thus look only at full-time positions, the most optimistic possible scenario shows more than five times as many people in need of jobs as there are available openings. If we use the more realistic poverty thresholds, the need for decently paying jobs outweighs the supply by more than seven to one, in the best case. And under quite reasonable assumptions, the demand for jobs outpaces supply by ratios of between twelve and twenty-five to one.[48]

Once these numbers are taken into account, the incidence of full-time, year-round workers who remain poor is less surprising.[49] Similarly, the high failure rates of job training programs seeking to place graduates into jobs become less puzzling. Analysts who presume a high level of unmet labor demand are faced with the paradox of explaining how high poverty rates could coincide with large numbers of unfilled job openings; in response, they have turned to a variety of theories focusing on skills, cultural, geographic, or organizational mismatches. With more realistic data in hand, the various facets of the labor market are no longer paradoxical, but describe a single reality: the reality of widespread deficient demand.

Data and Politics

The most remarkable characteristic of federal job training legislation is not that it overestimates the supply of jobs but that it never makes this calculation. In congressional hearings leading up to the adoption of JTPA, training advocates spoke of "skill shortages in critical and growth industries,"[50] insisting that "workers must be retrained for the new and expanding sectors of the economy," and that training would "facilitate the movement of these workers into jobs for which demand exceeds supply."[51] Yet nowhere in these hearings was any statistical evidence offered as to exactly how many trainees the economy might potentially absorb. The JTPA legislation itself mandated the secretary of labor to establish "a nationwide computerized job bank . . . matching the qualifications of unemployed, underemployed, and economically disadvantaged individuals with employer requirements and job opportunities, and . . . containing occupational projections of the numbers and types of jobs . . . as well as labor supply information by occupation."[52] But this master comparison of supply and demand has never been done; thus employment policy continues to be made in the absence of any firm data comparing the number of annual job openings with the number of people in need of work.[53] In her Senate confirmation hearing, Secretary of Labor Chao testified that "in America today, there are tens of thousands, perhaps hundreds of thousands, of high-tech jobs that cannot be filled [due to a lack of skilled workers]."[54] For the secretary of labor to be unable to estimate the number of unfilled job openings *within an order of magnitude* reflects the extent to which federal policy makers have been operating in a statistical vacuum.

In part, the failure to place training policy within such a statistical framework is due to the simple fact that no reliable source of job vacancy data exists. Yet it is curious that the government has historically shown a decided lack of interest in developing such data, which are much more widely collected in western Europe. As far back as 1962, the President's Committee to Appraise Employment and Unemployment Statistics reported that "[no] suggestion was more frequently voiced to this Committee than that calling for job vacancy statistics."[55] In the decades since, repeated studies and government panels have identified this need as one of the critical holes in knowledge about the economy. In the early

1990s, the Bureau of Labor Statistics determined that it would be possible to institute a national count of job openings by occupation and wage for an annual cost of only $12 million.[56] Given that the Labor Department at the time was spending over $5 billion a year on education and training programs, this might seem a small price to pay to know whether these funds were being wasted. Yet this proposal, like those of the previous three decades, was rejected by Bush administration officials as overly costly. In 1998, Congress appropriated just over $3 million for a pilot vacancy survey; however, the survey includes no information on the occupation, wages, or full-time/part-time status of the job openings surveyed and thus will be of little practical use to policy planners. In part, the limitations of this survey reflect an apparent lack of interest on the part of those driving federal employment policy. Despite the fact that detailed vacancy data might grant vision to the data-blind administrators of training policy, neither the officials responsible for JTPA nor those overseeing federal welfare-to-work policies lobbied for a more expansive survey.[57]

There is reason to wonder whether the failure to collect job vacancy statistics reflects political rather than budgetary concerns. Evidence exists that standards of measurement for other poverty-related statistics have been manipulated in order to downplay the extent of economic hardship in the country and to minimize the number of people eligible for means-tested benefits. Several government studies of the poverty thresholds have recognized that both the official food budgets and the food share of family expenditures are unrealistically low, but recommendations to correct these inaccuracies have been repeatedly rejected, at least once for the explicit reason that higher poverty thresholds would significantly expand the number of people eligible for economic assistance.[58] The definition of "unemployment" likewise has been periodically revised in order to minimize bad news.[59] And congressional debates over the use of sampling in the 2000 Census suggest that conservative legislators would prefer a less accurate count of the population to an improved measure that would increase the count and thus the funding for and representation of the urban poor.[60] Clearly, there is at least a potential government interest in avoiding a more systematic collection of vacancy data: if it were plainly and easily demonstrated that the population in need far outweighed the number of decently paying job openings, the public perception of poverty might shift away from an emphasis on individual initiative and toward greater expectations of government responsibility.

Whether or not the absence of vacancy data is politically motivated, it seems clear at a minimum that employment policy has been made on the assumption that one doesn't *need* vacancy data in order to know what should be done with the nonworking poor. The assertion that decently paying jobs are available thus seems to be the product of ideological conviction rather than empirical investigation. Indeed, the strength of this conviction renders it impervious even to those data which are available. Because the employment status of poor people is imagined in moral rather than economic terms, federal policy treats the poor as if they occupy a labor market of their own, unaffected by cyclical trends in the rest of the economy, in which job opportunities are always plentiful. The drafting of JTPA legislation took place during the height of the 1982 recession, when the national unemployment rate had climbed above 10%, its highest level since the Great Depression. In congressional testimony, Labor Secretary Ray Donovan readily admitted that training by itself could not reduce the overall unemployment rate—that is, middle-class unemployment—until the economy had recovered.[61] Yet the legislation assumed that training alone was sufficient for poor people. There was thus no waiting period for cutting welfare benefits and no provision of temporary jobs for the poor. On the contrary, only one month before the passage of JTPA, Senate Republicans rejected a proposal to create temporary public works jobs to see poor people through the recession.[62] The logic of training policy, then, was based on the curious theory that while there may not be enough jobs for experienced, middle-class workers, there are enough jobs for uneducated poor people, once trained.

Once the actual data are taken into account, the central illusion of job training policy becomes apparent. There are, in fact, a significant number of jobs with moderate wages for which poor people might reasonably qualify given adequate training. Indeed, considering that it is so much cheaper to train someone for an existing job than to create a new one, and that in any case the entire federal training budget is only sufficient to serve 5% of the eligible population, job training may represent a rational use of available resources. Yet the existence of decently paying jobs obscures as much as it reveals, for the total number of job openings remains only a small fraction of the number of people who need them. Policy makers have, at best, allowed themselves to become misled by believing that what might potentially work for this fraction can also work for the whole. But while it may be true for any single individual that there are jobs available if you work hard and get good training, it cannot be true for the population as a whole.

For the past twenty years, the national debate on employment policy has largely revolved around the question of exactly which type of training program can best facilitate the transition from dependence to self-sufficiency: Should training be voluntary or mandatory? Is it best done in a classroom or on the job? Should training focus on occupation-specific skills or on general workplace behaviors? How long should the programs last, and how much follow-up should be done after placement? How can job training efforts be linked with local economic development initiatives? How can they be coupled with childcare and transportation subsidies to allow single mothers to participate? These are the questions which have absorbed policy planners and which have occupied numerous blue ribbon panels, interagency task forces, conferences, journals, and academic curricula. Spirited debates and competing schools of thought, each with their leading advocates and body of research, have sprung up within this framework of analysis.

In light of the data presented above, however, the emphasis given these questions seems eccentric at best. There is a role for job training, and the effort to design effective training programs is an important one. As a primary focus of employment policy, however, it is mistaken. For if the data on job openings are even roughly accurate, then even the best training program will never be able to address more than a small fraction of the poverty problem. The intuition that as long as there are want ads in the newspapers, there must be jobs for anyone who really wants to work turns out to be illusory—there *are* jobs, but only for the number of people the ads specify; and this illusion masks a deeper truth, which is that for large numbers of the poor there are *no* decently paying jobs, no matter how hard they work or what training programs they enroll in.

CHAPTER TWO

How Important Is Education? Rhetoric and Reality in the Skills Mismatch Debate

> Our people . . . compete in a world where what you can earn depends largely on what you can learn.
> —President Bill Clinton[1]

> Low skills lead to low wages. . . . good jobs depend on people who can put knowledge to work.
> —Secretary of labor's Commission on Achieving Necessary Skills[2]

> Our responsibility is clear: . . . to make it easier for people to find good jobs by giving them the education and training they need to succeed.
> —President George W. Bush[3]

For the past twenty-five years, the wages of most American workers have been going backward. During most of the twentieth century, the earnings of almost every group of workers increased steadily, and it became natural to expect that each generation would become better off than its predecessors. Beginning in 1973, however, this trend was reversed. Between 1973 and 1999, the real wages of the average American worker fell by 5%.[4] Moreover, the problem was not restricted to pockets of concentrated poverty. While some people prospered, fully 70% of all American workers saw their wages fall between 1973 and 1995; even with the boom of the late 1990s, a majority of workers ended the century making less than they had in 1973.[5] The earnings of the average American *family* did improve slightly over this period, but only through a dramatic increase in the number of hours worked and the share of families in which both parents worked.[6] Much of the country, in other words, has had to run faster just to stay in place. Yet even with this additional effort, an increasing number of workers have been unable to keep up. The share of all employees whose wages were insufficient to lift a family of four above the official poverty line grew from 23.5% in 1973 to 26.8% in 1999.[7] The expansion of the late 1990s reduced unemployment to a historic low and began to improve the wages of those at the bottom. Nevertheless, of the jobs projected to grow the most in the late 1990s and early twenty-first century, fully half offer annual salaries insufficient to lift a family out of poverty.[8] The question of what caused this wage erosion and what might reverse it forms the central concern of economic policy.

As the opportunity for decent earnings became more and more elusive over the past two decades, federal policy makers increasingly pointed to workers' education as both the culprit behind declining wages and the hope for restored prosperity. Many economists declared that falling wages resulted from a slowdown in U.S. productivity, particularly compared with foreign competitors. While policy makers acknowledged the need to upgrade technology, workers themselves became the main explanation for the slowdown. In a series of landmark reports beginning in the first Reagan administration, a succession of high-profile commissions blamed the decline in wages largely on a mismatch between the skills possessed by the population and those demanded by employers; they urged workers to channel their economic anxiety into a renewed commitment to education and training. This "skills mismatch" thesis has been the subject of much debate over the past twenty years, yet it remains widely accepted in both the academic and popular press. Most important, federal employment policy remains committed to the proposition that education is the single most important requirement for poor Americans hoping to work their way out of poverty.

This assumption, however, flies in the face of the available evidence. This chapter reviews the central claims of the skills mismatch thesis as articulated since the early 1980s, testing them against empirical findings of the relationship between education and earnings. The evidence shows that education plays a relatively minor role in determining wages and that it cannot serve either as a convincing explanation for income trends or as an effective strategy for restoring Americans' earning power.

The skills mismatch thesis has become a convenient—and perhaps comfortable—explanation for falling wages and rising inequality. But more complex and more contested dynamics, such as racial and gender discrimination, the increase in temporary and part-time work, and the decline in unionization, all appear to play a greater role in determining the wages of most workers than does education. Poverty and unemployment will be more fruitfully addressed if policy makers focus attention on these issues rather than tinkering with education and training initiatives ad nauseam, as has been done for the last twenty years to little effect.

Table 2.1 Annual Earnings of Workers Aged 18 and Over, 1999

Level of education	Men	Women
High school dropout	$18,855	$12,145
High school graduate	30,414	18,092
Some college	33,614	20,241
College graduate	57,706	32,546
Advanced degree	84,051	46,307

Source: U.S. Department of Commerce, Census Bureau "Educational Attainment in the United States: March 2000 Update," table 9.

How Important Is Education as a Determinant of Wages?

There is no question that, on average, workers with more education earn higher salaries. As shown in table 2.1, for both men and women, workers at every level of education earn significantly higher wages than those at the level below them. In 1999, the wages of college graduates were 74% higher than those of high school graduates.[9] Thus it is intuitive for individuals to believe that a college education will position them to earn significantly higher wages. However, it is equally clear that many factors beyond education affect wages. As table 2.1 shows, the effects of gender, for instance, are sometimes more powerful than those of education—thus female high school graduates earn less than male dropouts, and women with postgraduate degrees earn less than men with B.A.'s alone. Indeed, while the data shown here are dramatic, the distribution of wages by other criteria—gender, race, age, industry, or degree of unionization, for example—are equally dramatic. Since these factors cut across all levels of education, the ultimate wage which any person earns is determined by the crosscutting interaction of all these factors.

Common experience provides many examples of less-educated workers earning more than their more highly educated counterparts: professional athletes earn more than the doctors who treat their injuries; prison guards make more than bank tellers; and first-year summer associates make more than law professors. These anecdotes are borne out in national statistics that show that higher education is neither a prerequisite for nor a guarantee of higher earnings. By 1996, one out of every six college graduates was in a job that paid less than the average salary of high school graduates.[10] Throughout the economy, the globalization of production, low rates of unionization in the service sector, and the increasing use of temporary and part-time labor have often kept wages low even for skilled workers in expanding industries. Indeed, the shift from manufacturing to service employment has been a shift toward jobs which simultaneously require higher education and offer lower wages than those they replaced.[11]

Thus while education and wages are indeed related, this relationship is cross-cut, mitigated, and often reversed by other determinants of wages. Many economists have focused on education because it fits well within the neoclassical paradigm of workers as "human capital."[12] While acknowledging the empirical evidence of offsetting factors, scholars have often treated these as temporary aberrations that will be eliminated in the course of market operations, or as distortions that mask the underlying truth of education's primacy.[13] So, too, while federal policy makers often acknowledge the effects of other factors, they return time and again to insist that education and training constitute the primary means through which welfare recipients may become self-supporting and the working poor may become middle-class.

In response to this unstinting belief in the importance of education, economists have conducted a series of studies that have consistently shown a lesser role for education in setting wages. The most important of these, undertaken by Rand economist Lynn Karoly, found that from 1967 through 1993 education and experience explained only a third of the variation in men's wages and less than a fifth in women's.[14] Karoly divided the labor force by level of education and experience, analyzing men and women separately. She then analyzed how much of the total distribution of wages could be accounted for by differences *between* these groups and how much resulted from variation *within* them. Between-group differences represent the effect of education and experience on wages; within-group differences represent the effect of other factors. Karoly's findings are dramatic: in 1987, 66% of men's and 80% of women's annual earnings were determined by criteria other than education or experience; the 1993 study showed these proportions holding steady.[15]

As shown in table 2.2, the difference in wages between high school and college graduates is significantly smaller than the differences among workers with the same level of education. Thus in 1999 the college–high school wage gap at the 50th percentile of earnings was $7.61 an hour, but the gap between high- and low-wage high school graduates was nearly twice as large—$14.79 an hour. Income inequality increased dramatically over the past three decades, but Karoly's analysis suggests that 70% of the increase occurred among people with the same level of education. Thus education is a significant factor in determining how much one earns, but it accounts for only about one-third of the story.[16] Moreover, these figures may actually overstate the importance of education in at least two ways. First, Karoly treats the fact that wages rise with experience as a function of human capital—skills learned on the job—but there is reason to believe that the effect of experience on wages has at least as much to do with seniority and salary incentives as with any acquisition of new skills.[17] Second, by treating men and women separately, Karoly's analysis ignores the effect of gender, one of the most important noneducation determinants of wages. If the effects of gender were added to this equation, and the effects of experience

Table 2.2 Wage Inequality among Workers with the Same Level of Education, 1999

Level of education	Hourly wage range			Wage gap within group
	10th percentile	50th percentile	90th percentile	
Men				
High school graduates	$6.54	$11.84	$21.33	$14.79
College graduates	9.62	19.45	40.75	31.13
College–high school wage gap	3.08	7.61	19.42	
Women				
High school graduates	$5.59	$8.95	$16.02	$10.43
College graduates	8.01	15.26	28.90	20.89
College–high school wage gap	2.42	6.31	12.88	

Source: Lawrence Mishel, Jared Bernstein, and John Schmitt, *The State of Working America, 2000/2001* (Ithaca: Cornell University Press, 2001), table 2.23, 161.

filtered out, the power of education to determine wages would be revealed to be even weaker than the figures projected here.

One might think that at this point the analysis was complete and the debate decided, clearly discrediting education as the primary determinant of wages and making for a mercifully short chapter. However, despite the apparent decisiveness of Karoly's findings, mismatch theorists have adhered to their conviction that education *must* explain earnings. Mismatch theorists fault the Rand analysis and others like it on three grounds.[18]

The first critique focuses on the supply of workers, arguing that the quality of education has deteriorated substantially in recent years, a fact that is lost or significantly understated in a study that examines the labor force as a whole, rather than just recent entrants. By aggregating workers who came of age in different eras, this argument goes, the data overlook a critical falloff in schooling quality in recent decades; once this decline is taken into account, it is asserted, insufficient education reemerges as the primary explanation for recent falling wages.[19]

The second challenge to Karoly's data contends that even if education standards have not deteriorated significantly, they have nevertheless failed to keep pace with a rapidly accelerating demand for educated workers. Many economists assert that the past two decades have witnessed the birth of a qualitatively new type of economy—a "knowledge" or "information" economy—focused on services rather than goods, innovation rather than production, and technical know-how rather than manual dexterity. Since aggregate economic data reflect an economy in flux, they underestimate the heightened importance of education in the emerging industries.

Finally, the Rand findings may be attacked on definitional grounds. Many mismatch theorists assert that the number of years one attends school—the measure used in Karoly's study and elsewhere—is too narrow a definition of education.[20] It does not capture differences in the types of schools workers attended, the curricula they followed, or the quality of education they received. Nor does it capture skills and training which might have been acquired in training programs outside the formal education system, through on-the-job training, or informally through contact with friends and relatives. Nor, finally, do years of schooling explain workers' attitudes—punctuality, loyalty, discipline, honesty, ability to follow directions or work in teams, and so on. Thus the third challenge to Karoly's findings contends that her studies simply mismeasure the problem, and asserts that, when the full range of skills is taken into account, it becomes clear that education and training remain the correct focus for employment policy.

As I will illustrate, none of these challenges holds up under inspection. Ultimately, no matter how the issue is defined or measured, the data fail to support any version of the skills mismatch thesis. Furthermore, on close examination, the mismatch argument appears to be driven more by ideological conviction than by empirical evidence. While various versions of the argument have been articulated at multiple points over the past twenty years, the debate reveals a pattern in which the mismatch thesis is repeatedly disproved, only to reappear, Hydra-like, in the guise of alternative claims. Thus early articulations held that there had been a significant decline in educational attainment. When this turned out to be false, the argument shifted to the suggestion that even if workers' education levels had not declined, the demand for workers with formal education had skyrocketed. When this claim, too, was found to be unsubstantiated, many theorists turned to yet more untestable assertions: that while no educational mismatch existed in the present, a future mismatch was inevitable—or, yet more hypothetically, a future mismatch *should* occur *if* employers were to retool for "high performance" production. Similarly, the argument about exactly which skills workers are lacking has metastasized from claims about formal education to measures of basic math and reading competencies and finally to vague assertions focusing on punctuality, discipline, and "higher order thinking skills." In each case, mismatch advocates have moved farther away from concretely testable propositions toward increasingly hypothetical or even normative claims. Thus theorists have responded to contradictory evidence not by questioning the logic of their assumptions but by reformulating the argument in terms that are less and less susceptible to empirical verification. This pattern reflects the political and ideological tenacity of the argument's proponents. Measured against more scientifically rigorous standards, the mismatch thesis cannot be substantiated, no matter how cleverly one juggles the terms of debate.

Supply-Side Explanations:
Have American Workers Become Less Skilled?

The skills mismatch thesis first became widely articulated in the early 1980s, at a time when the country had already lived through ten years of economic contraction and the unemployment rate had climbed to 10%. In its landmark report, *A Nation at Risk*, the Reagan administration traced slowing productivity to deteriorating standards of education, particularly in comparison with our foreign competitors:

> Our Nation is at risk. Our once unchallenged preeminence in commerce, industry, science, and technological innovation is being overtaken by competitors throughout the world. . . . while we can take justifiable pride in what our schools and colleges have historically accomplished . . . the educational foundations of our society are presently being eroded by a rising tide of mediocrity. . . . If an unfriendly foreign power had attempted to impose on America the mediocre educational performance that exists today, we might well have viewed it as an act of war. As it stands, we have allowed this to happen to ourselves. . . . We have, in effect, been committing an act of unthinking, unilateral educational disarmament.[21]

On close examination, it turned out that these claims were as groundless as Reagan's assertion that the want ads proved there were plenty of jobs for unemployed workers. U.S. education levels have in fact been rising steadily, not declining, for at least a century. Indeed, when the Bush administration commissioned a prominent research laboratory to corroborate the claims of *A Nation at Risk*, it received an unexpected response. "To our surprise," reported the research team, "on nearly every measure we found steady or slightly improving trends."[22] The average education of American workers increased from 9.2 years in 1940 to over 13 years in the 1990s.[23] The Reagan administration's warnings prompted renewed attention to high school dropout rates, particularly in urban centers. Yet while dropout rates remain a serious concern, the fact is that they, too, have been improving steadily. As shown in table 2.3, the proportion of American workers with a high school diploma has risen steadily and dramatically over the past thirty years. Furthermore, this increase in average education has been realized by every gender, racial, and economic group.[24] Even among welfare recipients, education standards have improved significantly, with the share of recipients who hold high school diplomas increasing from 42% in 1979 to 70% in 1995.[25] Thus the argument that American workers have become less educated cannot be substantiated either for the workforce as a whole or for any significant subgroup.

Nor has the quality of education declined. The available evidence suggests that the caliber of education has remained constant or improved slightly over the

Table 2.3 Percentage of People Aged 25 and Over Who Have
Completed High School, 1970–2000

Year	Percent
1970	55.2
1975	62.5
1980	68.6
1985	73.9
1990	77.6
1995	81.7
2000	84.0

Sources: U.S. Department of Commerce, Census Bureau, "Social
and Demographic Tables," table A-2, internet release December 10,
1998; U.S. Department of Commerce, Census Bureau, "Educational
Attainment in the United States, March 2000," Report P20-536,
December 2000.

past thirty years. Achievement test scores show mixed results, but generally indicate that the reading and math proficiency of seventeen-year-olds has held steady or increased slightly since the early 1970s. From 1971 to 1999, the share of white seventeen-year-old students who read at the "intermediate" level or above increased from 83.7% to 87%, while that of black students rose from 40.1% to 66%. SAT scores improved for every ethnic group over the course of the 1980s, and average scores for the nation as a whole have risen slightly through the year 2000.[26]

Nor is it true that the composition of the labor force has shifted such that less-educated segments of the population have come to dominate the supply of new workers, an argument put forward by the Reagan Labor Department in 1987 in its landmark *Workforce 2000* report. In a section titled "Demographics as Destiny," the report compared the makeup of the 1985 workforce with the profile of those expected to enter the labor force over the following fifteen years. In one of their most dramatic assertions, the authors projected that while "native white males" constituted nearly half of the current workforce, they would make up only a small fraction of net new entrants:

The cumulative impact of the changing ethnic and racial composition of the labor force will be dramatic. The small net growth of workers will be dominated by women, blacks, and immigrants. White males, thought of only a generation ago as the mainstays of the economy, will comprise only 15 percent of the net additions to the labor force between 1985 and 2000.[27]

Based on this projection, the Labor Department forecast an impending skills crisis created by the predominance of traditionally less-educated workers among new entrants to the labor force. In truth, however, the changes in labor force composition have been quite modest. On close examination, the pronounced changes forecast by *Workforce 2000* turned out to primarily reflect the report's eccentric methodology.[28] Using more straightforward measures, it becomes clear that the labor force is becoming moderately, but not dramatically, more diverse, and that it remains heavily dominated by white workers.[29] Indeed, when this landmark report was updated in 1997, its authors dramatically backpedaled on their earlier claims, conceding that "ethnic and racial diversification is proceeding slowly if steadily." The revised report forecasts that the white non-Hispanic share of the workforce will shrink moderately, from 76% to 68%, over the next twenty-five years.[30]

Thus there is no evidence to believe that falling levels of education—whether measured by years of schooling, achievement levels, or demographic composition of the workforce—are to blame for the worsening economic position of American workers. While there are many reasons, both economic and noneconomic, to be concerned with the quality of education, the source of stagnant or deteriorating wages must be sought elsewhere.

Demand for Technical Training, College Diplomas, and General Education Skills

Computerization and the Demand for Technical Skills

A skills mismatch can be caused by either a shortage of supply or an excess of demand. By the early 1990s, most analysts came to agree that there had been little serious deterioration in the supply of educated workers. Instead, they turned to the argument that technological changes had dramatically increased the demand for skilled labor. Even if the education of the labor force had improved modestly, they argued, it had nevertheless fallen far behind the requirements of employers. Many economists have focused specifically on the spread of computer technology as a development that both dramatically increased the demand for skilled technicians and significantly raised the technical knowledge required of workers generally. Mismatch theorists have asserted that wages are falling for those workers who fail to keep up with technology's advance, and conversely that those who have dedicated themselves to continued training may look forward to higher salaries.

In the congressional hearings leading up to the adoption of the Job Training Partnership Act (JTPA) in 1982, a variety of witnesses identified computer programmers, systems analysts, word processors, data processors, medical and laboratory technicians, machinists, and electricians as among the "new and expanding sectors of the economy" in which "demand exceeds supply."[31] As one supporter of JTPA explained,

> Employers are looking for engineers, technologists, computer analysts, and medical workers, while unskilled and semi-skilled workers are increasingly unable to find work. In our country today, good jobs are going begging while millions are out of work because of a mismatch between the skills of the work force and the requirements of the work place.[32]

The shortage of highly skilled technicians has remained a recurrent theme of employment policy, and indeed, employers report that scientific and technical positions are the hardest to fill.[33] In 1998, the computer industry successfully lobbied Congress to expand the number of work visas for foreign programmers. The evidence suggests, however, that there is no actual shortage of programmers or systems analysts. Rather, technology companies have preferred to hire lower-wage foreign programmers while thousands of more experienced (and more expensive) American programmers remained unemployed.[34] More important, while it may well be true that some employers face shortages in occupations such as nursing and computer programming, most technical professions are quite small as a share of the overall workforce, and therefore the total number of such jobs going begging has never constituted a significant job pool. For instance, the combined total of jobs for mathematicians, computer scientists, computer programmers, numerical control tool programmers, science technicians, electrical and electronic technicians, health technicians, and health assessment and treating occupations amounted to only 4.1% of the total workforce in 1984. After twenty years of unprecedented growth, this share is projected to grow to only 6.4% by the year 2006.[35] Thus even if firms faced shortages in such positions, satisfying that demand would not help the bulk of American workers stuck in the low-wage labor market.

The emphasis on computer skills gained added credence from the work of Princeton economist Alan Krueger, who tested the impact of computer use on wages and found that workers who used a computer on the job earned 10% to 15% more than otherwise similar employees.[36] Because the study did not independently control for occupation, however, it appears that some of the effects attributed to computers are actually coincidental effects of occupational structures. For instance, Krueger reported that the type of computer use that has the single greatest effect on wages is electronic mail. Yet it's hard to believe that e-mail is the critical productivity factor for most of its users. It seems more likely that there are certain highly paid occupations in which use of e-mail is a required part of the job yet is a relatively incidental factor in determining these professionals' wages. Acting on just such a hunch, two other scholars tested

Krueger's theory by calculating the effect of pencil use on wages, and found that pencil use is as accurate as computer use in predicting wages.[37]

In the wake of Krueger's study, a growing number of economists have focused on technological change and the increased use of computers as the dominant source of rising skill requirements and growing wage inequality over the past twenty years.[38] The manufacturing sector in particular is thought to have undergone dramatic upskilling in response to new technologies. For instance, Johnston and Packer point out that "assembly-line workers in many manufacturing plants are learning statistical process control, a system that is beyond the reach of those without a solid grounding in mathematics."[39] This sounds impressive, but what exactly are we to imagine? Will the majority of blue-collar production workers be required to learn probability theory and regression analysis? From the data available to date, it appears that the effect of changes in production techniques has been much more modest. Indeed, there is considerable debate as to whether changes in manufacturing technology have led to up-skilling or de-skilling of the workforce. One prominent study found that the development of numerically controlled machine tools has had a modest negative effect on skill demands, estimating that a machine shop converting from zero to 100% use of numerical control would experience a 2% to 3% decline in skill requirements.[40]

Beyond these technical occupations, some economists have projected a near explosion in demand for more general skills, as even nontechnical employees are called on to perform increasingly sophisticated work. Mismatch theorists have asserted that the economy is undergoing a radical transformation in the way the mundane tasks of factory workers, secretaries, and service workers are performed, such that technical knowledge is becoming a necessity not only for specialists but for the bulk of ordinary working people. The rhetoric of the early 1980s embodied a Disney-esque sense of futurism. In the JTPA congressional hearings, for instance, one witness testified that "Our society is undergoing a transition to a technological and information-based society that is reshaping our nation. . . . Xerox has predicted that 60 million Americans will be linked to electronic work stations by 1995, and that 36 million workers will need to be computer literate."[41] Similarly, another expert projected that

[The] accelerating shift to automation in plants and offices promises to bring . . . technical growth . . . in areas related to communications, robotics, service, and energy. . . . these enterprises will provide us with electronic yellow pages, newspapers, textbooks, mail and teleshopping. These and other communications-related businesses and industries will greatly increase the demand for system analysts, computer programmers, word processor operators and computer graphics personnel.[42]

From the vantage point of being two decades into the future, the grandeur of these projections rings hollow. The year 1995 has come and gone; computer technology has spread tremendously; and many of us are indeed linked to "electronic work stations." Yet the future has turned out to be much more mundane, and much more similar to the past, than its champions imagined. We have achieved "teleshopping," but the reality of what it's like to use the Home Shopping Channel doesn't match the image of effortless, autonomous consumers freed from the drudgery of mundane work; we are not the Jetsons.

Most important, while the spread of computers has required many of us to learn new skills, it has not meant a dramatic increase in the level of education required for most ordinary jobs, whether in factories or in offices. It is instructive that the testimony cited above classifies word processors together with programmers and systems analysts as high-skill jobs of the future.[43] In 1982, the personal computer industry was in its infancy, and the lines between inventor and owner, hacker and programmer, database management and data entry, had not yet been firmly established. Clerical workers encountering computer systems for the first time had to learn not only the specific commands of a particular word processing program but also the basic concepts of how the new technology worked—the distinction between what part of the computer's operation was done by hardware and what by software, the difference between a program and a file, the relationship between having text on a screen and having it on a disk, the idea of a computer having "memory," and above all, the initially mysterious distinction between what would and would not permanently erase files. All of these questions created the impression, for a time, that even the most basic work with computers entailed considerable technical skill, and conveyed near-professional status on its practitioners. Over the course of the past two decades, however, the difference between hardware and software has become as intuitive for most new workers as that between engine and gears is for most automobile drivers; neither constitutes the type of "skill" one might put on a résumé.

Furthermore, as the technology has developed, "computer work" has been segmented, with technical knowledge restricted to a relatively small group of highly skilled, highly paid specialists, while the vast majority of daily computer operations are carried out in relatively low-wage occupations with modest educational requirements.[44] Thus while the early job training advocates were correct in foreseeing the spread of computer technology, the belief that this would create a new labor market characterized by high-wage jobs with dramatically increased educational requirements has proven false.

After more than a decade of research, economists have produced scant evidence of a technology-based skills mismatch. Instead, recent mismatch arguments have often proceeded by adding up the components of wage determination that can be attributed to known factors and then assuming that the unexplained residual *must* be the result of technology.[45] But when scholars invoke invisible evidence and imagined causes, we have left the realm of scientific inquiry and reverted to ideological assumptions that, though comforting to proponents, tell us nothing about the facts of the labor market.[46]

The College Premium and the Demand for Higher Education

As computer technology became more commonplace, economists increasingly backed away from the claim that the new machines had created a widespread boom in demand for high-wage technical workers. Nevertheless, mismatch theorists asserted that the demand for skills—and particularly for higher education—was accelerating rapidly. The primary evidence these theories rested on was the fast-increasing "premium" paid to college-educated workers.

Over the past thirty years, the gap between the wages of college graduates and those of workers with only a high school diploma has reached its widest point in the history of these data. Following neoclassical theory, economists widely interpreted this trend as evidence of a rapid acceleration in the demand for skilled labor. From 1979 to 1999 the wage "premium" for a college degree increased by nearly 70%.[47] If the "price" of college-educated labor was rising steeply, it would seem to mean that employers' demand for higher skills was rising faster than supply. A wide range of scholars have taken this as evidence not only of growing demand for college graduates in particular, but also of a more fundamental increase in demand for education at all levels of the labor force.[48] As Bush Labor Department analysts argued, "Increasing returns to college education indicate strong demand for . . . skills," and conversely, "The decline in the earnings of unskilled or low-educated youth . . . is primarily due to a shift in demand toward more highly skilled labor."[49] Similarly, *Fortune* editor Thomas Stewart concluded that the "education premium proves the growing role of knowledge in creating value and wealth."[50]

On closer consideration, however, the college premium data are riddled with both methodological and substantive problems that raise serious doubts about the premium's presumed meaning. To begin with, when examined in historical context, the increase in the college premium turns out to be much more modest than that portrayed in many policy reports (see table 2.4). The most commonly cited statistic regarding education and earnings is the dramatic increase in the premium since 1979.[51] However, the use of 1979 as a baseline exaggerates the trend considerably. The college premium fell significantly over the course of the 1970s as an oversupply of baby boom college graduates entered the labor market. The year 1979 marked the trough of this decline; much of the increase from 1979 to 1999 is a measure of overeducation in the 1970s rather than of increased demand in the 1980s and 1990s. Thus the premium increased dramatically in the early 1980s, but didn't regain its 1967 level until 1987.[52]

Table 2.4 Hourly Wages by Level of Education, 1973–1999 (constant 1999 dollars)

Year	High school dropout	High school graduate	Some college	College graduate	Advanced degree	College premium	College premium as % of high school wage	Percent change in premium from previous period
1973	$11.64	$13.34	$14.37	$19.46	$23.53	$6.12	46%	
1979	11.58	12.99	13.89	18.21	22.24	5.22	40	−15%
1989	9.73	11.86	13.32	18.68	24.08	6.82	58	31
1995	8.57	11.33	12.67	18.80	24.80	7.47	66	10
1999	8.83	11.83	13.37	20.58	26.44	8.75	74	17

Source: Lawrence Mishel, Jared Bernsten, and John Schmitt, *The State of Working America, 2000/2001* (Ithaca: Cornell University Press, 2001), table 2.18, 153.
Note: Percent change in college premium from 1973 to 1999 = 43%, and from 1979 to 1999 = 68%.

Similarly, the gender distribution of the college premium also sheds doubt on its significance. A number of premium studies have drawn conclusions based on data for male workers alone.[53] Although these data are interpreted as a sign of "the rapid growth in demand for skilled workers" generally, adding in the data on women calls this logic into question.[54] Since years of schooling is a gender-neutral measure of skills, if employers are rapidly increasing their demand for educated workers we should see similar patterns of employment demand among women and men. But tables 2.5 and 2.6 show that the ways the increased college premium came about were markedly different for men and for women. For men, the gap was created by a severe deterioration in the earnings of high school graduates, along with a modest increase in college earnings. For women, the pattern was reversed: no change in high school wages but a large increase in college earnings. The explanation generally given for the rising college premium is a "decline in the earnings of unskilled or low-educated youth . . . primarily due to a shift in demand toward more highly skilled labor."[55] If this is the case, why didn't the wages of female high school graduates fall at rates similar to those of men?

The differential pattern of men's and women's wages suggests a more commonsense explanation. Since men began the 1970s with a much greater share of relatively high-wage manufacturing jobs requiring modest education, it is logical that their wages fell most dramatically as these positions were reduced through automation, layoffs, concession bargaining, and the relocation of jobs abroad. By contrast, female high school graduates began the decade concentrated in lower-wage service occupations which did not undergo similar transformations. Similarly, since men were already well-positioned in college-educated professions, they gained only modestly compared with women, who began entering

Table 2.5 Average Hourly Wages, by Education and Gender, 1973–1999 (constant 1999 dollars)

Year	High school dropout	High school graduate	Some college	College graduate	Advanced degree	College premium	College premium as % of high school wage
Men							
1973	$13.61	$16.14	$16.50	$22.26	$24.72	$6.12	38%
1979	13.36	15.65	16.28	21.28	24.21	5.63	36
1989	11.03	13.77	15.18	21.42	26.64	7.65	56
1995	9.43	12.78	14.26	21.14	27.50	8.36	65
1999	9.78	13.34	15.12	23.52	29.66	10.18	76
Women							
1973	$8.21	$10.16	$10.98	$15.20	$20.13	$5.04	50%
1979	8.57	10.16	10.92	13.82	17.70	3.66	36
1989	7.66	9.90	11.47	15.52	20.23	5.62	57
1995	7.19	9.73	11.15	16.22	21.35	6.49	67
1999	7.39	10.17	11.75	17.50	22.61	7.33	72

Source: Lawrence Mishel, Jared Bernstein, and John Schmitt, *The State of Working America, 2000/2001* (Ithaca: Cornell University Press, 2001), tables 2.19, 2.20, 155–56.

Table 2.6 Percent Change in Real Hourly Wages by Education Level and Gender, 1979–1999

	Men	Women
High school graduates	−17.2%	0.01%
College graduates	5.6	15.1

Source: Lawrence Mishel, Jared Bernstein, and John Schmitt, *The State of Working America, 2000/2001* (Ithaca: Cornell University Press, 2001), tables 2.19, 2.20, 155–56.

many professions in large numbers only during this period. It is not surprising, then, that the earnings of male high school graduates would fall most and those of female college graduates would rise most. However, these dynamics point to institutional rather than educational determinants of wages: the initial gender distribution of jobs was largely unrelated to skills, and the differential histories of the manufacturing and service sectors have more to do with the globalization of production, weak plant closing legislation, and falling unionization rates than with changes in the educational requirements of particular jobs.

This gender discrepancy points to a broader problem with the college premium thesis. Across the labor market as a whole, there are a variety of groups that experienced rising or falling relative wages. If a widening wage gap is sufficient evidence of a shortage of one group of workers, why have mismatch theorists focused only on the college–high school differential and not on other equally significant premiums? As one scholar notes,

> If rising wages for male college graduates relative to male high school graduates are simply interpreted as evidence of a shortage of male college graduates, why are rising wages of female high school graduates relative to male high school graduates not viewed as evidence of a shortage of female high school graduates? . . . Using as a base, men with fewer than 4 years of high school, should the case be made that there was a shortage of all other occupational groups, including male high school graduates?[56]

The "premiums" paid to union members, manufacturing workers, and full-time employees have all increased in recent years, yet no one suggests that employers face a shortage of full-time, unionized factory workers. In this context, the exclusive focus on education seems eccentric. Yet if the simple fact of rising relative wages is not enough to establish a labor shortage for these groups, neither can it be taken as proof of increased demand for college graduates.

The comparison with other premiums points to the most important reason not to take the college premium as evidence of rising employer demand for education. The premium is a relative measure; it can grow either because of increasing wages at the top or falling wages at the bottom. If the college premium increases due to setbacks in the lower end of the labor market, it cannot be interpreted as evidence of increased demand for college workers. In fact, over the past thirty years, the real wages of high school graduates fell by 11.3%, while those of college graduates rose by 5.7%.[57] Thus 60% of the change in the premium over this time was due to a worsening situation for high school graduates rather than to increasing wages for college-educated workers. For male workers—the primary concern of mismatch theorists—the trend is even starker. Since 1973, the college–high school wage gap for male workers has increased by $4.06 an hour; nearly 70% of this change is due to the bottom falling out of the high school market, rather than rising wages for college workers (see table 2.5).[58] In this light, the rising college premium cannot be interpreted as a growing demand for higher education.

When the actual numbers are consulted, it is clear that there has been no shortage of college-educated workers. From 1979 to 1999 college graduates in the labor force grew from 17.9 million to 38.9 million, an increase of over 100%.[59] Instead of being the subject of intense bidding, however, a significant share of these graduates have been unable to find jobs in occupations that make use of their degrees. By 1990, almost one in five graduates—more than 5.7 million college-educated workers—were unable to find college-level work; this total included 75,000 college graduates working as street vendors or door-to-door salespeople, 166,000 as truck and bus drivers, 83,000 as maids, housemen, janitors, or cleaners, and 688,000 who were unemployed.[60] These numbers held constant throughout the 1990s, and the Department of Labor projects that in the first decade of the twenty-first century, while the retirement of educated baby boomers will create more openings in college jobs, the number of new college graduates will continue to grow faster than the number of jobs requiring a college degree.[61] As economist Daniel Hecker notes, these data suggest that "employers chose not to hire large numbers of available college graduates for college-level jobs, even though the graduates were willing to work at wages well below the going rate for those jobs."[62] The authors of *Workforce 2000* described an emerging economy in which "for the first time in history, a majority of all new jobs will require postsecondary education."[63] In absolute terms, however, the economy seems to have moved in just the opposite direction. Rather than workers with college degrees being the objects of a bidding war, the college diploma has become increasingly less effective in guaranteeing middle-class wages even for those who already hold it.

College-educated professionals continue to earn significantly more than high school–educated workers. Yet even this gap does not necessarily reflect the economic value of skills. Indeed, it is possible that the growing income gap between workers with and without a college degree has less to do with differences in education than with the relative protections offered different occupations. While many of the institutions which protected the wages of production workers have been eliminated in the name of "competitiveness," professional earnings remain safeguarded by elaborate systems of immigration control, licensing, educational credentials, and legal mandates. Much of what lawyers do can be competently carried out by paralegals; many medical procedures can be performed by nurses or technicians; and much college instruction can be done by graduate teaching assistants. And certainly, any number of fully credentialed professionals in developing countries would gladly come to America for a fraction of the pay enjoyed by their local counterparts. The earnings of professionals have been artificially propped up not by the rarity of their skills but by their ability to erect institutional barriers to competition. If American professionals were forced to compete on the same basis as production workers, the wage gap between college and non-college-educated employees might be considerably narrower.[64]

The Limits of the College Job Market and the Value of Education for Nonprofessional Workers

The single most important fact about the college–high school wage differential is that the total number of jobs requiring a college degree is clearly limited. The link between education and income, like the availability of jobs in general, plays off the illusion that what's true for an individual is also true for the population

Table 2.7 Employment by Required Level of Education, 1998 and Projected 2008

Education required	1998		2008	
	Jobs (in thousands)	Share of total	Jobs (in thousands)	Share of total
Professional degree	1,908	1.4%	2,215	1.4%
Doctoral degree	996	0.7	1,228	0.8
Master's degree	940	0.7	1,115	0.7
Work experience plus B.A.	9,595	6.8	11,276	7.0
Bachelor's degree	17,379	12.4	21,596	13.4
Associate degree	4,930	3.5	6,467	4.0
Total, bachelor's degree or more required	30,818	21.9	37,430	23.3
Total, associate degree or more required	35,748	25.4	43,897	27.3
Total	140,514	100	160,795	100

Source: U.S. Department of Labor, Bureau of Labor Statistics data reported in Douglas Braddock, "Occupational Employment Projections to 2008," *Monthly Labor Review*, November 1999.

as a whole. But while it is the case for any single individual that a college degree may lead to a high-paying job, the structure of the labor market is such that the total possible number of professional jobs is limited to 20% to 30% of the workforce (see table 2.7).[65] In this sense, the college premium ultimately is irrelevant to the vast majority of American workers. In terms of federal employment policy, the important question is not the effect of a college degree on earnings, but rather the effect of lower levels of education on the earnings of workers in occupations where higher education is unnecessary.

Job training advocates have asserted that the economy is changing in ways that make education increasingly important for *all* workers. *Workforce 2000*, for instance, notes that the majority of new jobs have been created in clerical, retail, and service occupations, but insists that "even for these jobs ... workers will be expected to read and understand directions, add and subtract, and be able to speak and think clearly. ... jobs that are currently in the middle of the skill distribution will be the least-skilled occupations of the future, and there will be very few net new jobs for the unskilled."[66] In this view, the growing income inequality that marked the past few decades—and the deterioration in wages for the majority of nonsupervisory workers—is explained by the shift from low-skill manufacturing jobs to higher-skill service and technology jobs. "Like the farmer before him," explains Stewart, "the factory worker ... is becoming an artifact of a bygone age, carefully preserved on WPA murals."[67] The new jobs require new skills, with those who haven't mastered them left behind, and those who can supply them rewarded handsomely.

The claim that the past twenty years have seen a dramatic shift toward higher-skill jobs is easy to test. The Labor Department's Dictionary of Occupational Titles (DOT) measures the level of skill required for each individual occupation in the economy, according to several different definitions of skill. By totaling skill requirements across all occupations, we can produce a snapshot of the average level of skill required for the economy as a whole in any given year; comparing these economy-wide averages from year to year shows whether the economy as a whole is shifting toward higher- or lower-skilled work. If the mix of jobs in the economy has become concentrated in more demanding positions, the overall average level of skill required should be increasing. Moreover, if mismatch theorists are correct in asserting that increasing income inequality since the 1970s can be traced to an accelerating shift toward skilled occupations, we should see economy-wide skill indices that are not only rising, but rising faster as time goes on.

The most thorough analysis of this argument has been performed by economist David Howell in a series of collaborative studies.[68] Howell's first study focused on changes in the job mix over the period 1960 to 1985.[69] The findings, shown in table 2.8, indicate that skill requirements rose steadily, but very gradually, throughout this period.[70] For instance, the average level of "substantive complexity"—a measure of cognitive skills—increased by roughly seven-tenths of a percentage point per year between 1960 and 1970. The table shows four different measures of job skill; for all except motor skills, the average level of skill required for the economy as a whole increased modestly in all three of the time periods measured. However, the increase in skill requirements was so gradual that it was easily matched by the increasing skills of the workforce. Indeed, the average education of the labor force (measured by years of schooling) grew faster than most skill indices in all three periods analyzed. Nor is there any evidence that younger workers in particular failed to keep pace with the demand for skills; the education levels of workers aged twenty-five to twenty-nine increased even more rapidly than those of the workforce as a whole. Finally, the data show that the *rate* of increase in skill requirements is declining rather than accelerating, with the largest growth in demand for skills occurring in the 1960s and the most modest growth in the first half of the 1980s.

Howell's findings also suggest that demand for higher skills is largely restricted to upper-echelon occupations (not shown in the table). The fastest-growing skill indices in the 1980s were those for substantive complexity and general educational development, the two measures of cognitive skills. But while demand for these skills increased slightly among professional and managerial workers in the early 1980s, it actually decreased among nonsupervisory workers.[71]

In a more recent study, Howell examined the relationship between skills and wages over the 1980s and 1990s. He measured the skill levels required by hundreds of occupations, according to both the level of formal education

Table 2.8 Average Annual Increase in Skill Requirements, Due to Changes in Occupational Job Mix, and Average Annual Increase in Education and Earnings, 1960 to 1985

Measure	1960 to 1970	1970 to 1980	1980 to 1985
Skill requirements			
Substantive complexity	0.69%	0.46%	0.28%
General educational development	0.36	0.22	0.13
Interactive skills	0.26	0.22	0.03
Motor skills	0.07	−0.14	−0.04
Education of workforce			
Median years of education	1.32%	0.33%	0.16%
(workers 25+ years old)			
Median years of education	2.01	0.41	0.16
(workers 24–29 years old)			
Earnings			
Full-time, full-year earnings	0.28%	0.25%	0.09%
Annual earnings	0.33	0.20	0.02
Hourly earnings	0.44	0.18	0.00
Relationship of skills to earnings			
Ratio of annual earnings increase to increase	47.8%	43.5%	7.1%
in substantive complexity requirement			
Ratio of annual earnings increase to increase	91.7	90.9	15.4
in general educational development			

Source: David Howell and Edward Wolff, "Trends in the Growth and Distribution of Skills in the U.S. Workplace, 1960–1985," *Industrial and Labor Relations Review* 44, no. 3 (1991): 486–502.

required and the level of basic English and math skills required.[72] He then measured how employment and wages grew or shrank in each occupation over the periods 1984 to 1992 and 1989 to 1997. According to mismatch theorists, the demand for skills has grown faster than the supply, thus bidding up the wages for skilled workers. If this theory is correct, wages should be increasing most in the most highly skilled jobs and increasing least (or decreasing) in the lowest-skilled positions. However, the results of this study, shown in table 2.9, suggest a different story. While education does help explain which occupations had growing or shrinking wages, it explains only a fraction—somewhere between 5% and 29%—of the variation, depending on which measure is used. These results are in keeping with the findings for 1960 to 1985. What is most striking is that, rather than accelerating, the share of wage growth that can be accounted for by skills or education declined noticeably from the 1980s to the 1990s.

Taken together, data from these studies point to four important conclusions. First, while the demand for skills has grown continuously, it has not outpaced the abilities of the labor force. Second, the growth in demand for skills has been

Table 2.9 Share of Wage Growth Explained by Job Skills, 1984 to 1997

Job Skill	1984 to 1992	1989 to 1997
Years of schooling		
Men	18.0%	7.1%
Women	29.0	8.2
Functional literacy		
Men	13.3%	6.1%
Women	18.1	5.5

Source: David Howell, Ellen Houston, and William Milberg, "Demand Shifts and Earnings Inequality: Wage and Hours Growth by Occupation in the U.S., 1970–97," CEPA Working Paper No. 6, Center for Economic Policy Analysis, New York, N.Y., 1999, table 7.

slowing down rather than accelerating. Third, the demand for skills has been least pronounced among nonsupervisory employees in occupations that do not require a college degree. And, finally, while mismatch theorists assert that skills are becoming a more important determinant of wages, the historical trend is in the opposite direction, toward an increasing *decoupling* of skills from wages, particularly after 1980.[73]

Is Math the Answer?

As with the earlier data of Karoly, it might seem that Howell's findings have definitively laid to rest the mismatch thesis. Indeed, this work clearly refutes the most common claim of mismatch theorists, namely that the increasingly unequal distribution of income reflects a shift in demand toward higher-skill, higher-wage occupations. Nevertheless, economists have continued to explore the possibility that the demand for skills has increased in ways not captured by this analysis. While Howell's data demonstrate that there has been no marked shift toward more highly skilled occupations, some economists maintain that demand for skill has increased *within* existing occupations. It is difficult to imagine what set of skills might have become more important within occupations without also causing a shift in demand between occupations, but several studies have suggested that the growing importance of math skills might be causing this effect. While there is some evidence that math ability (independent of years of schooling) affects employment and earnings, the relationship between math scores and nonsupervisory earnings is ambiguous. Educational analysts Levy and Murnane, whose work has gone furthest to identify the link between math ability and wages, conclude that "improving schooling . . . is unlikely, by itself, to be a powerful strategy for restoring real earnings to their level of 20 years ago . . . [even] helping all students to achieve mastery of basic mathematics skills would contribute only modestly to restoring the earnings of high school graduates."[74]

"Unobserved Skill": The Final Formulation of the Mismatch Thesis

As discussed above, two-thirds of the increase in income inequality since 1970 has occurred among people with the same levels of education and experience, and no known measure of human capital can explain more than a small share of the distribution of wages. Thus for skill to be the prime determinant of wages, there must be some critical dimension of skill that has eluded detection in the studies done to date. Based on this assumption, a number of economists have taken to asserting a growing demand for "unobserved skills." Levy and Murnane speculate that the "unobserved" phenomenon might reflect "increasing demand for interactive skills, defined as skill in mentoring, negotiating, instructing, supervising, and persuading."[75]

Other economists have advanced similar and increasingly fanciful notions of personal behavior and character traits as the root of wage determination. Moss and Tilly, for instance, suggest that what entry-level workers really need are "soft skills," which they divide between "interaction" (the ability to deal with customers and to display "friendliness, teamwork, ability to fit in, and appropriate affect, grooming, and attire") and "motivation," defined as "enthusiasm, positive work attitude, commitment, dependability, and willingness to learn."[76] Likewise the National Center for the Educational Quality of the Workforce focuses on the importance of "behavioral skills" such as "showing up on time, following instructions, and taking pride in a job's outcome."[77] Finally, management guru Daniel Goleman insists that the critical trait demanded of workers is "emotional intelligence," defined as a combination of "self-confidence, empathy, the need to get results, constant improvement, influence, and teamwork."[78] Even though traditionally defined, "observable" skills show no signs of a mismatch between supply and demand, theorists assert that there is indeed a mismatch if we account for these more important, if less visible, criteria.

As may be apparent, the definition of these unobserved "soft skills" is expressed in terms so vague as to leave one wishing for a definition of the definition. Indeed, while insisting that unobserved skills are real, Levy and Murnane sum up the research on this topic by concluding that "the growth in within-group earnings inequality has many potential explanations, but . . . is not well understood."[79]

One immediate problem with the assumption that the increase in within-group inequality reflects unobserved skills is that inequality began increasing in the early 1970s, whereas the premium for formal education only increased after

1979. Thus whatever the "unobserved" skills are, they must be independent of formal education. Moreover, the demand for both education and occupational skills grew most in the 1960s, tapered off in the 1970s, and slowed further during the 1980s and 1990s, while inequality was unchanged during the 1960s, grew moderately in the 1970s, and accelerated in the 1980s and early 1990s.[80] Thus for the unobserved skills thesis to be true, there would have to be a critical dimension of workplace skills that (1) is not captured in measures of formal education, achievement test scores, or the Dictionary of Occupational Titles's skill indices; (2) predated the rising return to formal education by a decade; and (3) is inversely related to the demand for observed skills. It is not surprising, then, that economists have difficulty specifying what set of talents might meet this description.

In summary, while skills unrelated to education or training undoubtedly play a role in the determination of employment and earnings, there is no reason to believe that they constitute the driving force behind the income trends of the past two decades or that acquiring new skills is the path to upward mobility for the majority of American workers. After reviewing all available evidence, it appears most likely that there is no critical hidden skill that is the primary determinant of wages, but rather that incomes are shaped more powerfully by factors unrelated to skill.

What Do Employers Really Want?
The Mismatch between Wages and Discipline

Attitudes before Skills

The ultimate measure of labor market demand may be the simplest: direct surveys of employer needs. For the past twenty years, employers have regularly complained about the quality of labor, and critical skills shortages have been the subject of frequent news stories. But while there are certainly individual cases of employers unable to find adequately trained workers for new technologies, surveys provide no evidence of a broader trend of this type. In 1990, the Commission on the Skills of the American Workforce surveyed a wide range of businesses. For the bottom third of the labor market—comprising 40 million jobs—the commission found no increase in skill requirements at all: "a pleasant personality behind the service counter, physical stamina on the construction site or a steady hand on the wheel tend to be the important requirements."[81] While the commission found sporadic shortages among more highly skilled workers, it saw no suggestion of a system-wide upgrading of skill requirements. The commission concluded that there was "no . . . major change in skill requirements on the horizon. . . . With some exceptions, the education and skill levels of American workers roughly match the demands of their jobs. . . . Despite the widespread presumption that advancing technology and the evolving service economy will create jobs demanding higher skills, only 5 percent of employers feel that education and skill requirements are increasing significantly."[82]

Similarly, a 1991 survey of human resources directors in 400 major corporations found that the vast majority of positions could be filled without difficulty, and that occupations which required the greatest recruiting effort were concentrated among high-skill professions rather than ordinary production or service jobs.[83] Overall, 82% of these firms agreed with the statement that "in spite of all the talk of coming labor shortages, this is not yet a serious problem for [my] company," and 77% reported that they did not expect difficulty attracting enough entry-level workers with adequate math and verbal skills.[84]

When employers are surveyed regarding the specific skills they seek, there is little evidence for the sorts of technological mismatch often envisioned by training advocates. Even basic literacy and mathematics skills do not number among the most commonly voiced concerns of employers. Rather, employers seem primarily concerned with workers' attitudes. This emphasis on attitudes is found in virtually every major report on actual employer demands.[85] As the Commission on the Skills of the American Workforce reported:

> While businesses everywhere complained about the quality of their applicants, few talked about the kinds of skills acquired in school. The primary concern of more than 80 percent of employers was finding workers with a good work ethic and appropriate social behavior: "reliable," "a good attitude," "a pleasant appearance," "a good personality." . . . Although a few managers are worried about literacy and basic math skills, education levels rarely seem a concern. Employers do not complain about an inability to do algebra or write essays.[86]

Likewise, a survey of New York City employers spanning a wide range of industries found that "the most important hiring criteria across all occupational categories have to do with personal characteristics such as work attitude, work habits, punctuality and overall personality."[87] Table 2.10 shows these employers' ranking of hiring criteria for workers in service occupations. Asked to rank twenty-three qualifications, employers reserved their top marks for workers' attitudes. By contrast, educational and technical requirements were much less important: the "work habits" were considered almost twice as important as whether or not applicants had completed high school. Indeed, a wide range of criteria, including grooming, drug screening, and "applicant's realistic expectation of wages" were all judged considerably more important than any measure of education or training. As table 2.11 shows, employers surveyed by the

Table 2.10 Importance of Specific Factors When Evaluating a Job Applicant in Service Occupations (reported by New York City employers, 1994, all industries)

Factor	Mean importance ratings on 0–100 scale
Punctuality	98
Work attitude	93
Work habits	93
Overall personality	85
Stable work history	84
Speaking ability	84
Result of interview	84
Grooming/dress	81
Employer references	80
Applicant's realistic expectation of wages	76
Specific employment experience	69
General employment experience	68
Drug screening	64
High school/GED degree	54
Proximity of home	52
Result of testing	51
Vocational/technical training	45
Some college	32
Technical certification	29
College degree	24
Basic computer skills	22
Advanced degree	18
Advanced computer skills	15

Source: New York City Department of Employment, 1994.

Table 2.11 Most Important and Least Important Skills for Future Employees Reported by Michigan and Rochester, New York, Employers

Michigan	Rochester
Most important "skills"	
No substance abuse	No substance abuse
Honesty, integrity	Follow directions
Follow directions	Read instructions
Respect others	Follow safety rules
Punctuality, attendance	Respect others
Least important "skills"	
Mathematics	Natural sciences
Social sciences	Calculus
Natural sciences	Computers
Computer programming	Art
Foreign languages	Foreign languages

Source: Sandia Laboratories, "Perspectives on Education in America," *Journal of Educational Research* 86, no. 5 (1993): 295.

Table 2.12 Relative Ranking of Factors in Making Hiring Decisions, National Employers Survey, 1997 (5 = very important; 1 = not important)

Applicant characteristic	Rank
Applicant's attitude	4.6
Applicant's communication skills	4.1
Previous employer recommendation	3.9
Previous work experience	3.8
Industry-based credentials (certifying applicant's skills)	3.2
Years of completed schooling	2.9
Academic performance (grades)	2.5
Score on tests administered as part of the interview	2.3
Experience or reputation of applicant's school	2.0
Teacher recommendations	2.0

Source: Daniel Shapiro, "Connecting Work and School: Findings from the 1997 National Employers Survey," National Center on the Educational Quality of the Workforce, www.irhe.upenn.edu.

Michigan state legislature and the Rochester, New York, Board of Education reported similar sentiments.

The single most comprehensive survey of employer needs was carried out by the U.S. Census Bureau, in conjunction with the National Center on the Educational Quality of the Workforce.[88] Asking employers to rank the most important criteria for hiring new employees, they found "applicant's attitude" to be the single most important, followed by a series of measures designed to gauge general work habits rather than academic skills (see table 2.12). The National Survey authors conclude that firms "pay little attention to measurements of school performance. What is frankly more important to employers is how the applicant presents himself or herself—in terms of attitude and communication skills—and whether or not he or she has a successful history of previous work experience."[89]

Indeed, while employers often complain that entry-level workers possess poor skills, it appears that almost none care enough about academic skills to consult the high school transcripts of job applicants. In 1997, the National Alliance of Business, the Business Roundtable, and the U.S. Chamber of Commerce together launched a major public relations campaign whose goal was to convince 10,000 employers—just two-tenths of one percent of U.S. employers—to begin asking for school records as part of their hiring procedures. Four years later, they were less than one-third of the way toward this goal.[90] Nor do employers appear to be significantly concerned with upgrading the academic skills of employees once hired. Of all the training received by nonsupervisory employees, only four-tenths of one percent is devoted to remedial math or reading classes.[91]

The relative unimportance of skills for most employers is further evident in the choice of so many corporations to relocate production to third world countries where workers are less educated but cheaper, instead of using better educated but pricier Americans. This trend is most evident in the manufacturing sector—the very sector where, according to advocates of the mismatch thesis, technological upgrading and rising skill requirements have affected the labor market most. If the mismatch theory rests on demonstrating that manufacturing procedures have changed in a way that requires a higher-skilled workforce, the flight of jobs abroad may prove lethal to this theory. By 1999, there were nearly 4,500 foreign-owned production facilities in the Mexican maquiladora zones alone, employing 1.2 million workers at $4 per day.[92] Many of the nation's leading industrial companies—including Ford, General Motors, General Electric, Westinghouse, Goodyear, and Johnson and Johnson, to name just a few—have directed investment to these super-exploited production platforms; General Motors alone operates fifty-four maquiladora factories employing 75,000 workers.[93] In 1999 General Electric took things one step further when it began a systematic pressure campaign aimed at forcing its own suppliers to move to Mexico and use the labor savings to cut prices. Among the compelling reasons for relocation cited by GE are a workforce that is "50% under age 20, average pay $6 per day, [and] friendly unions."[94]

It is important to remember that maquiladora plants are not restricted to lower-skill methods or less sophisticated technology than those used in American plants. Virtually every step of the process in automobile manufacturing, for instance, is done both in the United States and in Mexico. However, while corporate representatives complain about American skills standards, it appears that identical production methods may be profitably carried out using a workforce dominated by teenage girls.[95] Furthermore, there is no evidence that Mexican hires are screened for the ability to write paragraphs, convert fractions into decimals, or engage in collaborative problem solving; indeed the only known criterion is that female workers are often required to undergo monthly pregnancy tests as a condition of employment.[96] It is possible, of course, that better-educated Americans are more productive workers—but it appears that the vast wage gulf between first- and third-world wages far outweighs the benefits of a well-trained workforce.

Even within the United States, some of the most sophisticated high-tech companies have chosen to manufacture their products in the most low-skill manner possible. Thus in 1999 the Labor Department announced an investigation into charges that Hewlett-Packard, Sun Microsystems, and other prominent high-tech companies had violated minimum wage and child labor laws by paying Asian immigrant families to assemble electronics products in their homes on a piece-rate basis.[97] Clearly these companies are capable of designing higher-tech production processes around the abilities of more highly educated (or at least English-speaking) workers. It may not be surprising that it is more profitable to rely on the lowest-tech, lowest-skilled, and lowest-wage forms of production, but this fact underscores how marginal the demand for skill is even in the most sophisticated parts of the manufacturing sector. With all the talk of "clean-room technicians" and the glamour associated with the computer industry since the beginning of the training debate, who in the early 1980s would have guessed that computer electronics assembly at the end of the twentieth century could turn out to be so similar to textile production at its beginning? Perhaps more than any other example, this case points to the fact that technology is not an independent force that automatically leads to more autonomous and higher-wage work. Rather technology always develops within a given political and economic context, and in the context of a weak labor movement and an unrestrained drive to maximize profits, companies will find ways to organize both high-tech and low-tech production along lines that keep wages low and workers dependent. The fact that employers prefer to hire workers who are cheap, desperate, and uneducated rather than secure, knowledgeable, and well-paid suggests that the "soft skills" they look for in job applicants have more to do with subordination than with team-building.

"Soft Skills": New Age Discipline?

The workplace attitudes demanded by employers constitute what Levy and Murnane term "the new Basic Skills."[98] They and other mismatch theorists take great pains to explain that these skills represent something other than simple discipline. The National Center for the Educational Quality of the Workforce, for example, maintains that employers do not want people who simply follow orders, because such people may be too passive and lack the initiative required for success. Employers certainly do want people to follow orders given, and the center's reports are filled with evidence of the premium placed on obedience.[99] These scholars insist, however, that in addition to obedience, there is another set of crucial traits that employers seek, and that these traits are at the heart of the current skills gap. Rather than simple submission, the key personality traits for a successful employee are held to be "conscientiousness," "dependability," and, above all, "motivation, the driving force behind the need to achieve."[100]

But how different, really, are these traits from what employers have always wanted? When we look behind the labels applied by academics to the words of employers themselves, the "new basic skills" seem in fact to be closely related to the old "skills" of deference and discipline. In the retail sector—one of the most important industries for entry-level workers—descriptions of "interactive skills" seem to dissolve upon inspection into nothing more novel than a servile attitude and a perma-smile. A senior manager in one major retail chain, for instance, invokes the slogan "fast, fun and friendly" to define the type of employee her corporation looks for: "I tell my . . . personnel managers, 'If they don't smile, don't hire them.' I don't care how well-educated they are, how well-versed they are in retail, if they can't smile, they're not going to make a customer feel welcome. And we don't want them in our store."[101] The fact that companies look for enthusiasm and commitment in addition to simple discipline does not seem to herald a fundamentally new economy in which workers are called on to be independently creative and collaborative. Rather, it may be a sign that employers have become even more ambitious in the extent to which they seek to mold employees' wills and personalities. From the worker's point of view, however, the fact that one is now expected to be enthusiastic about assembling products, stocking shelves, or typing letters may represent not an increase in freedom but a decrease—the employer now seeks to control not only the work that one produces, but also the thoughts that are in one's head.

Army, Prisons, Maquiladoras: Training Ground for Soft Skills?

Ultimately, the most commonly voiced business concerns seem to point back to the oldest of employer mantras: employees just aren't working hard enough. In this sense, it is revealing to note how often both employers and mismatch theorists point to the military as an example of effective training. For example, one survey reported that employers were optimistic that urban teenagers could ultimately make suitable employees because they "saw evidence in successful military service that the potential worker was both disciplined and trainable."[102] The National Center for the Educational Quality of the Workforce suggested that Congress institute a youth national service program that would enable a teenager to "demonstrate his or her capacity for work." "What we have in mind," explained a center working paper, "is to make national service more like military service, in that successful completion of a volunteer assignment would be viewed by the employer community as evidence that the volunteer . . . is ready for work."[103]

But if the skills in demand are those learned in boot camp, this suggests that the new "skills" are in fact indistinguishable from simple discipline.

Similarly, employers' bottom-line hiring criteria are revealed in the growing number of companies that have turned to prison labor as the ultimate in disciplined workforces.[104] For most prisoners, work offers the only possible means of making money and one of the only sources of relief from the boredom of incarceration. In addition, many prisons have made phone calls, visiting hours, exercise time, and other perks dependent on performance at work. Thus prisoners generally constitute a highly motivated workforce. If employers truly faced an urgent need for highly *skilled* employees (not to mention employees who are emboldened to critique production methods without fear of offending the boss), prisons are one of the last places one would expect them to look. If, however, the true concern is with simple discipline, it makes more sense to exploit the low wages and guaranteed obedience of prisoners. It is telling, therefore, that the companies that use inmate labor seem to find that it satisfies many of the hiring criteria included under the rubric of "soft skills." There is, obviously, no problem with punctuality in prison. Beyond this, prisoners seem to have the motivation, drive, and "work ethic" that employers often find lacking in the free labor market. The former head of Wisconsin's corrections system praised prison industries for enabling inmates to develop exactly those "work habits" that training advocates identify as critical: "learning discipline, how to follow directions [and] how to work with others."[105] The Federal Prison Industries' marketing campaign boasts not only of its "high-quality, competitively priced labor," but also of its "unwavering commitment to customer service."[106] The owner of a data processing company that operates in San Quentin prison likewise explains the advantages of convict labor by noting that "we have a captive labor force, a group of men who are dedicated, who want to work."[107] "Any person in here has a strong desire to work because this is by far the best game in town," concurs the manager of an IBM supplier. "The productivity and quality of this work force is as good as, if not better than, any that I've ever worked with." Indeed, IBM awarded its prison supplier a quality award for delivering defect-free cable.[108]

If private employers find the "motivation" and "work ethic" they need in prisons, it suggests that the "interactive skills" and "teamwork" they seek are not a matter of *skill*, but rather of *will*. Anyone, it seems, can be a good team member, if only he or she is desperate enough for the job or institutionally deprived of the means to resist.

Money Changes Everything: Skill Gap vs. Wage Gap

The extent to which "work ethic" is a matter of will rather than skill is further evident in the power of good wages to produce effects that training programs seem incapable of producing. It is striking that in entry-level occupations, if wages are raised just slightly above the average, the apparently intractable behavioral problems of "low-skill" workers seem to disappear. Moss and Tilly, for instance, surveyed two distribution warehouses in the same Latino neighborhood in Los Angeles, both employing large numbers of current and former gang members. In the first, managers "complain sarcastically about employees' laziness, their propensity for theft . . . and even the poor personal hygiene of the workforce," and the company struggles with a 25% turnover rate even after redoubled effort to screen new hires for the most stable employees. The second warehouse drew on the same labor force but paid entry-level workers several dollars an hour more than their competition. At this company managers had few complaints about the workers, and the turnover rate was just 2%.[109] This finding reflects what most of us take to be common sense: traits such as discipline, loyalty, and punctuality are not "skills" that one either possesses or lacks; they are measures of commitment that one chooses to give or withhold based on the conditions of work offered. It is troubling, then, that even when employers complain about skills shortages they often refuse to raise wages as a means for solving the problem.[110] If the critical "skills" at issue involve the willingness to embrace a subordinate position in a corporate hierarchy, it may be unsurprising if employers view the demand for higher wages itself as a sign of insolence or overreaching, and thus regard wage increases as a self-defeating strategy for obtaining the "skills" in question. Yet it is not surprising that workers would withhold this level of commitment in jobs offering low wages and little prospect for upward mobility. Given the dramatic deterioration of wages over the past twenty-five years, the comments of employers suggest a mismatch of an entirely different sort—a gap between the loyalty and commitment firms seek and the wages they offer.

What Is "Skill"?

The notion of "skill" has long been one of the most elusive and hardest-to-define concepts in labor economics.[111] In the academic focus on "unobserved skills" and in employers' demand for "work habits," the mismatch debate has converged on attitude and discipline as the central definition of skill for nonsupervisory workers. But this formulation makes nonsense of the very category it seeks to explain. If discipline is a "skill," we have defined away any possibility for a class of "unskilled" occupations. In this case, "skill" means nothing more than "whatever employers want." But once skill is defined in terms of workers' willingness to acquiesce to workplace authority, it becomes impossible to distinguish between the claims of human capital theory—that wages are determined by the objective skills workers bring to a job—and those of labor process theory—that wages are determined by the subjective, political position which workers occupy in the hierarchy of the firm. These two previously opposing claims have now been collapsed into one. Or rather, having exhausted all alternative definitions of "skill" that might explain the wage trends of the past twenty years, human capital theory has been reduced to labor process theory in drag. Rather than seeking to revive the corpse of human capital theory through creative redefinition, it might be more prudent to admit the obvious: the category of "skill" falls apart in the bottom half of the labor market, and there is little it can tell us about wages in this sector.

In some ways, it doesn't matter whether or not we term punctuality or discipline a "skill." Whatever it is called, it is clearly something other than what training proponents initially had in mind. From a policy perspective, the only reason to be interested in skills is the extent to which they enable otherwise impoverished citizens to make a decent living. At the start of the 1980s, job training focused on traditionally defined skills for the same reason that generations of parents urged their children to learn a trade: the skill of tool and die making or computer programming or nursing was something that would enable one to earn a decent living by equipping one with a trade that would always be valued in the labor market. Clearly, whatever punctuality is, it is not a skill in the policy-relevant sense. It may or may not be a prerequisite for getting an entry-level job, but in itself it offers no grounds for upward mobility and no hope for living-wage employment. That the original idea of a skill as a *trade* has been replaced by the notion of "behavioral skills" reflects the fact that there are not enough job openings in well-paid technical occupations to accommodate the full population that training policy aims to serve. It also indicates that the search to identify the right skill set that might enable low-income Americans to attain decently paying jobs is at a dead end.

Whose Problem Is It, Anyway?

Much of the mismatch literature is based on the assumption that the problem of falling wages must somehow be traced to workers' skills. For example, labor economists Richard Freeman and Peter Gottschalk frame their most recent overview of employment policy around the concern that "the American economy is in danger of leaving its low-skill workers behind"; the 300-page book that follows is laid out as a series of potential policy responses to the problems of less-educated workers.[112] But the most glaring fact about the past thirty years is that median earnings have fallen for half of all American workers, including the bottom 60% of male workers.[113] From 1973 to 1999, real wages fell not only for high school dropouts but also for both high school graduates and those with one to three years of college. Indeed, it was only in 1998 that the wages of college graduates recovered their 1973 level.[114] Leaving aside managerial and professional employees, the average wages of *all* production and nonsupervisory workers—accounting for 80% of American workers—fell by an average of 5% during this time.[115]

The wage problems of the last three decades cannot be confined to the "less skilled" among us, unless "less skilled" is defined to include anyone without a graduate degree. It is true that the least educated workers have suffered the greatest damage. But framing the problem as "how to explain the misfortunes of less educated workers" produces an eccentric analysis, and ultimately misses the point. It suggests that there is a fundamentally different explanation for the impoverishment of the bottom quarter of the workforce than for the falling real wages of the middle class. The right question is "how do we explain stagnant or falling wages for 80% of the American workforce?" This question points us away from a focus on skills and toward attention to more institutional determinants of wages, and, in so doing, points toward a policy agenda that unites rather than divides those who have suffered the effects of economic restructuring.

Unions, Employment Policy, and Discrimination: Institutional Determinants of Wages

Rather than education, the wages of nonsupervisory workers are powerfully shaped by a range of legal, political, and institutional factors unrelated to skill or education. Furthermore, while the economic return to skill is often treated as an immutable aspect of market life—a fact of nature which we may like or dislike, but are powerless to change—all of these other, institutional factors are fundamentally shaped by political choices. Thus a shift in emphasis from educational to institutional determinants of wages is also a shift from an analysis in which workers can do nothing but accommodate themselves to the demands of the market to a framework in which workers may use workplace and political organizing in order to help shape the economic opportunities they are offered.

The Union Premium

While the data linking education with earnings show inconclusive results, the relationship between unionization and wages is unambiguous. Across the economy as a whole, the salaries of union members are significantly higher than those of their nonunion counterparts in almost every major occupational and industrial category. As seen in table 2.13, union wages were 28.4% higher than those for unorganized workers in the year 2000. Since union members are also far more likely than others to win employer-provided pension and medical benefits, the union premium for total compensation is almost twice as large as the wage premium alone.[116] To some extent, the union difference reflects the concentration of organized labor in higher-wage occupations. However, even confining the comparison to union and nonunion workers with the same occupation, industry, work schedule, geographic region, and company size, unionization raises wages by 21% and total compensation by 28%.[117]

The union differential is even more dramatic in the service occupations that are projected to provide the bulk of new jobs for non-college-educated workers. The union premium for service occupations averaged 69.4%, with weekly earnings of $554 and $327 for union and nonunion workers, respectively. Moreover, while white men continue to dominate the best-paying union jobs, the importance of unionization appears to be greatest for minorities and women. In 2000, weekly earnings for male union members exceeded those for nonunion men by 19.2%, but women union members earned 30.5% more than their nonunion counterparts. Similarly, the weekly earnings differential was 26.7% for

Table 2.13 Median Weekly Earnings of Union and Nonunion Workers, 2000, by Race, Gender, Industry, and Occupation

	Union members	Unorganized workers	Wage difference	Union premium
Total	$696	$542	$154	28.4%
Men	739	620	119	19.2
Women	616	472	144	30.5
White	716	565	151	26.7
Men	757	641	116	18.1
Women	631	482	149	30.9
Black	596	436	160	36.7
Men	619	479	140	29.2
Women	564	408	156	38.2
Hispanic	584	377	207	54.9
Men	631	394	237	60.2
Women	489	346	143	41.3
All private sector workers	663	530	133	25.1
Clerical occupations	588	453	135	29.8
Precision production	784	570	214	37.5
Operators and laborers	605	411	194	47.2
Service occupations	554	327	227	69.4

Source: Bureau of Labor Statistics, "Union Members in 2000," news release, January 18, 2001.
Note: Data are for full-time wage and salary workers aged 16 and over.

white workers, 36.7% for black workers, and 54.9% for Hispanic workers. Thus the effects of unionization are most powerful among exactly those sectors of the population that job training has sought to assist.

Table 2.14 shows that, for non-college-educated workers, unionization is often much more important than skills or education. For nonunion high school dropouts, for instance, the advantage of finishing school is an increase of $2.25 per hour, while organizing one's workplace will benefit the worker more than twice as much. Similarly, high school graduates contemplating getting some college training short of a B.A. would actually do three times better to organize than to go back to school.

The past two decades have seen a severe decline in the union share of the workforce, from 25% in 1978 to just under 14% in 2000. This decline has fallen hardest on blue-collar men between the ages of twenty-five and thirty-four—exactly the segment of the population that experienced the most severe decline in real wages over the period. One calculation estimates that for male workers, up to 25% of the growth in the college premium can be attributed to declining unionization.[118] In fact, a comparison of wage trends in the United States and

Table 2.14 Median Wages by Education Level and Union Status, 1997

	Nonunion	Union	Wage difference	Union premium
High school dropout	$6.50	$11.20	$4.70	72%
High school graduate	8.75	12.79	4.04	46
1 to 3 years of college	9.87	13.30	3.43	35
College graduate	14.83	14.75	−0.08	−1
Advanced degree	19.23	20.00	0.77	4

Source: Kent State University analysis of U.S. Census Bureau, Current Population Survey data. Reported in Glenn Gamboa, "Unions: Long Considered Protection for the American Job, Organized Labor Enrollment Now Is at Its Lowest Point in History," *The Columbian*, July 16, 1999, C1.

Canada suggests that higher unionization rates in Canada were instrumental in enabling that country to avoid the wage collapse that struck American workers, despite contending with generally similar economic trends and demand for skills.[119]

The union premium points to a critical fact obscured by mismatch theories. In traditional human capital theory, competitive markets guarantee that wages are exactly equal to workers' marginal productivity, with little possibility for excess profit. Since the profit margin is so narrow, the only way workers can increase their wages is by increasing their skills and productivity, thereby allowing firms to generate increased revenues. If workers somehow managed to force employers to increase wages faster than productivity, they would simply end up endangering their employers' financial viability and, ultimately, their own jobs.

In this view, wages are determined by a technical formula rather than a political struggle. The union premium, however, shows that at least a substantial number of American employers are operating according to different rules. If unionized workers earn significantly higher wages than unorganized employees in the same occupations and industries, this must mean that at least some employers are enjoying significant profit margins, and that the wages of labor are determined in important part by the struggle over how those profits are divided. In this sense, the union premium points to a critical gap between neoclassical theory and the actual functioning of most firms; in the real economy, political contests have a significant role to play in determining who makes what.

More than a third of nonunion workers have stated in polls that they would like to be represented by a union.[120] However, the chances of realizing this desire have been undermined by both private practice and public policy. Approximately 10,000 Americans are illegally fired each year for participating in organizing drives; since federal labor law contains no provision for punitive damages, unscrupulous employers are free to violate the law more or less with impunity.[121]

At the same time, under the Reagan and Bush administrations the wait for National Labor Relations Board rulings on such illegal firings increased to twenty-four months.[122] Under both Democratic and Republican administrations, Congress has refused to change the law so that unions could simply be certified when a majority of workers have signed union cards ("card-check") or to mandate impartial arbitration for first contracts (both are standard in Canada). This has left workers vulnerable to management intimidation and prolonged legal delays en route to union recognition, and has meant that an increasing share of unions that succeed in winning recognition nevertheless fail to obtain a first contract.[123] Following the Reagan administration's firing and replacement of striking air traffic controllers in 1981, a growing number of employers turned to permanent replacements as a means of breaking employee unions. In the absence of legislation banning striker replacements—which President Bush vetoed and President Clinton failed to push past a threatened filibuster—the right to strike has been largely eviscerated, further undermining workers' leverage in the contest to divide corporate profits.

Toleration of Exploitation Abroad

While policy makers have aggressively promoted the globalization of production, they have often been unwilling to regulate even the most extreme forms of labor exploitation in other countries. Federal officials have long been reluctant to enforce sanctions for labor abuses, established in the General System of Preferences trade program, against U.S. allies such as Guatemala and Indonesia.[124] Nike's profits were built, in part, on Indonesians working ten-hour days for $1.13 per day, six days a week, in a country where independent unions are illegal. In China, Nike's workers have been beaten, subjected to forced overtime, and often paid wages below the country's minimum of $1.90 per day.[125]

Not only have American firms taken advantage of third-world desperation, they have also conspired to keep wages low through political repression. In Guatemala, American-owned plants making clothes for Leslie Fay, Esprit, and Appel and paying workers $4 per day have fired employees for attempting to organize a union. Also in Guatemala, contractors for shirtmaker Phillips-Van Heusen fired workers for organizing, issued death threats against union supporters, sent spies to union meetings, and required new hires to join a management-controlled company union. When, despite all this, Phillips-Van Heusen workers won an election to form an independent union, the company closed shop rather than negotiate with its own employees.[126] Even Levi's, the self-styled conscience of the garment industry, has chosen exploitation over fostering skills and teamwork. Despite a landmark agreement with its U.S. union that granted work rule flexibility and team-based reorganization, and despite record sales, the company announced in 1997 that it was laying off more than

6,000 U.S. workers, shifting their jobs to lower-wage, nonunion plants abroad. Five months later, Levi's announced that it was resuming operations in China, reversing a much-heralded commitment to avoid that nation's manufacturing in recognition of its poor human rights standards.[127]

While the U.S. Labor Department has stepped up efforts to encourage limits on child labor, both the Bush and Clinton administrations rejected proposals for a ban on imported goods produced by child labor, and the terms of membership established by the World Trade Organization preclude future administrations from considering such a policy.[128] The government's refusal to impose trade penalties against countries where workers are denied the right to organize means that Americans are forced to compete against wage levels set not only by the impoverished living standards of developing countries but also by government-sponsored labor repression.

Even within U.S. borders, the federal government has permitted or sponsored extreme forms of labor exploitation. In the sugar cane industry of central Florida and in the textile factories of the Northern Marianas, for instance, tens of thousands of foreign workers have been imported to toil at sub-minimum wages, subject to harsh discipline backed by the constant threat of deportation.[129] In both cases, the operations are wholly legal, facilitated by federal waivers of immigration and minimum wage regulations, and in both cases the misery of these workers undermines the ability of others to earn a living wage in these industries.

Weakened Minimum Wage

For American citizens working at home, dramatic changes in employment practices have driven increasing numbers of workers down to the lowest level of competition. The tight labor market of the late 1990s finally reversed the long-term decline in wages, and began to improve earnings for workers in the bottom part of the labor market. Even with these improvements, however, real wages for most Americans remain significantly below their level of twenty-five years ago. A significant factor in this equation is the federal minimum wage which, frozen during the course of the 1980s, lost 40% of its value by the end of the decade. Increases in the minimum wage in 1990–91 and 1996–97 were a key factor enabling low-wage workers to realize earnings gains in the late 1990s. Nevertheless, by 2001 the minimum wage was still 31% below its 1968 value in real terms (see table 2.15). If the minimum wage had kept pace with inflation since the 1960s, 30% of the current workforce would now have wages below the adjusted minimum. In other words, nearly one-third of American workers are now working for wages that would have been illegal thirty years ago.[130]

This deterioration has had dramatic effects. Contrary to popular perception, more than 70% of minimum wage and near–minimum wage workers are adults,

Table 2.15 Real Value of the Minimum Wage, 1968–2000 (1999 dollars)

Year	Minimum wage
1968	$7.07
1979	6.53
1989	4.50
1999	5.15
2000	4.85

Source: Economic Policy Institute.

and 48% work full-time.[131] In 1979, a full-time, year-round worker earning the minimum wage could keep a family of three above the poverty line; by 2000, such a worker was left $3,000 below poverty.[132] Raising the minimum wage by one dollar per hour would increase the earnings of more than a tenth of all American workers; yet the national business lobbies have joined Republican leaders in opposing all proposed increases as well as any attempt to index the minimum wage to the rate of inflation.[133]

Unregulated Use of Temporary, Part-Time, and Contingent Labor

The wages of many workers have similarly been depressed by employers' extraordinary expansion of their use of temporary, part-time, and other contingent workers, accounting for up to a third of all new hires and providing a workforce that is low-cost, flexible, and easily disciplined.[134] On average, part-time workers earn 20% less than full-time workers with similar levels of education and experience. Of course, contingent workers also have fewer benefits; less than 9% of temp workers get employer-paid health insurance, and less than 6% are covered by pension plans. Even within the same occupations, part-timers make significantly less than full-time workers doing the same job. Moreover, the increase in part-time work depresses the wages of full-timers as well. One early study found that full-timers who worked in sectors where more than one-third of the workers were part-time earned $1.21 less per hour than identical full-time workers in other industries.[135]

The decision to hire contingent workers is a choice made by thousands of individual employers. On a national scale, however, the expansion of both part-time and temporary employment has largely been fueled by the absence of regulations—common in Western Europe—guaranteeing equal hourly wages and prorated benefits for full-time and part-time workers, and mandating genuine time limits for the use of "temporary" labor.[136]

Child Labor and Lax Enforcement of Wage Regulations

Perhaps most disturbingly, the past two decades have seen a resurgence in child labor, with up to 2 million American children employed illegally.[137] In Manhattan, children as young as eight are employed in garment factories. The Labor Department estimates that at least half of all garment factories in the country are violating wage or safety laws, possibly including child labor laws, but the department is unable to monitor more than a fraction of such employers.[138] The increase in many forms of exploitation—child labor, subminimum wages, abuse of undocumented workers—is further encouraged by the dramatic underfunding of Labor Department investigators, leaving employers free to violate laws with virtual impunity. At the end of the Reagan-Bush era, while job training was being trumpeted as a critical commitment to the well-being of working families, the Department of Labor was reduced to 3,000 staff inspectors for the entire country, one-fourth as many as the Fish and Wildlife Service. By 1999, that number had been cut to less than 1,000, and nineteen states had ten or fewer compliance officers responsible for monitoring all workplace regulations.[139]

Race and Sex Discrimination

Finally, race and sex discrimination remain fundamental characteristics of the American labor market. The skills mismatch thesis often serves as an alternative to theories of race discrimination as an explanation for the concentration of black and Latino workers in low-wage jobs. If discrimination still poses a systemic barrier, training programs would be largely futile. On the other hand, if there is a skills crisis in black and Latino communities, what appear to be racist hiring practices may simply reflect the educational deficiencies of these workers. The emergence of job training as the dominant policy for minority workers reflects, in part, a conviction that race discrimination is a less important factor in job opportunities than is lack of skills. Thus the Reagan and Bush administrations simultaneously promoted job training while dramatically scaling back enforcement of equal employment opportunity regulations.[140] Similarly, in 2001 Labor Secretary Elaine Chao began her tenure by stressing the need for skills training while insisting that "demand for qualified labor . . . is so great that all historical barriers of race and gender . . . are almost irrelevant."[141]

However, the evidence suggests not only that race-based hiring cannot be explained by differential skill levels but, on the contrary, that race-based hiring often makes skills irrelevant. For instance, in the nation's largest labor market, California, a study of entry-level workers found that black and Latino youth had improved significantly on every possible measure of skill, both absolutely and relative to white workers, and yet found their wages falling farther behind white wages. The effects of race outweighed those of education, with minority workers at every level of education losing ground to similarly trained whites.[142] While revelations of discrimination are often reported as isolated cases of aberrant behavior, evidence suggests that race-based hiring and promotion practices remain a widespread feature of the labor market. Whenever tests have been conducted in which identically qualified black and white candidates applied for the same job, a pattern of discriminatory hiring has been revealed across a wide range of entry-level occupations.[143] It is clear that more vigorous enforcement of anti-discrimination laws is a prerequisite to enabling minority workers to realize any payoff to skills.

Similarly, the gender earnings gap remains pronounced at all levels of education. For nonsupervisory workers, the relationship between education and earnings is weakest in traditionally female occupations. Howell and Wolff note that the trend of rising skills accompanied by falling wages was most pronounced among childcare workers, hairdressers, cashiers, office machine operators, receptionists, and typists—all occupations overwhelmingly staffed by women.[144] Failure to pass the Equal Rights Amendment, coupled with the absence of effective comparable worth laws, has enabled employers to pigeon-hole women in low-wage occupations without fear of government reprisal. Indeed, one study found that effective pay equity policies would enable up to 40% of poor working women to leave public assistance.[145]

The combination of enduring forms of discrimination and deterioration of legal and policy protections in the labor market has created an institutionalized insecurity for the majority of the working population, an insecurity that does not recede even when the unemployment rate reaches historic lows. Indeed, as Federal Reserve Chairman Alan Greenspan has noted, this "heightened sense of job insecurity and, as a consequence, subdued wage gains" was instrumental to the inflation-free expansion and galloping stock market of the late 1990s.[146] All these institutional dynamics have two things in common. First, it is likely that almost any of them has a greater effect on the employment and earnings of non-professional workers than does job training. Second, they all involve a conflict of interest between workers and management, and the solution to any one of them requires that workers organize in opposition to business lobbies and that elected officials choose sides in this struggle. If job training is a diversion, these are the issues it serves to obscure.

Conclusion: The Politics of the Skills Mismatch Argument

As American wages were falling over the past thirty years, most citizens witnessed a variety of immediate causes which seemed to account for the trend.

Mass layoffs and relocation of jobs abroad; the institution of all-temp and all-part-time workforces; the use of striker replacements and the imposition of concession bargaining; continued discrimination against women and minorities; the deregulation of industries and the lack of constraints on cannibalistic mergers and acquisitions—all of these provided immediate, tangible, and logical explanations for the setbacks most Americans experienced. Throughout this period, however, business organizations and federal officials have sought to convince the public that our eyes have deceived us. In fact, they argued, these seemingly obvious causes of decline were either incidental to or mere symptoms of the deeper malaise, namely, the failure of workers themselves to provide adequate skills to fuel the growth of high-wage employment. This has been the function of the mismatch thesis.

As this chapter has shown, the definition of exactly which skills are in demand has undergone multiple revisions. When it became clear that average education levels were improving rather than deteriorating, mismatch theorists asserted that the *quality* of education had deteriorated. When data revealed that achievement test scores and other measures of education also showed signs of improvement, they then asserted that while the average quality of education might be adequate, the labor market was becoming increasingly dominated by traditionally low-skill groups, and therefore the average education of the *workforce* was deteriorating. When demographic studies showed that shifts in the composition of the labor force had actually led to more *highly* educated workers, training advocates shifted away from supply-side arguments entirely, arguing instead that, even if the average education of the workforce was improving, it was not improving fast enough to keep pace with employer demand.

At first, training advocates focused largely on demand for highly skilled technical workers. While the image of high-tech skill shortages has remained popular, most analysts quickly recognized that technical occupations accounted for a very small share of the labor market and shifted their focus to the shortfall of general educational skills. Many theorists suggested an excess demand for college-educated workers, while others stressed the growing importance of a high school diploma. When studies revealed that most of the growth in income inequality occurred among workers with identical levels of education, economists moved away from looking at years of educational attainment toward an emphasis on educational content, most often meaning English, math, and "reasoning" skills. And as employer surveys have shown that few firms are overly concerned with even these academic skills, training advocates have increasingly identified the critical traits in demand as "interpersonal," "problem-solving," and "behavioral" skills. Thus training advocates have consistently moved toward theories that are less and less susceptible to empirical verification.

Chapter 1 explained how training advocates have also continually revised their theories about the timing of the skills–workers mismatch and their definition of what evidence is required to prove or disprove the existence of shortages. After two decades of continually revising the skills mismatch thesis in order to account for contradictory evidence, the intellectual trajectory of this idea is finally exhausted. When scholars agree that there has been no deterioration on the supply side, and when every possible definition of highly demanded skills has been tried on and found not to fit, leaving as "skills" only descriptions of workplace attitudes that are indistinguishable from employers' age-old desire for hard work at low wages—at this point, there is nowhere further for the skills thesis to go. Because training policy still plays a political function, funding for program evaluations remains available, and articles on training policy continue to appear. But as vital intellectual inquiry, the skills mismatch thesis has reached a dead end.

In the debate over economic decline, the skills mismatch thesis has served as a demobilizing and ultimately disempowering rhetoric. The focus on skills has diverted public attention away from the more fundamental causes of inequality and poverty. In addition, in all its incarnations, the skills thesis has encouraged us to believe that economic improvement requires a politics of acquiescence in, rather than challenge to, private profit strategies.

From its inception, the skills mismatch argument has been filled with the language of futurism. Whatever the facts of the moment, we have been constantly told that the near future will be unlike anything we have known to date—that the impact of technology and the demand for education will set the future qualitatively apart from the present. After many years of speculation, the high-skill, high-wage jobs whose promise lies at the heart of job training ideology remain stubbornly elusive. In the 1982 JTPA hearings, one expert warned that "by 1995 . . . 36 million workers will need to be computer literate."[147] In 1995, however, corporate representatives were still testifying about the need to begin "preparing our children for the high-skill jobs of tomorrow."[148] Like Annie's "Tomorrow," it seems that the high-wage jobs are always a day away. Rather than standing on the brink of radical transformations, it appears most likely that while the future will bring continuous changes, it will mostly be quite like the present.

Millennial rhetoric has been used most often to evoke the image of the new, democratized workplace. Here, the most important break from the past concerns precisely the role of power in determining wages. We all know how wage increases were achieved in the "old" economy—workers organized and went on strike, child labor was banned and the minimum wage established, discrimination was outlawed and comparable worth pursued. While education certainly played an important role in raising standards of living, the most important wage gains were won through workplace and political battles over the institutions of the labor market. The remarkable difference in the "new" economy, we are told, is that such conflict has become unnecessary. At the Clinton administration's Conference on the Future of the American Workplace, the president responded to reports of "empowerment" initiatives by declaring that "the most interesting thing . . . is that what turned out to be good for the company turned out to be good for the employees."[149] And in ushering in the new Bush administration labor policy, Secretary of Labor Elaine Chao distinguished "the labor struggles of the early part of the last century" from the current economy, in which "the forces of labor and the forces of management . . . must come together and work cooperatively in order to compete successfully in the world economy."[150] The new economy is imagined to work in ways that guarantee the alignment of employers' and workers' interests; based on this vision, workers are encouraged to eschew the type of oppositional militancy which alone has ever provided meaningful power. Yet the truth is that in this way above all others, the future will be very much like the past. The earnings of workers will be protected not through a redoubled commitment to our education, but only by engaging in a political struggle over the terms of our employment.

Does Job Training Work? Lessons from the Job Training Partnership Act

> We threw out the old, inefficient CETA program and put in its place the Job Training Partnership Act, which provides . . . marketable, up-to-date skills.
>
> —President Ronald Reagan[1]

> For . . . years now, the Job Training Partnership program has been equipping the disadvantaged . . . to enter the work force, to start that climb up out of the poverty trap. JTPA—it works. The proof is its 68 percent success ratio, and we're working to make the program even stronger.
>
> —President George H. W. Bush[2]

> Three quarters of the money spent on poverty research would be better spent if it were just given to poor people.
>
> —Mollie Orshansky[3]

In the original legislation creating the Job Training Partnership Act, Congress declared the program's goals to be "the increased employment and earnings of participants."[4] Since that time, the federal government has spent over $85 billion on JTPA and its successor program, the Workforce Investment Act (WIA).[5] In this chapter, I seek to establish whether this money has been well spent or wasted: How have federal job training programs affected the employment and earnings of those who participate in them? Have the programs achieved their stated goals?

The analysis that follows focuses on JTPA, but it is intended to shed equal light on WIA, which succeeded JTPA in 2000 as the framework for federal job training.[6] After seventeen years, JTPA was the longest-running jobs program in the nation's history and thus offers the best source of systematic and scientific data on the effectiveness of training. Moreover, the types of training offered under WIA are virtually identical to those under JTPA; the primary innovations are administrative rather than substantive, including, most importantly, the creation of training "vouchers" designed to increase individual choice in selecting from among various training options. The range of services that one may choose between remains the same as under JTPA—classroom training, job search assistance, on-the-job training, and a variety of "other services" including remedial education and "job readiness" training. So too, the population served by WIA is largely the same as that of JTPA, with the new legislation mandating priority treatment for poor people and welfare recipients. If anything, WIA may have more modest impacts on participants' earning potential, since the new program emphasizes more superficial job search assistance rather than intensive training. Thus throughout the analysis that follows, the results shown for JTPA also represent the best available estimate of what can be expected from WIA.[7]

My aim in this chapter is to address both the specific question of JTPA's performance and the broader question of how well job training has worked generally. JTPA not only marked a departure from the job creation policy of CETA—it also marked a radical restructuring of training programs themselves. Under CETA, training was carried out by public and nonprofit community agencies, and funding was based on an examination of the specific services and quality of training that agencies provided their clients. The disappointing performance of CETA and earlier training programs was often attributed to the natural inefficiency of government operations, to an inappropriate focus on the process of training rather than its outcome, and to insufficient involvement of the private sector in shaping programs to meet the needs of local employers. By incorporating these concerns into its program structure, JTPA was designed to succeed where other training programs had failed. Under JTPA, training was privatized, contracted out to a variety of organizations including for-profit vocational schools. Furthermore, the criteria for awarding contracts no longer focused on the specific services provided participants. Rather, contractors were freed to run almost any type of program, as long as they met federal goals for placing graduates into private sector jobs. Finally, JTPA legislation required every locality to establish a Private Industry Council (PIC) endowed with substantial authority for planning, budgeting, and establishing criteria for awarding contracts.

Because of these features, an evaluation of JTPA provides not only a report card for a specific training program, but—by measuring the results of a program which was designed for superior performance—also provides a best-case test of the potential effectiveness of training programs in general.

In this chapter I provide an overview of the JTPA/WIA system, including its particular nature as a privatized program. I then examine the program's implementation and compare the legislation's stated intent with its actual record of operation. I then present the findings of the Department of Labor's comprehensive evaluation of JTPA, the only scientifically valid evaluation of the program. Finally, I compare the results of JTPA with those of other job training programs, in order to determine the extent to which the JTPA findings can be taken as a measure of the effectiveness of training in general.

The evidence presented below indicates that JTPA has failed to achieve its goals. Furthermore, this failure reflects the structural constraints of job training policy rather than the difficulties of program implementation. There is widespread evidence of fraud and abuse in the job training system, yet even those programs that have been operated honestly and competently (by far the majority) have proven incapable of raising participants' earnings by a significant amount. Indeed, while federal records make it difficult to directly compare JTPA costs and benefits, it is quite possible that poor people would have been better off had the money spent on JTPA instead been simply applied to participants' heating and food bills.

Finally, the results of JTPA training are consistent with those of a wide range of training programs for low-income workers. Thus the failure of JTPA cannot be traced to idiosyncratic problems of program design or operation. Rather the results indicate that, while training may be an effective strategy for modestly improving the earnings of a small number of workers, even the best-run training programs cannot provide a stepping-stone out of poverty for any significant number of Americans. The lesson of JTPA's failure is not to design a more efficient training system but to turn away from training toward confronting the institutional roots of unemployment and poverty.

The Job Training Partnership Act: Background and Structure

The Job Training Partnership Act created seven separate training initiatives (see table 3.1).[8] In the analysis that follows I focus exclusively on the programs operated under Title IIA, which is by far the largest single component of JTPA.[9] Title IIA represents the most logical object of study in that its programs are most analogous to training undertaken by other government agencies and its administrative structure most completely embodies the program innovations at the heart of the JTPA system—devolution of authority to the states, performance-based contracting, and private sector oversight. Finally, Title IIA alone has developed a participant base large enough to allow statistically significant studies; for this reason, the Department of Labor's comprehensive review of JTPA focuses exclusively on Title IIA programs. For all these reasons, the remainder of this chapter addresses job training as it has operated under Title IIA of JTPA.

Table 3.1 JTPA Funding and Participants, 1999

	Budget (in millions)	Number of participants
State and locally operated programs		
Title IIA, adult training	$955	383,000
Title IIB, Summer Youth Employment	871	530,000
Title IIC, youth training	130	116,000
Title III, dislocated workers	1,406	666,000

	Expenditures (in millions)	Number of participants
Federally operated programs		
Job Corps	$1,308	70,000
Indian & Native American	58	15,000
Migrants & Farmworkers	79	20,000

Source: U.S. Department of Labor, Employment and Training Administration, FY 1999 Final Appropriations Action: Summary of Significant ETA Items.

Eligibility and Participation

JTPA Title IIA programs are open to a wide range of low-income Americans. The primary eligibility criterion is that participants be "economically disadvantaged," generally defined as living in families with incomes below the federal poverty line.[10] In addition, 65% of participants must face one or more "barriers to employment," including "limited English proficiency, or [being] displaced homemakers, school dropouts, teenage parents, handicapped, older workers, veterans, offenders, alcoholics, or addicts."[11]

Funding Formula: "Defederalism"

JTPA was the first of the Reagan administration's "New Federalism" initiatives, and it entailed the largest funding restructuring of any social policy area in the president's first administration.[12] At the heart of the new program's design was a radical reduction in federal government involvement in the development, operation, and oversight of program activities. In many ways, JTPA was designed to function more as a funding stream than as a federal program. Thus, training funds are distributed as block grants to each of the fifty states. The federal role is limited to providing the funding, establishing formulas for funds to be distributed between the states and to localities within each state, setting performance criteria that programs must meet to be compensated, and providing minimal oversight to monitor local compliance with these regulations. Everything else—the choice of which occupations to train people for, the development of training curricula, the establishment of specific performance standards

Table 3.2 JTPA Title II Performance Standards, 1998–99

All adults	
Participants employed 3 months after graduation	60%
Weekly earnings at follow-up	$289
Welfare recipients	
Participants employed 3 months after graduation	52%
Weekly earnings at follow-up	$255
Youth	
Entered employment	45%
Positive termination	72%

Source: U.S. Department of Labor, Employment and Training Administration, "Job Training Partnership Act (JTPA) Title II and Title III Performance Standards for PYs 1998 and 1999," *Training and Employment Guidance Letter* No. 12–97, June 30, 1998.

for each contract, and the actual recruitment, training, and placement of participants—is left up to local authorities.

Performance-Based Contracts

One of the central innovations of JTPA was to give contractors maximum possible discretion in crafting the content of training. To this end, the authors of JTPA rejected the fee-for-services approach of CETA contracts and instead demanded that fees be paid for results only. The goal of performance-based contracts was twofold: to guarantee results by insisting that program operators not get paid unless they placed graduates into jobs; and to create market-driven curricula, allowing operators to respond to labor market signals by providing whatever type of training they thought would lead to job placements. Table 3.2 shows the performance standards Title II program operators were to meet in 1998–99.[13]

Privatization of Training

One of the goals of JTPA was to increase private sector participation in providing training, reflecting the belief that the private sector is more efficient and that competition for contracts brings forth the most effective trainers in a free market. Indeed, the transition from CETA to JTPA was remarkable for the extent to which training contracts shifted away from nonprofit community-based organizations and toward proprietary vocational schools. Within two years of the changeover, proprietary schools had become major training providers for 39% of all state and local training authorities, a greater share than that held by either state employment service offices or the community college system.[14]

Governance: Local Government and the Private Industry Councils

At the local level, job training is administered in "partnership" by local governments and Private Industry Councils (PIC).[15] Addressing a common complaint that CETA training programs were out of touch with the real needs of employers, JTPA for the first time mandated a statutory oversight role for private sector representatives. According to the authors of the legislation, a strong private sector role is desirable "because it is the private sector which will employ the graduates of the training programs, and it is only those who will employ the graduates who can really define the kinds of training programs that are needed."[16] To this end, the original JTPA legislation mandated that each local labor market area establish a PIC, a majority of whose members were required to be representatives of private employers.[17] Thus while the PIC is not responsible for day-to-day monitoring of program contracts, it has considerable influence in shaping the broader agenda for training in the local market.[18]

Training Services Offered

Participants in federal training programs are offered four broad types of service. The most intensive is classroom training, in which participants spend up to six months learning a particular trade. Among the most common courses are those for clerical and office skills, production work, food service, custodial services, and training as nurses' aides or home health aides.[19] Alternatively, participants may be enrolled in on-the-job training, in which JTPA funds are used to subsidize the wages of a trainee employed in a private firm. The most superficial service is Job Search Assistance, in which participants who already have sufficient skills receive help in looking for job openings and contacting potential employers. Finally, for participants who are not yet ready for skills training, JTPA offers a range of employment preparation services, including English as a second language or GED classes, résumé writing and interview skills workshops, "world of work" acclimation, and unpaid "work experience."

Reality Check: How Does the JTPA System Actually Function?

I argued above that JTPA was adopted for ideological rather than economic reasons. This view is strongly supported by evidence from the program's implementation. From its beginning, the operation of JTPA was marked by a level of inefficiency and abuse so blatant, and so long ignored, as to suggest that the government was not primarily interested in whether or not the program succeeded.

To begin with, funding for Title IIA programs was set at woefully inadequate levels, never sufficient to serve more than 2% of the eligible population.[20]

Beyond this, central features of the legislation's design created predictably perverse incentives which worked against the program's stated goals. The combination of token funding and performance-based contracts led to widespread "creaming," as program operators recruited the most capable of the eligible population, those most likely to have gotten jobs on their own even without training. The absence of provisions for childcare, transportation, or stipends weeded out many of the most needy applicants from any but the most short-term, superficial services. Similarly, the emphasis on job placement and cost containment led operators to concentrate on short-term, inexpensive services such as job search assistance, despite evidence suggesting that more costly services like classroom training yielded greater long-term benefits. The refusal of the Department of Labor to intervene in monitoring the local contracting process led to predictably high levels of fraud and waste as providers were overpaid and firms were subsidized for on-the-job training of workers they would have hired anyway. Finally, the Reagan administration's refusal to fund follow-up research meant that for the first five years of JTPA's operation, it was impossible to tell— at any level of the system—which programs were truly effective. As a result of all these problems, JTPA failed to serve those most in need of training, failed to provide the most effective services to those who were enrolled, and wasted a large share of its funding.

Token Funding

Job training is the primary labor market policy through which the federal government seeks to expand employment opportunities for the long-term unemployed, discouraged workers, welfare recipients, high school dropouts, and other poor Americans seeking to work their way out of poverty. For such an ambitious agenda, actual funding for JTPA has been embarrassingly inadequate. Funding for JTPA or WIA as a whole has never been sufficient to serve more than 5% of the eligible population, and for Title IIA it was lower still—enough for roughly 2% of those eligible. Indeed, despite trumpeting the need for training, officials in the Reagan, Bush, and Clinton administrations all reduced real funding for JTPA, as shown in table 3.3, such that by 1999 the program was serving only half as many participants as when it began.[21]

Creaming

The limited funding for JTPA has enabled program operators to be extremely selective in choosing participants. This practice is compounded by the use of performance-based contracts, in which providers' fees are based on the share of trainees they place into jobs. These factors together create a tremendous incentive for providers to "cream" the eligible population, enrolling only the most

Table 3.3 Appropriations and Participants in JTPA Title IIA Programs, 1985 to 1999 (including Title IIC since 1993)

Fiscal year	Budget authority (constant 1990 dollars, in millions)	Adult participants	Youth participants	Total participants
1985	$2,279	551,372	404,039	955,411
1986	2,101	604,896	462,482	1,067,378
1987	2,108	609,727	490,995	1,100,722
1988	1,991	600,406	493,293	1,093,699
1989	1,877	554,391	446,017	1,000,408
1990	1,745	510,785	424,272	935,057
1991	1,694	442,087	384,324	826,411
1992	1,637	414,403	381,896	796,299
1993	1,530	239,505	164,320	403,825
1994	1,415	229,643	189,950	419,593
1995	971	329,329	178,180	507,509
1996	824	301,700	124,400	426,100
1997	838	310,900	106,500	417,400
1998	868*	321,200	106,500	427,700
1999	857*	383,000	116,000	499,000

Sources: Budget figures are from 1998 Green Book, U.S. House of Representatives, Committee on Ways and Means. Adult and youth participants 1993–97 are from 1998 Green Book. Participant figures are from U.S. Department of Labor, Employment and Training Administration (ETA). Budget and participant figures for 1998 and 1999 are from ETA, "FY 1999 Final Appropriations Action: Summary of Significant ETA Items," October 22, 1998, and from ETA, "Summary of Impact of Final Action on FY 1998 Appropriations Bill."

*Budget figures for 1998 and 1999 were deflated by the author, using the consumer price index for urban areas, to translate into constant 1990 dollars.

qualified applicants with the least need for daycare, transportation, or other special services, virtually dictating that single mothers or others with special needs will be underserved.[22] It is difficult to measure the system-wide effects of creaming, since program operators do not keep data on applicants who are rejected. Yet nearly every case study of Title IIA programs finds evidence of creaming.[23] In some ways, creaming is more or less forced by federal funding guidelines: the fact that JTPA and WIA—unlike CETA—provide no stipends for training participants puts training off limits to those who cannot afford to stop working in order to go to class.

Finally, the emphasis on placement has encouraged providers to cater to employer racism by enrolling disproportionate numbers of white workers. Thus in the first year of the transition from CETA to JTPA, the number of African Americans enrolled in training fell by 50%, with even greater drops in Hispanic enrollment. Both racial and gender discrimination have been greatest in on-the-job training, where program operators are eager to provide private employers with the workers they want. Two early studies found that fully two-thirds of on-the-job trainees were white men.[24] One training provider reported employers who insisted on three white workers for every black worker they agreed to hire, and Orfield and Slessarev determined that "the most serious problem for black trainees coming out of the programs was employer discrimination."[25] This problem was compounded by staff cuts in the Department of Labor's Office of Civil Rights and by the department's refusal to enforce civil rights regulations in the JTPA system. As with other aspects of program management, the Reagan administration insisted that it was the states' responsibility to monitor civil rights compliance. Orfield and Slessarev concluded that "during the first two years of JTPA . . . the programs operated as if the [civil rights] laws had been repealed."[26]

Over the course of the program's life, JTPA regulations were progressively tightened in order to limit the extent of creaming. Most important, the 1992 amendments required that 65% of adult participants be facing one or more "barriers to employment" (such as low education) in addition to being low-income. Yet even when providers recruit an appropriate share of minorities, women, welfare recipients, and high school dropouts, they still may choose the most capable individuals from among these groups. Within each of these groups, there is considerable variation in education and experience, and since there are so few training slots compared with the number of people in need, it is relatively easy for program operators, while conforming with the regulations, to practice selective recruitment. In extreme cases, program operators screen up to twenty-five eligible applicants for each training slot they fill.[27]

The creaming problem is likely to be worse under WIA than JTPA, since the new program has looser eligibility standards. WIA regulations state that low-income individuals and welfare recipients have "priority" for training services but do not require that any specific portion of funding be reserved for them. Furthermore, the new legislation does away with JTPA's requirement that participants face "barriers to employment" in addition to low income.[28] Thus the incentive and opportunity for creaming under WIA will be even greater than in the past.

The practice of creaming is not only detrimental to those weeded out; it likely defeats the purpose of training for low-income workers. Evaluations have consistently suggested that programs have the greatest impact when they provide intensive services to the most disadvantaged workers.[29] Yet the structure of performance-based contracts encourages providers to concentrate services on those who need them least. Moreover, when needier workers are served, they are often steered into the cheapest and most superficial programs, as contractors are reluctant to risk resources on what they perceive as an unreliable population. After five years of JTPA operation, the Senate Labor Committee reported that "88% of dropouts served by JTPA received *no* remedial education at all. Nearly one in three JTPA participants who could be considered most in need received only job search assistance and *no* other form of training or education."[30] Nearly a decade later, despite repeated statements of commitment to serve those most in need, the practice of training providers was not much different: only 29% of Title IIA participants judged to have deficient basic skills were provided with basic skill training, and one-third were provided no services at all beyond a brief assessment of their existing skills.[31] Thus JTPA concentrated public resources on exactly those workers who could most likely find jobs without the program's help. In this way nearly all training providers meet their job placement quotas, but this accomplishment is often chimerical. As one critic argues, "If the National Weather Service operated like JTPA, it would claim credit for the sun rising each morning."[32]

Emphasis on Short-Term Services

The combination of reduced funding and increased emphasis on job placements as the measure of success has led to a reduction in the quality of training offered under JTPA. From the peak of CETA activity under the Carter administration to the inception of JTPA, job training resources measured in real dollars per unemployed person were cut by 80%.[33] Under those conditions, program operators increasingly rely on short-term, inexpensive services that are unlikely to give participants new skills but that offer low-cost means for placing trainees into jobs. Under WIA, intensive training classes have been made entirely optional, creating an incentive for fiscally strapped states to offer no services beyond low-cost assessment and referral. While this strategy may succeed in meeting immediate job placement goals, it offers little hope of improving individuals' long-term employability. Studies of CETA suggest that—while no form of training has raised average participant earnings above the poverty line—classroom instruction has the greatest relative success in increasing trainees' long-term wages; but the structure of performance-based contracts has rendered extended classroom training inefficient for program operators.[34] Thus the average classroom training program was one month shorter under JTPA than under CETA.[35] In addition, the shift from CETA to JTPA saw a drop in the share of participants who are referred to classroom training at all, with a dramatic increase in the number enrolled in short-term job search assistance programs, which make no claim to impart new skills of any kind.[36]

Fraud, Abuse, and Mismanagement in Training Contracts

From its start, JTPA was plagued by widespread abuse and mismanagement. In many ways, these problems—the very problems whose publicity ruined CETA's reputation—were a direct product of the defederalism strategy. The effort to eliminate the federal government's role in writing or enforcing training contracts opened a wide terrain in which abuse often goes unmonitored. The insistence that no level of government concern itself with the type of services being provided—as long as placement quotas are met—encourages contractors to overcharge for superficial services provided to people easily placed into jobs. And the emphasis on performance quotas has led to widespread manipulation of placement data by both contractors and government agencies.

At the heart of this problem is the federal government's reluctance to provide detailed oversight of state and local programs. As part of general cutbacks in training funds, the transition from CETA to JTPA saw the Department of Labor's Employment and Training Administration staff cut by nearly 50%, making it impossible for ETA to adequately monitor local training contracts.[37] At the same time, cuts in federal revenue-sharing have left state and local governments incapable of overseeing contracts themselves.

While the government has never made a system-wide audit of JTPA contracts, local audits have consistently found widespread inflation of program accomplishments. Provider staff have manipulated data in several stock ways in order to secure ongoing funding. Most commonly, providers avoid listing participants as officially enrolled in programs until they actually get a job; those who don't find jobs are excluded from the total count of participants used to calculate placement rates. This practice is so common that the Department of Labor's National JTPA Study found that the total number of program participants was understated by nearly 20%.[38] A second strategy for boosting placement rates is to manipulate the time period in which placements are measured. While graduates are counted as "employed" on the first day their jobs begin, those who do not find jobs are commonly kept in a "holding status" for several months, which is counted as part of their training period; only if they remain unemployed for several months after graduation are they counted as not placed. Trainees who find jobs through their own efforts in this period—not necessarily related to any effect of training—are nonetheless counted as "placed" by the training provider.[39]

The shortage of oversight staff at all levels of government allows contractors to inflate placement rates with virtual impunity. One study by the Department of Labor's inspector general found that state and local governments regularly failed to verify job placement rates claimed by contractors; when verification was attempted, the study found that fully 25% of all job placements claimed under Title IIA were invalid.[40] Similarly, a U.S. General Accounting Office (GAO) survey found that for two-thirds of JTPA contracts, local governments had either paid providers before they achieved the performance stipulated in the contract or had simply never verified the job placement figures. In extreme cases, providers who failed to meet the terms of their contracts had their contract standards retroactively revised so that payment could be made despite the program's failure.[41]

An additional source of abuse is the diversion of JTPA funds to nontraining expenses. One audit found that nearly 15% of the Title IIA budget was being charged for illegitimate expenses.[42] In order to test the extent to which funds might be vulnerable to such misuse, the Department of Labor measured JTPA contracts against a checklist of sixteen basic contract elements considered vital for the safeguarding of public funds. In a survey of nearly 4,000 contracts, the Department found that "83 percent of the contracts, representing . . . 52 percent of the JTPA funds reviewed, failed to adequately protect JTPA funds."[43] Yet this knowledge has not led to increased funding for contract audits under either JTPA or WIA. Thus while the system's shortfalls are widely acknowledged, they continue to go largely unchallenged. In his 1997 report to Congress, the Department of Labor's inspector general voiced concern that program funds continued to be misappropriated for personal expenses, first-class travel, expensive hotels, or outright embezzlement by training providers.[44]

Fraud and Abuse in On-the-Job Training

On-the-job training (OJT) programs have consistently reported the greatest success in raising the earnings of JTPA participants. But since they have also been the most common sites of program fraud, this success is suspect. Since OJT is essentially a program of federal wage subsidies to private employers, there are many opportunities for abuse—and in some cases, outright corruption. In at least two instances, program staff were convicted of conspiring with employers to list fictitious individuals as OJT participants, with the wage subsidy split between employer and staffers.[45] In other cases, local governments have paid OJT subsidies for individuals already on a firm's payroll. When Compaq threatened to move its operations out of Houston, for instance, the Private Industry Council induced it to stay with a package of incentives that included OJT subsidies for existing workers. Compaq testified at the time that "there has been no change in training procedures. Because the JTPA is an easy government program to work with, we feel we should take advantage of it." In a slight twist on this story, a Pennsylvania company officially "closed" on one day and reopened the next, collecting JTPA wage subsidies for rehiring its own workers.[46] While it is impossible to know how common this type of fraud is, one GAO survey found that half of the local governments surveyed had at least one OJT contract for workers who were already employed in the occupation for which they were being trained.[47]

The more common forms of abuse in OJT involve practices that are both legal and technically permitted under JTPA guidelines but that clearly subvert the program's goals. In many localities workers have been hired as OJT trainees for occupations in which they had substantial previous experience. For example, one program subsidized a four-month training contract for a delivery driver

Table 3.4 Sample On-the-Job Training Contracts for Low-Skill Occupations

Occupation	Days of training subsidized
Fast-food worker	40
Hotel maid	65
Meat wrapper	65
Kitchen helper	71
Laundry attendant	73
Rug cleaner	80
Car wash attendant	129

Source: U.S. General Accounting Office, *Job Training Partnership Act: Inadequate Oversight Leaves Program Vulnerable to Waste, Abuse, and Mismanagement* (Washington, D.C.: U.S. General Accounting Office, 1991), 23.

who had previously worked as a delivery driver for five years; another contract provided three months' custodial training to someone who had already been a custodian for almost twenty years.[48] A program for farm workers gave employers a $1.4 million training subsidy for workers who had been selected specifically on the basis of their previous experience in the type of work performed.[49] All told, the GAO estimates that "about one-fourth of the . . . individuals for whom work histories were available had at least one year of prior experience in the job for which they were being trained."[50]

By far the most common form of OJT fraud, however, is the practice of inflating training times for low-skill occupations. Over 40% of all on-the-job training has taken place in occupations such as custodian, housekeeper, and laundry worker.[51] In many cases these occupations require virtually no training at all; yet local governments have agreed to extended employer subsidies for training in these positions. All the occupations listed in table 3.4 are defined by the Dictionary of Occupational Titles as requiring a maximum of thirty days' training, and field research indicates that many require less than two days.[52] The GAO's survey found that fully 73% of all OJT contracts in low-skill occupations provided for excessive periods of training, with contracts averaging six weeks longer than needed. That means that more than one-third of the budget for low-skill OJT was spent on excessive wage subsidies.[53]

Waste in On-the-Job Training

Underlying the various forms of fraud which have plagued the OJT system is a more fundamental form of waste: most of those placed into jobs would have been hired anyway. In some cases, OJT has been used explicitly as an economic development incentive, offered to companies as a means of lowering their normal training costs in return for expanding local employment.[54] Even without this special intent, however, the normal creaming process of the JTPA system results in OJT slots being used for those who already meet employers' normal hiring criteria. There are no systematic data on this issue, but an early study reported that fully 60% of employers who received OJT subsidies stated that they would have hired the same individuals even without the subsidies, and roughly the same share of firms retained trainees after the subsidy ran out.[55] This suggests that the apparent success of on-the-job training may be almost entirely illusory, and the program may accomplish nothing more than subsidizing private sector employers, enriching poverty entrepreneurs, and offering local governments an easy way to claim paper success in combating unemployment.

The Aggregate Impact of Operational Problems

The lack of centralized data makes it impossible to conduct careful cost-benefit analyses of JTPA. However, using the studies cited above as a rough measure, it is clear that mismanagement accounts for a very substantial share of the program budget. Adding together the impact of only three of the problems discussed above—inflated claims of job placement, illegitimate costs charged to contracts, and OJT subsidies for individuals who would have been hired anyway—yields a maximum estimate of up to 50% of Title IIA funds that were wasted through fraud or mismanagement.[56] While the total impact of mismanagement is uncertain, it is clear that JTPA has suffered from more than minor implementation problems—indeed, it has wasted money on a vast scale.

Taken together, the range of problems which have plagued JTPA suggest that the success or failure of job training holds no critical importance for those who oversee it. Over time, Congress has amended the JTPA regulations to address a number of the most pressing problems, including creaming, inappropriate service, and data collection. However, the slow response by Congress—and WIA's recent reversal of several hard-won reforms—suggest that reforms are not driven by an urgent need to satisfy any business demand for trained workers. The government's refusal to strengthen the program even in ways that do not require congressional action (such as improved fiscal oversight) suggests further that JTPA's value is more symbolic than economic.

The National JTPA Study

The mismanagement of JTPA funds means that a substantial part of the program's resources have been wasted. But even those resources devoted to job training yielded little in the way of increased earnings, according to the National JTPA Study, the Department of Labor's major review of the program, completed

Table 3.5 Thirty-Month Earnings Gains of JTPA Title IIA Enrollees

	Control group earnings	Enrollee earnings	Enrollee earnings gain	Enrollee earnings gain	Margin of error for enrollee earnings gain
All adult women	$12,387	$14,224	$1,837	14.8%	$866
All adult men	19,922	21,521	1,599	8.0	1,427
All female youth	10,298	10,508	210	2.0	1,049
All male youth*	17,286	16,418	−868	−5.0	1,724
Adult women					
Classroom training	$11,378	$12,008	$630	5.5%	$1,106
OJT/JSA**	15,027	17,319	2,292	15.3	1,688
Other services	10,242	14,191	3,949	38.6	2,056
Adult men					
Classroom training	$18,062	$19,349	$1,287	7.1%	$2,610
OJT/JSA**	21,512	23,621	2,109	9.8	2,203
Other services	19,082	20,023	941	4.9	2,686
Female youth					
Classroom training	$9,440	$10,279	$839	8.9%	$1,305
OJT/JSA**	14,835	14,256	−579	−3.9	3,107
Other services	8,319	8,286	−33	−0.4	1,856
*Male youth**					
Classroom training	$16,111	$16,362	$251	1.6%	$3,161
OJT/JSA**	24,113	21,101	−3,012	−12.5	3,666
Other services	13,257	12,819	−438	−3.3	2,432

Source: Larry L. Orr et al., *The National JTPA Study: Impacts, Benefits and Costs of Title II Year-Round Programs: A Report to the U.S. Department of Labor* (Bethesda, Md.: Abt Associates, March 1994), exhibits 4.6, 4.17, 5.7, 5.17.
*Excludes male youth with prior arrest records (see appendix B).
**On-the-job training/job search assistance.

in 1994. Because it is the only program evaluation based on a controlled experiment, this study provides the best available assessment of the effectiveness of job training as a whole. Conducted by the nation's premier program evaluation consultants at a cost of roughly $25 million, the National JTPA Study followed 20,000 JTPA applicants over a period of two-and-a-half years.[57] In order to test the impact of JTPA, the study compared the earnings of JTPA graduates with those of similar workers who did not participate in training.

As shown in table 3.5, the most consistent finding of the national study is that JTPA had very modest effects on participants' earnings. Of the sixteen categories of program participants shown in this table, in only four cases—all adult women, all adult men, women in OJT/job search assistance, and women in "other services"—were the differences between participants' earnings and nonparticipants' earnings statistically significant.[58] The largest gains were realized by adult women, who earned nearly 15% more than those not in the program, followed by adult men, who earned 8% more than their counterparts. For both male and female youth, the program had no statistically significant impact, either for the group as a whole or for any single subgroup. If the data are believable, the program was actually detrimental for male youth, with those who went through the program earning less than those who did not.[59]

These results are striking, since the study's authors analyzed the experience of youths across a broad range of demographic criteria, including race, education, work history, and family income, in order to determine which groups had benefited most from the program. After measuring impacts for thirty-nine separate subgroups, the authors concluded that "the lack of program effectiveness for youths was pervasive. . . . In fact, we cannot identify *any* group of youths who benefited, in terms of earnings gains, from participation in JTPA."[60]

The single most effective service appears to be "other services" for adult women; participants in this group are reported to have earned nearly 40% more than their counterparts. However, a detailed examination of the data reveals that this finding is the result of questionable methodological assumptions and cannot be considered reliable (see appendix B). Excluding this category, the most effective strategy for both women and men is on-the-job training; women in OJT earned 15.3% more than the control group, and men 9.8% more. Classroom training was the second most effective service, with women earning 5.5% more than nonparticipants and men 7.1% more.

The program's effects are even more disappointing when measured against the income needed to escape poverty. Table 3.6 shows the annual earnings of JTPA participants and nonparticipants as a percentage of the poverty line for a family of three.[61] For adult women—the single most successful group in the study—participation in JTPA raised annual earnings from 47.6% to 54.6% of the official poverty line, or from 27.2% to 31.3% of the Original Orshansky threshold. Thus though adult women benefited from participating in JTPA, their gain was meager compared to the income needed to support a minimally decent standard of living. Indeed, on average, participants in every demographic group remained eligible for JTPA even after graduating from the program.[62] Unsurprisingly, then, the program produced no statistically significant effect on welfare benefits, for any demographic group.[63]

While the national study shows JTPA to have minor effects on participants' earnings, there is reason to believe that even these results overstate the program's real impact. The study contains several controversial methodological assumptions that bias the results in the direction of higher program impacts. These assumptions are discussed in detail in appendix B. While some of these issues reflect genuinely difficult methodological puzzles, in which a variety of

Table 3.6 JTPA Title IIA Participants, Earnings Gains Compared to Poverty Threshold*

	Control group annual earnings	Control group earnings compared to poverty	Enrollee annual earnings	Enrollee earnings compared to poverty	Earnings gain compared to poverty
Based on official poverty threshold					
Adult women	$4,955	47.6%	$5,690	54.6%	7.1%
Adult men	7,969	76.5	8,608	82.6	6.1
Female youth	4,119	39.5	4,203	40.3	0.8
Male youth**	6,914	66.4	6,567	63.0	−3.3
Based on Original Orshansky poverty threshold					
Adult women	$4,955	27.2%	$5,690	31.3%	4.0%
Adult men	7,969	43.8	8,608	47.3	3.5
Female youth	4,119	22.7	4,203	23.1	0.5
Male youth**	6,914	38.0	6,567	36.1	−1.9

Source: Earnings data from Larry L. Orr et al., *The National JTPA Study: Impacts, Benefits and Costs of Title II Year-Round Programs: A Report to the U.S. Department of Labor* (Bethesda, Md.: Abt Associates, March 1994).

*Poverty thresholds used are for a family of three in 1990.
**Male youth excludes those with prior arrest records.

assumptions might be equally legitimate, each was resolved in a way that inflated the program's estimated impact. If any of these issues had been treated differently, the impacts shown in table 3.6 would be considerably smaller.

Training and Skills

To the extent that JTPA did raise participants' earnings, it is not clear that the increase reflects the impact of skills training rather than simple job placement services. If workers in the program are given solid skills that employers need, they should be able to command higher hourly wages than nonparticipants. However, the data suggest that this happens in a minority of cases. Averaged across all types of training, 60% of the increase in men's earnings, and 80% of that for women, was due to increased employment rather than higher hourly wages.[64] If JTPA participants cannot earn higher hourly wages than nonparticipants, the program has failed at enabling workers to move into new strata of the labor market. These data suggest that the primary effect of JTPA may have to do not with enhancing skills but rather with simply rearranging hiring queues, giving program participants priority at getting jobs that, in the absence of JTPA, they or someone like them would have gotten anyway.

Indeed, one of the striking findings of the national study is that education seems to have little effect on the wages of trainees. JTPA appears to have been extremely effective in increasing the education of participants. As shown

Table 3.7 Educational Attainment of JTPA Participants and Control Group

	Share with GED or high school diploma after 30 months		Educational gain of JTPA participants	
	Control group	JTPA enrollees	Percentage points	Percent increase
Adult women	20.4%	39.2%	18.8	92.2%
Adult men	16.3	30.7	14.4	88.3
Female youths	31.7	42.3	10.6	33.4
Male youth non-arrestees	36.3	37.0	0.7	1.9
Male youth arrestees	28.9	30.6	1.7	5.9

Source: Larry L. Orr et al., *The National JTPA Study: Impacts, Benefits and Costs of Title II Year-Round Programs: A Report to the U.S. Department of Labor* (Bethesda, Md.: Abt Associates, March 1994), exhibits 4.8, 4.18.
Note: Data are for educational attainment 30 months after application to JTPA.

in table 3.7, the share of adult participants who earned a GED or high school diploma within thirty months after applying to JTPA was nearly twice as high as that of nonparticipants. While education gains for youth were not as dramatic, they were still significant, with female participants achieving a gain of 33.4%. It is noteworthy, however, that these educational accomplishments did not translate into more significant earnings gains. Adult women, for instance, increased their educational attainment by 92.2% but saw their earnings rise by only 14.8%. This finding is consistent with the analysis presented in chapter 2, suggesting that education is a relatively weak determinant of wages for non-college-educated workers.

The marginal relevance of skills and education is further underscored by the enduring impact of race and gender on the earnings of low-income workers. The gender gap is quite dramatic. Upon entering the program, men and women had similar levels of education, work experience, and previous training.[65] Nevertheless, as table 3.8 shows, men earned substantially more than women in every category of service provided. Compared with the effect of gender, the impact of training was very modest. Table 3.8 shows that, while JTPA training had a 14.8% impact on adult women's earnings, the impact of gender difference was more than four times as great. In each of the service groups, women who participated in training earned less than men who were excluded from training. Indeed, the lowest-earning category of untrained men earned more than the highest category of trained women. These results suggest that those who are interested in addressing the feminization of poverty might do better to focus their energies on comparable worth initiatives rather than job training.

Similarly, there is some evidence that race may have a greater impact than education on participant earnings. For adult men, the best educated going into

Table 3.8 Impact of Training and Gender on JTPA Earnings (total earnings after 30 months)

	Control group earnings	Enrollee earnings	Program impact ($)	Program impact (%)	Gender Impact ($)		Gender Impact (%)	
					Control	Enrollees	Control	Enrollees
All adult women	$12,387	$14,224	$1,837	14.8%				
All adult men	19,922	21,521	1,599	8.0				
All adults					$7,535	$7,297	60.8%	51.3%
All female youth*	10,298	10,508	210	2.0				
All male youth*	17,286	16,418	−868	−5.0				
All youth					6,988	5,910	67.9	56.2
Adult women								
Classroom training	$11,378	$12,008	$630	5.5%				
OJT/JSA**	15,027	17,319	2,292	15.3				
Other services	10,242	14,191	3,949	38.6				
Adult men								
Classroom training	$18,062	$19,349	$1,287	7.1%				
OJT/JSA**	21,512	23,621	2,109	9.8				
Other services	19,082	20,023	941	4.9				
All adults								
Classroom training					$6,684	$7,341	58.7%	61.1%
OJT/JSA**					6,485	6,302	43.2	36.4
Other services					8,840	5,832	86.3	41.1

Source: Larry L. Orr et al., *The National JTPA Study: Impacts, Benefits and Costs of Title II Year-Round Programs: A Report to the U.S. Department of Labor* (Bethesda, Md.: Abt Associates, March 1994), exhibits 4.6, 4.17, 5.7, 5.17.

*Excludes male youth with prior arrest records.
**On-the-job training/job search assistance.

the program were those referred to classroom training, of whom 75% were high school graduates; by comparison, only 68% of men in OJT had high school degrees. Yet OJT provided by far the largest increase in earnings. The backgrounds of the two groups were similar in nearly every respect, including work histories and the number of barriers to employment. The one outstanding difference was that 69% of OJT participants were white, compared with only 46% of classroom trainees.[66] This may reflect the bias of program staff or that of employers who prefer to hire white workers. In either case, the result is that less-educated white male participants could expect to do better than more-educated nonwhites.

In her Senate confirmation hearings, Secretary of Labor Elaine Chao suggested a view of the economy in which the demand for trained workers is so great as to make affirmative action unnecessary. "Demand for qualified labor . . . is so great," she explained, "that all historical barriers of race and gender and disability are almost irrelevant."[67] The results of JTPA, however, suggest both that the need for affirmative action has not disappeared and that the impact of such efforts is likely to outweigh those of training.

Cost-Benefit Analysis: Is JTPA Worth It?

It is clear from the National JTPA Study that JTPA has had very modest impacts on participants' earnings. But how these gains compare to the program's costs is unclear due to limitations in the data. The national study offers a partial analysis that looks at the incremental costs and benefits associated with participating in JTPA rather than other, less intensive training programs; the results of this incremental cost-benefit analysis are presented in table 3.9. Here, the incremental costs of the program have been balanced against participants' incremental income gains, including earnings, taxes, and public assistance payments, in order to yield a measure of net social benefits. For women and men, the study

Table 3.9 Net Social Benefits of JTPA Title IIA Programs

Category	Net social benefits
Women	$532
Men	570
Female youths	−1,170
Male youth non-arrestees	−2,904
Total*	−152

Source: Larry L. Orr et al., *The National JTPA Study: Impacts, Benefits and Costs of Title II Year-Round Programs: A Report to the U.S. Department of Labor* (Bethesda, Md.: Abt Associates, March 1994).
*Weighted average based on enrollee shares.

reports net benefits of $532 and $570 respectively over the thirty-month period. For both female and male youth, the program was a large net loss. Combining all groups of participants, the incremental analysis suggests that program costs outweighed benefits for Title IIA as a whole.

A number of methodological problems suggest that the program's benefits may be even less than those presented in table 3.9.[68] Ultimately, it is impossible to determine definitively to what degree JTPA funds were well spent or wasted. However, given the combination of methodological concerns outlined above and the effects of fraud and mismanagement discussed earlier, it is quite possible that JTPA participants would have been better off if the whole program had been scrapped and the funds simply designated to support people's housing and subsistence needs.

How Typical Is JTPA? Evidence from Other Training Programs

The history of job training evaluations indicates that the results of the National JTPA Study are well within the normal range. Over the past forty years, there have been many hundreds of job training program evaluations. This literature addresses a wide range of programs and populations, and employs a variety of statistical methods. Nevertheless, one point of consensus emerges: almost all varieties of education and training services have resulted in small or insignificant earnings gains. Indeed, not a single study suggests that job training has enabled impoverished Americans to earn their way out of poverty. The debate over competing models of training revolves around a narrow range of possibilities: the difference between successful and failed programs is that the former take participants 2% to 10% closer to the poverty line, while the latter have no effect at all. That the range of results has been so consistent, over four decades and scores of competing program models, strongly suggests that the results of JTPA reflect the fundamental limits of training rather than idiosyncratic problems of program design or management. The following sections survey the results from adult, youth, dislocated worker, and welfare training programs.

Programs for Economically Disadvantaged Adults

In the aftermath of the national study's disappointing results, the GAO conducted a five-year study to see if the impact of JTPA might be more evident over the longer term. Unfortunately, payroll records showed that even five years after enrolling in JTPA, no population group showed a statistically significant improvement in earnings. Even if the reported gains had been statistically significant, they were not economically significant: for adult women, for instance, the difference between participating in JTPA and not, measured over five years, is the difference between making 57% versus 53% of the poverty line.[69]

Apart from JTPA itself, the largest source of literature on adult training programs is from the CETA period. While these studies did not use controlled experiments, there is broad agreement that the results of CETA programs were very modest. Barnow reviewed eleven evaluations of CETA training, concluding that the programs increased earnings by an average of $200 to $600 per year.[70] The National JTPA Study's summary of CETA evaluations found "results for male participants which ranged from small earnings *gains* to large earnings *losses*, depending on the study. For women, there were conflicting results, but they were inconclusive."[71] In addition, nearly every study found that the primary benefit of training was increased employment rather than higher hourly wages.[72]

For adult training programs as a whole, an optimistic estimate suggests that a given investment in training results in an increase in annual earnings equal to 10% of the original cost. That is, a program that expends $2,500 per person in training services will increase participants' annual income by $250.[73] At this rate, for a participant who starts off $5,000 below the poverty line, WIA would have to enroll that worker in a program that cost $50,000 per person, approximately twenty-two times the amount now budgeted for adult WIA participants.[74]

Youth Training Programs

While the national study's results for youth seem surprisingly negative, they are quite consistent with the experience of earlier programs. Youth participants in the Supported Work program of the 1970s lost $1,000 per year compared to the control group. In the more recent JOBSTART program, male youths lost $461 a year compared to the control group, despite a program cost of $5,000 per participant.[75] The federal Summer Training and Education Program (STEP), combining minimum wage jobs with remedial English and math training, further confirms the weak relationship between education and employment for youth trainees. While participants significantly increased their math and reading levels, these did not translate into long-term job gains. Three years after finishing the program, participants' rates of employment and of high school graduation were identical to those of nonparticipants.[76] Reviewing a wide range of previous evaluations, the national study concludes that "the findings of previous experimental evaluations of employment and training services for out-of-school youths . . . are consistent with the present result for JTPA. All have found that male youth participants suffered earnings losses while female participants experienced only very small earnings gains and that, for both, the programs resulted in sizable net social costs."[77]

Dislocated Worker Programs

Training for workers who are laid off as a result of plant closings or foreign competition has been offered since the recessions of the 1970s. Outside of JTPA, the major federal initiative for dislocated workers is the Trade Adjustment Assistance program (TAA), which provides extended training for workers laid off as a result of foreign trade. In 1991, the Department of Labor found that while workers who underwent TAA retraining did slightly better than those who did not, fewer than one in five trainees found jobs that paid 80 percent or more of what they had earned before being laid off.[78] Recent results from JTPA are more positive, but they still show that less than half the participants were able to land jobs paying at least 90% of their old wages or that offered any kind of fringe benefits.[79] In a review of six smaller state programs for dislocated workers, Leigh found similarly modest results: job search assistance had a small but positive effect on workers' earnings, while neither classroom training nor on-the-job training had any significant impact.[80] Under WIA, the services offered to dislocated workers are identical to those for low-income adults; thus there is no reason to expect that the program will produce better results than those reported in the National JTPA Study.

Programs for Welfare Recipients

The heyday of welfare training programs ran from the early 1980s through the mid-1990s, as the federal government encouraged states to experiment with training recipients for jobs in the private sector. The 1996 welfare reform act moved states away from skills training and toward an emphasis on simple job placement services, so it is the earlier efforts that provide the most useful comparison with JTPA and WIA. The most comprehensive review of training programs for recipients of Aid to Families with Dependent Children (AFDC) is that done by Gueron, who summarized the findings in seven state demonstration programs.[81] The programs, which provided a combination of work experience, job search assistance, basic education, and occupational training, represented a cross-section of state innovations designed to enable public assistance recipients to work their way out of poverty. As shown in table 3.10, this goal proved unattainable. While participants in some of the programs realized substantial gains compared to those in the control group, none of them came close to earning above-poverty wages. The single highest-earning group of participants earned only 42.3% of the official poverty line after completing the training program; by comparison with control group members, who came from similar circumstances but did not go through the program, even the most effective program raised participants' earnings by only 7.5% of the poverty line. As with nearly every other form of training, to the extent that welfare-to-work programs have

Table 3.10 Annual Earnings Gains from Welfare Recipient Employment Programs

	Control group earnings as % of poverty*	Program participant earnings as % of poverty*	Difference as % of poverty*
AFDC training programs, 1980s			
Arkansas	13.1%	17.2%	4.1%
Baltimore, Md.	36.1	42.3	6.2
Cook County, Ill.	14.7	14.8	0.1
San Diego, Calif., I	23.4	28.7	5.3
San Diego, Calif., SWIM Program	25.7	33.2	7.5
Virginia	28.5	31.7	3.2
West Virginia	5.3	5.4	0.1
Welfare-to-work strategies, early 1990s			
Work-first programs			
Atlanta, Ga.	27.1%	30.7%	3.6%
Grand Rapids, Mich.	30.0	32.9	3.0
Riverside, Calif.	22.3	26.4	4.0
Portland, Ore.	29.8	38.4	8.5
Education or training programs			
Atlanta, Ga.	27.1%	30.7%	3.6%
Grand Rapids, Mich.	30.0	31.3	1.3
Riverside, Calif.	16.5	17.7	1.3
Columbus, Ohio, I	36.7	40.2	3.5
Columbus, Ohio, II	36.7	39.3	2.6
Detroit, Mich.	26.5	30.1	3.6
Late 1990s TANF Programs			
Jobs-First GAIN (Calif.)	24.9%	31.3%	6.4%
Family Transition Program (Fla.)	28.3	35.2	6.9
Family Investment Program (Minn.)	39.0	43.2	4.3
Jobs First (Conn.)	47.3	52.6	5.3
Welfare Restructuring Project (Vt.)	34.5	38.8	4.3
New Hope (Milwaukee, Wisc.)	60.1	65.3	5.2

Source: Author's calculations based on Judith Gueron, "Work and Welfare: Lessons on Employment Programs," *Journal of Economic Perspectives* 4, no. 1 (1990): 79–98; Stephen Freedman, "The National Evaluation of Welfare-to-Work Strategies: Four-Year Impacts of Ten Programs on Employment Stability and Earnings Growth," report prepared for U.S. Department of Health and Human Services and U.S. Department of Education, Office of Vocational and Adult Education (New York: Manpower Demonstration Research Corporation, 2000); Stephen Freedman, Jean Tansey Knab, Lisa Gennetian, and David Navarro, "The Los Angeles Jobs-First GAIN Evaluation: Final Report on a Work First Program in a Major Urban Center" (New York: Manpower Demonstration Research Corporation, 2000); Dan Bloom and Charles Michalopoulos, "How Welfare and Work Policies Affect Employment and Income: A Synthesis of Research" (New York: Manpower Demonstration and Research Corporation, 2001).
*Official federal poverty threshold for a family of three.

increased participants' earnings, they have done so primarily by increasing employment rather than hourly wages.[82]

Even the most successful welfare training programs have shown only modest effects. In the early 1990s, California's Greater Avenues for Independence (GAIN) program was touted as a national model of effective welfare reform. However, while GAIN participants earned 16.6% more than control group members, this increase lifted them only 2.6 percentage points closer to the poverty line, raising their earnings from 15.7% to 18.3% of poverty (not shown in table 3.10). Even in the state's most successful county, the income of program graduates amounted to only 23.7% of the poverty line.[83] Similarly, Massachusetts's celebrated "ET Choices" program, which provided the most comprehensive range of training and support services for welfare recipients, produced an annual earnings increase equivalent to less than 10% of the poverty line.[84]

During the 1990s an increasing number of states established "work-first" programs that eventually became the model for federal welfare reform. While some of these programs included education and training, most concentrated simply on putting welfare recipients to work as quickly as possible—in any job, at any wage. These programs were based on the belief that what welfare recipients needed most was the discipline, punctuality, and socialization that can come only from work itself. State officials set out to show that work experience would prove a more marketable "skill" than anything gained in the classroom. However, results from across the country show that work-first programs have failed just as dismally as the education and training programs that preceded them.

In 2000, the Department of Health and Human Services published its national evaluation of welfare-to-work strategies, which tracked 30,000 welfare recipients in seven states over a six-year period.[85] The results are not encouraging: averaged across all programs, welfare-to-work strategies increased participants' earnings by less than $500 per year. The single most successful program, operated in Portland, Oregon, increased earnings by $1,000 per year—but still left participants making less than 40% of the official poverty line. Even the more recent initiatives touted as national role models have produced similarly anemic results. In the late 1990s, Los Angeles's revised Jobs-First GAIN program reported that participants earned $800 per year more than welfare recipients who did not go through the program. This result was hailed by the Manpower Demonstration Research Corporation as "particularly impressive for a welfare-to-work project in a large urban area." But the increase amounts to only 6.4% of the poverty line and left graduates making less than one-third of poverty.[86] Innovative programs in Florida, Connecticut, Vermont, Minnesota, and Wisconsin all produced similar results.[87]

Because welfare reform has been such a high-profile political issue, a significant amount of money has been spent conducting controlled experiments to measure program results. Unfortunately, as table 3.10 shows, these studies have overwhelmingly confirmed the same depressing truth as the National JTPA Study: there is no training strategy—whether focused on education, occupational training, or the "skills" of workplace discipline—that has enabled participants to work their way out of poverty.[88]

The Workforce Investment Act

For the most part, the government offers the same services to the same people under WIA as it did under JTPA. However, where the two programs differ, the changes are likely to make WIA even less effective in enabling poor people to obtain decently paying jobs. Specifically, in terms of the problems of creaming, incentives to provide low-cost services, and oversight of contractor performance, WIA appears to mark a step backward.

First, the new program encourages exactly the type of superficial services that had been banned under JTPA. WIA offers three levels of service for the poor and unemployed: "core" services such as a brief skills assessment and job search assistance; "intensive" services such as a detailed skills assessment or training in punctuality or interviewing skills; and actual training, which may include remedial education, occupational skills, or "job readiness" training.[89] The 1992 amendments to JTPA banned training programs from offering job search assistance without substantive skills training, on the grounds that simply helping with job placement could not equip participants to land better-paying jobs than they had held previously. Under WIA, however, 80% of participants are slated to receive exactly the type of superficial services that these amendments had banned.[90] It is difficult to know how many WIA participants will get real training, but the administrative structure of the program encourages an emphasis on superficial services.

First, while state and local governments must provide all three types of service, the Department of Labor has no requirements regarding what share of funding should be devoted to each. Thus states may choose to restrict substantive training to a small part of the overall program. Second, WIA mandates that training only be provided to those who have proved unable to find decent jobs through the more superficial "core" or "intensive" services. Thus most WIA offices practice a form of diversion, in which applicants are first given brief counseling and told to go look for a job; only after returning for the third time (following both "core" and "intensive" services) are applicants eligible for actual education or training. The Department of Labor's own review of WIA implementation warns that "much of the system has adopted some form of 'work first' approach . . .

that stresses the importance of a quick entry or re-entry into the workforce. Consequently . . . training would be viewed only as a last resort."[91] Partly owing to this work-first philosophy, the department notes, a significant portion of the WIA budget went unspent in its first year of operation.[92]

Those who receive job search assistance without substantive training can expect the same disappointing results that led Congress to ban this approach under JTPA. However, it is possible that WIA officials will never be held accountable for these outcomes. Theoretically, WIA offices are charged with tracking the employment and earnings of everyone served, with continued funding predicated on meeting performance standards. But participants who receive "core" services are often never registered as participants at all. The Department of Labor's own review notes "a reluctance in local areas to officially register people in WIA because of concerns about their ability to meet performance goals. . . . Some local areas are basing their decision to register a person on the likelihood of success, rather than on an individual's need for services."[93] Thus WIA program staff appear to recognize the limitations of job search assistance but are responding not by improving services but simply by not counting those likely to fail. The ultimate program results reported from such operations will be artificially high. However, it is perfectly legal and within the WIA rules for program operators to pad their numbers in this manner.

Even where WIA offers substantive training, the program is likely to suffer from greater creaming problems than JTPA. The 1992 JTPA amendments sought to control creaming by requiring that 65% of program participants face one or more "barriers to employment" (such as low education) in addition to having low income. WIA has no such restrictions. Indeed, it is not even clear how many participants must have low income, since the law merely requires that states give "priority" to poor people if funding is limited but provides no definition for what "priority" means in practice. Thus program operators—whose budgets remain sufficient to serve only a small fraction of the eligible population— are free to select those most likely to succeed out of a large pool of potential trainees.[94]

Finally, WIA officials will likely find it even harder to monitor contractors' performance or measure overall program success under the new law. The law appears almost allergic to setting standardized terms for program measurement, insisting instead that individual states and localities must define the program on their own terms. For instance, the Department of Labor has refused to provide a standard definition for who is a dislocated worker or a displaced homemaker, who is eligible for training services, what types of for-profit or nonprofit organizations can be contracted for training, whether participants should be allowed to choose how to spend training vouchers, and even when a participant must be counted as enrolled in a program. In response to state and local confusion on these issues, the department may offer "guidance" or publicize "best practice" alternatives, but it refuses to actually issue rules. To the extent that each state and locality operates under different rules, it will be harder to monitor contractor performance in a coherent manner, and it will be nearly impossible to measure the success or failure of WIA as a national policy.

For all these reasons, then, WIA appears unlikely to correct either the administrative waste or the poor performance that have marked the history of JTPA.

The Limits of Job Training in a Job-Shortage Economy

There are two final problems that cast doubt on the achievements of all job training programs, regardless of the population served. First, the programs as a rule are very small, rarely serving more than 5% of the eligible population. This makes it impossible to extrapolate from local successes to policy conclusions for the population at large. In a labor market with a limited number of decently paying jobs, the fact that a well-run program places a small number of people into jobs cannot be taken as evidence that similar success would result from an expanded program. Thus the token funding of virtually all programs serves, in part, to exaggerate the effectiveness of training. Evaluations that conclude that training raises wages by 10%, for instance, hold out the promise that at least this modest achievement could be realized by all low-income workers if more training funds were forthcoming.[95] In fact, however, it is likely that program results would steadily deteriorate as the operation expanded in scale.

A second, even more fundamental question is whether training serves to create new jobs or simply rearranges the hiring queue in low-wage labor markets. The idea of job training is that a shortage of qualified labor has left firms with such excess labor demand that they immediately expand production as soon as any qualified worker becomes available—including even the minimally qualified graduates of WIA programs. Every evaluation of job training implicitly assumes that the jobs filled by trainees were created especially for them rather than taken away from alternative job candidates.[96] Even for welfare training, Gueron "assume[s] that the increased employment of welfare recipients did not come at the expense of nonrecipients."[97] But this assumption is unwarranted. Gueron imagines that new jobs were created for welfare recipients that would not have existed but for their availability to work. Yet this population—even after training—is among the least skilled and least experienced segment of the labor force. It is hard to imagine what special talents trainees possess that would warrant a company's creating positions just for them. If the jobs taken by trainees are not newly created, however, then trainees' success must come at the expense of other, equally qualified job seekers. In this case, the sole result of "training" is to determine who has access to the limited supply of jobs, rather than to increase the overall level of economic opportunity. The only reason job training programs are able to report success is because the nontrainees who lose out in this competition are not counted in the programs' cost-benefit analyses. If we measure job losers as well as gainers, the net result of such programs is zero. Since there is little evidence of jobs being newly created for the graduates of training programs, it seems most likely that programs indeed serve a purely distributional function. To the extent that this is true, all of the earnings gains claimed by all job training programs are illusory.[98]

Why Did JTPA (and Other Programs) Fail?

The disappointing results of training programs have often been taken as evidence of flaws in program design or management. Even after reports of widespread failure, public officials often insist that the basic policy model is sound, if only certain kinks could be worked out.[99] There is certainly much evidence of mismanagement, incompetence, and abuse within the job training system. However, the long history of training suggests that the programs' failure ultimately has more to do with the structure of the labor market than with the skill or integrity of program managers. In an economy where, as we saw in chapters 1 and 2, decently paying jobs are in short supply and skills are a relatively minor determinant of wages, job training programs are asked to perform an impossible task. The mandate to enroll impoverished and inexperienced workers in short-term training programs and then place them in decently paying jobs is an equation that simply cannot add up. Even fraud and mismanagement may be more the result of labor market conditions than of moral failure. If the labor market were as training advocates imagine it to be—if there were indeed large numbers of employers clamoring to hire moderately skilled workers at livable wages—it would be easy for providers to satisfy their performance standards without manipulating data. It is the absence of real job opportunities that forces so many programs to fabricate data in order to create the appearance of impressive placement rates.

Similarly, the extent to which OJT is used to subsidize employers' normal hiring practices rather than to create new opportunities for otherwise unemployable workers reflects the paucity of demand for genuine on-the-job training. If there were in fact a large group of employers facing urgent skills shortages that could be addressed through OJT, and they discovered that the funds needed to meet their requirements were instead being wasted on wage subsidies for fast-food chains, the business community would demand program changes and increased accountability. The fact that there has been no such clamor from the U.S. Chamber of Commerce, National Association of Manufacturers, or other business organizations responsible for nominating PIC members suggests that employers are not lacking workers with occupation-specific skills.

As successive generations of job training programs fail to produce the hoped-for results, policy makers have cycled through a stock repertoire of procedural fixes that promise to solve the problem. CETA, organized to remedy the overly fragmented training system of the 1960s, was criticized as overly consolidated, and too centrally planned, and thus its successor, JTPA, was designed to delegate authority to the states. JTPA in turn has been faulted for insufficient coordination, to be remedied by consolidated "One-Stop" centers under WIA. Similarly, CETA was criticized for focusing on the content of training services at the expense of job placements; JTPA was charged with focusing exclusively on placement rates and ignoring the quality of services provided; in 1992, JTPA programs were banned from providing only job search assistance without any real skills training; then the 1996 welfare reform act and 1998 WIA encouraged work-first programs that downplayed skills training in favor of job search assistance. Finally, for the past twenty years policy makers have called for a privatized job training system that would respond to private sector demand for occupation-specific skills. JTPA's block grants and performance-based contracts made up just such a system, but even this structure has been criticized as too reliant on government planning. Thus WIA has instituted training "vouchers" which will allow participants to take funds to a training provider of their choice—even though the proprietary training schools that may benefit from this system have a terrible track record of job placement.[100] In this way, lawmakers have responded to repeated program failures by calling for procedural reforms that have already been tried and proved ineffective.

The lesson of the National JTPA Study is that there is no managerial fix which can create dramatically more effective training programs. JTPA itself was designed to address most of the key criticisms of earlier programs: its curriculum was dictated by the private sector and its services were bid out to the most competitive providers; it insisted on bottom-line results and paid only for success; it allowed widespread experimentation and innovation at the state, local, and individual program level; and, since the 1992 amendments, it encouraged providers to serve those most in need of help. The failure of JTPA does not signal the need for further tinkering with program design. Rather, the lessons of the national study reflect the true limits of job training policy as a whole. The search for more effective management may improve results by several percentage points, and this would be a welcome development. But ultimately it is impossible to transform job training into a system that will accomplish what its champions promise.

Training advocates assume that certain mechanisms are at work in the labor market—firms seek workers with identifiable skills and expand to make use of them—and then wonder why the programs they establish cannot seem to take advantage of this dynamic. As long as they hold fast to this neoclassical view of the economy, all program failures are interpreted as problems of design or implementation: policy makers simply have not yet figured out how to tap into the mechanisms which *must* be there. The truth is that, to borrow from Gertrude Stein, "there's no *there* there."[101] There is nothing to "get right," because the central mechanism that training advocates imagine does not exist. Employment does not expand to match supply, and in the nonprofessional labor market, neither employment nor wages can be explained by reference to human capital.

The Need for Further Research?

Over the past thirty years, scores of studies have evaluated job training. In the national study's review of previous research, the authors concluded that, due to the absence of experimental controls, these three decades of research were largely wasted: "Because the data and the statistical techniques used to control for selection bias in these studies were inadequate, little systematic knowledge emerged from them."[102] Similarly, the National Research Council reviewed over 400 evaluations of training programs for youth and concluded that "despite the magnitude of the resources ostensibly devoted to the objects of research and demonstration, there is little reliable information on the effectiveness of the programs."[103] The national study itself was designed to respond to these problems. However, one year after the study was completed, a congressional report still concluded that "although the federal government spends billions of dollars annually to support employment training programs, little is known about their long-term effects."[104]

In the conclusion to the national study itself, the authors explain that "the study findings . . . cannot provide a blueprint for action. They can only identify issues to be addressed in the future, which must, in turn, be based on the development and rigorous testing of new approaches to serving the labor market needs of disadvantaged persons."[105] The authors conclude that "the principal implication of this study . . . is that the Department of Labor must find ways to improve program performance. . . . we urge the Department of Labor to undertake a systematic program of controlled experiments designed to test alternative ways to serve those groups."[106] It may be unsurprising that a firm which makes its living conducting evaluations would conclude with a call for further research. But the program's results suggest that research funds are wasted. If the national study had never been done, and its $25 million budget had simply been distributed to the trainees involved in the study, each enrollee would have received $3,600, or nearly three times the earnings gain actually realized through participation in JTPA.[107] In this context, to divert poverty funds away from real social support in order to fund research is to take money away from people in desperate need and devote it to projects which have proven incapable of advancing the struggle against poverty. Despite the national study's unprecedented scale and methodological rigor, it reached the same conclusion as the vast majority of studies conducted over the past thirty years: that is, the results are inconclusive. It is time to turn away from the belief that the shortcomings of evaluation studies reflect solvable methodological problems, and to face the fact that studies are inconclusive because the programs' impacts are extremely meager. Given the evidence of likely JTPA impacts, and the long history of inconclusive evaluations, to spend more money on evaluations of training programs is not part of an anti-poverty agenda; it is simply welfare for academics.

The Politics of Job Training: Why JTPA's Problems Will Never Be Fixed

For much of the past thirty years, job training has been plagued by a series of structural problems that have hampered its effectiveness. Above all, job training has been carried out through a highly fragmented system in which multiple agencies have each run their own independent programs. In 1999, responsibility for training was divided among twenty-two different offices within the Labor Department plus fourteen other federal agencies outside the department.[108] In addition, many services are offered simultaneously—with no coordination—by federal, state, and local agencies. Thus in any given locality, the board of education may be running a school-to-work program for at-risk youth while the department of employment conducts training for laid-off defense workers, community colleges enroll adult students in job training, halfway houses mount programs for drug addicts, food stamp and welfare offices offer training for public assistance recipients, and homeless shelters provide training for the indigent. Most of these programs are funded at token levels and serve a small fraction of their client populations.

Most recently, WIA seeks to solve the problem of fragmentation by establishing "One-Stop" centers that will serve as points of access for welfare recipients, unemployment insurance claimants, and the long-term poor alike.[109] For the most part, though, the One-Stop center serves merely as a central office from which those interested may be referred to the various training programs—which continue to be operated by separate agencies, each according to its own guidelines. While WIA may centralize the information on what types of training are available, it has not consolidated the funding streams for training programs. The act does not insist that training be carried out by a single agency and bar others from funding duplicative programs, nor does it stop federal, state, and local officials from running overlapping or contradictory initiatives. Thus a congressional report concludes that even under WIA, job training remains a system of "separate programs that are focused on the same population, each with its own outcome and performance data."[110]

This fragmentation of services partly explains the difficulty of measuring the effectiveness of job training as a whole. But the problem is much worse than simply being unable to add up the effects of various agencies' programs. In 1997, a congressional review of JTPA programs found that fewer than half of those surveyed had obtained data on whether their graduates ever got jobs.[111] An internal Department of Labor assessment concluded that the unreliability of local program reports made it impossible to assemble an accurate picture of the program as a whole. "Adequate management controls were lacking at every level" of the system, the department's inspector general reported, and as a result, the national data were "inaccurate, incomplete and not in compliance with JTPA requirements."[112] The record of other training programs is even more bleak: for better or worse, JTPA probably established the *best* monitoring system of any training program. In a report titled *Multiple Employment Training Programs: Most Federal Agencies Do Not Know If Their Programs Are Working Effectively*, the GAO concluded that, after thirty years of experimenting with program design and performance monitoring, the government still has basically no idea whether or not its training programs are working.[113] In terms of program effectiveness, then, job training policy is carried out in a systemic haze that no one seems willing or able to dispel.

Measuring the success or failure of a multi-billion-dollar program may be a complex undertaking, but it's not rocket science. The fact that the Department of Labor lacks such basic information, and that this lack, while noted, has gone uncorrected for thirty years, suggests that it is simply not important enough to those in power to find out the answer to this question.

The ongoing series of policy adjustments aimed at redressing JTPA's structural problems seem to suffer from a similar lack of purpose. Proposals that sound bold on paper end up being carried out through such partial and half-hearted measures that they are inevitably doomed to be ineffective. The most dramatic such instance is JTPA's system of performance-based contracts, formulated as a radical solution to CETA's disappointing results. Performance-based contracts are supposed to guarantee success because training providers get paid only if an adequate number of trainees are placed into real jobs at real wages. In practice, however, the Department of Labor's performance standards have been adjusted from year to year in order to match the actual accomplishments of training providers in the recent past. Performance standards are generally set at a level equal to the 20th to 35th percentile of past performance—that is, at a level surpassed by 65% to 80% of contracts in the past two years.[114] Thus when contractors were unable to place a sufficient number of welfare recipients into decently paying jobs, the government did not cut off funding and demand better performance—it simply lowered the performance standards so that contractors could report success without changing their operations.[115] Even when programs clearly fail to meet established standards, they are unlikely to face financial penalties. In order to be judged a failure, a state must fail to meet at least 50% of the individual federal performance standards. Even then, the sole remedy is for the federal Department of Labor to offer technical assistance aimed at improving the next year's performance. State funding may be cut only after two successive years of program failure—and then only by a maximum of 5%.[116] Thus the procedural fix of performance-based contracting—the notion that funding guidelines in and of themselves would guarantee that poor people obtain decently paying jobs—has been fundamentally undermined by the practice of program administrators.

Perhaps the most telling such instance is the recent refusal of training providers to report their track records to WIA officials.[117] As part of the voucher program, WIA requires all providers to report their graduation rates, along with the employment and earnings of graduates six months after leaving the program. This information is then made available to the public at large, so that trainees can spend their vouchers intelligently. However, many programs have simply refused to provide the information, with the result that some states now face a growing shortage of eligible training providers. In part, programs have balked at assuming the cost of extensive follow-up interviews without a guarantee that WIA vouchers will be used for their services. Even beyond the cost, though, training operators have good reason to avoid publicizing their track records. For instance, JTPA's performance goals in 1999 aimed at having 60% of trainees employed three months after graduation; the earnings goal was set at less than $15,000 per year.[118] Programs that are comfortable with this standard as a federal requirement may nevertheless be loathe to advertise a 40% failure rate to the general public. It is not clear how this conflict will be solved, but in 2001, several states were considering applying for a waiver of this part of the law, allowing them to continue funding training programs without requiring performance reports. Thus WIA seems set to perpetuate a long history of bending administrative standards in order to continue funding a failed policy.

Across the country, well-intentioned policy analysts are engaged in an ongoing search for solutions to the operational problems of the job training system. These analysts must assume that training is what it claims to be: an honest attempt at improving the economic lives of poor Americans. From this perspective, the central question of training policy appears to be, How can we solve the technical problems that prevent JTPA or WIA from achieving their aims? From a broader perspective, however, this is the wrong question. The technical snafus are only symptoms of much deeper problems—in the very assumptions that drive job training programs as a whole.

In this sense, it is useful to compare JTPA with other areas of federal policy making. Job training proponents often treat their programs' shortcomings as the inevitable implementation problems faced by any large-scale public effort. But not all large federal programs look like JTPA. On the contrary, there is a clear contrast between those initiatives that succeed in their basic missions—and whose success is measurable—and those that flounder around year after year, seemingly unable to cure their ills or even to obtain a clear diagnosis of what's wrong. A mundane bureaucracy such as the Department of Transportation, for example, presumably has its share of inefficiency and fraud, but its basic mission gets accomplished: roads are built, lanes are expanded, potholes are filled, and the traveling public gets where it needs to go. Moreover, all of this is carried out without either the confusion or the hype characteristic of job training. If the DOT were run as job training is, the national budget for road construction would be parceled out to each state and local government, where it would again be divided among a host of private contractors. Each contractor would build roads of different widths and gradients, and there would be no coherent system for making sure that the end of one road lined up with the beginning of another. All of this activity would be carried out in a statistical haze where no one was ever sure exactly how many miles of road were laid or which drivers they served, and state governments would describe the situation in Pollyannaish reports entitled "California DRIVES" or "The Road to the Twenty-first Century," promising that programmatic success was, so to speak, just around the corner.

Why is job training beset by these types of problems while the Department of Transportation is not? The answer to this question lies not in the technical details of program implementation but in the political logic underlying each program. The primary goal of those who fund and control the DOT is, actually, to make sure that roads get built. While mayors and governors may post billboards advertising their sponsorship of new construction projects, transportation is not generally considered a politically crucial policy area in which politicians need to claim success. JTPA follows an opposite logic on both these counts. For those who control training policy—congressional funders, local administrators, and their business advisors—it is not strictly necessary that poor Americans be able to work their way out of poverty.[119] It is important, however, that politicians be able to claim credit for seeming to do something about the problem—and job training has proven extremely useful for establishing this credit. In virtually every city and state in the country, elected officials need to point to some credible effort at combating poverty and unemployment. In addition, since job training has been promoted as a key response to so many social problems (homelessness, high school dropouts, drug addiction, crime, and welfare dependence, among others), each agency that serves these particular populations finds it politically important to showcase some training initiative. Therefore the logic of job training as a *political* strategy leads to program authority being divided among the federal, state, and local levels of government and among myriad agencies within each level. This is why federal officials will never ban local governments from running duplicative programs, why local officials are content to run small-budget programs, and why programs continue to be re-funded even when it is not clear that they're working.

From a programmatic viewpoint, it makes no sense to divide the job training budget among a host of underfunded, token programs operated by a myriad of local authorities. From a political viewpoint, however, the logic of the system is unassailable.

In this context, the curiously intractable problems that have plagued JTPA and WIA become easier to understand—and the futility of searching for a technical fix is laid bare. The seeming mystery of job training's long history of frustration is resolved when we understand those responsible for it not as social engineers engaged in a design problem but as political actors engaged in a public relations drama—a charade, one might say.

CHAPTER FOUR

Power and "Empowerment": The Final Frontier of Job Training

Democracy in the workplace . . . is rapidly being introduced as an economic imperative instead of a social ideal.

—Clinton advisor Doug Ross[1]

The new economy is revolutionizing the workplace. We now live in a world where workers are being empowered to be managers. . . . As we invest in critical job training, we are giving workers the bargaining power they need to custom-design their jobs.

—Secretary of Labor Elaine Chao[2]

Where workers used to have to go up the managerial hierarchy . . . they now make their own decisions. . . . Companies . . . don't want employees who can follow rules; they want people who will make their own rules.

—Michael Hammer and James Champy,
Reengineering the Corporation[3]

Thinking generally slows this operation down.

—McDonald's manager[4]

For most of its history, job training has been conceived of as a program for marginal workers. Policy makers have assumed that, except during temporary cyclical downturns, the normal rate of economic growth would provide ample opportunity for all but the most handicapped workers. It was only those who lacked even the most basic levels of education and experience who were considered to need the remedial assistance provided by programs such as JTPA.[5] Over the course of the past twenty-five years, however, large numbers of reasonably well-educated and often highly experienced workers have also been left out of the country's economic expansion. Even while the national unemployment rate fell dramatically, millions of previously middle-class Americans lost jobs in manufacturing industries and found themselves stranded, unable to support their families in the low-wage service sector. In part, the government responded with initiatives to provide training in high-wage technical trades. Both the Trade Adjustment Assistance program and JTPA's Dislocated Worker program were often thought of as efforts to convert laid-off steelworkers into software engineers.

However, as policy makers realized that the demand for technicians could not absorb more than a small fraction of those seeking work, they shifted the focus of training away from occupation-specific skills, as discussed in chapter 3. Instead, for experienced workers—whether unemployed and looking for work or currently on the job and hoping to avoid layoffs—both public and private training efforts have increasingly focused on "problem solving," "teamwork," and "thinking" skills as the keys to economic security in the emerging economy. Such training aims to equip workers for employment in firms organized around a new set of principles—offering higher wages and increased autonomy, and variously described as "high performance," "empowerment," or "Total Quality Management"—that training boosters assert is coming to characterize a wide swath of the economy.

According to this latest incarnation of the skills mismatch thesis, the nature of economic competition at the turn of the twenty-first century has changed such that intellectual rather than technical skills are now the key to worker productivity. In this view, new forms of competition require employers to adopt organizational reforms that encourage all workers to contribute to innovations in product design and guarantees of product quality. For this system to succeed, proponents argue, it has become critical for nearly all workers to develop the "higher order" intellectual skills that were previously restricted to management. In this sense, the new theory attempts to solve the puzzle of "unobserved skills" discussed in chapter 2: it is the skills of creativity, innovation, and teamwork— unquantifiable by any existing skill measures—that both explain increased wage inequality among workers with similar education and offer the best hope of renewed prosperity in the postindustrial economy. Thus the study of high performance production represents a kind of final stand for the skills mismatch thesis. If there is a chance that skills training can guarantee steady jobs at good wages, it should be revealed in the practices of firms operating on this model; by contrast, if even "high performance," "empowered" workers remain economically insecure, it is hard to imagine what sort of further revision could breathe new life into the theory.

Beyond the promise of increased wages, proponents of high performance training also suggest that it will revolutionize power relations in the workplace, granting employees a hitherto unimaginable degree of autonomy, creativity, and dignity on the job. These are ambitious claims, but in one sense they are a logical extension of job training ideology. The assumptions undergirding training policy are fundamentally related to questions of power, in that they promote a view of unemployment in which conflict is anachronistic. Job training has long been presented as an *alternative* to political mobilization: rather than fight employers over labor conditions or regulations, employees will achieve greater gains by joining with management to pursue increased skills, productivity, and hence wages. Indeed, if mismatch theorists are right, attempts to mobilize political power on behalf of institutional protections of wages are doomed to backfire, as firms find themselves unable to retain untrained workers at higher wage rates. The promise of training suggests that workers' political power is irrelevant at best and counterproductive at worst. Proponents of high performance take this logic one step further: not only is it unnecessary for workers to exert power against management, these theorists argue, but it is specifically by *cooperating* with the profit-maximizing goals of their employers that workers can achieve the greatest measure of power on the job. In this chapter, I examine both of the primary claims of empowerment boosters. First, have firms which have adopted "high performance" methods increased their demand for skills among nonsupervisory workers? And second, has "empowerment" changed power relations within the firm, such that workers' mobilization or militancy is no longer needed?

When asked to identify the exact skills required for high performance, employers often refer to general capabilities such as "problem solving" or "teamwork." It is difficult to know what these terms mean in the abstract, and difficult to verify the mismatch theorists' claims that these skills are in short supply. While there is ready statistical evidence of employers' actual demand for college graduates, for example, it is impossible to know whether employers truly seek "problem solvers" or "empowered workers" without a more concrete understanding of how employees are actually used in the workplace. It is only by looking at actual work conditions, across a variety of industries, that we can realistically assess the claims of this latest mismatch thesis.

Unfortunately, the reality of workplace conditions does not live up to the rhetoric of high performance. The evidence presented below suggests that the majority of employers have little need either for democratization or for significantly higher-skilled employees. While "reengineering"—the high performance buzzword of the early 1990s—has often increased productivity, its effect on the demand for skills has been marginal. For many firms, empowerment programs seem primarily designed to serve the goals of public relations or employee indoctrination.[6] Even where "empowerment" has involved a genuine reorganization of work along lines that require increased teamwork and employee responsibilities, the effect on demand for *skills* has been modest. Most important, even the "best practice" companies have never granted employees fundamental control over their work lives. Partly for this reason, empowerment programs have guaranteed neither the wages of their participants nor even their jobs; indeed, many of the most renowned "high performance" firms have steadily reduced the size of their workforces.[7] There is no reason to believe that even the most successful reengineering will be able to restore the incomes of working class Americans.

To arrive at this conclusion, I first provide the historical and theoretical background of the management theories that fall under the rubric of "high performance" or "Total Quality Management."[8] I then examine workplace conditions in industries where I believe the rhetoric of empowerment has been used primarily for ideological purposes as well as in those where the strategy has been adopted in a more meaningful manner. I devote considerable attention to the impact of recent technological and organizational trends on the autonomy and democratic rights of nonsupervisory workers. The evidence shows that, for the most part, even those firms that proclaim a commitment to empowerment have subjected their employees to forms of control just as complete as—if not more intensive than—in the past. Because of the inherent conflict of interest between employer and employee, there is an unavoidable contradiction between the theory of high performance and the reality of power relations in the workplace. I conclude that the empowerment movement as a whole fails to deliver a convincing rationale for training as a key strategy for restoring American workers' earning power.

Historical Background: The Evolution of "High Performance" and the Re-enchantment of Work

Beginning in the first Clinton administration, government officials offered a new twist to the rationale for job training. Where the preceding Republican administrations had placed the blame for unemployment solely on the deficiencies of workers, the New Democrats apportioned blame equally between workers and firms. In this vision, workers lack the skills required for "the workplace of the future," but most companies have also failed to restructure their operations in ways that would make use of more high-skilled workers. Thus we are stuck in a chicken-and-egg dilemma in which companies will not retool until they know the skilled workforce is there, and workers will not invest in further training until they know jobs are really available. The solution, we are told, is to move ahead on both fronts at once: to redouble government efforts in education and training, while convincing private employers to retool for high performance production. Thus, while admitting that existing skill levels are adequate for current employer demands, the New Democrats nevertheless suggested that we are on the brink of a new industrial revolution in which advanced skills—

both technical know-how and the ability to function as part of a creative problem-solving team—will be critical for all but the lowest-wage occupations. The Clintonites' romantic view of the economy has also been embraced by scores of management gurus, who continue to trumpet this vision in a steady stream of inspirational how-to books.

This vision of the "new economy" has been most clearly articulated by former Secretary of Labor Robert Reich in *The Work of Nations*.[9] Reich explains that in the old economy of mid-century, profits derived from economies of scale. Most of the value added to a product came from mass production, with product design and marketing strategies remaining largely unchanged for long periods. In the new economy, however, value is added not by the mass production process but by the continual innovation of design and marketing specialists. Reich terms this a shift "from high volume to high value."[10] His examples point to the profits to be made in specialized production:

> The most profitable textile businesses produce specially coated and finished fabrics for automobiles, office furniture, rain gear, and wall coverings . . . the highest profits in telecommunications derive from customized long-distance services like voice, video and information processing. . . . The fastest-growing trucking, rail, and air freight businesses meet . . . needs for specialized pickups and deliveries, unique containers, and worldwide integration of different modes of transportation.[11]

In each of these industries, profitability derives from creative innovation: "All that really counts is rapid problem-identifying and problem-solving—the marriage of technical insight with marketing know-how, blessed by strategic and financial acumen."[12] This, Reich suggests, is what accounts for the growing disparity in wages between the college-educated professionals he terms "symbolic analysts" and the non-college-educated production and service workers: the nature of production has changed such that, in the new economy, it is actually the professionals who are creating the value.

Reich insists, however, that "all of America's routine production workers could become symbolic analysts."[13] The process through which this transformation might occur is intimately related to the principles of Total Quality Management (TQM) as articulated by the grandfather of all management gurus, W. E. Deming.[14] At the heart of Deming's vision is the conviction that firms must increasingly compete through the quality rather than the price of their products. To produce consistently high-quality goods and services, ordinary workers must be involved in the production process in new ways. Rather than stressing strictly quantitative goals for the majority of workers and enforcing quality control through inspection of final products, workers at every stage of the operation must be involved in guaranteeing quality. That means that workers must have greater knowledge about the overall production system, do more work in teams, and be equipped to undertake a wider range of jobs as production needs vary. Beyond this, if a firm's advantage comes from constant quality improvements and design innovations, management cannot afford to do without the insights of workers who have the most immediate knowledge of the company's operations. Therefore TQM requires that managers create an atmosphere of openness and cooperation in which workers feel free to contribute ideas and recommendations without fear of retribution.

Thus the "high performance" workplace has two aspects that together provide the basis for the most recent articulation of the skills mismatch thesis. First, management theorists have projected that workers in general need to become involved in many more aspects of their firm's operation than ever before and to be prepared to take responsibility for a wide variety of tasks previously reserved for management. As the Secretary's Commission on Achieving Necessary Skills (SCANS) suggests, in the emerging economy, "All employees will have to read well enough to understand and interpret diagrams, directories, correspondence, manuals, records, charts, graphs, tables, and specifications . . . . Virtually all employees will be required to maintain records, estimate results, use spreadsheets, or apply statistical process controls as they negotiate, identify trends, or suggest new courses of action."[15] Second, in addition to this set of managerial competencies, training advocates emphasize the need for workers to master the social skills of teamwork, cooperation, flexibility, and creative problem solving. Even for ordinary production workers, scholars assert that the skills now in greatest demand include "reasoning, interpersonal skills, working in a team, using information systems, setting priorities, [and] personal work behaviors."[16]

In the TQM vision, the qualities demanded of managers—design innovation, productivity improvements, and a constant vigilance regarding quality—are also demanded of every employee. However, neither attention to quality nor contribution of ideas can be extracted from workers through simple coercion. Rather, these will be forthcoming only if workers are secure in their jobs and are treated with respect in the course of the workday. Taken together, these dynamics entail a suspension of the hierarchical power relations that have previously governed the workplace. Authoritarian managers end up only sabotaging themselves: as they alienate workers, they undermine the basis on which their own performance is judged. Because firms' interests lie in promoting workers' creativity, the nature of work is fundamentally changed in the new enterprises. Thus Reich describes "the 'flat' organization of high-value enterprises," where "one of the best-kept secrets among symbolic analysts is that so many of them enjoy their work. In fact, much of it does not count as work at all, in the traditional sense. . . . The 'work' . . . often involves puzzles, experiments, games, a significant amount of chatter, and substantial discretion over what to do next. . . . many symbolic analysts would 'work' even if money were no object."[17]

Here Reich touches on a central claim about "empowered" workplaces. For the vast majority of Americans, work's best promise has been a steady paycheck and reliable benefits. In the early 1980s, the proponents of high performance began to offer something more: not only money, but meaning; not only dollars, but dignity; not only a paycheck, but power. In Reich's description, the reengineered companies come close to Marx's meshing of work and play. After lifetimes of subordinated, mind-numbing labor, American workers are told that the right skills will not only bring high wages; they will also set us free. As one observer noted, this message was at the core of the IBM advertising campaign that single-handedly launched the personal computer era:

A Chaplinesque figure sits before the soft, off-white keyboard and ice-green screen, his face consumed with wonder and delight. Plucked from his imprisoning assembly line, stripped of his overalls and dressed in a pinstripe suit (so suddenly that his work boots remain, old and worn, a fitting contrast to the high-tech polish of the computer), the character made famous by Chaplin in *Modern Times* is plopped down in the middle of the twenty-first century. "How to test drive the IBM Personal Computer," the headline reads, only the first in a long line of references to that twentieth-century archetype of freedom and mobility, the automobile. Liberated from the drudgery of his factory job, his chair tipped back, his hat blown clean away by a passing breeze, our former assembly-line worker is off on a wild, exhilarating ride into the future of work. . . . Designed to sell computers, this ad sells a promise as well. Charlie Chaplin was the first popular media figure to express the reality of alienating work on the assembly line. . . . yet, here, Chaplin's factory worker finds fulfillment (and, from the look of his suit, a considerable raise in pay) through the wonders of new technology. The computer delivers him from the prison of dirty, boring, alienating work. . . . the former critic of work becomes a persuasive advocate for technology and for the corporation itself. Through technology and the corporation that provides it, Chaplin seems to be telling us . . . our work can become a realm of freedom—fluid, infinitely mobile, freighted with enormous possibility.[18]

Thus in the reengineered workplace—at least as imagined by its boosters—skills are both more important than ever and more rewarding than ever. Furthermore, while this vision may appear utopian, empowerment advocates have argued that it is the inevitable product of market forces. In the words of the SCANS report, "workplaces organized along the lines of the traditional mass production model can no longer prosper. Like the dinosaur with its limited intelligence, doomed to extinction at the hands of smaller but craftier animals, the traditional model cannot survive the competition from high-performance organizations."[19]

Theoretical Background: High Performance and Human Capital

While the practices of TQM emerged from corporate efforts to redress falling productivity rates in the 1970s, the intellectual basis for the vision of a conflict-free workplace predates these developments, tracing its roots to the human capital theory of neoclassical economics. In neoclassical thought, labor is a "factor of production" like any other. As land commands a higher or a lower price depending on its fertility and metals depending on their strength, workers are paid more or less according to the skills they bring to a job. Workers, like all other inputs, are paid their marginal product. In the neoclassical vision of the workplace, there is no role for power relations. Rather, earnings are directly and simply determined by one's contribution to production. In such an economy, management has no reason to hesitate in granting power to workers. In competitive markets, whoever manages the firm will be obliged to pay each factor according to its productivity. If empowering workers increases productivity, it will directly and simply serve the firm's interests.

It is this vision of the firm as unmediated by power relations (or at worst, where power relations appear as an unnecessary bad habit left over from earlier times) that animates advocates of high performance. Indeed, the most celebrated "excellence" firms have been described in terms that match this vision. The early reports from Silicon Valley told of "egalitarian and flexible" firms that were "less concerned with the normal trappings of rank."[20] And Business Week describes the celebrated General Motors Saturn plant as a place where "teams of workers largely govern themselves."[21] These breathless descriptions of high performance assume that power relations are not fundamental to the firm and can therefore be suspended without violating the firm's mission.

In reality, however, there are at least two dynamics that perpetuate power relations within firms and that therefore place limits on the extent to which American companies can share power with their employees. First, to state the obvious, firms and workers are in a constant struggle over wages. It is usually impossible to calculate the exact marginal productivity of any worker, and even where it is possible, there is no guarantee that wages will be set accordingly. Firms pay workers as little as they can get away with; workers seek as much as they can extract. While the firm's total revenues are at least partly determined by its overall productivity, the division of these revenues is the subject of political contestation. Therefore, at least in this area, management has a conflict of interest with workers and cannot give over substantial power without sacrificing some of its own most important objective: profit.

Second, both neoclassical theory and modern empowerment advocates ignore the crucial distinction between human labor and all other "factors of production." Whereas land, minerals, and energy are all inert, the fact of human consciousness and intentionality adds a unique dimension to our participation in the production process. With any other input, a firm buys a quantity of material and gets what it pays for. With workers, however, there is a critical disjuncture between what the firm buys and what it hopes to obtain. The only thing that can be guaranteed in a labor contract is that the employee will come to work for a certain number of hours and agree to do as told. But this is insufficient for an employer, who also needs the worker's effort and initiative, concentration and commitment—factors that cannot be specified in a labor contract and must therefore be extracted through a system of workplace control.

In nearly every workplace, it is in management's interest for workers to constantly work as hard and as conscientiously as possible. Conversely, it is in workers' interest to conserve work effort to some degree or another, whether to protect their health, minimize stress, save energy for nonwork activities, or simply allow for conversational breaks with fellow workers. This conflict of interest makes every employer-employee relationship what Bowles and Gintis term a "contested exchange"; and it requires that management establish some system of workplace control in order to guarantee the desired level of work effort.[22]

The combination of these dynamics—the struggle over wages and management's need to control workers' effort—points to the limitations of empowerment. While the goals cited by Reich and others may be laudable, it is naive to believe that they will be simply instituted through the normal competition of the market. Rather, when empowerment goals come in conflict with firms' other imperatives, we should expect employers to enact empowerment only within the confines of their overarching mission.

In what follows, I hope to illustrate the impact of this conflict of goals in the daily reality of working life. I begin by presenting two case studies of industries in which the goals of empowerment have been almost completely trumped by those of social control and profitability. While the cases examined (fast food and airline reservations) are not necessarily representative of employers outside these industries, I believe that they offer particularly illuminating examples of the extent to which employers have instituted the trappings of high performance while actually limiting the skills and autonomy of employees. Moreover, since these are financially successful industries, their records challenge the assumption that the dinosaurs of mindless work and autocratic power must be driven out in the normal course of market competition.

The Non-Empowered Workforce: High Performance as Rhetoric

McDonald's and the Fast-Food Industry

It may be thought that the situation of McDonald's employees is too extreme to serve as an example for anything beyond itself. The jobs are well known to require few skills and to provide meager wages. Indeed, the popular reference to "McJobs" suggests that the chain defines the lower pole of the labor market rather than a representative middle. Nevertheless, the case of McDonald's offers a number of important insights regarding the nature of "quality" in the service sector and the extent to which the goals of quality and productivity truly require higher skills or workplace democracy.

McDonald's is a highly successful corporation that has been expanding for fifty years both in the United States and abroad; the company boasts that one-seventh of all American workers have at some point been employed there.[23] Though its practices are now widely imitated, McDonald's management methods marked a revolution in the restaurant industry. Before the chain came into existence, hamburgers were thought to exemplify exactly the kind of good that could not be mass-produced: each short-order cook had his or her own slightly idiosyncratic style, and each customer wanted a burger cooked to personal taste—rare or well done, with or without onions, and so on. By installing new technology and radically reorganizing work, McDonald's showed that it was possible to produce and market uniform, high-quality fast food. The company has followed the edicts of TQM, using computers to continually enhance quality control and improve productivity. McDonald's workers are organized in teams and are often cross-trained for multiple tasks. Yet it is hard to call these employees "empowered."[24]

The McDonald's workplace is divided roughly in two, between food preparation and counter service. The production of food is almost entirely mechanized. In order to guarantee consistent quality standards, there is virtually no room left for human judgment. A series of lights and buzzers tells workers exactly when the fries are ready and when the burgers need to be turned. Ketchup dispensers are designed to release exactly the right amount, in the approved flower pattern, on every burger. Detailed work regulations specify the exact method workers must follow in almost every step of production: the correct arm motion to use in salting a batch of fries, the right quantity of chopped onion to put on a burger (twelve bits per patty), and the correct sequence in which customers' orders must be assembled.

At the counter, workers are similarly controlled by a combination of computer technology and detailed performance guidelines. Counter workers log onto a cash register with an individual identity code, and all the registers are fed through the store's central computer. McDonald's software provides managers with reports that identify the sales at each employee's register, broken down for each half-hour period. If a worker is slow at assembling orders and therefore reaches a smaller number of customers than others, it will show up in her sales figures. If the store is conducting a special campaign to promote Bacon Double Cheeseburgers, managers can count the exact number sold, in which shifts and by which workers. Further, the cash register itself is used as a tool to promote sales: registers are commonly programmed so that, for instance, when a customer orders a burger, fries, and cola, the buttons for ice cream, cookies, and apple pie will automatically light up, prompting the worker to suggest dessert.

Although McDonald's workers are organized into teams and cross-trained, no increase in skill requirements is involved, since workers are trained to do each other's jobs rather than to take over managerial responsibilities, and since each of the jobs involved can be learned in less than a day. Workers are encouraged to take responsibility for guaranteeing that the operation as a whole runs smoothly, but this primarily means that all workers are expected to clean counters, mop floors, or restock supplies whenever they are not otherwise busy. "If there's time to lean, there's time to clean" is a favored McDonald's slogan, and its effectiveness is evident in the fact that all cleaning is accomplished in the course of normal shifts; no workers are ever paid overtime to stay after and clean up.

McDonald's counter workers must contend with a further dimension of control unique to the service sector. In worksites where employees deal directly with the public, their attitude toward customers is itself part of the product. When diners enter McDonald's, they are not merely buying hamburgers; in some broader way, they are also buying the "McDonald's experience." It is up to the workers to create this experience. But management cannot rely on workers to do this on their own initiative or through their own judgment. Part of what is supposed to be enjoyable about entering a McDonald's is the experience of being treated with deference, of being *served*. If employees were free to use their discretion, this experience might be less intensely pleasurable. At a minimum, employee discretion would result in customers being treated differently depending on the particular store and time of day they entered; since the core of McDonald's promise is the guarantee of uniform quality around the world, such variation would threaten the company's marketing strategy.

In order to standardize this dimension of service, McDonald's has gone to great lengths to control workers' interaction with the public. Employees are subject to strict dress codes (women cannot wear earrings and men's hair cannot touch their shoulders) and are required to wear first-name-only identification tags, thus establishing the implied power relationship—the customer is "sir" or "ma'am," while I am "Gordon." The counters are disproportionately staffed by women, on the assumption that they have already been socialized to project caring and deference. Furthermore, almost every customer interaction has been anticipated and pre-scripted at McDonald's corporate headquarters. Employees are not allowed to ask "Can I help someone?" or "What'll it be today?"—these are considered disrespectful and impersonal. They must ask "May I help you, sir/ma'am?" And employees are regularly reprimanded for not smiling.

Thus quality-centered management has not brought greater autonomy to McDonald's workers, but just the opposite. Managerial control of servers extends even beyond the realms imagined in *Modern Times:* workers are required to take an instrumental attitude toward their own personalities, manufacturing and projecting emotions as part of their job, and being policed, promoted, or fired on the basis of this performance.[25] Furthermore, it is not enough to merely follow conversational scripts without also producing the appropriate emotions. Thus, although conversations with McDonald's customers are almost entirely pre-scripted, the company is concerned that they not *sound* canned; thus workers are instructed to "act natural" and "be yourself" while delivering their lines.[26] Since it is hard to act genuinely enthusiastic while actually being angry, depressed, or alienated, the drive to control the quality of customer service interactions ends up being a drive to control the internal emotional states of workers.[27]

In return for all this effort, McDonald's workers get a surprisingly bad deal. All nonsupervisory workers are part-time and generally are paid at or near the minimum wage, with no health insurance, paid holidays, vacation, or sick days. Workers are granted a fifteen-minute paid break for four hours of work, plus an additional five minutes for each additional hour; thus even an eight-hour shift includes only thirty-five minutes of paid break time. Work schedules change from week to week at the discretion of managers, and workers are often asked to come in early, stay late, or leave early, depending on customer volume. Since managers are under constant pressure to minimize labor costs relative to sales, staffing plans are generally set at levels that guarantee that workers will be constantly running.

Why, given these conditions, do McDonald's employees work as hard as they do? In part, workers' motivation is driven by the very type of employee involvement and customer feedback hailed as defining features of high performance. Leidner suggests that customer feedback at McDonald's is uniquely facilitated by the restaurant's architecture, featuring an innovative design that allows customers to view everything counter workers do and much of what grill workers do. When customers pile up in front of a register, counter workers feel intense pressure to please the people they are dealing with. As a result, they are driven to bag fries, make drinks, assemble orders, and urge on the grill staff to produce as quickly as possible. If the restaurants were arranged so that counter people were responsible only for taking orders and making change, and all other work was conducted behind a wall, the system would break down: no matter how uncomfortable the counter worker felt about growing lines, this pressure would not be passed on to those actually responsible for getting the order ready. Thus McDonald's enrolls its customers as a critical arm of managerial control.[28]

An in-depth study of Burger King suggests that team ideology has also played a powerful role in keeping fast-food workers motivated. The Basic Restaurant Operations Course required of all would-be Burger King managers outlines a strategy for keeping employees motivated without raising their wages.

Incredibly, the course draws on Maslow's theory of self-actualization, defined by Burger King as "the need to grow and become what one is capable of becoming."[29] Clearly, fryolater workers are unlikely to feel that they have achieved their telos. Yet, no less than high-tech design firms, fast-food chains use the ideology of teamwork to encourage workers to find greater meaning in their calling. "Let's think of, say, a Roman ship that's being rowed by galley slaves," explains a former Burger King manager. "You want them to work hard . . . [but] how do you get them to smile?"[30] Fast-food corporations teach managers that if they give workers personal sympathy and appreciative comments and make them feel that they're in the loop on restaurant decision-making, employees will give their all even at low wages and stressful conditions. Thus Burger King scholar Ester Reiter explains that "just as almost all discretion is removed from the job, workers are told how important each of them is to the restaurant's success."[31] From the corporation's viewpoint, the rationale for employee inclusion is baldly cynical. "Employees who . . . feel a part of store life, develop a sense of loyalty and pride," explains the Burger King management training course. "As a result, they work harmoniously with management."[32] For many workers, the desire for management appreciation may be powerful enough that the corporate strategy is indeed effective, as least for as long as workers last on such a job.

At both McDonald's and Burger King, then, fast-food operations suggest that technological innovation, quality-centered management, teamwork, and enhanced customer feedback—the very core attributes of "high performance"— may be entirely divorced from either the skills employers require or the wages they offer. The fast-food case demonstrates that it is possible to improve quality and productivity without increasing employees' skills or power; that quality control in the service sector may involve an extension of managerial control into previously personal aspects of workers' lives; and that both customer feedback and the internalization of corporate goals may be used to elicit harder work with no corresponding increase in wages.

Airline Reservations

The history of airline reservation agents' work over the past twenty years reflects a process of de-skilling, in which computerization has been used to limit rather than expand workers' autonomy and in which management has willingly sacrificed quality of customer service in order to increase control over the quantity of transactions conducted. Until the early 1980s, reservationists were paid well and accorded a semiprofessional status. As Barbara Garson explains, "they were valued because they had to learn all the company's routes, fares and policies. Then they had to apply this knowledge while responding on the telephone to the thousands of turns that even the simplest conversation can take. It seemed that this would always involve a great deal of personal judgment."[33] It is exactly this element of unpredictability, and the ensuing reliance on the discretion of workers, that airlines sought to prevent. In a system where every call was idiosyncratic, it was impossible for companies to accurately control the quality of service provided, set goals and procedures for improved productivity, or calculate the exact number of workers needed for a given shift. Thus over the past twenty years, airlines have used computer technology and work reorganization to remove these uncontrollable elements from the reservations system.[34]

In the new system, reservation agents log onto a computer console when they report to work. From the beginning to the end of their day, every movement they make is monitored and accounted for. The console divides agents' time into four modes: speaking with a customer, waiting for a new call to come in, "after-hangup time" during which agents process the information just received, and break time. Workers are allowed eleven seconds of "after-hangup time" between calls and twelve minutes of personal break daily; two instances of being unplugged without authorization are cause for disciplinary action.[35] Workers are evaluated against quotas for the percentage of time spent in each mode and the average time spent per call. In addition, agents are required to function as active salespeople, and the airlines have developed standard sales techniques which must be included in every conversation—"tone of voice," "probe," "used the customer's name," "close," and so on. As they work, reservationists are secretly monitored by supervisors who grade them on the consistency with which they employ these methods. The success of this system in reducing reservations work to a series of mechanical tasks not reliant on the independent discretion of employees is evident in the choice of at least one major airline to use California prison inmates as telephone booking agents.[36]

There is no question that the quality of service provided to customers is worse under the new system than under the old. For example, Garson describes an "old-fashioned" Air Canada reservationist who unplugged his console for fifteen minutes in order to type out fare information for a man who wanted it mailed to his son in Germany. This type of personal consideration—or even lesser irregularities such as helping a customer decide between alternate dates, routes, and fares, or developing a personalized sales pitch—is made largely impossible by the new management techniques. Indeed, it is exactly the type of flexible problem solving championed by high performance advocates that has been eliminated from airline reservations work. Even management recognizes this loss of quality: several airlines have instituted separate reservation systems in which higher-paying customers can speak with less-monitored agents. Yet on the whole, airlines have benefited from these changes. In many cases, the wages paid to reservation agents have been cut in half. Even more important, the airlines have gained a critical dimension of control over their product. As Garson notes, "standardization . . . allow[s] [management] to count, time and grade each phone call. It was more important to have a quantifiable phone call than a flexible agent."[37]

Summary: Total Quality Management in Non-Empowered Workplaces

At its boldest, the vision of empowered production suggests that we have entered a fundamentally new stage of economic development, in which it is in the *nature* of profit-seeking enterprises to require democratization, worker autonomy, and "higher-order thinking skills." The cases of fast food and airline reservations illustrate several principles which challenge the applicability of high performance theory to a wide range of the economy. First, there is no necessary connection between quality or productivity on the one hand and workers' skill or empowerment on the other. Second, even where quality does require some level of empowerment, quality to the customer is not necessarily the most important goal for the firm. Proponents of Total Quality Management suggest that in postindustrial economies, firms must compete on the basis of quality rather than price and therefore that market forces will drive all firms to adopt the highest-quality production techniques. But this analysis ignores the fact that the demand for quality service, like that for quality goods, is highly segmented. Not everyone flies first-class. Both manufacturing and service firms have long learned to divide their customer base between those who demand the best—and can pay for it—and those who must settle for less. Competition does not, apparently, force airlines to provide all callers with flexible, skilled, helpful reservationists. Thus even where quality would be improved by worker empowerment, this good may be trumped by more urgent imperatives of the firm.

I believe the lessons illustrated by these industries apply to the majority of American workplaces. Across the economy, successful companies are proving that quality, productivity, and profitability do not require per se that workers obtain higher skills or be granted greater autonomy. On the contrary, abundant examples point to a trend in the opposite direction, toward ever greater and more detailed control over the work lives of employees. Random drug testing has become a commonplace feature of employment. Telephone operators and home-shopping clerks are routinely monitored by supervisors who secretly listen in on their conversations.[38] Trucking companies have installed monitors that report on drivers' average speed, engine-idling time, and length of breaks.[39] Government social workers have been subject to time and motion studies and are now evaluated on a system of transaction quotas and timed productivity.[40] Flight attendants are instructed in precise scripts to use with disgruntled customers.[41] Hotel porters are required to read guests' luggage tags and comment on the virtues of the chain's hotel in their hometowns.[42] Supermarket checkout clerks are required to smile at each customer—and managers insist it's not a smile unless your teeth are showing—and to make eye contact for at least three seconds. (The employer in question refused to drop this policy even after female clerks complained that it led to sexual harassment.)[43] Retail firms increasingly employ undercover "shoppers" and employee-specific customer-feedback forms in order to evaluate and discipline store workers.[44] Office word processing systems are equipped with features that count the keystrokes and time the pace of clerical workers.[45] And the practice of denying employees bathroom breaks has become so widespread that in 1998, OSHA was forced to issue a policy statement requiring employers to provide "timely access" for employees who need to go.[46]

For nonprofessional workers, the reengineered workplace may look less like techies in tennis shoes brainstorming new product designs and more like the back-office panopticon which one study describes as the prototype of high-tech, low-empowered workplaces:

> Imagine an enormous office that looks like a classroom during exam period. Desks face the front of the room; the windows are blacked out. In "the cage" (an old banking term for the money-handling area), workers slip open envelopes, remove checks, and sort the remaining contents at the rate of three envelopes a minute. At the desks, clerks enter the amount on each check into a computer system. Clerks have a quota of eighty-five hundred keystrokes an hour. Everyone's performance is monitored. A manager watches from a platform elevated above the room that workers call "the pedestal" or "the birdhouse." Other supervisors monitor workers from the back of the room, and a black globe containing television cameras hangs from the ceiling. . . . the manager, using the cameras, can zoom in on any individual's desk and see exactly what they're working on and . . . employees are forbidden to talk to co-workers about anything other than the task at hand. The owner explains that "I'm not paying people to chat. I'm paying them to open envelopes."[47]

The drive for increased control over employees can be seen in employers' broader political strategies as well. Corporate lobbies have generally sought not to expand power-sharing relations with their employees but rather to eliminate those rights workers have already won. Union-busting remains standard practice in every industry and occupation; by the early 1990s, anti-union consulting had grown into a $1 billion industry.[48] Virtually every major business organization joined in the effort to defeat the 1994 striker replacement bill, thus guaranteeing that even where workers have unionized, the right to strike is largely eviscerated.[49] Further, the national business lobbies have sought to protect employers' ability to violate federal labor laws with little repercussion, fighting the Clinton administration's efforts to ban repeat violators from bidding on federal contracts—a proposal they labeled "blacklisting."[50] One of George W. Bush's first acts as president was to fulfill this business demand and revoke the Clinton-era regulation.

Beyond the question of unionization, employer organizations have used their political clout at both the federal and state levels to disempower their employees in myriad smaller ways. At the national level, employers are seeking to eliminate the Davis-Bacon prevailing wage law, to bar expansion of the Family and Medical Leave Act, and to make it easier for employees to be denied benefits by reclassifying them as independent contractors.[51] Under the rubric of flexible scheduling, manufacturing employers have sought to circumvent the eight-hour day and avoid the requirement to pay a higher rate for overtime work.[52] In Washington state, Microsoft and other high-tech employers have lobbied successfully to exempt computer analysts, programmers, and developers from the right to overtime pay.[53] And for professional employees, business groups have defended the growing practice of requiring employees to sign away their legal right to sue in the event of employment discrimination.[54]

Perhaps the most ominous example of the trend toward employers' increased control over rather than empowerment of employees is the dramatic growth in the surveillance of workers' activities. Retail outlets have long used hidden cameras not only to prevent shoplifting but also to monitor the behavior of sales staff. Some stores have added hidden microphones to record the nature of service workers' interactions with customers.[55]

The practice of spying on employees has spread most dramatically in the white-collar office sector. Employer surveys report that 30 percent of large corporations conduct some form of electronic surveillance of their employees, including searches of voice mail, e-mail, and computer files.[56] Indeed, many offices use software that not only allows supervisors to read workers' e-mail but also analyzes the flow of communication within the office, highlighting who is speaking with whom and identifying cliques of disgruntled workers.[57] Networked communications software allows managers to check on any employee's work in progress at any time, without the worker's knowledge. Standard office telephone systems record the origin, destination, and duration of every call made, both externally and within the firm, thus allowing top managers to track patterns of communication among their subordinates. Similarly, security systems that replace door keys with identity cards also generate a report tracking employees' movements throughout the workplace. A group of hospitals took this technology one step further, insisting that all nurses wear battery-powered badges, detectable by infrared monitors installed throughout the hospital, so that their movements between patients, supplies, and doctors could be monitored, analyzed, and, presumably, measured against new efficiency standards.[58] Finally, the technology we all knew must be coming seems to be creeping closer to reality: several London banks and technology companies have announced that they are investigating methods for implanting microchips under the skin of their employees, in order to more perfectly monitor their whereabouts and activities. A British professor defending the proposal had a chip implanted in his own arm to show that it was "not such a big deal," noting that the microchip was not that many steps away from the tracking devices many employees are already required to wear.[59]

While the extent of workplace spying is hard to measure, the technology is still being developed, and both the National Association of Manufacturers (NAM) and the U.S. Chamber of Commerce have opposed congressional proposals to limit surveillance. The NAM argues that surveillance is an important part of American companies' "fight to remain competitive."[60] Indeed, the boundaries of acceptable surveillance have extended so greatly over the past ten years that by 1998 the scope of debate in the California Assembly was restricted to the question of whether electronic spying should be allowed in toilets and locker rooms where employees might be undressing; the chamber of commerce opposed even such a limited ban, charging it went "too far" in restricting employers' right to spy.[61]

Thus highly successful firms have demonstrated that there is no necessary link between productivity and workplace democracy. Indeed, the rhetoric of teamwork and participation has often been deployed cynically, even by employers who are openly committed to the disempowerment of their workers. For example, in 1994 the management of Briggs & Stratton, an engine manufacturer and Milwaukee's biggest employer, demanded that its union reopen contract agreements nineteen months before they were due to expire. Despite the fact that the company had realized two consecutive years of record profits, management demanded the virtual elimination of seniority rules as well as the suspension of restrictions on moving jobs out of Milwaukee—language that had been granted in return for earlier employee concessions in wages and health care. The company threatened that if the union didn't cooperate, its jobs would be moved to Mexico. While the company was thus seeking to eviscerate both the living standards and the bargaining power of its workers, CEO Fred Stratton complained publicly that the union leadership was "archaic and adversarial," decrying its insistence on a "we-versus-them mentality and an adversarial approach."[62]

Polaroid Corporation, an early leader in employee participation, provides a similar example of the uses of empowerment rhetoric as a disguise for management control. For over forty years Polaroid operated an employees committee for its 8,000 workers. While workers were invited to elect representatives to the committee, management appointed the top officers, controlled the agenda, and had veto power over the committee's recommendations. In 1992, employee Charla Scivally was elected as a secretaries' representative and proposed a series of democratizing reforms including employee election of officers, roll call voting, term limits, financial disclosure, and open meetings. Company management rejected all these ideas, stating that election of committee officers would be "contrary to the collaborative heritage" of the company. In response, Scivally initiated an organizing drive to establish an independent union, which management denounced as "a reversal of 40 years of building a participatory process." The union gathered 1,200 signatures but was unable to force an election. Shortly afterward, Scivally was fired.[63]

Even among the most highly educated of workers—those supposedly most in demand—"empowerment" is commonly used as a ruse to avoid giving workers meaningful forms of power. When Yale University's graduate student teachers struck for union recognition, the school's administration vehemently opposed collective bargaining, instead inviting the teachers to elect representatives to a joint "policy" committee. Administrators insisted that they were interested in the "full participation" of teaching assistants and that the committee would provide "a genuine voice" for the concerns that underlay the unionization drive. University managers insisted on the right, however, to appoint three-quarters of the committee's members and to veto any recommendations it might generate. Over the ensuing years, the committee repeatedly overruled graduate teachers' proposals regarding salary, job descriptions, and grievance procedures. When a majority of graduate student teachers became convinced that the committee process was bankrupt, and engaged in another strike in 1995, the university announced that strikers would be banned from future teaching and might be expelled, and the administration encouraged faculty to write negative letters of recommendation for Ph.D. candidates who participated in the strike. Yet throughout this entire period, administrators never abandoned the public insistence that they were committed to a process of "inclusion" and "consensus."[64]

Thus in all these cases, from the ivory tower to the golden arches, the rhetoric of empowerment is deployed cynically, and serves above all to mask the ongoing attempts to disempower workers.

Innovative Practices: The Empowered Workforce

While the cases described above likely represent the majority of American workplaces, in a significant number of firms—primarily large corporations in the information-processing or durable goods industries—"empowerment" has been more than a rhetorical strategy. The record in these companies is mixed and complex.[65] In many cases, workers have been given increased autonomy in the day-to-day conduct of their work, and their suggestions regarding productivity have often been sought out and implemented. For a significant number of workers, these innovations have led to improved work satisfaction.[66] On close examination, however, even these firms have rarely increased workers' actual power over key economic decisions affecting their livelihood. Moreover, there is no clear effect on skill requirements in these firms. Technical skills have been raised in some jobs, lowered in others, and left untouched in many. There is little evidence of a widespread increase in the managerial or interpersonal skills required for nonsupervisory workers. Thus even in the best firms, the institution of Total Quality Management has not lived up to its boosters' promise of increased skills, wages, and autonomy.

The most serious TQM programs have been instituted by companies seeking to impact aspects of productivity which cannot be technologically or bureaucratically controlled. Particularly for union employers, the early 1970s' rash of strikes over working conditions signaled the need to win employees' *voluntary* participation in productivity improvements. As Wells notes,

> The benefits management derived from its old system of control over its workers had reached their limit, yet there remained a domain of potential productivity that had not been tapped, a domain that contained the intimate knowledge that the workers had of their tools and the products they made with those tools. It included the ability to report or not to report, to rectify or not to rectify, a host of production problems, and the ability to make an effort that simply could not be coerced. . . . this frontier could only be crossed with the voluntary cooperation of the workers.[67]

Firms facing this situation needed three things from their employees. First, they needed their employees' knowledge about how the work actually got done. In most firms, workers had developed informal routines for accomplishing their tasks faster and more easily than under the formal procedures. Particularly in the office and service sectors, managers had charged their workers with handling certain types of transactions, but they were unaware of exactly what steps were involved in these procedures. If work was to be redesigned along more efficient lines, it was critical that managers acquire the knowledge of how work was actually done, including all the shortcuts workers had developed over the years. Second, companies needed workers to take responsibility for policing each other—guaranteeing high effort and few errors. By the mid-1970s, the average costs of supervision had grown significantly as a percentage of operating expenses, and it was clear that heavy-handed forms of control generated resentment and lethargy. If these firms were going to get employees to work harder and pay more attention to quality, it could not be done by increasing the ratio of supervisors to workers, but by the opposite: encouraging workers to supervise themselves and each other. Third, companies needed workers to internalize the firm's goals as their own. This was necessary not only so that workers would become self-policing but also so that they would accept the periodic reorganization and rescheduling of work, be willing to bend work, seniority, and overtime rules for productivity's sake, and continue to contribute their recommendations for productivity improvements on an ongoing basis.

Tapping Employee Knowledge

Not all employers who have instituted a quality program have pursued all three of these goals. For a great many firms, it is unnecessary or unprofitable to involve employees in an ongoing process of cooperation. In these cases, the process has stopped at the first step: managers have involved employees in participatory discussions in order to acquire their knowledge about how work could be most efficiently organized; after this was achieved, the reorganization was carried out wholly at the discretion of management, and workers were resubmitted to a new regime of often more totalized control. One of the earliest empowerment projects was carried out in the New York offices of Citibank. In a project code-named Paradise, bank clerks were transformed into "work station professionals" with advanced computer technology and responsibility over a far greater range of customer transactions. Employees were solicited for information as to how their tasks could be organized most efficiently; however, they were never given decision-making authority over the design of the reorganization. Over the course of this process, more than half the workers lost their jobs, and the remaining clerks were hooked up to computer systems that monitored every detail of their workdays. When Paradise was completed, one manager commented that "we know what is being done every minute and how it is being done. There is a much more efficient hierarchy of control."[68]

Thus companies may require employee input in order to reorganize production most efficiently—but that reorganization may result in layoffs or heightened management control. To accomplish this balancing act without provoking a workplace rebellion, managers have borrowed a traditional strategy of union-busters: the soft sell.[69] Here, participation is used largely to momentarily lull employees into believing that power relations have been reformed, just long enough to extract their knowledge of operating procedures before reestablishing control. One office automation consultant explains how she encouraged workers to reveal their informal practices: "You don't want [workers] to feel that they don't have control of their jobs anymore. I wanted to make them feel they had a little input into the decisions. Of course, they really didn't. There was a management task force for that. So it was sort of window dressing."[70]

One of the most carefully studied cases of "high performance" is the series of agreements negotiated by AT&T with its unionized employees. During the 1980s and 1990s, AT&T and its spun-off subsidiaries laid off nearly 400,000 workers.[71] Under these conditions, the companies' unions negotiated a network of joint labor-management committees to oversee productivity and the reorganization of work. Beginning in the early 1980s, AT&T established more than a thousand employee committees in its workplaces. However, as in the banking industry, these committees were often used to elicit recommendations that resulted in speed-ups and increased control. As new computer technologies became available, they were used to minimize rather than maximize the number of highly skilled employees required. As with airline reservation agents, AT&T's paramount concern for telephone operators was to standardize procedures and reduce transaction times. In 1984, it was estimated that reducing the average directory assistance call by a single second would save the company $24 million per year.[72] Thus new technology was designed to monitor and control the exact number of keystrokes entered, calls answered, and seconds expended by each operator. Unsurprisingly, nearly 70% of operators have reported in surveys that "I feel like just another part of the machinery" and that "the machines and equipment control me."[73] All the Bell companies have realized impressive profit levels since the break-up.

Most important, AT&T's "high performance" agreements failed to prevent continuing layoffs. Indeed, after its Merrimack Valley, Massachusetts, plant won the Department of Commerce's Baldrige Quality Award, the company announced that 1,000 of the facility's 6,000 workers would be laid off. In later discussions, a spokesperson acknowledged that some of these layoffs resulted from suggestions offered by the workers' quality teams.[74] Nor is this pattern unusual—the companies most often cited as models of reengineering are often those that have eliminated large numbers of jobs. *Training and Development* magazine, for instance, includes AT&T, Xerox, General Motors, Levi Strauss, Boeing, Caterpillar, Sprint, and UPS in its elite list of "benchmark" firms known for excellence in workforce development; yet all these companies have undertaken either vicious anti-union campaigns or massive layoffs.[75]

Developing Self-Policing Employees

In addition to gaining workers' knowledge, employee participation programs have given many firms a means to enroll workers in the process of policing themselves. In companies that have carried TQM the furthest, operating procedures have been restructured around teams of workers who are collectively responsible for a major facet of production. While teams have increased the variety of work and in some places have led to increased worker satisfaction, they have also established a new structure of production incentives. Since teams assume collective responsibilities—and may be collectively rewarded for productivity increases—if any member is slow or absent, the burden on all the others is increased. Thus each team member has a strong interest in guaranteeing the performance of others. In addition, in unionized companies it is often union stewards who are subtly co-opted by being promoted to "team captain" positions with responsibility for guaranteeing the productivity of their area. As team captains they may receive special perks, participate in regular productivity meetings with other captains, and help shape agreements granting bonuses for increased productivity. Under these conditions, stewards who start off representing the oppositional interests of workers may end up functioning as an extension of management.

The "pre-empowered" workplace, by contrast, was often characterized by worker resistance, as in the case of these coil winders in a nonunion shop:

> While working as a coil winder in a big transformer factory, we workers faced the dehumanizing "science" known as Minutes Times Motion, which is where a computer estimates how long it should take to complete a task such as building a transformer. Every day, we would check the number and type of transformers built, and at the end of the week we would get a computer-generated analysis of our efficiency rate. If we "beat the clock," we would get a happy face on our evaluation report. . . . To get a grip on this bad situation, we required a total conspiracy amongst workers. Starting with the guy I knew the best, we each agreed to slow down production on one of the transformer types. . . . After a few frowning faces on our monthly reports and a talking-to by the supervisor, the management had to readjust their computer time accordingly. It makes management look bad to have a product constantly come in under production goals. . . . This victory encouraged other assemblers to do the same, with equally good results. As we became faster at winding, we would overproduce and thus we would have to store some units in our lockers. We soon saw the wisdom of having a bank of units, in case we didn't want to work as hard one day, or a friend needed one because they messed one up. We earned more free time at work, and were still working at 100 percent, as far as management was concerned.[76]

This type of collusion aims at a *worker's* definition of a quality work life: not only seeking less stress and more free time but also creating the room to maneuver that provides one a measure of dignity. Worker power in this factory meant becoming someone who is not on a constant treadmill but who (within the constraints of getting the job done) chooses when to work and when not, someone who can be a source of generosity toward friends, and someone who refuses to produce more without being paid more. It is exactly this type of slowdown, however, that team production makes increasingly impossible, because teams take on many of the responsibilities of low-level supervisors. While this expands the range of problems they are asked to address, it also undermines workers' ability to evade or insulate themselves from the full impact of management control.

Internalization of Corporate Goals

The most ambitious goal of empowerment programs is to ultimately eliminate the need for policing workers altogether, by socializing them to embrace the firm's goals as their own. Over the past twenty-five years the average American has come to spend the equivalent of nearly an extra month per year at work.[77] The expansion of work and the decline of leisure have been fueled by the cost-containment strategies of employers and the economic insecurity of workers. Yet as work has taken over more and more of our lives, employers have begun encouraging us to think of our jobs not as forced drudgery but as a site of self-expression and personal meaning. In addition, as the bonds of place, family, and community have weakened, employers have increasingly portrayed the workplace as the new meaningful community. The message of countless management boosters is that we should think not that work is taking over our lives but that work *is* our lives.

One early observer describes Silicon Valley's famously participatory corporations as peopled with émigrés who had uprooted themselves from communities around the world and relocated to an environment that was socially barren but for the company:

> The new worship of work amounted to a movement to personalize it, to take on as one's own the absorbing challenge of computer work, and thus to become an intimate part of something larger, something meaningful. It was the practical response of isolated people to the vacuum of community, the erosion of traditional ties, and the suspension of social coherence. . . . Despite their "corporate cultures," the electronics firms had done little more than . . . created something of an oasis amid the loneliness.[78]

For many workers—particularly young, single, and mobile professionals—the promotion of the corporation as community may speak to a preexisting anomie. If the chance to belong to a community is the carrot, the stick is the specter of layoffs and dislocations, even at the most profitable firms. Thus even workers who have social lives outside work may embrace the ideology of corporate community as a means of rationalizing the extreme hours demanded by their employers.

Much of the empowerment ideology is aimed at creating this same sense of attachment, loyalty, and identification among nonsupervisory workers; ultimately the goal is to make everyone feel about their jobs the way the owners of a Mom-and-Pop grocery feel about their store. At this level, too, there is both carrot and stick. Many workers spend so much of their lives being disrespectfully ordered about, asked to repeat unchallenging tasks with mind-numbing regularity, that the experience of being given responsibility or asked for opinions can be genuinely exciting. Most workers want to believe that management cares about them, that their opinions are valued, and that previously repressive bosses are sincere in saying they have realized the logic of democratization.[79] After years of subordination, the allure of being treated with respect and taking a managerial perspective on workplace problems is powerful. Coupled with this carrot is the stick of fear: workers may be convinced that their employer needs more productivity in order to maintain jobs, or they may simply believe that they will be fired if they do not participate in the new regime. In either case, the fear of hardship combined with the allure of authority leaves many workers hungry to embrace a pro-corporate identity.

The aim of empowerment programs is to tap this hunger on behalf of higher productivity. This is the message of the best-selling *In Search of Excellence*: "If people think they have even modest personal control over their destinies, they will persist at tasks. They will do better at them. They will become more committed to them . . . [the] drive for perceived control [is] one of a tiny handful of fundamental motivations."[80] Empowerment programs that have achieved this goal have produced genuinely mixed results. On the one hand, a significant number of workers have been able to put more of their talents to use and have been treated with at least somewhat greater respect in the course of their daily tasks. On the other hand, the identification with employers has been used to extract ever-greater work effort without corresponding pay increases. As one clerical worker commented on Hewlett-Packard's much-touted quality program:

> They are constantly telling you how important you are to the company. You would think that what I'm doing would shut them down in a minute—if I took a vacation or something. They try to make you feel that. They want you to be the person who shows up on Saturday and Sunday and who works until eleven o'clock at night—and not just once in a while but constantly. They demand so much from . . . from your *life!*[81]

For companies that are truly on the margin of economic viability, such strenuous efforts may be in workers' interests in some sense. But some of the largest empowerment programs—including those at Hewlett-Packard, AT&T, Xerox, and General Electric—have been operated by highly profitable companies that have nevertheless pushed workers to extreme conditions in search of ever greater productivity.

Thus even at those companies for whom "high performance" denotes actual work reorganization and not just rhetoric, the new work systems have not delivered on the promise of widespread autonomy and prosperity for skilled workers. Many companies have indeed reconfigured production processes, and in some cases this has entailed new and higher skills for some set of workers. Nothing in this process, however, has guaranteed an alignment of corporate and employee interests. Reorganizations have been driven by the need to maximize profits; workers' skills or participation have been expanded only where this fit with the employer's financial strategy. And in most workplaces, despite employers' commitment to quality and innovation, there remains a poor fit between the interests of workers and those of owners.

Empowerment and Power: The Limits of High Performance

It seems that there is virtually no company, however egregious its labor practices, that does not promote the rhetoric of teamwork and democratization. Even General Electric CEO Jack Welch, whose penchant for layoffs earned him the moniker Neutron Jack, and who helped lead an unprecedented round of downsizing during the profitable years of the late 1990s, is a self-styled empowerment booster. "The most important thing a leader has to do," Welch declares, "is to . . . treasure and nourish the voice and dignity of every person." His official biography explains further that "[Welch] had the ambitious goal of removing the 'boss element' from General Electric . . . to give everyone a say in the way the organization was managed. . . . Now the boss stands in front of the employees, to listen to *them*. In this new world of role reversal, who is the boss, and who is the underling?"[87]

What accounts for the apparent contradiction between corporate words and deeds? In many cases, the contradictions accurately reflect the dilemma that corporate managers face: how to encourage employees to work enthusiastically and contribute valuable ideas, while maintaining maximum control over hiring, firing, and workplace politics. This tension is captured by the CEO of another "model" company, in explaining the constraints placed on empowered teams: "It's absolutely clear within each team what people are expected to do. Then within that framework, it's a free-for-all. . . . If you maximize freedom without a framework, you have chaos. But if you can create a framework and then maximize the freedom, you can create the fastest-learning and fastest-improving organization."[83]

But what is this caged freedom? Naturally, participants in empowerment programs are authorized to make suggestions regarding only a narrow range of topics related to profit maximization. Workers are asked to engage in "problem solving," but the problems—as well as the range of acceptable solutions—are always defined by management. Workers cannot, for instance, call a meeting to discuss how forced overtime affects their family lives, or the need for more generous health and pension benefits, or whether the company should keep production in the United States rather than shifting it to Mexico, or which political campaign it should contribute to. Nor, clearly, can workers suggest that the company settle for more moderate profits in order to make work life less stressful. All these are issues that matter greatly in the lives of employees, yet because they run counter to the company's financial goals, they are off limits. Yet when workers are asked to enthusiastically offer suggestions that increase profitability but to stifle any ideas that might limit profits—even if the latter correspond to deep personal needs—this is not "power." This is co-optation.

In fact, the primary goal of empowerment programs is not necessarily to elicit ideas for new methods of production—these are few and far between—but rather to motivate employees to work harder at doing the same thing they always did. Even for workers who may never offer an idea, the spectacle of participation is designed to make them feel more committed to the firm. As Slater reports, CEO Welch knew that "an engaged, conscientious worker is a more motivated, productive worker. It's really no more complicated than that. . . . Workers want to feel needed and important, a simple fact that business leaders can exploit."[84]

Even at companies with award-winning quality programs, when committees come up with suggestions that would improve workers' lives but would also cost money, they are generally rejected out of hand, even if they involve workers' health or safety. The celebrated "high performance" NUMMI plant, for instance, was cited by California state inspectors for substandard ergonomic design leading to repetitive motion injuries and for refusing to respond to workers' complaints on this issue.[85] General Motors rejected a paint shop team's proposal to build an enclosed lunch area to protect food from dangerous fumes.[86] The Silicon Valley workers who assemble microchips have been forced to handle highly toxic materials without adequate protections, despite multiple employee protests to managers.[87] And when a Hewlett-Packard team proposed to reduce stress by increasing office workers' privacy, they were told that this went "beyond the scope" of the quality program.[88]

Most important, workers have been granted no power whatsoever over the actual design of reengineered corporations. In 1998, GM's Saturn car plant—the poster-child of empowered teams—imposed a family-killing schedule on employees, requiring them to work ten-hour shifts and rotate between day and night shifts every few days. When the company refused to respond to employee complaints, workers elected new union leaders who promised to be more confrontational in advocating employee interests.[89] Northwest Airlines heralded its labor-management cooperation when employees agreed to contribute nearly $900 million in wage concessions to help the company through financial crisis. Once the airline returned to profitability, however, managers no longer cared to hear workers' suggestions about anything but cost-cutting; the company's CEO defiantly declared that he would weather a strike rather than raise wages significantly for flight attendants whose salaries started in the low teens and who had not seen a raise in ten years.[90] So too, the authors of the best-selling *Reengineering the Corporation* cited Kodak as one of the model firms with hierarchies so flat that "intrusive supervisors and managers have no place in the reengineered work processes."[91] But empowerment did not extend to the most fundamental form of power: the ability to preserve one's livelihood. In the late 1980s,

18,000 Kodak employees lost their jobs, and in 1997 the company announced that it would eliminate 16,000 more, the nation's single largest downsizing of that year.[92]

Thus even the most empowered workers have at best fought a rearguard action designed to minimize the fallout from layoffs and speedups. A counter-example from Australia depicts what true worker empowerment might look like. This case also illustrates that the way a company organizes production is dictated neither by the nature of the technology nor by the competitive position of the firm but largely by management's political concerns for controlling the workplace. Howard describes the reorganization of the Australian telephone company in the 1980s. Immediately after management announced its impending computerization plan, the communications workers' union denounced management's design, insisted that no plan be implemented without workers' approval, and developed a counterproposal for a different design. Through a series of job actions, the union won government agreement to stage a competing trial run in which alternative offices were run according to management's and the union's plans, in order to test the productivity of each. Ultimately, the union negotiated a compromise that fell short of its own proposal but was far preferable to management's initial design.[93] This case differs fundamentally from even the most progressive American empowerment program in that workers established a right to negotiate over the very design and implementation of new technology.

A similar case posing questions of skill, technology, and control can be found in the struggles of university professors to deal with the new technologies of distance learning. University faculty are among the most highly trained employees in any industry, and their craft has long been considered impervious to Taylorization. The work of crafting syllabi, planning lectures, devising papers and exams, and advising students seems to be irreducibly idiosyncratic and personal. In addition, university faculty have long been considered the original instance of independent employees and flat hierarchies; they literally provide the model of "collegiality" that other workplaces seek to emulate. However, universities' growing interest in distance learning as an academic profit center has called these relationships into question. At UCLA, faculty have been required to place their lecture notes on web pages, where they become the intellectual property of the university, which may then use them in profit-making courses without the professor's consent or participation. Another school notified junior faculty that all their course lectures would be videotaped. If they refused, they could be fired; once they agreed, they could be replaced by a video version of themselves. This move toward for-profit distance learning has begun to initiate a dramatic restructuring of academic work, along the same lines as that carried out in airline reservations, nursing, and other less-skilled occupations. With few exceptions, neither the credentials nor the collegiality of faculty has protected them from restructuring, downsizing, and commodification. One exception to this trend is at York University in Toronto, where teachers conducted a two-month strike to win contractual guarantees that new educational technologies would not be imposed without faculty consent.[94]

The successes of the Australian communications workers and the Canadian professors were due largely to the strength of their unions. By contrast, despite rhetoric to the contrary, empowerment programs have not brought American workers more of the strength needed to negotiate technological change, but rather have contributed to their further powerlessness. Workers' bargaining leverage ultimately derives from the solidarity of collective action and the negative power of disobedience and disruption. TQM fundamentally undermines both these bases of workers' power. High performance organization encourages workers to develop a primary work identity as members of their team. Managers frequently arrange productivity competitions between various teams and shifts, and even workers covered by union contracts may receive extra rewards based on team performance. At GM, managers went so far as to establish separate eating areas for each team and to paint each work area a different color.[95] Team members are encouraged to concentrate only on the requirements of their particular work area; in extreme cases, productivity improvements in one team may lead to downsizing in another. In addition, the members of competing teams naturally develop a platform of requests particular to their areas, and in plant-wide meetings, the representatives of different teams often end up competing against one another for scarce resources. In all these ways, worker solidarity is fragmented, and the ability of workers to act collectively on behalf of shared goals is undermined.[96]

Similarly, the creation of teams, quality circles, and joint committees often serves to fragment unions' internal cohesion. If unions do not put their own leaders into positions of authority within these committees, they risk the development of an alternative leadership cadre that competes with union authority. But when union activists do join committees, it is easy to become co-opted. Team leaders enjoy the exercise of authority and a variety of perks, including time spent not doing direct production work. Since holding this position is generally contingent on management approval, however, union stewards who become team leaders often develop a strong incentive to perform their duties according to management's standards. In this situation, fellow team members may come to regard the steward with ambivalence, uncertain whose side he or she will take when a worker's interests conflict with productivity goals. Even at the highest levels of union leadership, the question of how to participate in quality programs has often divided activists into competing factions and created personal enmity between people who must work together for the union to succeed.

To the extent that they undermine the capacity for collective action, employee participation programs have ultimately proved disempowering for workers. Indeed, it is telling that most TQM initiatives resemble nothing so much as the strategies that management consultants have used for decades to prevent workers from forming unions. Martin Levitt, for instance, ran union-busting seminars that used much the same language as contemporary quality programs. Levitt is explicit about the goal of these seminars:

> managers learned the tricks of evading the so-called union problem: by appearing to listen to their employees and to encourage openness, by making policies simple and clear, and by relaxing some rules. . . . But the objective was not to empower the employee, as I pretended, but to shut him up. Let him talk, sure, and let him feel he's being heard—in fact, actually listen to him when it suits you. . . . Just be selective. Give the workers just enough rope so that they believe they are off the leash, just enough to fool them into scorning the union. The golden rule of management control . . . [is] Incorporate dissent, institutionalize it.[97]

The fact that managers have been practicing this strategy for most of the past century suggests that the impetus for "empowerment" may be largely unrelated to technology, globalization, or any other characteristic unique to the current economy. Indeed, even those companies that boast award-winning quality programs, proclaiming their commitment to an empowered workforce, have simultaneously pursued anti-union and anti-worker strategies wherever possible. For instance, even while AT&T has trumpeted its cooperation with the Communication Workers of America, it has also steadily transferred its work to a nonunion subsidiary and reclassified remaining workers into nonunion positions, resulting in a severe decline in the unionized share of the company's workforce.[98] At the competition, things are even worse. Sprint established a quality program, featuring a network of employee committees and a stated desire for wide participation; simultaneously, the company engaged in a vicious anti-union campaign, including the harassment of union sympathizers and the illegal closure of a facility on the eve of a union vote.[99] Similarly, when workers at the heralded NUMMI plant voted to strike over grievance, discipline, and overtime policies, management distributed leaflets suggesting workers might lose their jobs if they struck and encouraging loyal workers to resign their union membership.[100] In the most explicit such incident, General Motors circulated a memo to all its North American executives suggesting that Quality of Work Life circles be used to convince workers that union negotiating demands would damage the company.[101]

If it is true that companies' competitive edge depends on the full participation of their employees, and therefore on democratization of the workplace, these actions by model employers appear contradictory. For this reason, empowerment advocates are often in the position of having to explain what appears to be the false consciousness of employers, who persist in anachronistic, authoritarian habits opposed to their presumed best interests. However, when we understand that productivity and quality do not necessarily require democracy, when we account for management's critical interest in maintaining social control of the workplace, and when we recognize the genealogy and strategic uses of employee participation, the behavior of companies that bust unions while championing quality programs becomes both intelligible and coherent. A number of economists have asserted that companies face a choice between a "high-skill, high-wage" path of trained and empowered employees or a "low-skill, low-wage" path of untrained, contingent labor. The evidence presented here, however, suggests that employee participation programs do not necessarily define an alternative to the path of layoffs, wage cuts, and anti-unionism. Rather, they may *complement* these tactics as part of an overarching corporate strategy aimed at increasing productivity, cutting costs, and guaranteeing maximum management discretion.

Conclusion: Empowerment and Skills

In conclusion, the "high performance" thesis seems unable to deliver on its promise. While there are a significant number of individual success stories, there is no reason to believe that reengineered production signals a new economy in which skills training will guarantee decently paid jobs. Nor does the track record of "high performance" suggest that power is less relevant to the workplace of the twenty-first century than to that of earlier times. Cross-training efforts of empowerment programs have generally entailed workers learning each other's jobs rather than taking on the tasks of management planning; therefore, even those companies that best exemplify the high performance ideal have not experienced a dramatic increase in either the technical skills or the basic education required of workers. Instead, even here the "skills" in greatest demand are workplace attitudes.

Finally, then, the assertion that the state of workers' skills—even "high performance" skills—offers a convincing explanation for falling wages or a promising avenue for economic recovery must be abandoned. In its claim to finally transcend the roots of workplace conflict, and in its ultimately untestable definition of skills, the thesis articulated by Reich and others serves as a logical culmination of job training ideology. The assertion that employers' self-interest lies in a highly skilled, high-paid, and democratic workforce offers workers a powerfully appealing vision at a time when their lived reality has become increasingly desperate. Yet this promise turns out to be nothing more than a naive vision of romantic economists and a cynical tool of management control. The nebulous nature of the vision insulates it from empirical rebuttal. But it also makes "high performance" a poor program for workers who must conduct their own problem-solving in the real world.

CHAPTER FIVE

The Politics of Job Training:
The Legislative History of JTPA

[JTPA] would give people something to run on. It would help with the rich/poor thing; the bill helps do something about the poor. It would help with unemployment; the bill helps people without jobs. It will help with the whole compassion argument. It's a natural.

—JTPA author Senator Dan Quayle, explaining why the Reagan administration should support job training legislation.[1]

When President Reagan signed the Job Training Partnership Act (JTPA) into law in October 1982, he trumpeted the new program as a much-needed answer for the record number of Americans out of work in the country's worst unemployment crisis since the Great Depression. Heralding "the opportunity this approach holds for millions of Americans," the president declared that "long-time workers who've lost their jobs because of new technology, women who can't find work because their home-making skills aren't marketable, young people who aren't hired because they have no experience—all will be helped by this program."[2]

The hope held out to the unemployed of 1982 was radically different from the government's response to earlier recessions. In the late 1970s, the Carter administration had reacted to unemployment by directly funding nearly three-quarters of a million public service jobs reserved for the economically disadvantaged. Now, Reagan insisted that public jobs were both undesirable and unnecessary. Rather than wasting taxpayers' money on temporary jobs that imparted no marketable skills, the president proposed to equip the unemployed for jobs in the private sector. "This is not another make-work, dead-end bureaucratic boondoggle," he insisted. "This program will train more than one million Americans every year in skills they can market."[3] At the heart of the new policy was the promise that private employers were ready to hire those in need of work, if only they were adequately trained. Indeed, over the next few months, the president repeatedly responded to questions about the potential effect of a training program in the face of 10% unemployment by pointing to the help-wanted ads and suggesting that jobs were available for anyone with the skill and drive to work.

In the years since 1982, the notion that a significant share of unemployment stems from a mismatch between the needs of business and the qualifications of workers has only grown stronger. Job training—originally conceived as a program for the urban poor—has come to be promoted as a policy for an increasingly broad group of workers, including those laid off by defense cut-backs, foreign trade, and environmental regulations. In all these cases, the logic of training policy rests on the assumption that the private sector economy is fundamentally sound and that unemployment and poverty stem primarily from the failure of would-be workers to qualify for the growing number of higher-skilled jobs that employers are eager to fill.

The promotion of training as a dominant policy response to poverty and unemployment began with the passage of JTPA. In this chapter, I ask why job training emerged as a central policy direction in 1982. Neither at that time nor since has there ever been economic evidence that a significant share of poverty or unemployment could be traced to a skills mismatch. Rather, JTPA was passed, and job training ideology was promoted, by people who could not reasonably have believed that it would solve the problems it purported to address. Thus JTPA constitutes a political rather than an economic response to unemployment. From the beginning, its primary aim has been to insulate both private corporations and public officials from the political response to economic hardship. Job training became the country's dominant labor market policy not because anyone deeply believed in its efficacy but because it represented the path of least political resistance, on which Republicans and Democrats, governors and mayors, big business and local community organizations could come to agreement. Indeed, JTPA's political popularity stems primarily from its capacity to direct public attention away from the notion that government or business could or should address the problem of unemployment in a deeper way, and to focus it instead on the failures of individual workers.

Job Training Despite the Evidence

One of the most remarkable aspects of JTPA's history is that repeated reports of the program's failure seem to have little effect on its political popularity. A striking instance is the debate over the amendments to JTPA adopted in 1992. The amendments were designed to minimize program fraud and creaming and to focus more resources on those groups in greatest need of training, including teenagers.[4] The bill established a new program for year-round training of youth and increased the overall share of JTPA resources targeted to high school dropouts. At the time these amendments were being debated in Congress, the Department of Labor had just released a draft version of its National JTPA Study, showing that youth were the single least effective focus for JTPA resources, and indeed that youth who participated in training programs ended up with lower earnings than those who did not. These findings were made available to the members of the Senate and House committees overseeing JTPA and were widely circulated among interest groups following the legislation.

The national study clearly suggested that money targeted to youth was at best a total waste; it concluded that resources should instead be directed solely to adults, at least until a more effective youth program could be developed. Yet rather than admit that the government had no idea how to improve the employment prospects of poor youth, both the congressional committee members and concerned lobbyists reacted to the report's findings by insisting that the legislation be passed quickly, before an official release of the study might force a reconsideration of the amendments. Senator Kennedy, then chair of the Labor and Human Resources Committee, acknowledged that he had been briefed on the report, but insisted that the existing amendments "already addressed the program's problems." A representative of the National Alliance of Business noted that "the findings might not be what people want to hear" but urged that the bill be passed anyway. The consensus seems to have been summed up by the U.S. Conference of Mayors, whose representative insisted that "we've got it, now let's just be done with it."[5] These actions are made more intelligible by the fact that the debate took place within a month after the 1992 Los Angeles riots. Faced with the specter of urban upheaval, lawmakers' first concern was to show that they could do *something* in response to the riots. At that point, to announce that the government's youth programs were failing would generate either intense political embarrassment or increasing pressure to address urban poverty through more controversial and expensive means. Rather than face these prospects, lawmakers from both parties, joined by representatives of the nation's mayors and governors, chose instead to endorse a program that they had strong reason to believe would fail, in order to at least appear to have a response to urban poverty.[6]

The story of the 1992 amendments offers one of the most striking illustrations of political concerns trumping sound economic policy in the development of training legislation. Indeed, from its earliest history JTPA appears to have been shaped more by political imperatives than by economic aspirations. When Ronald Reagan was elected president in 1980, neither the Democratic nor Republican parties held job training to be a major legislative priority. The 1980 Democratic Party platform included support for the Comprehensive Employment and Training Act (CETA), which was begun under Nixon and was still in effect, but its primary employment policy was to call for enforcement of the Humphrey-Hawkins full employment goals and a $12 billion public jobs program.[7] The Republican platform focused on increasing jobs through reductions in personal and business taxes.[8] When the Reagan administration assumed office, it proposed to address unemployment through broad economic stimulus rather than training programs. Labor Secretary Raymond Donovan identified not workers' lack of skills but rather inflation, taxation, regulation, and government spending as "the four horsemen of the economic apocalypse" and "the root of our employment problem."[9] Indeed, Reagan's transition team recommended eliminating all federal training programs and establishing enterprise zones as the government's anti-poverty employment strategy.[10]

Nor was the private sector pushing job training as a top priority for the new administration. When the Business Roundtable issued its 1981 *Policies Proposed to Promote Growth in the Productivity of U.S. Industry*, it focused on capital investment, monetary policy, and government regulation. Training was nowhere mentioned as an economic need.[11] Nor did training figure anywhere in the National Association of Manufacturers' 1980–81 Program to Revitalize American Industry.[12] Similarly, the U.S. Chamber of Commerce's chief lobbyist on JTPA stated that job training was "way down at the bottom" of the chamber's legislative priorities.[13] While the AFL-CIO was generally supportive of CETA, its agenda focused on labor law reform and improved workers' compensation and unemployment insurance.[14]

Even the man who was to author JTPA, Senator Dan Quayle, began the 97th Congress with no particular interest in training and, in fact, no interest in serving on the Labor Committee at all.[15] Indeed, Robert Guttman, Quayle's chief staffperson on the Labor Committee, characterized JTPA as a subject of universal disregard. "There are some issues that most people just don't care about," Guttman explained. "Job training is an issue nobody's going to give you a PAC contribution over."[16]

More important, when job training was discussed in 1980, it was considered strictly as social policy, with no particular connection to economic development. Even the most vocal advocates of CETA training never suggested that the program represented an urgent need of business. Thus training appears in the Democratic platform under the heading of "Economic Inequities Facing Minorities" and in the Republican platform under the category "Employment Safety-Net."[17] Quayle himself viewed training as "part of equal employment opportunity . . . a kind of Republican affirmative action."[18]

Nor did the business community advocate a skills mismatch explanation for unemployment. Business as a rule drew a sharp distinction between education and training for low-income workers—perceived as a social welfare program—and the much more limited need for technical training to fill occupations with labor shortages. Business participation in job training programs began in 1968, when President Johnson created the National Alliance of Business to marshal the private sector response to the wave of urban riots sweeping the country. For the next twelve years, business support for training was regarded as a form of philanthropy or social volunteerism. When a pilot Private Sector Initiative Program was created within CETA in 1978, the business community regarded it as an opportunity to demonstrate their social conscience rather than to satisfy any demand of their own for skilled workers. Addressing a Business Roundtable conference called to discuss the new program, GM chair Thomas Murphy framed the issue as a question of "what . . . the business community [is] doing to help these poorly educated and unskilled young people."[19]

At the start of the 1980s there were indeed increasing numbers of employers who complained of technical skills shortages. But they never suggested that the plight of impoverished workers could be alleviated by training them for these positions. For one thing, the magnitude of these shortages was extremely limited. For instance, the single most commonly cited shortages were for tool and die makers and other skilled machinists. In 1981 the National Tooling and Machining Association estimated that its member firms could increase employment by 32,000 if trained workers were available; in a booming economy, this number could be as high as 75,000.[20] Yet in that same year over 8 million Americans were officially unemployed. Thus even the most optimistic projection of demand for machinists would provide for less than 1% of the population in need.[21] Unsurprisingly, then, a 1978 U.S. Chamber of Commerce survey of employers found wide agreement that unemployment could best be solved by providing financial incentives for business expansion rather than training for the jobless. Employers insisted that "unemployment doesn't occur because of a lack of trained workers; it occurs because of a lack of jobs."[22]

In addition, the occupations facing significant shortages generally required experienced workers with extensive and costly training. Since federal training programs were generally targeted to the least educated and least experienced workers and were limited to relatively short-term and inexpensive services, even those firms that confronted labor shortages in skilled occupations did not believe they could meet these through the anti-poverty training programs. During the transition from CETA to JTPA, businesspeople repeatedly stressed that the need to respond to urban poverty and the demand to fill skilled occupations represented two distinct and fundamentally incompatible rationales for training. This tension was most commonly voiced in debates over how training resources should be targeted. If the program was intended to meet the needs of employers, it should provide funds for long-term training, and eligibility should be open to a wide range of experienced and educated workers, who were not necessarily poor. By contrast, if the program was aimed at relieving urban poverty, participation must be restricted to the poorest and least experienced workers, and if the services were to reach a significant number of people within realistic budgetary constraints, they must be confined to low-cost and short-term interventions.[23] Throughout this period, then, businesspeople conceived the needs of employers and those of the poor as two distinct issues. As late as the spring of 1982, the Business Roundtable called on the government to establish two separate training programs, one addressing "critical skills shortages" and the other geared toward the "remedial education and training needs" of impoverished Americans.[24] Thus the experience of both the poor and businesspeople testified to the impossibility of solving unemployment or poverty through a "matching" process: the level of excess demand was extremely limited, and where firms did need workers, they did not need—and most often could not use—the graduates of public training programs.

Given both the near-universal lack of interest in training and the absence of any economic rationale to believe that it could effectively address poverty, why was there any support at all for a new training program? How did the House, Senate, and president all come to trumpet JTPA as a critical new initiative? How did the idea of a "skills mismatch" become a reigning theory of unemployment? Most important, how did job training come to be promoted as a solution to unemployment and poverty? The answers to these questions can be found in the history of the legislative actions that replaced CETA with JTPA. This transition occurred in two phases: the elimination of Public Service Employment in early 1981, and the adoption of JTPA in the fall of 1982. In the discussion that follows, I describe the motives and activities of each of the major players who participated in these events.

The Privileged Position of Business

To understand the legislative history of JTPA, it is critical to pay special attention to the role of the national business lobbies, for several reasons. First, job training was promoted by the Reagan administration on the grounds that, alone among all possible employment policies, it not only helped the poor but also met a critical need of private employers. To assess this logic, it is necessary to examine the behavior of employers' representatives themselves. Beyond this, the national business lobbies represented the single most influential constituency of both the administration and the Republicans in Congress.[25] In the last years of the Carter administration, business lobbies had won a series of critical victories against the labor and consumer protection movements, which enabled them to shift from a defensive posture aimed at holding off encroaching regulation to an aggressive and pro-active agenda. In the first Reagan administration, this resurgent power was at its height.[26]

The U.S. Chamber of Commerce, Business Roundtable, National Association of Manufacturers (NAM), and others were critical to the election of both Ronald Reagan and a host of Republican senators and congresspeople. Corporate PACs gave nearly $20 million to congressional candidates in 1980, more than twice as much as in 1978, and much of this was expressly aimed at creating a pro-Reagan legislative majority.[27] These organizations were even more critical in generating political support for the president's landmark 1981 Omnibus Reconciliation Act, which locked in the administration's basic agenda of tax and spending cuts and included the elimination of Public Service Employment.[28]

In return for this support, the administration pursued an unprecedented agenda of pro-business legislation. On the eve of the 1981 budget fight, a White House strategist rallied several hundred corporate lobbyists for the upcoming crusade. "Like the Confederacy, you have only won defensive victories. If you will march with us this time," he promised, "you will win offensive victories."[29] Indeed, business did win a series of critical victories in the early Reagan years, including tax cuts, accelerated depreciation, deregulation, relaxed anti-trust statutes, and the withdrawal or loosening of government regulation from a wide range of economic arenas. The president appointed members to the Equal Employment Opportunity Commission, the National Labor Relations Board, and the Occupational Safety and Health Administration who viewed their purpose as the dismantling of these bodies' original goals; as a result, all three agencies were largely gutted as organizations that could effectively challenge business prerogatives.[30] Similarly, Reagan appointees to the federal judiciary brought about a marked pro-business tilt in the interpretation of labor law.[31] Thus business was both the Reagan administration's most powerful ally and its most consistent beneficiary.

When JTPA was being crafted in 1981 and 1982, the political strength of the business community was at its height, as was the conservative domination of Congress. The business lobbies were one of the key constituents consulted both by the Department of Labor and by the Senate Republicans who primarily authored JTPA.[32] As discussed above, the business lobbies were generally uninterested in training legislation. Throughout the debates leading to JTPA's enactment, it was primarily Democratic legislators and the representatives of local governments and community organizations who were the most vocal proponents of federal training programs. Nevertheless, the business lobbies' willingness to endorse these proposals was critical to the passage of JTPA. In 1981 and 1982, business lobbies and the administration alike were urgently committed to cutting all nonessential domestic programs in order to close the budget deficit, reduce interest rates, and restrict the government's role in the economy. In this context, the fact that business leaders did not oppose training is highly significant in itself. Nearly every other program designed to aid the poor or unemployed—including welfare, unemployment insurance, workers' compensation,

Trade Adjustment Assistance, daycare, food stamps, and low-income housing—was attacked by both the administration and its business allies. Thus the decision to allow training to continue, and indeed to trumpet its value as a response to the 1982 unemployment crisis, stands out as a strategic choice that begs explanation.

In what follows I first analyze the elimination of Public Service Employment (PSE) and the logic that drove each party to support this move. I then address the question of why training programs were not eliminated altogether along with PSE, and how JTPA eventually came to receive such widespread support.

The Elimination of Public Service Employment

At its height in 1978, CETA supported 725,000 public service jobs in local governments and nonprofit organizations across the country, making it larger than all the War on Poverty programs combined. PSE began as a modest component of CETA but was greatly expanded to cope with rising unemployment during the Carter years; the PSE share of the CETA budget rose from 34% in 1975 to nearly 60% in 1978.[33] For the Democratic administration, the policy of public service employment held a number of attractions. First, in an economy characterized by both stagnant growth and inflation ("stagflation"), direct federal job creation was thought to be the most reliable means of combating unemployment without risking the increased inflation likely to result from broader macroeconomic stimulus. Second, the jobs reached one of the party's core constituencies. While public works construction programs often employed better-paid white male workers, public *service* positions were far more likely to be filled by female, minority, and low-income workers. Finally, CETA funds were disbursed directly from the federal Department of Labor to local city officials. This funding formula in part reflected the origins of training programs as a federal effort to rush money to cities struck by riots. In addition, though, the funds represented an important source of patronage and fiscal support for big-city Democratic strongholds. As the cities of the Northeast and Midwest faced growing fiscal crises in the mid-1970s, CETA became an increasingly important source of support for Democratic mayors.

However, by 1978 unemployment rates had fallen considerably, and the program was plagued by increasing charges of fraud.[34] Facing pressure to control abuses and to contain the federal deficit, President Carter scaled back PSE; by 1980, the PSE share of the CETA budget was back to 40%. While this was a substantial drop-off, public service jobs remained a critical component of federal labor policy. When Ronald Reagan took office in January 1981, nearly 400,000 Americans were employed in PSE jobs, at an annual budget of $3.1 billion.[35]

The Reagan Administration

For the incoming Reagan administration, the elimination of public service employment was driven by a convergence of fiscal, ideological, and political goals. The president's budget agenda was driven by his core commitment to a 30% tax cut. With interest rates already high and concern in the business community growing over the mounting federal deficit, it was critical for the administration to offset its tax policy with corresponding spending cuts.[36] Even those members of the administration who believed (with economist Arthur Laffer) that tax cuts in themselves would eventually generate increased revenues knew that the financial markets would respond to the first signs of trouble without waiting to test the theory. Barely two weeks after Reagan's election, incoming Budget Director David Stockman warned the president-elect of an impending "economic Dunkirk":

> The pre-eminent danger is that an initial economic policy package that includes the tax cuts but does not contain decisive, credible elements concerning outlay control . . . will generate pervasive expectations of a continuing "Reagan inflation." . . . If bold policies are not swiftly . . . implemented in the first six months . . . political realignment could be thoroughly dissipated before the Reagan administration is even up to speed.[37]

With the administration committed to expanding defense spending, every domestic program that lacked hard-core political backing was targeted for cutbacks or elimination. In this context, PSE represented the fattest and most politically expendable budget item for an administration in desperate need of victims. In preparing Reagan's first budget presentation to Congress, Stockman identified PSE as one of the obvious "big ticket" items where savings could be found.[38]

Beyond fiscal considerations, the elimination of PSE fit with the administration's ideological agenda; indeed, it is likely that PSE would have been eliminated even if Reagan had faced a budget surplus. The conservative critique of CETA held not simply that the program was ineffective but that it subsidized laziness and promoted a "culture of poverty." Republican guru George Gilder, whose *Wealth and Poverty* was personally handed out by the president to each member of his incoming cabinet, insisted that "by paying the minimum wage and more for work far less stressful than the . . . other menial jobs available in the lower reaches of the private sector, the CETA jobs . . . deprive the poor of an understanding of their real predicament: the need to work harder than the classes above them in order to gain upward mobility."[39] Similarly, an Office of Management and Budget (OMB) statement in early 1981 charged that social welfare programs posed "serious challenges to basic social values of independence and self-support."[40] The move from job creation to job training was designed to weed out laziness and encourage self-discipline. Thus the Department of Labor's assistant secretary for employment and training explained the elimination of public service jobs by insisting that training programs should help "those who want to get ahead, not resurrect those who don't care."[41]

Finally, the elimination of PSE served important political goals for the Reagan administration. PSE had functioned as a critical source of support both for urban Democratic regimes and for the community organizations which had long rallied low-income and minority workers in support of progressive economic policies. With Reagan's election, the radical right called for an aggressive program of "defunding the left."[42] While never articulated as official administration policy, the goal of denying federal funding for liberal opponents was vigorously pursued by Budget Director Stockman and others, and the elimination of PSE must be seen as a significant part of this project.[43] The policy of defederalism—shifting responsibility for social programs out of the federal government and onto the shoulders of state and local authorities—helped create budgetary shortfalls at the state and local levels; this forced even liberal governors and mayors, particularly in big cities with significant demand for social welfare services, to adopt conservative programs of fiscal austerity.[44] In addition, Reagan officials sought to silence their opposition by directly undermining the organizational capacity of anti-poverty and other liberal advocates. Among the administration's first domestic priorities was the abolition of the Community Services Agency and the Legal Services Corporation, which had long supported class action suits aimed at expanding the economic rights of poor Americans.[45] The president further issued an executive order barring organizations that engaged in "advocacy, lobbying or litigation" from participating in the federal employees' general charity campaign; the order barred groups such as the NAACP Legal Defense and Education Fund, the Women's Legal Defense Fund, and the National Black United Fund. Similarly, the OMB sought to prohibit any organization that received federal funding from engaging in activities aimed at influencing public policy.[46] As a result, many organizations that had traditionally spearheaded the opposition to conservative policies found themselves financially crippled. The National League of Cities, for instance, was forced to cut its staff from 130 to 50[47] and the U.S. Conference of Mayors from 110 to 42.[48]

The elimination of public service employment fit neatly with this political goal of "defunding the left." PSE jobs were heavily concentrated in urban Democratic areas and liberal social welfare agencies. Among the organizations engaged in job training, those hardest hit were the national black organizations. As a result of CETA cuts, the Reverend Leon Sullivan's Opportunities Industrialization Centers lost 40% of its national affiliates and had its staff cut by 100. The National Urban League likewise had its budget sliced in half and was forced to dismiss 80 staff people.[49] The administration sought to eliminate all CETA funding for the AFL-CIO; under court pressure a compromise was reached which left the labor federation with 15% of its former budget.[50] All told, the demise of public service employment eliminated nearly 270,000 jobs from community-based organizations.[51] Thus for the Reagan administration, the abolition of public employment simultaneously promoted the president's fiscal, ideological, and political agendas.

The Business Community

Like the Reagan administration, the national business community was concerned to close the budget deficit and thus supported the elimination of public service jobs for strictly fiscal reasons. But the elimination of public employment also fit more specifically into the corporate agenda for employment policy. The business community's primary goal in labor legislation was to restrict working people's bargaining leverage in relation to employers. One component of this agenda was to limit the power of organized labor. For unorganized workers, the business lobbies sought to weaken federal laws that provided institutional support of wages and employment security, including minimum wage laws, prevailing wage regulations, and plant-closing legislation. Finally, for the target population of PSE—workers at the bottom of the labor market and impoverished Americans who remained outside the labor force hoping to get in —business sought to limit or dismantle those sources of federal support that strengthened workers' ability to choose when, whether, and at what wage to accept a job. Increasingly, this agenda aimed to leave potential workers no choice but to accept whatever job employers offered, no matter what the conditions or how low the wage.[52]

As discussed in chapter 2, businesses' primary concern with entry-level workers is neither their technical nor their academic skills but their commitment, punctuality, and discipline. When a 1978 U.S. Chamber of Commerce survey asked employers about their criteria for hiring graduates of government training programs, the survey recorded considerable consensus that "proper attitudes and work behavior counted more than any other qualifications."[53] Most important for employment policy, the survey found that discipline problems were commonly believed to be *caused* by social welfare programs: "a great many businessmen feel that poor work attitudes are the direct result of easy access to government welfare payments, unemployment insurance, food stamps and other transfer payments."[54] In keeping with these convictions, the Business Roundtable's employment policy recommendations suggested that "efforts should be made . . . to remove the disincentives to seek employment from programs such as unemployment insurance, welfare and public service jobs created to provide work for the unemployed."[55] In the early years of the Reagan presidency, the administration and the business lobbies together worked to enact this agenda. One of the business lobbies' central goals was a moratorium on raising the minimum wage, which the chamber of commerce described as its "No. 1, 2, 3, 4 and 5" priorities in employment policy.[56] Similarly, all the major national business organizations lobbied for repeal of the Davis-Bacon Act, which requires that the government pay prevailing wage rates—usually union scale—on public construction projects.[57] Reinforcing the centrality of worker discipline in the corporate agenda, the Business Roundtable also suggested that the government offer "short-term military experience which might provide a valuable transitional step for many youths into the full-time world of work."[58] For its part, the administration proposed to abolish the eight-hour day as the standard for overtime pay on federal contracts and proposed—with the strong backing of the fast-food and amusement park industries—that the child labor laws be relaxed to allow fourteen- and fifteen-year-olds to work longer hours and in a wider range of jobs.[59]

For the nonworking poor, the business lobbies advocated policies designed to limit the ability of potential workers to remain outside the labor market rather than accept substandard work. The 1981 budget package established a national ceiling on benefits under Aid to Families with Dependent Children (AFDC) and sharply reduced the amount of earnings AFDC families could retain without losing benefits. These changes together substantially reduced the number of working-poor families eligible for AFDC.[60] The administration and business together sought a variety of restrictions on workers' compensation programs.[61] Funding for the Trade Adjustment Assistance program, which provided extended unemployment benefits to workers laid off as a result of foreign trade, was cut by nearly 80% in 1981.[62] Finally, the administration proposed sweeping restrictions on unemployment insurance (UI), including a requirement that anyone receiving UI for more than three months accept any available job paying at least the minimum wage.[63] For business, these policies not only represented valuable budgetary savings but, more important, they changed the dynamics of the labor market. NAM chair Luke Williams lauded the administration's UI policies, for example, for making it "as difficult as possible to collect benefits if there [are] job openings available."[64]

The elimination of public service employment was consistent with the business strategy of limiting the options that allowed potential workers to hold out for higher wages in private industry. Indeed, business opposition to PSE predated the Reagan administration and the fiscal constraints imposed by its tax cut.[65] The centrality of disciplinary concerns in the opposition to PSE is perhaps best illustrated by the contrasting support for workfare initiatives. Early in 1981, the Reagan administration asked Congress to establish mandatory workfare requirements for AFDC recipients; congressional Democrats rejected this proposal but agreed to grant the governors leeway to establish state workfare programs, an innovation which was warmly welcomed by the administration.[66]

Yet state officials reported that the workfare jobs occupied by participants in the Community Work Experience Program (CWEP) were often identical to those filled under PSE.[67] Thus the president's shift from lambasting these positions as "dead-end" "make-work" under PSE to praising them under CWEP did not reflect any change in the content, supervision, or skills training involved in this work; rather, the sole difference was that the workers were paid for their effort under PSE and worked for free under CWEP.[68] If CETA's public service jobs did not make workers marketable in the private sector, neither could CWEP—except to the extent that employers might be impressed by the willingness of AFDC recipients to apply themselves with no salary, and might be put off by workers who had developed higher expectations. Whether the administration or the business community truly believed that CWEP would produce better-socialized workers, or whether they simply wanted to force "slackers" back into the labor market through the unpleasantness of workfare, is impossible to know. It is clear, however, that both for the administration and for the business lobbies, the critical concern with a public jobs program was the extent to which it promoted discipline or laxity, rather than the skills it provided to participants.

Thus for the business community, the elimination of PSE accorded with the goals of shrinking the federal budget, minimizing governmental intervention in the labor market, and, most important, enforcing market discipline on potential workers.

Congressional Democrats

The Democratic leadership in Congress had traditionally been strongly supportive of public service employment. It was through prolonged struggles with the Nixon administration that the Democratic Congress succeeded in establishing PSE as a component of the original CETA legislation. Representative Carl Perkins, chair of the House Education and Labor Committee, and Senator Edward Kennedy, chair of the Senate Labor and Human Resources Committee, were both outspoken supporters of public employment. Representative Gus Hawkins, chair of the House subcommittee that oversaw job training, had termed CETA "pathetically underfunded" at its height in 1978 and had sought to increase the number of public service jobs to one million.[69] Hawkins consistently fought to maintain PSE as part of the new JTPA system, and Democrats in both houses proposed a series of public employment initiatives throughout the unemployment crisis of the early 1980s.

Democratic support for PSE reflected a combination of interests. For members of the party's liberal wing, the program embodied philosophical principles of social welfare and economic opportunity that had been central to their ideology since the New Deal. Beyond this, PSE represented one of the largest discretionary programs targeted to traditional Democratic constituents in low-income and working-class communities. Apart from the general benefit of channeling resources to these constituencies, PSE provided critical support for the community-based organizations that served these neighborhoods and that often constituted important political coalitions in urban areas. Finally, PSE served as a crucial form of fiscal assistance to city governments, many of which had used the program to offset civil service cuts forced by the wave of mid-1970s fiscal crises.[70] This convergence of interests made most congressional Democrats committed supporters of PSE. But in 1981, a combination of developments made it impossible for the Democratic leadership to successfully defend the program.

To begin with, the 97th Congress was operating under unprecedented pressure to cut the federal budget. The end of the postwar economic boom was reflected in growing federal deficits beginning in the late 1970s. While the Carter deficits appear almost trivial compared with those of the Reagan era, the political pressure to eliminate the deficit was a constant theme of the Carter administration and was further fueled by the populist tax revolt embodied in the 1978 passage of California's Proposition 13. With the election of a president who had made this theme one of his campaign's central messages, the Democrats were backed into a corner, forced to defend social service programs against the charge of federal profligacy.

The Democrats' ability to resist this pressure was undermined by the 1980 elections, which cut their majority in the House from 117 to 49; the incumbents defeated in this turnover included the majority whip, the chair of the Ways and Means Committee, and the chairs of the subcommittees overseeing public assistance, unemployment compensation, and labor standards.[71] While still nominally running House business, the liberal party leadership lost effective legislative control to a working majority of Republicans and conservative Democrats.[72] Moreover, the political resolve of the remaining Democrats was severely weakened by the elections. On the eve of the 1981 budget debates, an aide to House Speaker Tip O'Neill explained the leadership's commitment to "recognize the cataclysmic nature of the 1980 election results. The American public wanted this new president to be given a chance to try out his programs. We [aren't] going to come across as being obstructionists."[73] Similarly, Democratic Congressional Campaign Committee chair Representative Tony Coelho explained the party's support for business tax cuts by noting that Democrats had "had our asses kicked" and were thus eager to be seen as "business Democrats."[74] Thus the leadership approached the budget fight with no pro-active agenda and little confidence. As one of the House Democratic whips conceded, "We have no game plan. We're just going to get killed."[75]

The weakness of the Democrats was exacerbated by a new budget reconciliation process used for the first time in 1981. Under the new system, the Reagan administration was allowed to package its entire program of tax and spending cuts into a single vote. This unprecedented procedure enabled lawmakers to avoid the potentially costly act of casting votes against individually popular programs and allowed the administration to frame the debate in terms of overall fiscal discipline. In addition, it removed effective control from the various authorizing committees and vested it instead in the budget committees and in votes of the entire chambers. Once the overall budget targets were approved, the individual committees—which previously had maintained primary control over the funding of programs under their jurisdictions—had no choice but to institute the mandated level of cuts. This shift in authority worked to the disadvantage of liberal interest groups supporting CETA, who had developed strong relationships with the authorizing committees but were much less significant players in the budget committee. Conversely, the new procedure strengthened the hand of business organizations, for whom lobbying against a myriad of individual programs was both inefficient and politically costly but whose influence could be effectively concentrated on the single up-or-down vote of the body as a whole.[76]

While the Democrats thus faced pressure for across-the-board cuts, the prospects of saving PSE were particularly weak as a result of CETA's reputation for fraud and abuse. In reality, numerous reviews found that instances of fraud in CETA were rare. But these reports did nothing to shore up its reputation; an early 1981 poll found overwhelming public support for cutting the program.[77] The reports of CETA fraud were often framed in terms that fit within the broader late-1970s backlash against feminism, sexual permissiveness, and civil rights, as reflected in such nationally galvanizing controversies as Allan Bakke's attack on affirmative action, the northern white riots against school integration, and the unexpected defeat of the Equal Rights Amendment. One of the most widely cited articles criticizing CETA included the following descriptions of programmatic abuse:

> [CETA funds supported] a nude sculpting workshop . . . in which naked men and women ran hands over one another's bodies, and body drumming classes, in which inner-city youth were taught how to slap various parts of their bodies rhythmically. . . . In Atlanta, CETA funds paid the former leader of the Black Panther party, an avowed Marxist-Leninist, $475 a month to, as he said "keep an eye on city, county and state governments and their jiving of the masses."[78]

Thus the images of CETA waste and fraud brought together the conservative critiques of government inefficiency, big-money liberalism, black militancy, and sexual deviancy in a single explosive issue.[79] In an increasingly conservative political atmosphere, continuing charges of corruption helped shape the perception of CETA as the paradigm of government waste and rendered the program almost impossible to defend. By 1978, CETA's reputation was so closely identified with fraud that one House Democrat noted, "The way to show you're against abuse is to be against this program."[80]

Largely in reaction to reports of fraud, the 1978 reauthorization of CETA amended its eligibility requirements to restrict participation to the economically disadvantaged. Whereas public service jobs had previously been open to anyone who was unemployed for seven days or more—with no income restriction—the 1978 amendments limited job slots to those with incomes below the poverty line; as a result, the number of people eligible dropped from 18 million to 6 million.[81] These changes addressed the problem of cronyism and responded to critics' charges that anti-poverty funds were being wasted on middle-class beneficiaries. But they also rendered PSE much less useful as a tool of city governments. It was now impossible to use CETA jobs to rehire laid-off city workers or to distribute patronage among non-poor constituents—and thus one of the program's primary bases of political support was undercut.[82]

Finally, the weakness of Democratic resolve in support of PSE may in part reflect the political marginalization of poor communities. The 1960s social movements sparked an increase in both voter participation and nonelectoral political action on the part of poor and minority Americans. With the abandonment of the War on Poverty and the defunding of community action programs, participation in both electoral and protest politics declined significantly in low-income communities. As Mollenkopf and others have noted, the community organizations which rallied poor people in political protest during the 1960s were transformed into nonmobilizing social service agencies during the 1970s.[83] By the time PSE was threatened with termination, even Democrats whose districts included large poor populations may not have confronted the level of political pressure these communities had exerted a decade earlier. Indeed, while the record of congressional hearings on CETA and JTPA includes the testimony of numerous "community based" training agencies, it does not contain any representatives of grassroots organizations of poor people. Thus the political need for either Democrats or Republicans to respond to conditions of urban poverty may have been mitigated by the growing disenfranchisement of the urban poor.

In May 1981 the House passed the Reagan administration's first budget resolution, rejecting the Democratic leadership's alternative proposal, which itself had accepted 75% of the administration's desired cuts. Notably, while the Democrats frequently criticized Reagan's termination of PSE, their own budget proposal did not restore the program; by this point, the pressures had become too great for even the supporters of PSE to mount a serious effort in its defense.[84] Several weeks later, the Budget Committee chair informed an angry gathering of the U.S. Conference of Mayors that it was useless to lobby for restoration of

PSE.[85] Thus despite the ideological commitment of the House leadership and considerable constituent demand to support the program, House Democrats were faced with a convergence of pressures which rendered them incapable of defending PSE.

Liberal Interest Groups: Local Governments, Community Organizations, and Labor

Those with the strongest self-interest in preserving public service employment were the city governments that received PSE funding; the community organizations that operated the programs and employed most of the participants; and, to a lesser degree, labor unions that benefited indirectly from the expansion of labor market demand. Indeed, all of these organizations did join in an effort to save public employment.[86] Their efforts were limited by several factors, however. For one, many of those most affected were also fighting a host of other cutbacks, including issues with more immediate impact than that of CETA. Local officials had seen federal revenue-sharing cut in 1979 for the first time in three decades and were facing the prospect of further cutbacks by the new administration.[87] The AFL-CIO was concentrating on administration proposals to cut Trade Adjustment Assistance, unemployment insurance, black lung benefits, and OSHA, each of which was perceived to be more consequential than the loss of CETA jobs.[88] Moreover, both labor and local governments had significantly weaker interests in public service employment after the 1978 amendments.

The community organizations that operated CETA programs, and that derived a substantial portion of their budget from PSE, mounted the most serious defense of the program. Even here, however, recognition of the overwhelming opposition to PSE, together with the particular limitations of the 1981 budget process, quickly led the various members of this coalition to split apart, each seeking first and foremost to guarantee its own continued funding and authority.[89] By May 1981, a conference of PSE supporters produced bleak predictions of the difficulty of forming effective coalitions in the face of shrinking resources.[90] And by July, this prediction was borne out in hearings of the Senate Labor Committee, as various organizations proposed contradictory funding formulas, with each advocating that a greater share of resources be designated for its constituents.[91]

Thus the combination of the president's early political momentum, the Democrats' weakness in the House, the power of the national business lobbies, the generic pressure for spending cuts, the unique packaging of the budget legislation, and CETA's reputation for fraud and waste all converged to guarantee the elimination of public service employment in 1981.

Why JTPA?

Given the politics of the first Reagan administration, one would expect that PSE would have been eliminated. It is far more surprising, however, that any ongoing training program would have been funded by the administration, particularly given the growing deficits and increasing pressure for spending cuts throughout the president's first term. Indeed, it is remarkable that less than a year and a half after the abolition of PSE, JTPA was trumpeted as a major administrative initiative. Moreover, given the bitterness and divisiveness that marked the debate over PSE, it is striking that the passage of JTPA the following year elicited universal approval from parties which had previously been dramatically pitted against one another.

The training components of CETA that remained in place following the elimination of PSE were scheduled to expire at the end of September 1982. Thus almost as soon as the 1981 budget battles were concluded, each of the relevant parties began anticipating whether, and in what form, federal training programs would be continued. By the spring of 1982, Congress was considering three separate proposals for continued federal training programs—authored respectively by House Democrats, Senate Republicans, and the administration. The bill that the president ultimately signed was authored by Senator Dan Quayle and approved by the Senate in a remarkable 95–0 demonstration of bipartisan support. In the sections that follow, I discuss the motives that drove the Democratic and Republican leaderships in Congress, liberal interest groups, the business lobbies, and the Reagan administration all to support JTPA in the wake of CETA's demise. Over the course of this analysis, I pay particular attention to the political developments which led the administration and its business allies— the primary forces behind the budget agreement that ended PSE—to become advocates of federal job training.

Congressional Democrats

While the liberal Democratic leadership remained supportive of public service employment and the principles articulated in the Humphrey-Hawkins Act, by 1982 they understood that such proposals stood no chance of passage. The functional debate for Congressional Democrats was not between public employment and job training but between job training and nothing. The development of CETA replacement legislation proceeded under the omnipresent threat of a presidential veto, and the administration was promoting a legislative agenda which made even a modest training program seem like a major progressive accomplishment.[92] During the period in which JTPA was being debated, the president proposed an end to federal responsibility for AFDC and food stamps, the imposition of mandatory workfare requirements for recipients, and the establishment of a guest worker program for low-wage Mexican immigrants. The Democrats ultimately succeeded in resisting these initiatives, but the fact that they enjoyed serious consideration indicates that the center of political debate had shifted to a point at which liberal employment initiatives were no longer tenable. Liberal Democrats were so marginalized in the 97th Congress that the best they could hope for was to stave off the complete elimination of federal employment programs.

Many Democrats remained harshly critical of administration policies, and indeed the party pressed repeated proposals for public jobs programs throughout 1982 and 1983. When the House finally passed its version of JTPA, Representative Paul Simon insisted that the bill was "so far from what we ought to be doing in this nation at this time that it is pathetic."[93] However, these protests took on an increasingly pro forma tone. The Democratic members of the Senate Labor Committee, for instance, issued a statement insisting that "the federal government has a responsibility in recessionary times to create jobs for the long term unemployed," but they declared their support for JTPA despite these misgivings, "because we believe it is essential to continue the federal government's commitment to training disadvantaged and unemployed persons."[94] In April 1982, Representative Hawkins deleted the provision in the House JTPA bill calling for the restoration of public service jobs.[95] Thereafter, the party's leaders concentrated on wresting as much as possible from what they acknowledged would be a narrow training program. For the remainder of the legislative season, the Democratic leadership focused on three goals: guaranteeing wages or stipends for training participants, protecting the authority of local governments in the training system, and increasing the overall funding available for the program.[96]

In pursuing these goals, Democrats often sought to couch their arguments in terms of the newly dominant conservative ideology. In so doing, they followed a well-worn historical path. Mucciaroni notes that Democrats adopted conservative rhetoric in urging passage of the Emergency Employment Act of 1971, the first public employment project since the New Deal. Their argument "was usually couched in terms of assisting the long-term, hard-core unemployed, who were associated with structural, rather than cyclical unemployment, a rhetorical posture at least partially designed to calm Republican fears of establishing a WPA-like program."[97] Presumably, Nixon-era Democrats believed that Republican rhetoric would enable them to win reforms which would be unachievable if presented as a straightforward response to a shortage of jobs. While this strategic judgment may have been sound, the party paid the price of helping to solidify an ideological consensus which limited the future possibilities for creating public jobs. Similarly, liberals in 1982 apparently hoped to achieve their legislative aims by cleverly disguising liberal policies in conservative logic. In the process, it was, ironically, Democrats who became the most forceful advocates of the skills mismatch argument. In arguing for the higher funding provided in the House bill, congressional Democrats pointed to "structural forces [that] have increased the number of . . . persons without skills entering the labor force, including minority youth, who are in need of training to compete for jobs in a technologically advanced society."[98] Even New York liberal Ted Weiss advocated support for training on the grounds that "continued investment in human capital . . . is a traditional and necessary supply side investment that we must continue to support if we are serious about regaining economic growth."[99]

As it developed over the course of the congressional session, the debate over employment and poverty boiled down to a disagreement as to exactly which traits of poor workers made them unemployable—taking for granted that it was a deficiency in workers rather than employers that accounted for economic stagnation. Conservatives asserted that the poor suffered primarily from motivational problems, which could be cured by cutting the social benefits that undermined the work incentive. Liberals argued that poor people already wanted to work but needed skills training before this noble desire could be realized. This "compassionate" approach was best articulated by Senator Kennedy, who characterized the unemployed as "men and women [who] have searched the want ads and pounded the pavement. They know that most jobs today are only available to people with skills. Without specialized training, they cannot qualify as computer programmers, or medical technicians, or machinists. . . . The jobs are there, but the skilled individuals are not."[100] The Democrats apparently hoped that the cleverness of their reasoning would trap conservative opponents, forcing them to concede that a well-funded training program was entailed by their intellectual principles or to face the embarrassment of logical contradictions. While liberals may have succeeded in subjecting opponents to the pressure of public discomfort through these tactics, the Democratic advocates of JTPA, like their counterparts of 1971, helped to consolidate an understanding of unemployment which would frustrate more serious responses to poverty for decades to come.

In this way, the Democrats strived to make the best of a bad situation, forcefully advocating continued federal support for training while conceding both the essential programmatic structure and the core ideological principles of the Republican agenda.

Community Organizations

Those with the greatest stake in the development of JTPA were the community-based organizations who had run the CETA programs and who relied on training funds for a substantial part of their budgets. However, these organizations came to the table with relatively little clout. While many of them had originated as vehicles of popular protest, by 1982 the "community-based" designation was something of a misnomer. Many groups were staffed by professional social servants who lacked the skills, networks, or orientation to mobilize grassroots activism. When JTPA was being debated, the primary tools these organizations could wield were their ties to a weakened Democratic Party, the ability to embarrass opponents of anti-poverty programs, and in some cases the support of a middle-class minority community. While these made the community organizations a force that had to be included in negotiations, they amounted to relatively modest leverage in the crafting of legislation. Moreover, these organizations' political role had evolved along lines which rendered them less directly accountable to poor communities. For the most part, the nonprofits engaged in training were no longer poor people's organizations. They were rather the organizations of middle-class people who were committed to, and financially supported by, providing services to poor people. Thus it is unsurprising that, rather than mounting a radical attack on the logic of training itself, the community organizations primarily focused on those details of JTPA which directly impacted their own funding and authority.

Virtually every national advocacy organization for poor people attacked the administration for cutting anti-poverty resources in the midst of a recession and called for restoration of PSE. However, these organizations were in no position to mount a principled attack on the logic of training policy. For many community-based agencies, the very survival of their organizations hinged on the ability to forge a training bill that could achieve bipartisan support. Thus rather than focusing on more radical critiques or more progressive demands, their lobbyists concentrated on the question of their organizations' role in Private Industry Councils, the extent to which local governments would retain authority for letting contracts, and the overall level of funding devoted to training. A program restricted to training was not what the community-based organizations wanted. It would limit their resources and would not meet the needs of their constituents. But in the context of service cuts on all fronts, they championed the need for training as a critical obligation of the federal government.

Thus, like the congressional Democrats, the community organizations contributed some of the most forceful "skills mismatch" rhetoric in the debate over JTPA. SER-Jobs for Progress, for instance, stressed the "modern-day paradox, [in which] we find ourselves in the singular situation of having the highest number of unemployed workers in the industrialized world, while also having the longest list of highly skilled positions going unfilled."[101] In this way, the organizations that were most fundamentally opposed to a training-centered poverty policy came to serve as the most vocal advocates of its logic.

Similarly, the national community organizations also supported narrow targeting of training resources to the poorest groups.[102] In an ideal situation, the bargaining leverage of poor communities would be strengthened through a coalition with working-class organizations. In the context of shrinking resources, though, community organizations and labor unions developed competitive interests. The community nonprofits sought to prevent a diversion of funds to retraining better-off, unionized workers—projects much less likely to be routed through their offices. Paradoxically, the arguments these groups used to defend a narrowly defined training program also served to reinforce conservative assumptions about the causes of poverty. The community organizations in part defended their role by stressing the difficulty of serving poor people. As one spokesperson explained, the private sector "does not want to train unequipped, unsophisticated, unskilled, inexperienced, and jobless persons. In fact, they will not do the training, even when lured by tax credits and other incentives."[103] By characterizing training participants as "the 'hardest-to-employ,'" the community organizations sought to mark out territory which they alone were qualified to occupy.[104] It is difficult to assess the extent to which this language reflected the true perceptions of training providers or whether their exaggerated claims were simply designed to scare away competitors. It is clear, however, that by articulating this argument, the very organizations that served as the representatives of impoverished Americans helped to consolidate an ideology that intensified the political marginalization of their clients.

Senate Republicans

Throughout the 1970s, congressional Republicans characterized urban unemployment as a result of workers' shortcomings. In 1980, the party's platform stated that "Republicans . . . realize that a job alone will do very little to move a disadvantaged young person beyond the poverty line," suggesting that the roots of poverty lay in personal handicaps rather than a shortage of jobs.[105] In keeping with this logic, the new Senate leadership joined the president in criticizing PSE as a "program in which persons were paid to perform work regardless of whether it increased their employability," again emphasizing the focus on "employability" rather than actual employment.[106] In crafting legislation to replace CETA, Republicans saw the program's goal as preparing marginal workers for available jobs, rather than supporting those for whom no job opportunity existed. Senator Quayle thus explained his support for JTPA by noting that "a rising tide does not lift all boats; we must caulk the leaking seams so that all have a chance to share in our prosperity."[107]

Like the administration, many Republican lawmakers were at best uninterested in training. As the economy worsened, though, politicians who faced reelection in 1982 felt increasing pressure to respond to the growing crisis. When President Reagan took office in January 1981, the unemployment rate stood at 7% and the inflation rate at 12%. By September 1982, however, unemployment had passed 10% while inflation had fallen to 4.4%. This reversal produced a dramatic shift in the nation's priorities. As Congress entered the 1982 legislative season, opinion polls showed that the public viewed jobs, rather than inflation, as the most pressing problem facing the country.[108] By February, 63% of the public said they disapproved of the president's response to unemployment, and 59% said more money should be spent on job training.[109]

The need to formulate a political response to unemployment drove many Republican lawmakers to support training despite their previous lack of interest in the subject. The task of producing the specific vehicle for addressing this need fell to Senator Quayle, who as chair of the Subcommittee on Employment a d Productivity authored the original legislation and shepherded it through a full year of bipartisan negotiations and threatened vetoes.[110] Throughout the course of 1982, Quayle hammered out a series of compromises with both Senate and House Democrats that preserved the essential Republican principles of the bill: a strong private sector role, the shift of funding from cities to states, institution of performance-based contracts, and a near-total ban on wages or stipends for training participants. Nevertheless, the administration repeatedly threatened to veto the legislation over the compromise provisions.[111] Throughout the year, Quayle persisted in the faith that ultimately the need to respond to unemployment would outweigh the White House's objections: "I kept saying to myself 'they can't veto the bill—not with 10.1 percent unemployment.'"[112]

While the administration remained ambivalent about training throughout most of 1982, and the business lobbies supported the program in principle without ever marshaling significant resources on its behalf, it was Republican senators and congresspeople who faced the most consistent need to produce some kind of jobs bill. Preparing for the 1982 legislative session, the House minority leader warned that "when we get into next year, it's going to be tougher than a son of a buck. Unemployment is going to be the most serious problem, and I don't want the White House to minimize the fact that they could be faced with hostile members in January."[113] Representatives from hard-hit industrial states faced particularly difficult prospects. As Connecticut Republican Chris DeNardis insisted, "Unemployment is rapidly becoming the major political problem of this administration. No one has ever lost an election because of an unbalanced budget, but we could lose because of unemployment."[114] Thus Quayle aide Robert Guttman explains that while the business community initially "was not that interested" in training legislation, it was Republican Senators who "wanted to say 'we're doing something about unemployment,'" and "business went along with that."[115]

In this sense, Republicans facing reelection in 1982 served as the most immediate channel through which public discontent found political expression among the ruling coalition. For both the administration and the national business organizations, the unemployment crisis represented a significant but distant danger. By forcing the administration to confront this danger as an immediate political crisis, Republican lawmakers played a critical role in forging bipartisan support for training.

The Business Lobbies

The national business lobbies were enjoying a period of unprecedented triumph in 1981 and 1982, achieving a series of victories on the issues of greatest priority for their members, including tax and regulatory reform. There is no reason to believe that the business organizations felt a need to pursue job training legislation as an urgent requirement of member firms. On the contrary, both economic evidence and the direct testimony of employer representatives indicate that federal training programs were regarded as irrelevant to the interests of business. Throughout the 1981–82 debates over JTPA, the business community was focused instead on controlling the growing federal deficit and identifying domestic spending cuts. Thus business support for JTPA appears paradoxical.

To understand the business community's support for JTPA, it is necessary to begin with the legislation's origins in the Private Sector Initiative Program (PSIP), a precursor to JTPA established as part of the 1978 reauthorization of CETA. PSIP—which mandated the creation of Private Industry Councils aimed at encouraging business participation in training—marked the Carter administration's attempt to make CETA more businesslike and to demonstrate its support for market-driven responses to unemployment. In budgetary terms, PSIP was an almost insignificant component of CETA.[116] But in championing the superior efficiency and job-placement skills of business, and by establishing a program that took authority away from local government officials and vested it in Private Industry Councils, PSIP marked an important shift in the government's implicit philosophy about training. When the Reagan administration and Senate Republicans set about to create a new job training law, they largely looked to this model. Indeed, with some modifications, JTPA is PSIP expanded to a national scale. By examining business leaders' response to this pilot legislation, we may shed light on their later thinking regarding the full-blown JTPA.

In 1978, national business leaders were recovering from a crisis in public confidence. The protests of the late 1960s, including scores of demonstrations aimed at corporations involved in the Vietnam War, remained a recent memory in the minds of most executives.[117] The early 1970s had brought an unprecedented wave of government regulation of industry, including the establishment of the Environmental Protection Agency, the Occupational Safety and Health Administration, and the Consumer Product Safety Commission.[118] In addition, the decade had spawned a host of new advocacy groups and public interest lawyers devoted to limiting the prerogatives of corporate management.[119] The public reputation of business was further tarnished, and the activity of business lobbies subjected to heightened scrutiny, by the revelation of illegal corporate contributions to the Nixon campaign and the conviction of high-level business leaders in schemes to bribe foreign government officials.[120] Simultaneously, the oil crisis of 1973–75 fed widespread speculation that "big oil" was intentionally exacerbating the shortage in order to gouge the public.[121] This string of scandals had a dramatically negative effect on the public perception of business. The share of Americans who believed that "business tries to strike a fair balance between profits and the interest of the public" fell from 70% in 1968 to 18% in 1973. By 1976, 82% of the public thought that big business had "too much power," making corporations the least trusted among twenty-four groups included in the survey.[122]

Business faced still more problems with workers, wages, and federal employment policy. As the economy stagnated, workplace tensions soared. In 1974 workers staged the greatest number of strikes since the end of the Second World War. In the same year, the business lobbies lost hard-fought battles over an increase in the minimum wage and the Employee Retirement Income Security Act (ERISA), which expanded pension protections.[123] The Nixon administration's institution of wage and price controls represented the most direct government intervention in the market economy since the New Deal, and in 1975 the prospect of increasing government controls received a critical boost with the government's establishment of the Initiative Committee for National Economic Planning, headed by Nobel laureate economist Wassily Leontief.[124]

This state of affairs changed dramatically in the late 1970s. From 1976 to 1978, the national business community, including the NAM, U.S. Chamber of Commerce, and Business Roundtable mounted successful counterattacks against both labor law reform and the Humphrey-Hawkins Full Employment Act. The campaign against the labor law bill, which would have made it easier for workers to win union representation, represented the biggest mobilization of corporate pressure to date.[125] The gutting of the Humphrey-Hawkins bill capped a thirty-year fight against Democratic attempts to institute a legal right to a job and to establish the government as employer of last resort.[126]

These victories marked a critical turning point in business's political fortunes. However, they also provided highly visible illustrations of corporate opposition to employment assistance in a period of increasing joblessness. In this context, business representatives were eager to find initiatives which, without forfeiting their newfound advantages, would defuse accusations of greed and display a corporate commitment to the public interest. It is this political need which PSIP served to address. At a Business Roundtable conference on PSIP, General Motors chairman Thomas Murphy thus articulated the problem that conference participants hoped the new legislation would address:

Concerned individuals in society and government quite legitimately turn to business and demand to know why we don't do something about [the unemployment] problem. Some of these people, for whatever reasons, believe the private sector is unconcerned about the problem and uninterested in helping develop solutions. One manpower expert recently told a Congressional committee that, "This is simply and basically because the interest of the private sector is by and large in making a profit and not in the social betterment of the most disadvantaged." Unfortunately, that impression of business is shared by many Americans. . . . [We must overcome] the myth that the profit motive and concern for the disadvantaged are mutually exclusive.[127]

In this context, PSIP was enthusiastically greeted as "a unique opportunity for American business to collaborate . . . in a highly essential, highly visible and positive effort, appropriate to its abilities, resources and powers."[128]

While businesses already contributed regularly to various social causes, employment policy was an area in which corporations could portray a central aspect of their regular operations as serving a public function. Support for youth basketball or hospitals might suggest that businesspeople were willing to share some of their winnings with the less fortunate. But the notion that employers' self-interest could help solve the unemployment crisis offered a much more fundamental shift in public relations: a suggestion that business by its *nature* served the public good. For this reason, PSIP was embraced as a vehicle for insulating business from a wide range of public criticism, beyond the specifics of employment policy. Articulating the incentives to participate in PSIP, the National Alliance of Business suggested that "business, under fire on all sides as not adequately concerned with the public interest, needs . . . to 'carve out some of the high ground of public interest' for itself, so that it can speak with greater credibility in the councils of public policy. PSIP offers the greatest demonstration project ever of practical business concern with the country's interests."[129]

In addition to its public relations potential, PSIP served as a much preferred alternative to expanded public employment. Business had long argued that the private sector could do a better job than government in addressing employment issues. In 1978, while the Senate Labor Committee debated PSIP, it was simultaneously considering continued funding for PSE as well as the Humphrey-Hawkins bill. A key committee staffer stresses that it was "*in that context* [that] the Roundtable and NAB [National Alliance of Business] came saying 'give business a chance at this.' "[130] Thus PSIP offered a double opportunity: the chance to bolster business's public image and also to minimize government involvement in the labor market.[131]

By the time PSE was eliminated in 1981, the political landscape had changed significantly. The Reagan administration had banished the prospect of social democratic initiatives and ushered in a new ideological climate in which businesspeople were cast as heroes rather than villains. Yet the very successes of business in the first Reagan administration threatened to provoke the anti-business sentiment that had proved so potent in the recent past. Thus in the fall of 1981, GE chairman Reginald Jones reminded a Roundtable gathering that

[while] at the moment it may appear that we have a more favorable climate . . . business—especially large corporations—has always been regarded as somewhat suspect in the minds of the public. The worst thing we could do is become complacent. We've got to continue to work very hard to meet the demands of the public. If they become disillusioned with supply-side economics, or the actions of business, the present environment could change very rapidly through the electoral process.[132]

The danger posed by business's very legislative success—and corporate leaders' continuing sensitivity to public criticism—was illustrated in the controversy surrounding the "tax leasing" provisions of the 1981 budget bill. Under this policy, unprofitable companies such as Ford and Chrysler received hundreds of millions of dollars in tax refunds, while profitable corporations such as IBM were able to pay virtually nothing. In April 1982, General Electric touched off a public outcry over revelations that despite earning substantial profits in 1981, the company's purchase of other firms' paper losses had enabled it not only to completely wipe out its tax liability but to collect a $110 million refund.[133] Such high-visibility corporate excesses at a time when millions of Americans were being thrown out of work threatened a sharp decline in public support for the business agenda.[134] Corporate leaders responded by voluntarily supporting the elimination of tax leasing provisions in the 1982 law. "The issue is the public perception that corporations are not paying taxes," explained one participant in an early 1982 NAM conference. While the business lobbies remained committed to eventual "elimination of the corporate income tax," he added that staking out a hard-line position at that point "virtually invites Congress to come back" with even more stringent demands.[135]

The same logic which animated the tax leasing debate—a commitment to fashioning an acceptable compromise rather than risk more radical public demands—seems to have driven the corporate response to job training legislation. As the unemployment rate rose toward historic levels in 1982, the government came under renewed pressure not only to retain training programs but to fund public works. In this context, business leaders pointed to the ability of private employers to absorb new workers as "a strong argument against massive Federal spending to *create* jobs."[136] In the face of rising concern among both Democratic and Republican lawmakers to "do something" about unemployment, JTPA appeared as the most effective option for business leaders who might otherwise have preferred no action at all on the issue. As one U.S. Chamber of

Commerce official explained, "You really can't say 'we're not going to do any-thing'" about unemployment; "even if you want to do nothing, you need a proactive position."[137]

Throughout this period, corporate leaders were not overly concerned with unemployment per se. A spring 1982 survey found that two-thirds of executives thought the president's program was working well, and 64% believed that "the fight against inflation must continue even if that means high unemployment."[138] Rather, it was in attempting to contain the *political* response to unemployment that business came to support JTPA. As the chamber of commerce's lead lobby-ist on the issue explained, "Significant members of the Chamber felt the job was just to defeat CETA and that's all. But we had to ask what's going to happen to the people . . . this wasn't all that far from the burning cities. . . . we wanted to look more socially responsible."[139]

Business representatives further realized that, in the absence of such a govern-ment program, employers themselves might be viewed as morally responsible for resolving the country's economic problems. The Reagan administration's initial legislative agenda called for the complete privatization of training through the replacement of CETA with a package of wage subsidies and tax incentives designed to encourage private sector hiring of disadvantaged workers. While this approach was ideologically appealing, it also implicitly assigned to business the political responsibility for solving the problem of unemployment. Faced with this choice, business representatives largely preferred to maintain the federal role in training. Though many executives might ideally have chosen to have no federal employment programs at all, they were unwilling to put themselves in a position of assuming blame for the country's spiraling joblessness.

The tension between business leaders' desire to restrict federal employment services and their commitment to avoiding responsibility for unemployment came to a head in the fall of 1981. In mid-September the administration once again floated a proposal to eliminate all remaining federal training programs.[140] At the same time, the president announced the establishment of his Private Sector Initiative Task Force, described by one of its staff as an attempt "to soften the impact of the budget cuts by demonstrating that the private sector—the business community—could help solve community needs."[141] Administration officials pushed hard for business to help out with the politics of retrenchment. The commerce secretary insisted that corporate executives had an obligation to "do the kinds of things you've always told the government you want to do—like providing more jobs. . . . the President has delivered what you have asked, and now it's time for you to deliver."[142] In keeping with this philosophy, the Labor Department suggested that in the future, the private sector might assume com-plete responsibility for job training.[143]

While business leaders supported the general principle of substituting private initiative for public responsibility, they were wary of the administration's rhetoric. As one business writer recorded, conservative members of the task force feared "that no amount of corporate philanthropy or community cooperation can begin to fill the gap created by government cutbacks, and that industry will be blamed for failure to accommodate unrealistic public expectations."[144] The Roundtable's Corporate Responsibility Task Force likewise warned that "if public expectations and perceived corporate performance are at odds, corporations will be attacked more and more on social and political as well as economic grounds. The result would be adverse public opinion leading to further government involvement in their operations."[145]

Thus throughout the recession, the Reagan White House and the business community were engaged in a peculiar dance, with the administration seeking to shift political responsibility for unemployment to the private sector and corporate leaders insisting on passing it back to the government. The secretary of labor maintained that "unemployment is primarily a business and labor problem," and that "it is not one that government can solve,"[146] while the Business Roundtable insisted that "the primary responsibility" for structural unemployment "must continue to reside in the public sector . . . because the magnitude of structural issues is beyond the capacity of private firms."[147] Ultimately, business was bound to win this contest, since without its acquiescence, the administration could not help but be held accountable for the state of the economy. But in anticipating the political consequences of complete privatization, business leaders appear to have developed a new appreciation for the federal role in employment policy.

While the legislation that Congress ultimately adopted was slightly more generous than the administration proposal supported by business, it retained the principles at the core of employers' concerns: strong PICs, a transfer of authority from local to state governments, decreased power for the federal Department of Labor, and the preclusion of nearly all stipends or wages for participants. In this way JTPA offered the business community something very similar to the benefits of the earlier PSIP: a relatively inexpensive means of addressing the politics of unemployment without strengthening either the bargaining leverage of potential workers or the role of the federal government in regulating labor markets. For these reasons, while the business lobbies remained essentially unenthusiastic about the prospect of continued training programs, they came to be vocal advocates of JTPA, ultimately playing a critical role in convincing the president to sign rather than veto the legislation.[148]

The Reagan Administration

Like the corporate community, the Reagan administration might logically have been expected to oppose new job training initiatives in the wake of PSE's demise. The 1981 tax cuts generated mounting pressure for the administration to shrink the federal deficit. With both Social Security and military spending declared off-limits, this pressure necessarily subjected all domestic programs to review for possible cuts or elimination. By the fall of 1981, the growing federal deficit had set off major declines in the financial markets. Business leaders, who had vigorously supported the president's budget package earlier in the year, began criticizing White House policy with increasing frequency. The fall-off in business support, together with the direct effects of depressed stock and bond markets, served to redouble the administration's commitment to identifying additional spending cuts.[149] The remaining CETA programs were an obvious target; simply by doing nothing—that is, by allowing CETA to expire the following year without initiating new training legislation—the White House could save $3 billion in annual expenditures. Indeed, it was exactly at this point that the administration floated proposals for a new round of cuts, including the elimination of all remaining federal training programs.[150] Clearly, training did not simply slip unnoticed into the 1982 budget; it was funded only because it met critical political goals.

For the administration, these goals emerged from the public response to the rising unemployment rate during 1981 and 1982. From the beginning of his administration, Reagan was sensitive to the danger that his policies might provoke a liberal backlash. Among the broad strategies outlined by his transition team was the warning that "the image of being . . . narrowly pro-business, and uncaring, could potentially derail the President's aspirations for a new direction for the country."[151] As the economy worsened this danger became more real. By September 1981, 52% of the public believed that Reagan was primarily concerned with the wealthy, representing an increase of nearly 30 percentage points in five months.[152]

Rising unemployment particularly threatened to alienate the blue-collar voters who had provided Reagan critical support in the 1980 elections. In February 1982, the president's pollster warned that "ratings from blue collar workers . . . have dropped precipitously over the past year. [Last year], 75 percent of the blue collar respondents felt that the program would help; now only 51 percent of them feel this way."[153] This development not only threatened to destroy a carefully cultivated base of support; it pointed to the prospect of a broader class realignment which might establish a powerful new alliance opposed to the Reagan agenda. As Barrett notes,

In the late seventies, at the height of the tax revolt, many working-class and other middle-income Americans rallied to the conservative side. . . . Thus they pitted themselves against the poor, the most obvious consumers of direct government services. The recession and two years of Reagan policies appeared to have checked the growth of that gap. Blue collar families were being reminded of the interests they shared with those one or two steps down the economic ladder.[154]

In February 1982, the senior White House staff gathered at Camp David to formulate a "political public relations strategy for overcoming" the backlash against supply-side policies. As part of that strategy, Presidential Assistant Richard Darman suggested that the administration

- Hype Federalism for as long as it will play.
- Develop and implement plans for minor (low cost) and symbolic actions for key constituencies—aged, Spanish-surnamed, white ethnics/blue collar, populist/rednecks, (other?).
- Distract attention from economic focus until the economy is clearly turning up—via a combination of foreign and domestic actions.[155]

As the unemployment crisis deepened and the deficit expanded over the course of the year, the pressure to develop a symbolic, low-cost response to joblessness grew increasingly intense. While important members of the administration continued to prefer to save money by eliminating training altogether, this position became increasingly less tenable. By September 1982, a White House strategist explained that "we have got to focus somehow on jobs, jobs, jobs. That is what the voters want to hear."[156]

In this context, to press for the total elimination of job training programs would have provoked unnecessarily extreme reactions. Perhaps if the Congress had passed enterprise zone legislation, the president might have been able to eliminate training programs while maintaining the administration's credibility on issues of economic dislocation. But in the absence of any alternative strategy for combating joblessness, the prospect of enduring a severe unemployment crisis with no program whatsoever posed political difficulties too great to justify. Ultimately, it was the budget hawk Stockman who "recognized the usefulness of the rhetoric" embodied in JTPA and convinced the president it was "a politically important issue" worthy of his support.[157] After months of threatening to veto the legislation, the president announced his support for JTPA in late September and signed the bill into law in early October 1982.[158]

After nearly two years of struggle, the final bill achieved a remarkable degree of bipartisan support. Indeed, in the immediate aftermath of JTPA's passage, the primary area of disagreement concerned conflicting claims of credit, as the president and the House leadership each held separate bill-signing ceremonies. In the ensuing months, community organizations celebrated the commitment to continued funding, and the business lobbies rallied their members to prove the new program a success by lending their support to local PICs.

For the president, JTPA offered a cheap solution to the politics of unemployment. Beyond this, however, the legislation served a number of affirmative goals of the new administration. In implying that unemployment could be substantially alleviated if only workers were more skilled, JTPA redefined the poverty discourse in terms that, while maintaining a role for federal action, located the primary source of hardship in the deficiencies of workers rather than the actions of business or the failures of government. In addition, JTPA represented the first of what Reagan hoped would be a series of New Federalist initiatives, replacing federally run programs with block grants to the states and devolving federal authority to the governors, and ultimately to the private sector.

For the president, the bill's most tangible function was to head off Democratic proposals for a more expansive jobs program. Immediately after announcing his support for JTPA, Reagan deployed the new initiative as a means of blunting demands for public employment. The day after his decision to endorse JTPA, Reagan challenged the Democratic leadership:

> Let me . . . speak a moment about one of our major concerns right now—jobs. You might have noticed the rhetoric from our liberal critics has already reached a crescendo. . . . Last week, they stampeded the House with another temporary, public make-work program for, at best, 200,000 people. . . . We've taken a different approach . . . a program . . . that will provide job training for one million people or more per year in the private sector. So, my question to the Speaker is, which is it going to be, Tip? Temporary or permanent? Two-hundred thousand or one million? Make-work or training for lasting jobs?[159]

Thus in contradiction to all available economic evidence, and in contrast to the Labor Department's careful disclaimers that training could only marginally impact unemployment, the president deployed JTPA as a policy which promised to return the country to gainful employment. For much of the previous two years, Reagan had disparaged training as an ineffective waste of taxpayers' money. And indeed, the evidence presented in earlier chapters suggests that this perception was largely accurate. That the president came to champion JTPA as a primary response to unemployment does not reflect the compelling arguments of its proponents. Rather, it reveals the legislation's purpose as an essentially political document, aimed at containing the response to economic hardship rather than addressing its root causes.

Conclusion: JTPA and the Triumph of Politics

On the surface, the most active proponents of JTPA appear to have been congressional Democrats, urban officials, and liberal interest groups. These are the organizations that spoke out most forcefully and consistently on the need for a continued federal training effort. Nevertheless, it is the Reagan administration, together with the business lobbies and Senate Republicans, who must be regarded as the critical actors in shaping JTPA. The coalition of Democrats and liberal lobbyists who championed training had also supported the continuation of public service employment. That JTPA passed where PSE was defeated is not due to the increased effectiveness of its liberal supporters but rather to changes in the political calculations of those who would have been JTPA's opponents. It is the actions of conservative politicians and business groups that ultimately determined the fate of federal job training.

Moreover, it is primarily the Reagan–business agenda that shaped the details of JTPA's structure. With a few concessions, the bill's final language remains almost entirely based on the core political goals of the administration and the business community, discussed above.

The record of congressional testimony leading to the adoption of JTPA is marked by a series of inconsistencies which point to the primacy of this political agenda in the program's structure. The first apparent contradiction concerns the overall level of funding for the program. In theory, JTPA was supposed to *save* the government money, as poor people left welfare and entered the ranks of taxpayers. Thus the Senate Republicans forecast that "the amount of savings to be accomplished in cash welfare payments . . . is expected to . . . at least equal the cost of [JTPA]."[160] On this basis, congressional Democrats argued that training should be supported at the highest possible level, since every dollar spent would save the government at least as much. Yet the administration bill, supported by all the business lobbies, provided by far the lowest funding of the three proposals on the table. At points, the logical contradiction inherent in this position led business representatives into embarrassing exchanges with House committee members. When the Business Roundtable testified in support of the administration's bill, for instance, Democrats asked whether the organization truly believed that, with unemployment at 9%, a program with such limited funding had "any realistic chance of succeeding in dealing with the vastness of the problem." The Roundtable reply clumsily eludes the question: "Yes . . . even though we are talking about five to seven million people in need of that training, and although the resources made available will most likely deal with only between 750 and 800 thousand—we think that the basic legislation is sound and embraces the correct principles."[161] Yet even when reduced to vague assertion, the business lobbies were unwavering in support of the administration's funding restrictions.

Second, both business representatives and the administration adopted seemingly illogical positions on the proper targeting of JTPA resources. The need for training was justified by repeated reference to shortages in skilled technical occupations. As discussed earlier, experience clearly indicated that a program targeted to the poorest of the unemployed would be least effective in meeting these hiring needs. Nonetheless, both the administration and the business lobbies supported eligibility criteria that reserved 90% of training funds for welfare recipients and dropout youth.[162] Indeed, all the corporate lobbies were adamant that, in the Roundtable's words, "the legislation now under consideration should primarily focus on training for the culturally and economically disadvantaged."[163] Thus the actually existing economic need for skilled technicians was subordinated to the political need to discourage a coalition between poor people and labor unions and to minimize federal intervention in the core labor market.

The third contradiction concerns the level of funding available per trainee and the payment of stipends or wages to program participants. It was widely acknowledged that longer-term training, facilitated by financial support for participants, had worked best to teach usable new skills. If companies had any hope of gaining useful technical employees from the program, their needs could be filled only through the extended programs made possible by wages for trainees. Such a provision would have greatly increased the program's expense, of course—and would have undermined the goal of imposing market discipline on the low-wage labor market.[164] Thus the administration, Senate Republicans, and corporate lobbies all supported a low cost per trainee and a complete prohibition on stipends.

In all these ways, the final JTPA legislation reads more like a record of political strategies than a blueprint for economic action. Indeed, the source of the bill's broad support may lie specifically in the fact that it provides a political response to unemployment without challenging any vital economic interests. Shortly after JTPA's passage, Senator Quayle attended a fundraiser at which he was hailed for his unusually bipartisan accomplishment. "I can't remember a bill," his host remarked, "unless it meant nothing to anybody, that passed the Senate 95–0."[165] The speaker, of course, meant to spotlight JTPA as the exception to this rule. In retrospect, however, it seems that the bill might simply provide further confirmation of the general trend. The fact that legislators who fought bitterly over virtually every other piece of employment and social policy were able to reach such broad agreement on job training testifies not to the program's centrality but, on the contrary, to its marginality: it does not strengthen the hand of the poor; it does not fundamentally alter labor market dynamics; it does not challenge the prerogatives of business; and it does not raise the expectations of government. The unique success of JTPA lies in the promotion of a fundamentally irrelevant policy as a critical solution to economic hardship, thus allowing lawmakers of both parties to survive the politics of recession by placating the poor without alienating the mighty.

CHAPTER SIX

Job Training after Welfare Reform:
Training for Discipline

> Work experience is the best training. Remember: "WORK IS IN. WELFARE
> IS OUT."
>
> —Notice to welfare recipients,
> Los Angeles County work-first program flyer

From its inception, job training policy has been closely linked to the institution of welfare. Almost all training programs have focused on welfare recipients as a primary target of services, and the enabling legislation of both JTPA and WIA identifies reducing welfare dependency as a key goal. In political terms, job training has often been promoted specifically as a response to welfare—a means of enabling participants to leave the rolls and become productive taxpayers. This relationship between training and welfare has been central to the political equation underlying support for a national training policy. Liberals have often defended training appropriations on the grounds that successful programs will save money by reducing the need for public assistance. For conservatives, training has often been viewed as the lesser of two evils: if it's necessary to provide some type of support for poor people, better to pay them to learn a trade than pay them to stay at home doing nothing. In both parties, it was long assumed that debates over training policy would always be framed by this trade-off between training and welfare.

For this reason, the 1996 law eliminating the legal entitlement to welfare has had far-reaching repercussions for training policy. The Personal Responsibility and Work Opportunity Reconciliation Act (PRWORA) abolished AFDC, replacing it with the Temporary Assistance for Needy Families program (TANF)—which does not guarantee any amount of cash assistance for poor families but does institute strict time limits and workfare requirements for welfare recipients. The shift from AFDC to TANF has wrought fundamental changes in both the programmatic content and the political context of job training as an anti-poverty strategy. In the aftermath of PRWORA, training policy has been reconfigured in two ways. First, the political landscape of anti-poverty policy has shifted. The ease with which welfare was eliminated proved that the very poor were even more politically expendable than previously assumed. And if there is less need for welfare, there is also less need for training programs as an antidote to welfare. Second, the "work-first" principle underlying most of the states' new welfare-to-work programs has led to the large-scale abandonment of both education and skills training in welfare-to-work programs.

For welfare recipients, the content of training has come to focus almost exclusively on an ideological agenda aimed at reinforcing the value of hard work at low wages. Far from a vehicle for upward mobility, welfare-to-work programs have come to serve primarily as a disciplinary mechanism for forcing participants to embrace their fate at the bottom of the labor market. Job training as it was initially conceived—providing the poor and unemployed with specific occupational skills that would enable them to earn a good living in the private labor market—has been largely abandoned. The retreat from this agenda reflects its proven ineffectiveness as an economic strategy. In its latest incarnation as a molder of workplace attitudes, however, job training has become something worse than useless; it has become reactionary.

How Did We Get Welfare Reform?
The Political Genealogy of PRWORA

The most immediate impact of the 1996 welfare reform was not the changes in welfare policy itself—though these were momentous—but rather the shift in the political power balance that it ushered in. The host of jobs programs enacted in the wake of the 1960s' urban riots aimed at calming the protests as much as at alleviating hardship. For decades, it was taken for granted that, even if programs were ineffective, some level of resources must be directed to impoverished communities, if only to avoid social disruption. During the Reagan and Bush administrations, federal policy increasingly pushed the envelope of this equation, enacting a series of retrenchments that in earlier times would have been unthinkable. The Reagan administration's chief welfare official explained that deep social service cuts became possible in the 1980s because "we're not seeing riots. We're not seeing people rushing the doors of Congress and the White House."[1] As poor communities became more depressed, inactive, and politically isolated, the threat of social unrest receded. In this sense, each series of cuts served as a test—almost all successful—of how far the government could go in eliminating support for poor communities without triggering a destructive response. Even with this continuing retrenchment, however, when the Clinton administration came into power it was still widely assumed that cutting poor families off AFDC with no guarantee of follow-up employment was beyond the pale of political feasibility. While conservative Republicans might introduce such tough-love proposals, they had no real hope of being adopted. It took a unique combination of circumstances to shatter this political axiom that had undergirded three decades of anti-poverty policy.

When President Clinton signed PRWORA—and when the 1996 Democratic Party convention proved, one week later, that he would pay a relatively small political price for doing so—he signaled a shift in the political balance of power that had long framed anti-poverty policy. But the bill he signed bore little resemblance to the president's initial plans for reforming welfare. The administration's original welfare proposal, presented to Congress in 1994, was to establish a two-year limit for public assistance but to couple this requirement with generous job training and health insurance benefits. Government jobs would be guaranteed for anyone unable to find private sector employment when their two years were up. The architect of this plan, David Ellwood, was a longtime poverty researcher appointed assistant secretary of health and human services in the first Clinton administration.[2] Ellwood, along with nearly all the administration's welfare policy makers, believed that the government's promise to serve as the employer of last resort was critical to truly enabling welfare recipients to support their families through paid work; the prospect of simply cutting people off after two years was, Ellwood declared, "appalling."[3] Indeed, this opinion was well-founded. Virtually every piece of empirical evidence available at the time of the welfare reform debate concluded that the PRWORA formula could not work. Liberal and conservative economists agreed that there were not enough decently paying jobs to provide employment for millions of welfare recipients.[4] As Secretary of Labor Reich pointed out at the time:

> Most of [the president's] economic advisers are ready to accept the necessity for eight million people to be unemployed in order to soothe the bond market and prevent even a tiny increase in inflation. . . . Welfare recipients will be at the end of any job queue. If *at least* eight million people have to be unemployed and actively seeking work in order to keep inflation at bay, the additional four million on welfare simply won't get jobs.[5]

In the same month that Clinton signed the welfare bill, New York City economists projected that, at the city's current rate of economic growth, it would take twenty-one years for all welfare recipients to get jobs—even if all the jobs created during this period were reserved exclusively for them.[6] The state welfare-to-work programs that TANF was modeled on had produced marginal effects in enabling recipients to work their way out of poverty.[7] Even the Republican staff director of the House Human Resources subcommittee acknowledged that, to date, no state had been able to place more than 10% of its welfare recipients into private sector jobs.[8]

In fact, the president vetoed a welfare reform bill in 1995 precisely because it lacked either the support services or the job guarantees needed to make welfare-to-work realistic. In November of that year, the Department of Health and Human Services (HHS) conducted a study that concluded that welfare reform without these features would drive an additional one million children into poverty.[9] How did it happen, then, that less than a year later the president signed into law exactly such a proposal?

The political foundation for radical welfare reform was laid in the 1994 elections, which produced a triumphant Republican Congress and a battered, defensive president. The Republicans were inspired by victory to push for a more radical welfare bill than they had proposed in the previous Congress. For the president, the 1994 humiliation led to a fundamental reassessment of political strategy. Immediately following the election, Clinton hired pollster Dick Morris as the chief architect charged with plotting his 1996 reelection strategy. On January 19, 1995, Morris held his first meeting with the president to outline the basic strategy they would follow for the next two years. "The core of the strategy," he reports, "was to embrace parts of the Republican initiative. . . . We would work to eliminate the deficit, require work for welfare, cut taxes, and reduce the federal bureaucracy."[10]

But it is not clear that even the Republican authors of PRWORA crafted it with the intent that it would become law. Clinton had vetoed similar legislation before, and there was good reason to believe he would do so again. Indeed, Republicans were divided on whether they preferred for Clinton to sign or veto the bill. For most of 1996, the Dole campaign and the congressional leadership were primarily interested in forcing a presidential veto, in order to produce a strong issue for the fall elections. Morris reports, "They looked forward with glee to his third veto of a welfare-reform bill. Their legislation would fail so their campaign issue might live."[11] For this reason, welfare reform was initially packaged in a larger bill that eliminated Medicaid entitlements to health care for poor children and nursing home care for the elderly—thus guaranteeing a certain veto. It was only in the summer of 1996, when it became clear that the Dole campaign was doomed and Republicans in Congress felt increasing pressure to avoid the do-nothing label, that the Senate leadership decoupled the welfare bill and allowed it to be voted on as a stand-alone proposal. Even in this form, however, the law was designed primarily to serve a political rather than a policy function. As Republican National Committee strategist Eddie Gillespie explained, "They tried to write a bill where [Clinton would] be hurt either way— that if he signed it he'd make his base crazy and if he vetoed it he'd be going against the mainstream."[12]

At the White House, many Democratic strategists thought that, while signing the bill might help the president's campaign, it would hurt the party's chances to retake Congress. George Stephanopoulos and others argued that signing PRWORA would "cut off at the knees" Democratic challengers for House seats, by removing a key issue in their case against Republican incumbents.[13] Ultimately, however, Clinton believed that he was boxed into a corner: he had failed to win support for his own more generous version of welfare reform, and—after making the commitment to "end welfare as we know it" his best-known campaign pledge—the president felt unable to defend a veto against the inevitable Republican charge that he was soft on welfare. Morris himself was emphatic on this point; he insisted that vetoing the welfare bill was the single worst thing the president could do for his campaign and projected that it would by itself transform a fifteen-point victory into a three-point loss.[14]

The president's ultimate decision to sign PRWORA was a purely political calculation. The majority of his cabinet—including Chief of Staff Leon Panetta, Housing and Urban Development chief Henry Cisneros, HHS Secretary Donna Shalala, Labor Secretary Reich, Treasury Secretary Robert Rubin, and Chief Economic Advisor Laura Tyson—urged him to veto the bill.[15] While these officials offered both substantive and political reasons for opposing the bill, PRWORA's supporters within the cabinet voiced only a political rationale for their position. No one, it seemed, believed in the legislation on its merits. On the contrary, one of the primary arguments advanced by those urging Clinton to sign the bill was that by securing his own reelection, the president would be in a position to correct the mistakes of PRWORA, and ultimately to enact something much closer to his original 1994 proposal, in his second term.[16] Nearly all of the poverty specialists in the Department of Health and Human Services were opposed to the new policy, and with good reason. The year before, when the president had vetoed the Republicans' welfare reform proposal, he had commissioned a study that showed the bill would push one million children into poverty. After deciding to sign a nearly identical bill one year later, the president avoided asking for a study of this bill's likely effects. Instead, HHS officials encouraged the Urban Institute, a liberal think tank, to conduct its own study, which concluded that eleven million families would be substantially hurt by PRWORA.[17] On this basis, all three of the administration's top welfare policy makers resigned in protest within one month of the president's bill signing.[18]

Despite this internal dissension, the president quickly shored up his support within the party. In fact, his timing was impeccable: he waited to sign PRWORA until the eve of the Democratic convention. In political terms, the signing and the convention were two parts of the same act. Immediately after the signing, the administration moved to soothe the backlash among alienated activists and to reunite the party stalwarts behind Clinton's campaign. Both Jesse Jackson and Mario Cuomo were enlisted to address urban, black, and Latino caucuses with the message that, although they disagreed with Clinton's decision, he still represented their best hope for future improvements in welfare policy. Jackson delivered a pivotal convention address, proclaiming that "we are mature enough to differ without splitting," and rallying the disaffected behind the lesser evil.[19] Within weeks, it was clear that this strategy had been successful. Liberal Democrats had nowhere else to go, and the prospect of a Dole presidency was enough to solidify them behind the Clinton campaign.

It was this one-two punch that finally ended the political equation that had supported three decades of anti-poverty policy. Job training and other forms of support for the poor were based on the assumption that poor people had to be given *something* to keep them from rebelling. PRWORA introduced a different political logic: that by following strict time limits it might be possible to simply cut the poor off from all supports, to give them *nothing*. The proof of this logic was not in securing a majority of Republican votes in Congress. While Republicans might be the most vociferous champions of cutting welfare, they were not the ones who would be expected to pay the political price, since the poverty population was by and large a Democratic constituency. It was only when a Democratic president endorsed the bill—and immediately proved that he could do so without paying a political price—that the rules of poverty politics were rewritten.

In essence, the hardest-line vision of Reagan Republicans, which proved politically impossible in the early 1980s, became the status quo fifteen years later. Beyond its effects on welfare itself, the politics of PRWORA undercut the basic logic of job training for poor people. As a result, the welfare-to-work programs under TANF have been notable for the extent to which they eschew any traditional education or training services whatsoever.

From Education and Training to "Work-First"

The new welfare regime aims, above all, to put poor people to work. At the federal level, TANF imposes a five-year lifetime limit on cash assistance, forcing most recipients into the labor market when their eligibility runs out. States are required to see that those who do receive assistance are working, looking for work or participating in unpaid work experience or "job readiness" training.[20] Many states have imposed even shorter time limits and stricter work requirements; by 1999 twenty states had mandated that even those merely applying for welfare must be engaged in job search activities while their applications are pending.[21] Poor people who do not meet these requirements find their applications rejected or grants cut. Thus the structure of federal and state regulations—even without any welfare-to-work programs—has helped push millions of poor Americans off the welfare rolls and into the labor market.

For those who remain on the rolls, most states have established programs based on a model commonly described as "work-first." In a marked shift from previous welfare training efforts, work-first programs include little or no actual education or training, focusing instead on placing participants as quickly as possible into the first available job—any job, at any wage. In part, the turn away from education and training is a response to the anemic results of earlier programs. Beyond this, work-first proponents offer two rationales for the new policy. First, they argue, for those reentering the labor market, the most important "skills" to obtain are not literary or technical but attitudinal. The corporate-funded American Enterprise Institute, for instance, stresses that "any entry-level job teaches the important skills of showing up for work, regularly and on time, suitably clothed and prepared to cooperate with other workers and to attempt to please customers."[22] Second, work-first supporters argue that getting a job right away provides a foothold in the labor market, from which one may start climbing a career ladder to middle-class earnings. Thus the Los Angeles County GAIN program insists that "even an entry-level job . . . will provide experience which will assist a parent in securing a better job later."[23]

It is noteworthy that work-first policies directly contradict the lessons drawn from JTPA's first decade of operations, embodied in the amendments of 1992. As described in chapter 3, JTPA was frequently criticized for allowing contractors to provide superficial services that had little impact on improving participants' employability. After repeated admonitions from both the U.S. General Accounting Office and the Department of Labor's own inspector general, Congress amended the JTPA legislation. The new regulations required that participants receive real skills training rather than superficial job referral services. Most important, the new law banned local governments from providing job search assistance, "job readiness" programs, résumé writing, or interview training without also providing substantive education or skills training. Program results showed that—while no type of training enabled participants to work their way out of poverty—welfare recipients who enrolled in real education or skills training earned relatively higher wages than those who were simply helped with referrals. For this reason, job search assistance as a stand-alone service was widely condemned as undermining JTPA's mission of enabling low-income workers to reach higher levels of the labor market.[24]

Under PRWORA, then, both federal and state officials have adopted exactly the model Congress banned in 1992—short-term, superficial job search assistance that may place participants into jobs but cannot equip them to get better jobs than they might previously have landed. In this sense, TANF marks the large-scale abandonment of job training as a strategy for upward mobility. Under the new law, the General Accounting Office reports, "training focuses more on job readiness than on acquiring new vocational skills, in some cases using unpaid work experience or community service work to teach job-readiness skills."[25]

In some states, the switch to work-first was driven largely by budgetary concerns. California's GAIN program, which provided the single most important model for TANF, began as a service-intensive program. Initial assessments showed a very high share of recipients in need of basic literacy, effectively transforming GAIN into a large-scale remedial education program. The state had not budgeted for such an effort, however—Los Angeles County, for instance, was never funded to serve more than 8% of its welfare population. Instead of increasing funding to educate illiterate recipients, California simply amended the GAIN legislation. Rather than assess the type of skills recipients would need to get good jobs and then provide the requisite training, the program would now focus on putting to work as many people as possible as quickly as possible in whatever jobs might be available. "Let the marketplace, not caseworkers, determine who is employable," insisted Governor Pete Wilson.[26]

Thus in shifting to a work-first policy, state programs abandoned the original intent of job training: to improve the wages and job prospects of participants above what they could otherwise attain. Of course there are jobs that welfare recipients can get without training, but they are overwhelmingly unstable, low-wage, no-benefit positions. To determine that recipients are "employable" in these jobs is meaningless in terms of the aim of self-sufficiency. And to declare this type of employability as the goal of welfare-to-work programs is to mark the end of any significant effort at education or training for the nation's poorest citizens.

Liberal policy makers appalled by the deliberate non-helpfulness of work-first programs might argue for a return to genuine skills training rather than attitude adjustment. But to the extent that public officials rejected education and training strategies based on these programs' history of failure, their actions reflected a correct perception. As detailed in chapter 3, several decades of welfare training programs—of all types—have proven universally incapable of providing participants with a way out of poverty. No kind of training provided to poor people, whether skills-based, education-based, or attitude-based, has succeeded in raising the average earnings of participants above the poverty line—or even significantly closer to it. Although training in occupation-specific skills or in general English and math helps a little more than job search assistance or "world-of-work" seminars, the difference is nowhere near enough to earn one way's out of poverty. The root of this failure lies in the shortage of decently paying jobs. Four decades of experimentation show that poverty and unemployment cannot be solved on the supply side, that is, by changing something about workers; instead, we must focus on the demand side of the labor market by working to improve the quality of jobs available to working-class Americans. To conclude, as welfare-to-work proponents do, that welfare recipients must simply be subjected to harsher discipline and forced into the lowest-wage part of the labor market is not to solve the problem posed by the failure of earlier programs. It is, rather, to give up on the problem entirely, and to reformulate the goal of welfare "training" as encouraging public assistance recipients to dutifully accept their lot at the bottom of the economy. Restoring education and training programs will not solve the problems faced by poor families. But the brazenness with which work-first advocates suggest that poor people should make do with whatever job is available marks a new low in public policy for those struggling to keep their families' heads above water.

How Have Former Welfare Recipients Fared in the Labor Market?

It comes as no surprise that welfare recipients' experience in the labor market does not match the hopes of work-first proponents. TANF was implemented during an unprecedented period of low unemployment, and the combination of strong economy and stricter policy led to a sharp reduction in the number of families on welfare—from 4.4 million in August 1996 to just 2.2 million four years later.[27] On this basis, politicians of both parties have declared TANF a resounding success. Representative Clay Shaw, one of the architects of PRWORA, declared the new policy "the most successful piece of legislation in this half century," and incoming Secretary of Health and Human Services Tommy Thompson dubbed it "the single most effective jobs program we have seen."[28]

Yet those who left the welfare rolls have largely been unable to find work that pays enough to support their families. In the expansion of the late 1990s, the unemployment rate fell, and wages increased, even for the poorest segments of the workforce.[29] These improvements were marginal, however, and did not change the facts described in chapters 1 and 2: there are simply not enough decently paying jobs in the economy, and no combination of tough love and time limits can turn low-wage jobs into something better. What happens to women who leave welfare is no mystery—they enter the same labor market already inhabited by millions of other poor women.[30]

The federal government has refused to collect systematic data on the fate of those who have left welfare under the new policies.[31] The available evidence, however, suggests exactly what one would expect: people have left welfare to enter a world of irregular, low-wage, and often no-benefit employment. For many, the loss of government assistance has been devastating; others have been able to make up for lost benefits with increased earnings. Few have found jobs that let them support their families above the poverty line. Nationally, 20% of all female-headed families suffered a loss in disposable income in the transition from AFDC to TANF, and the percentage of all poor children whose families went without cash assistance rose from 38% to 57%.[32] The median wage of those who left welfare for work during the TANF period was insufficient to lift a family of three out of poverty even if the mother worked fifty-two weeks per year—an unlikely prospect for most recent welfare recipients.[33] Less than one-quarter of those working had jobs with health insurance, and one state study found that only one-third got sick leave or paid vacation.[34] In addition, 25% of low-income working mothers were paid less than the federal minimum wage; while some part of this population may represent waitstaff and other tipped occupations exempt from the minimum wage, the data also suggest that poor women are likely to occupy jobs where enforcement of wage and hour regulations is lax.[35] As a result of these conditions, one-third of those who left welfare reported that they were forced to cut the size of meals, or skip meals entirely, in order to make ends meet. Forty percent of welfare leavers were unable to pay their rent, mortgage, or utilities within a year after ending welfare, and 7% were made homeless. Among the families of former welfare recipients, 41% of adults and 25% of children had no health insurance.[36] In 1998, Catholic Charities reported that 73% of parishes saw increases in the number of families seeking emergency food; in 1999, the U.S. Conference of Mayors reported that 85% of cities surveyed experienced a similar increased demand for emergency food.[37] Unsurprisingly, one-third of those who left welfare under TANF were back on the rolls within one year.[38]

In Wisconsin, whose reputation for innovative and aggressive welfare reform won Governor Tommy Thompson the nomination to become secretary of health and human services, the track record is even more disturbing. Under Thompson's guidance, the state cut its welfare caseload by nearly 70%. The number of people in poverty, however, declined much more modestly. Thus the state's policy in many cases amounted to no more than denying cash assistance to families who remained poor. As the caseload shrank, the percentage of poor families who were denied cash assistance rose from 40% to 75%. In Milwaukee, with the state's largest population in poverty, the Hunger Task Force reported a 48% increase in demand for food and shelter. Even more chilling, the city saw increases in the number of children placed in foster care, incidence of child abuse, and infant mortality rates for black families.[39]

Tellingly, the hardships of families that have left welfare do not appear to be due to a lack of skills or education. Indeed, the welfare population is surprisingly well educated. The premier study of those who left welfare from 1995 through 1997 found that more than 70% had high school diplomas, 27% had been to college, and 6% held college degrees. Similarly, of those who left welfare and were not working, only 1% said that their reason for not working was a shortcoming of skills or education.[40] Thus while individual welfare recipients may benefit from increased education, there is no reason to believe that increased skills of any kind—whether educational or attitudinal—can change the quality of jobs available to welfare leavers as a whole. The evidence suggests that we must look not at changing the workers but at changing the jobs.

The Impact of Work-First on the Entry-Level Job Market

It is clear that work-first does not improve welfare recipients' job opportunities, but it may nevertheless have an impact on the shape of the low-wage labor market. Unfortunately, welfare-to-work policies have often served the interests of the most marginal employers, in a manner that may restrict rather than expand the number of decently paying jobs. According to congressional Republicans, the point of welfare reform is to "reintroduce . . . families to the dignity of work."[41] For the most part, however, no introduction is needed. The vast majority of welfare recipients already have extensive work histories, and most move in and out of the paid labor market or work at least part-time while receiving welfare.[42] Long before work requirements became part of the welfare system, the majority of welfare recipients sought opportunities to leave the rolls for paid employment. For TANF to insist that work is preferable to welfare, then, is not saying anything new. What is new, however, is the insistence that welfare recipients must take *any* job, at *any* wage, no matter what strains it may put on their family's well-being.

Historically, the central problem encountered by public assistance recipients trying to get off welfare was the fact that most available jobs paid no more than welfare and offered few if any benefits. Moreover, it is not uncommon for poor mothers to be fired after missing one or two days' work to care for a sick child; once unemployed, one often has to endure several months of bureaucratic delay before receiving one's first welfare check.[43] As long as welfare was an entitlement, prudent mothers might choose to remain on relief rather than subject their families to such conditions. It is this calculation that TANF now aims to break. Under the new regime, the choice to resist the worst jobs is becoming increasingly untenable. In this sense, TANF provides a boon to the very worst sort of employers. For these firms—whether marginal or male-volent—TANF is a welcome source of market discipline that leaves them freer to impose extreme conditions on employees, knowing that without the fallback of welfare, women will think twice before missing a day at even these least desirable of jobs.

Similarly, state programs that provide transitional health insurance for working welfare recipients end up not only subsidizing low-wage employers but forcing workers into a position of increased dependence. In the low-wage labor market, very few jobs provide health insurance. Even when welfare benefits amount to less than what one would make at a minimum wage job, welfare remains very valuable for its medical coverage. Under work-first policies, however, this benefit is contingent on working at whatever job one is assigned to. This means that TANF recipients may be forced into low-wage jobs and then threatened with loss of their only source of health insurance if they quit or complain. In these cases, TANF serves to drive down the level of both wages and compensation that low-end businesses must offer. The prime beneficiaries of TANF, then, may be employers who offer the worst jobs in the labor market.

Perhaps the most dramatic such instance is Missouri's Direct Job Placement program, a joint venture between the state's welfare office and the poultry processing industry. Work in the chicken plants is exhausting and dangerous. For $6.75 per hour, workers hang 40 to 50 chickens per minute on metal hooks, for shifts of four to six hours without a break. In 1995, one-third of the employees in this industry suffered work-related injuries, and the companies experience chronic high turnover. Rather than face the prospect of having to raise wages or improve conditions in order to attract a more stable workforce, agricultural giants such as Tyson Foods and ConAgra have entered into agreements with the Department of Family Services, in which people applying for welfare are told instead to apply for jobs at one of the poultry plants. Since the jobs are, in the company's own words, "repetitive-motion, unskilled labor," nearly everyone is offered a job. And anyone who turns down such an offer is classified as having refused to work and is denied welfare on that basis.[44] In a small way at least, the ability of the state's most desperate workers to refuse such jobs and still receive AFDC increased the pressure for such employers to improve conditions. The elimination of that entitlement forces the most marginal workers into a brutal choice between health and health insurance.

To the extent that welfare-to-work policies remove the incentive for low-end or unscrupulous employers to raise wages, they restrict rather than expand the supply of good jobs. The most generous interpretation of TANF policies is that the program operates on the assumption that decently paying jobs are available and that the poor are best helped by establishing a work history in entry-level employment. But if the key barrier to success is not recipients' willingness to work but the quality of jobs available, these programs will backfire. It is still possible, of course, that individual welfare recipients will find their way to family-wage jobs with the help of TANF programs. As a broad policy, however, the strategy of forced work is likely to worsen conditions in the low end of the labor market and therefore worsen rather than improve conditions for the majority of the very poor.

The World of Workfare

For those families that remain on public assistance, federal and state officials require that able-bodied recipients be engaged in some form of "work activity." Across the country, states have established two broad categories of such activity: unpaid work experience, or "workfare," and short-term job search assistance, or "job readiness" training. Workfare programs have been concentrated in a few of the country's largest cities. While these account for a small percentage of TANF recipients, they grew significantly during the last half of the 1990s. The supporters of workfare—including Secretary Thompson—insist that it is a "training" program, although it includes little recognizable training in any traditional sense of the word. Across the country, tens of thousands of Americans have been set to work at menial jobs that can be learned in hours. Furthermore, since many workfare programs screen participants not for the skills they need but for those they already possess, thousands of impoverished workers are performing jobs that they had already done for years—with the caveat that they now do the work without pay. In both cases, no new skills are imparted, and there is generally no path that leads from workfare assignments to decently paying jobs.

New York City's Work Experience Program (WEP) is the largest workfare program in the country, with over 40,000 workers sweeping streets, cleaning parks, changing bedpans, and filing records in dozens of public agencies. City officials acknowledge that their records show no more than 10% of WEP workers going on to land regular jobs. Instead, WEP has been used to facilitate the elimination of tens of thousands of regular civil service jobs. All told, the Giuliani administration cut 20,000 city positions at the same time as expanding workfare.[45] In the city's Parks Department, virtually the entire regular workforce has been replaced with WEP workers—with the inevitable corollary that few regular Parks jobs remain that workfare participants might aspire to graduate into.[46] In 1997, the Parks Department gave full-time jobs to only ten out of its 7,000 workfare workers.[47] One Parks Department worker described the problem:

We were told that we would be on the WEP assignment for three months. It's supposed to be a training program. When you first hear this you say, "Hey, maybe there's some hope after all." It's a lie. You never get any training. The extent of your training is basically being given a broom and a dustpan. You can't go into the private sector submitting an application to be a computer technician when your training actually has been cutting branches and leaves and picking up dog feces. . . . You're in the WEP program and you're being trained to use Park equipment. But you are not going to get that job. The government says it is downsizing. So why are they going to hire you when they just got rid of somebody?[48]

On the other end of the spectrum, skilled positions are not used as training slots but are generally filled by those already familiar with the work. One WEP participant, for example, had twenty years' experience as a painting contractor before falling on hard times and finding himself serving as a workfare painter.

> When I went to my first orientation, I was told that if I worked hard and I did my job well I might get a job with the City. My first WEP assignment was at a senior citizens' center. I painted walls, plastered ceilings, and "tapped and floated" newly erected plasterboard walls. . . . my WEP supervisor also regularly asked me to order paint and materials from the same purveyors that I had built up a working relationship with over the past twenty years as a general contractor. On June 7, 1996, I received an award for my work at the senior citizens' center that was signed by Mayor Rudolph Giuliani. . . . At the conclusion of the award ceremony, my council member complimented me on my work and asked me if there was anything he could do for me. I told him that what I really wanted was a full-time job with the City. . . . Although he told me that he would see what he could do, he never contacted me. . . . The City is not going to pay me a real wage when it can get the same work by dividing my benefits by the minimum wage per hour.[49]

In response to these conditions, 20,000 New York WEP workers voted to unionize—by a 98% margin. The city government refused to recognize the vote, however, on the grounds that workfare is not real work but training, and therefore the "participants" do not share the right to collective bargaining afforded regular "workers."[50] The city government may have multiple reasons for resisting unionization; but its treatment of workfare participants makes clear that, whatever workfare is, it is not providing either skills or career paths for its participants.

In this sense, it is instructive to compare workfare under TANF with public service employment under CETA. Many of the critics who derided CETA for enrolling participants in "make-work" projects that imparted no marketable skills now champion workfare under TANF. Yet many of the jobs now being done by workfare workers are identical to those performed under CETA.[51] The only difference, it seems, is that CETA workers were paid regular wages, while workfare participants are not.[52] CETA workers were not only paid; they were paid decently. The business lobbies attacked Public Service Employment precisely because CETA offered an alternative to the lowest-wage jobs in the private sector.[53] It is understandable that employers might want to school poor people in the practice of low-wage discipline or to guarantee that they have no right of refusal for even the worst of job offers. But this cannot be the goal of public policy.

Beyond promoting workfare as a training ground for entry-level employment, each of the states also runs welfare-to-work training programs aimed at enabling recipients to transition to private sector jobs. They are "training" programs in name only, however, since they offer very little instruction in either occupational skills or remedial education. The PRWORA legislation explicitly bans states from counting basic education, math, literacy, or English as a second language courses as "work activities" for the purpose of satisfying federal workfare requirements. Some states have established similar policies at the local level. Massachusetts Governor Paul Celucci fired his entire board of welfare advisors when they suggested that hours spent in education should be counted toward satisfying workfare requirements.[54] In Wisconsin, Governor Thompson vetoed a bill that would have allowed vocational or technical college classes to count toward requirements, and the Milwaukee mayor's office denounced proposals that recipients enrolled in school might be excused from workfare as "a step back to the old welfare system. . . . a terrible mistake."[55] In New York, Mayor Giuliani forced thousands of city residents to drop out of college in order to work off their grants raking leaves or alphabetizing files.[56]

Similarly, the Department of Labor's Welfare-to-Work initiative, established in 1997 to fund programs for TANF recipients who need special help moving off the rolls, follows a work-first philosophy. While the Welfare-to-Work program allows states to offer education and training, it does not require these services; in an era of fiscal restraint, making costly programs optional is often tantamount to abolishing them altogether. Moreover, while the initiative funds job placement services, "job readiness" classes, and unpaid work experience, states are barred from using funds for education or skills training except for recipients who have already been placed into jobs.[57] The policy priority here is to put all welfare recipients to work. Only *after* they are working are states even permitted to provide real training—if they have enough funds left over to devote to this effort.

Even before TANF, welfare recipients rarely had access to intensive education or training. A 1993 review of state welfare-to-work programs found that on average, only 6.3% of participants were enrolled in training for specific jobs.[58] Similarly, in the model Los Angeles Jobs-First GAIN program, only 8.5% of welfare recipients received any education or training whatsoever.[59] Since 1996, traditionally defined training programs have virtually disappeared from welfare offices. In the three years following adoption of PRWORA, the share of welfare recipients across the country who received any sort of education or training services fell from 5.8% to 2.7%—even while the overall size of the caseload fell dramatically.[60] Indeed, the move to de-emphasize training went so far that an evaluation of the Los Angeles GAIN program found that welfare recipients in the control group were more likely to get basic education or vocational training than those enrolled in the program.[61]

Requiring recipients to toil at unpaid, menial labor may reflect social aims unrelated to the labor market—the conviction, for instance, that one should "give something back" in return for public assistance. Whatever the reason for the insistence on work-first, education and training have effectively disappeared from welfare policy.

Rather than focus on English, math, or occupational skills, welfare "training" is increasingly defined by a combination of harsh discipline and hokey motivational seminars. In the early 1990s, the federal government designated "low self-esteem" one of the "barriers to employment" that keep welfare recipients from securing gainful employment—thus enshrining in federal policy guidelines the conviction that it is the attitudes of poor Americans which are substantially to blame for their poverty.[62] In keeping with this assumption, state programs have placed self-help rhetoric at the heart of their welfare-to-work efforts. The very names of the programs indicate the centrality of motivational discourse to welfare reform strategies. A partial review of state welfare-to-work initiatives lists programs titled GAIN, GOALS, REACH, REACH UP, JET, MOST, PATHS, NEW JOBS, JOINT JOBS, KANWORK, Project First Step, Project Independence, and in two different states, Project Success.[63]

The primary service provided in these programs is job search assistance, described by the Manpower Demonstration Research Corporation as "sessions designed to build self-confidence and job-seeking skills."[64] But what is the real content of this training? One participant-observer provides a partial answer to this question in the following account of Wisconsin's Gateway to Opportunity, Advancement, and Lasting Success program (GOALS), one of the "motivational seminars" which have become mandatory under welfare reform regulations:

> During the first week of GOALS, about a dozen women and two men sit around a conference table at the Dane County job center. The instructor, who introduces herself as Kelly, shows flashcards. One flashcard says, You'll never amount to anything.
> "Has anybody ever heard this in your life?" she asks.
> No response.
> "Good! Because it's not true!"
> She holds up another flashcard: You can do anything you set your mind to.
> "How about this one? How often do we hear this?"
> No one says anything.
> This is day three of the two-week GOALS session. The topic: communication. From Kelly's point of view, things aren't going so well. "People aren't talking a lot," she says.

Several participants are clearly trying, though. Kelly holds up a flashcard that says, I'm so proud of you. "How do we feel when someone says this to us?" she asks.

"Good?" one participant offers.

"Yeah!" says Kelly. She hands out pieces of paper and asks everyone to write down the names of two people who have had a positive influence in their lives. "It's the person who believes in you," she says.

She writes 'belives' in magic marker on a flip chart, then crosses it out and writes 'beleives.' "Don't tell her," the woman in front of me whispers.

"What?" Kelly asks. "Don't tell me what?"

"You still spelled 'believes' wrong," someone says. Kelly stares at the flip chart.

"It's I before E except after C," another participant explains.

"That's okay," the woman in front of me says. "That's a hard one."

After a short break, Kelly lists some more rules for good communication. "Here are two of the hardest things to say in the English language," she says, and writes "Thank you" and "I'm sorry" on the flip chart. . . .

I interview some participants after class. "I don't want to knock the program or anything—maybe someone is getting their self-esteem raised," says one participant. . . . "But . . . they've given me an ultimatum: You either go to this class or it's your check."[65]

Across the country, Americans who are unfortunate enough to need public assistance are being forced to undergo "training" programs such as that mandated by GOALS—programs which have virtually no content apart from "can-do" hype. Under TANF, however, the goofiness of self-esteem training is backed by the ever-present threat of sanctions and the specter of time limits. The nation's largest welfare-to-work program, Los Angeles's Jobs-First GAIN, exemplifies this two-pronged approach, combining a "strong Work First message" with regular reductions in the grants of those who don't participate in job search activities. Fully 70% of recipients are threatened with sanctions in a typical program year, and 23% have had their grants cut as punishment for nonparticipation—more than double the rate of punitive sanctions issued before TANF.[66]

The content of GAIN's motivation seminars varies between cloyingly Pollyannaish and eerily Orwellian. In the six-hour orientation meetings, "the message [is] . . . upbeat, stressing how work can lift self-esteem and that a low-paying first job can lead to a better one in the future."[67] In one sense, the rhetorical hype serves to legitimate very low standards of program success. The program promises neither improved skills nor a living wage; expectations of the jobs that recipients are to be placed in are kept low, and are justified on the unlikely assumption of upward mobility. Indeed, the GAIN "message" rings with brutal cheerfulness, relentlessly hawking the idea that work is its own reward: "By working, you demonstrate the self-growth and independence which provide the positive role model that your children need to become successful, productive adults. Participants are encouraged to work full or part-time even if they want to pursue education or training. A job is an education too."[68]

The motto of GAIN is "A Job, Another Job, A Career"—suggesting that any job is a first step up the ladder toward a middle-class standard of living. The reality is that with few exceptions, most welfare recipients are unable to find decently paying jobs, and therefore are condemned to cycle through a continuing series of low-wage, no-benefit, dead-end jobs. It is for this reason that so many recipients are cynical or dismissive of welfare-to-work initiatives: the type of job they are pushed toward is exactly the type of job they have held previously and found incapable of supporting their families.[69] As a Milwaukee welfare administrator explains, "People are placed in low income and temporary jobs that they work a few days here and there for a few hours. There's no chance for stability at a job with a livable wage that will allow them to lead a wholesome life."[70] In this context, the hype surrounding "job readiness" activities becomes obnoxious. As one recipient recalls: "It was disgusting. Here were these women getting jobs at a fast food restaurant for minimum wage, and people were clapping and cheering. And then they would find out that they couldn't make it on that amount, so they would just come right back on welfare a month or so later. And that was the best they seemed to do. They didn't offer any real good jobs to anyone."[71]

The Political Content of Welfare Training Programs: Training for Discipline

If "job readiness training" is not preparing participants for living wage jobs, then what is its function? In program after program, it appears that welfare-to-work "training" serves largely as a disciplinary mechanism, aimed at disabusing participants of the notion that they can refuse, resist, or even complain about the type of job they are offered. Simply put, the goal of much welfare training appears to be to get poor people to embrace hard work at low wages, and to suffer this fate willingly.

Work-first programs begin from the assumption that welfare recipients must be made into attractive candidates for private employers—however employers may define their needs. In fact, employer surveys consistently report that the most important hiring criteria for entry-level jobs are attitudinal.[72] Employers who are considering hiring recent welfare recipients report that they look above all for "positive attitude," "reliable," "a strong work ethic," and "training in workplace expectations."[73] When we consider that these jobs are often unstable, with low wages, no benefits, and little prospect for advancement, the call for discipline and diligence becomes offensive. These are the worst jobs in the labor market—the lowest paying, the dirtiest, and the least secure, often with the most petty and personal supervision. For psychologically healthy adults, it may be appropriate to view such jobs with distaste and resentment. In a study commissioned by the Department of Labor, the American Society for Training and Development declared "self-esteem" one of the "basic skills" required by employers. However, it is unclear that self-respecting workers should be expected to embrace these jobs. On the contrary, one early study found that those with the highest self-esteem were *least* likely to accept the sorts of jobs being offered to graduates of government training programs.[74]

Indeed, if there is a chance of improving working conditions in low-wage industries, it may lie partly in workers' ability to participate in collective rebellion against employers who prosper on the backs of such standards. The goal of welfare-to-work training, however, is not to encourage *this* sort of self-esteem, but its opposite. The General Accounting Office stresses that one of the "soft skills" welfare recipients must acquire is "eliminating inappropriate responses to authority."[75] Similarly, a program lauded by the *Wall Street Journal*—Project STRIVE—aims explicitly at curbing "the self-defeating postures of passivity, racial blaming or the strut of 'attitude.'" Instructors explain that harsh, tough-love treatment is needed for participants such as Gloria, who "leans back with her arms crossed over her chest—just the kind of subtle gesture of defiance bound to irritate a supervisor on the job. Other participants will be challenged to recognize their own resistance to authority, displayed in their bored facial expressions, smirks, slouching and unconscious clucks of disgust."[76]

Thus the mission of "training" programs has been fundamentally transformed: no longer to provide the skills or education that might, in fact, enable participants to gain greater leverage in the labor market, but now to lower the aspirations of participants and produce a disciplined caste of low-wage workers.

In both the public and private sectors, the rhetoric of self-esteem and taking charge of one's life serves to mask the reality that "world-of-work" programs primarily train workers to be submissive: to follow orders, to accept the superiority of the boss's judgment, to affect personalities which are pleasing to those in power, and above all not to challenge the prerogatives of management. The difference between the "self-esteem" taught in such welfare-to-work programs and a less Orwellian approach may be seen when we consider what an alternative curriculum might look like. Educator Ira Shor suggests a humanistic world-of-work training aimed at "empowering" participants in a more straightforward manner.[77] Here, the work world is defined not by what management wants workers to think but by what information is truly useful to workers. Shor suggests that when approaching a specific occupation, students be sent out to interview workers currently employed in the field. He recommends that they ask:

What did you learn on the job compared to what you learned before you got the job? Was there a union at the workplace? Does the union make a difference?

If no union, does anyone think you need one? Is this a place that treats women and minorities equally? Is health and safety taken seriously here? What do people like about this work? What do they complain about? . . . What are your hours, your pay? . . . What do you have to do to get promoted? . . . Do you know how your work fits together into the larger operations of your company? . . . How does your company fit into the larger economy? . . . If you don't like something at work, can you change it?[78]

This approach to the "world of work" would uncover a range of information which is critical for workers but ignored or suppressed in management-oriented programs.[79] Beyond this, Shor's approach treats students as political citizens rather than merely as production inputs. The notion that workers should know something about how their jobs fit into the broader economy seems eccentric in a training program oriented to the needs of business, but it is essential for a public program which seeks to enable individuals to make sense of their work lives and achieve some measure of dignity on the job.

When contrasted with Shor's curriculum, it is clear just how hard TANF, WIA and other business-oriented training programs are working to suppress workers' self-esteem. The skills-as-discipline curriculum of training programs is a predictable result of a business-dominated employment system in an economy with a shortage of good jobs. If job training is ever effective for entry-level workers, its greatest impact is in periods of labor shortage. In an economy of limited opportunity, training has become not only irrelevant but increasingly reactionary, as a growing share of training resources is devoted to channeling economic discontent in directions which are benign to employers. To the extent that this project is successful, training becomes something worse than a misplaced hope; it becomes an ideological tool for preventing a political solution to the very problems of poverty which training policy purports to address.

CHAPTER SEVEN

Conclusion: Job Training as Political Diversion

> We need some job training, but we need the jobs after the training. . . .
> We've been trained to death.
> —Cincinnati community activist Linda Brock, commenting on
> the conditions that sparked a week of riots in spring 2001[1]

In the twenty years since the adoption of the Job Training Partnership Act, the ideology of job training has taken root as national common sense. When the legislation was first proposed, the administration conceived of it as a temporary intervention designed to address the worst effects of recession.[2] However, while the national unemployment rate fell significantly over the next two decades, poverty persisted at troubling levels.[3] Moreover, even for those who were gainfully employed, modest unemployment rates masked a steady deterioration in the quality of jobs available. Corporate downsizing and the globalization of production led to multiple waves of layoffs, affecting a growing share of the middle-class workforce. In this context, job training has become a permanent fixture of federal employment policy and a favorite response to the politics of economic anxiety.

The skills mismatch thesis, which the Reagan administration and its business allies stumbled into in the course of formulating a rationale for the privatization of CETA, has become an axiom of federal employment policy. Indeed, while Republicans and Democrats have argued over the exact funding level and program design of training initiatives, the central assumptions of a training-focused policy have retained remarkably broad support. Job training has come to be seen as the ultimate win-win policy, and thus remains a favorite of elected officials drawn to universally acceptable initiatives. In the years since 1982, a host of high-profile commissions have boasted of achieving consensus among business, labor, community, and public sector representatives on the need for training. In 1999, President Clinton enjoyed a rare moment of Republican support when he proposed an increase in the job training budget. The Republican chair of the House Committee on Education and the Work Force greeted the proposal warmly. "We will spar on a variety of issues this year," he predicted, "but not these. What the president is talking about today should enjoy broad bipartisan support."[4]

Chapter 5 highlighted the goals that Republican officials and business organizations achieved through the focus on training policy. Yet training has been promoted with equal vigor by Democratic officials, at both national and local levels. In 1982, congressional Democrats supported JTPA in the spirit of making the best of a bad situation: the program was far from what they wanted and believed necessary, but at least it preserved some federal role in employment policy, delivered resources to traditionally Democratic urban communities, and provided a modicum of support for their allies in city government and community organizations. What began as tepid endorsement, however, soon turned into enthusiastic embrace. Over the course of the past two decades, job training has become increasingly important to Democratic officials, particularly in urban and industrial parts of the country. Beginning in the mid-1980s, the decline of manufacturing coupled with continued cuts in federal revenue sharing left most big cities and industrial states facing near-permanent fiscal crisis. As poverty rates grew steadily, city and state officials were increasingly unable to respond with anything other than token, low-budget initiatives. Simultaneously, local officials faced the constant fear of corporate disinvestment, as large employers threatened to relocate to lower-wage, lower-tax, and less-regulated jurisdictions. This combination of conditions left even progressive officials in a position similar to that of the early Reagan administration: needing a politically convincing response to economic hardship which would not cost money and would not alienate the business community. In this context, job training emerged as something like the path of least political resistance even for those who might ideally have wished for something more ambitious. For Democrats no less than Republicans, the ability to go public with the claim to be doing *something* about poverty—while avoiding tax increases and the risk of disinvestment—proved invaluable.

Many liberals saw the elimination of CETA's public service jobs as a Republican policy which they hoped would be reversed when Democrats retook the White House. The history of the Clinton administration, however, shows the extent to which job training represents the convergence of political forces that bear equally on politicians of both parties. In its first year in office, the Clinton administration found itself facing budgetary and political constraints similar to those of Democratic mayors and governors during the 1980s. While the president's 1992 campaign platform had focused heavily on job training, it had also included a number of proposals which looked beyond training to more structural improvements in labor policy, including public job creation, increasing the minimum wage, and rewriting labor laws to ban striker replacements, facilitate new organizing, and outlaw "right to work" statutes.[5] However, it quickly became clear that these institutional proposals, which might actually change the balance of power between workers and employers, would be impossible to implement. The president's job creation program, already scaled back from a $50 billion public works agenda to a $16 billion "stimulus" package, was defeated by Republicans and conservative Democrats in the Senate. Labor Secretary Reich's call for a mandatory payroll "training tax" met such vigorous opposition from business that it was dropped without even being presented to Congress. And as the administration's discussion of labor law reform progressed, it shifted precipitously away from strengthening unions and toward expanding company-dominated "work committees."[6] With the election of a Republican majority in the 1995 Congress, the president was forced into an even more defensive posture, most clearly reflected in the adoption of PRWORA. It may be, then, that the Clinton administration, like local Democratic officeholders, focused on job training policy as that which is possible—not what they would have preferred in their heart of hearts, but an affordable policy on which everyone could agree.[7]

For both Democrats and Republicans, and for both public and private officials, job training has served primarily as a form of political diversion. At both the federal and local levels of government, the rhetoric of job training has encouraged a discourse about poverty and unemployment which minimizes the public's expectations of government. If poverty were viewed largely as the result of a shortage of jobs, and the government were held responsible as employer of last resort, scores of mayors and governors would have been thrown out of office in response to the dislocations of the past two decades. By instead promoting a view of poverty as largely rooted in the educational, cultural, and moral failings of poor communities, the assumptions underlying training policy suggest that the government could not be expected to provide more than marginal assistance toward solving this problem. This was the view urged by President George W. Bush in his first major address on poverty: "Much of today's poverty has more to do with troubled lives than a troubled economy."[8] If poverty stems from the personal and social pathologies of the poor, then government cannot reasonably be held accountable for ending it. In this way, in ideological as well as programmatic terms, job training has been politically functional for elected officials even when it produces meager results.

The essentially political logic of training policy can be seen, in part, in the shift of resources away from welfare recipients and toward dislocated workers. As described in chapter 6, the politics surrounding the passage of PRWORA signaled a shift in the political framework that had long undergirded training policy. The number of people in poverty significantly outweighs the number who have lost jobs due to plant closings. The former, however, have been shown to be politically expendable, while the latter often constitute the classic "swing" voters that every pollster places at the center of electoral strategies. Therefore, as the country was hit by a new wave of layoffs in the mid-1990s, politicians in both parties promoted job training as a response to economic anxiety among these middle-income voters.[9] The shift in political priorities was reflected in a dramatic reapportionment in the JTPA budget. From 1992 to 1999, funding for low-income workers fell by 40%, while that for dislocated workers nearly tripled.[10] WIA extends this trend even further, with 60% of all adult training funds reserved for dislocated workers.[11] Thus while officials across the country have declared training useless for the very poor, they continue to trumpet its promise for those who remain a core political constituency.

For conservatives, the expansion of dislocated worker training has served, in part, as a means of avoiding more structural responses to dislocation, just as a similar logic led the Reagan administration to support JTPA as a means of avoiding a public jobs program. One Senate Labor Committee staffer explained that funding for dislocated worker programs was significantly increased in the mid-1990s as a "way of getting away from plant closing" legislation.[12] As the export of jobs abroad accelerated after the passage of the North American Free Trade Agreement (NAFTA), corporations came to accept training programs as an unavoidable political cost of doing business. In explaining the Business Roundtable's support for retraining, for instance, one official pointed to the fact that 25% of member companies' revenues were generated from overseas operations. "We're sensitive to the dislocations issue," she explained. "If we want to be flexible to relocate overseas, we have to understand that there's a human toll, and be responsive to that."[13]

Unfortunately, however, while more resources may now be available for laid-off workers, the quality of training remains disappointing; under WIA, dislocated workers receive the same menu of services as low-income adults, with training increasingly focused on workplace attitudes rather than technical know-how. Program designers assume that laid-off manufacturing employees do not need to learn the arts of discipline and punctuality; thus these workers are spared the harshest forms of "work maturity" training. Their training focuses instead on the teamwork and problem-solving skills described in chapter 4.

In this sense, the logic of job training has been split into two divergent streams. For the poorest workers, training focuses solely on discipline, with no particular promise that it will lead to a better job. For more experienced and better-off workers, training advocates continue to promote the vision of the high-skill workplace described in chapter 4. However, at both ends of this continuum—the descent into discipline and the aspiration to empowerment—programs have moved toward a focus on workers' attitudes and away from the original conception of training in tool and die making, air conditioner repair, and other technical skills.

In the private sector as well, training has become an instrumental strategy for muting the backlash against large-scale layoffs and relocations; here, too, training has increasingly little to do with occupation-specific skills. Thus, for example, while AT&T and its spin-offs were laying off workers at the rate of 1,000 per month, the company established an Alliance for Employee Growth and Development to provide career counseling and résumé writing services for those let go.[14] Similarly, when Levi's closed its San Antonio plant to relocate the jobs to Costa Rica, it established a retraining program for the 1,100 workers left behind.[15] Recognizing that there are few decently paying occupations for which workers might be retrained, employers have increasingly developed training curricula which recall the self-help rhetoric of welfare programs. Thus when General Electric fired 600 workers at an air conditioner plant, it established a Reemployment Center to help those laid off secure new jobs. Rather than identifying occupation-specific skills in demand in the local labor market, however, GE adopted a therapeutic approach to training. As the plant's human resources manager explained, "The primary objective of training for displaced employees is helping these people to turn from feelings of confusion, despair, and depression to a sense of hope, planning and action."[16] General Motors' program for laid-off workers in Southern California was likewise conceived as a primarily psychological project. As the director of training explained, "Many students had been very angry because the bottom had dropped out of their world. . . . [But now] all the students have goals. They know that they need to get back out there and do something with their lives."[17] Similarly, the Labor Department under George W. Bush declared that its primary mission was not to actually provide jobs for unemployed Americans, but rather "to give workers constant hope in a changing world."[18] Thus in a low-skill, job-shortage economy, the primary function of training programs is increasingly the diversion of workers' anger away from the responsible company toward a benignly ineffective rhetoric of self-help.

While training programs have often been deployed in a cynical fashion, it is critical to note that the diversionary function of training programs does not necessarily entail a conscious conspiracy on the part of their proponents. Throughout this book, I have presented evidence that, at many points, job training was intentionally promoted as a means of staving off more progressive—and more effective—ways of addressing poverty and unemployment. However, I believe that in many cases those who championed JTPA, including both public officials and private employers, were at least partly motivated by a genuine desire to help the economically disadvantaged. The nature of ideology is to seamlessly blend material self-interest and heartfelt belief. For many of the actors in this story, the impossibility of encouraging unionization or restoring the minimum wage to its previous level appears not as a political choice but as part of the naturally given background which frames policy discussions. Within this framework, the possibility for at least anecdotal success—in which individuals' lives may be genuinely transformed—makes job training appear as the best option for well-intentioned people seeking to do good.

The thousands of job training specialists employed by local governments across the country are overwhelmingly people who have chosen this line of work out of an interest in improving social conditions, and they work hard to make the most of the resources they are afforded. And while the national business lobbies may be informed by a sophisticated political strategy, the same cannot be said of the thousands of people involved in small businesses who have served on Private Industry Councils. Overwhelmingly, those who devote their time to supervising JTPA or WIA training activities derive no direct benefit from the program.[19] It is likely that for some of these firms, the PIC offers an opportunity to generate favorable publicity or useful contacts. I believe, however, that a substantial number of board members are genuinely concerned with the plight of unemployed workers and join the PIC out of a sincere desire to do some social good. This reality reflects the subtlety of ideology. Businesspeople who are moved by economic hardship may start from the assumption that responses such as increasing welfare payments, mandating comparable worth laws, or restricting plants' ease of relocation are out of the question; indeed, they may have convinced themselves that the nature of market economies is such that these policies would ultimately redound to the detriment of poor people. The fact that training neither requires significant public expenditures nor increases the bargaining leverage of potential workers makes JTPA stand out as one of the policy responses which businesspeople can embrace unambiguously. PIC activities thus allow businesspeople to engage the issue of poverty in the role of magnanimous benefactors rather than stingy exploiters; who among us would not be seduced by such a powerful logic? I do not believe that PIC board members across the country are driven by a conscious, cynical plan to frustrate the aspirations of the poor. On the contrary, the ready availability of anecdotal success stories, coupled with the deep desire to believe in the positive effects of the market, leads many businesspeople to conclude that training can work despite their own first-hand knowledge of the limits of the labor market. Thus a Business Roundtable official notes that even executives whose own companies engage in significant downsizing are convinced that trained workers will be in great demand in the near (if unspecified) future.[20] I believe that many such CEOs are genuinely convinced of the truth of this scenario, despite the fact that it is manifestly contradicted by their own knowledge of the market. Similarly, when training programs do fail, this same complex of motivations leads businesspeople to conclude that the failure must result from poor program design or inefficient management rather than the underlying logic of training policy as a whole.

Thus I believe that many of JTPA's supporters among lawmakers, policy analysts, and business participants believed that they were acting in the best interests of poor people. Nevertheless, the question of these actors' intentions does not in itself determine the underlying meaning of job training. On the contrary, the structural constraints facing elected officials have led liberal mayors and conservative presidents to promote training for much the same purposes, despite manifest differences in political intentions. In all these cases, JTPA *functions* as political diversion just as surely when its proponents are convinced of its virtues as when they are cynically bent on manipulating public discourse.

The Death and Rebirth of Training Policy

As an economic policy, job training appears to be largely exhausted. Training providers have largely given up on the original notion of basic education or technical skills training, and over the past two decades scholarly research seems to have tried every possible version of the skills mismatch thesis without hitting on a believable formulation. Over the course of the past two decades, the mismatch argument has undergone a process of continual redefinition. The terms of the policy have repeatedly shifted, along three dimensions: the questions of what skills workers needed, what goals training programs should aim at, and how a program's success or failure should be measured. As described above, the skills deemed necessary for low-income workers have shifted from occupation-specific technical skills to basic English and math, then to résumé writing and interviewing skills, and finally to the attitude adjustment promoted in "job readiness" programs. Similarly, the initial goal of training programs was to increase the earnings of participants above what they could otherwise attain. Over time, however, programs retreated to the more modest goal of simply getting participants employed, or at least graduating them to other training. Finally, the question of how to measure the success of training has slipped from a bold insistence on measurable economic impacts to a fuzzy assertion that work experience may be its own form of success—providing enhanced self-esteem for the worker and a positive role model for her children. In this case, however, it is both impossible and unnecessary for social scientists to measure the success or failure of programs; work experience succeeds by definition.

Along all three dimensions, welfare-to-work programs under TANF mark the ultimate end point of this progression. For twenty years, failed programs and contradictory evidence have been met by creatively shifting the terms of the mismatch thesis and the parameters of federal programs. Finally, in the work-first provisions of TANF and WIA, the long evolution of meanings that has characterized the skills mismatch thesis has run out of options; everything has been tried and failed. When employment programs explicitly have no training content, declare their goal to be nothing more than putting people back to work in the same jobs they previously held, and defy any meaningful measurement of performance, there is nothing left that can credibly be described as a "training" agenda.

As an economic thesis, the notion that unemployment can be explained by a skills mismatch, and that some sort of skills training can provide a pathway to prosperity, is all played out. Every formulation of the skills mismatch thesis has been tried and failed, as has every variation of federal program design. However, as a political strategy, job training remains alive—because it continues to be useful. Despite largely abandoning JTPA's original notions of "skill," "training," and "success," job training continues to be re-funded with bipartisan support. Moreover, the broader axioms of training policy—that unemployment is due to the shortcomings of would-be workers, that the economy is changing in ways that demand ever-higher levels of skill, and that high school and college curricula must be brought more into line with the needs of private employers—remain widely popular and frequently articulated.

The long expansion of the late 1990s did not prevent a new round of high-profile layoffs. In the last three years of the decade, 7.5 million workers lost their jobs due to downsizing, plant closing, or relocation.[21] Indeed, the number of layoffs caused by international trade or relocation of jobs abroad was so high in 2000–2001 that a special federal training fund set up to ameliorate job losses resulting from NAFTA ran out of money halfway through the year.[22] These job losses prompted both private employers and public officials to devote renewed attention to training. As with earlier rounds of layoffs, the new programs have often been sponsored by the same companies responsible for downsizing; Boeing, for example, launched its Quality Through Training program after laying off 12,000 employees.[23] The incoming Bush administration stressed the need to train displaced workers in high-tech occupations despite the fact that the Information Technology Association of America announced that demand for high-tech workers was off by nearly 50% and despite the administration's own support for a policy of filling high-tech jobs through temporary work visas for lower-wage immigrants rather than longer-term training for unemployed Americans.[24] In practice, the new administration provided only tepid support for training; the president's first budget included a cut of nearly $500 million for WIA.[25] Nevertheless, as the unemployment rate rose and market analysts declared the nation nearing recession in 2001, the administration returned to a public emphasis on skills as the explanation for economic decline and the key to future improvement. "The number-one fact these [unemployment] numbers demonstrate," explained Labor Secretary Chao, "is this economy is undergoing a fundamental transformation—from manufacturing to services to information-based industries. It is an economy that increasingly favors higher skills and higher education."[26]

Similarly, training continues to be promoted as a key policy response to urban unrest. After Cincinnati was convulsed by a week of rioting and the imposition of martial law following the police shooting of an unarmed black teenager in April 2001, job training was advanced as one of the possible solutions for defusing the underlying racial tensions sparked by the shooting.[27] So too, the U.S. Conference of Mayors convened a Skills Summit in early 2001, declaring that "training the local workforce to stay competitive in a changing economy" was "the number one challenge" facing the nation's cities.[28]

Finally, even those officials responsible for welfare policy are signaling the beginnings of a swing back to education and training. In the late 1990s, when the economy was good and no one had yet reached the final time limits for welfare assistance, states had an easy time cutting welfare rolls. After six years of shrinking caseloads, however, eleven states saw their welfare populations increase in the year 2000.[29] As the economy worsened and time limits approached, a growing number of voices advocated a restoration of education and training to TANF policies.[30] Thus in 2001, Massachusetts Governor Jane Swift, a Republican, reversed state policy to mandate that time spent in training or education could count toward the work requirements of public assistance recipients.[31] Similarly, a 2001 report by the U.S. General Accounting office noted that "every state we visited . . . concluded that the Work First approach is not effective in helping certain types of [long-term] TANF recipients get and retain jobs"; in response, officials have "modified or enhanced their approach to better serve recipients for whom the Work-First approach is not successful."[32]

As the country faced the prospect of reauthorizing TANF in a recession economy, even poverty analysts who had recently proclaimed the death of education and training began hedging their bets. After several years of explaining why training was abandoned as a failed strategy, a number of scholars inexplicably reversed course to call for increased funding of education and training. For instance, in their comprehensive study of welfare-to-work strategies, scholars of the Manpower Demonstration Research Corporation declared that "education-focused programs . . . had almost no effect on earnings growth."[33] Indeed, they reported that education and training programs were even less effective than work-first. Nevertheless, within one year of publishing these findings, some of these same scholars called for a reauthorization of TANF with an expanded commitment to education and training.[34]

It is understandable that these scholars might have recoiled from work-first policies. After close to a decade of experimentation, it is clear that this strategy has failed just as certainly as training. Furthermore, these policies are often harsher, more punitive, and less humane than education programs and provide less opportunity for individual enrichment, literacy gains, or other forms of personal advancement. However, the answer to the failures or ugliness of work-first is not to resurrect training strategy. After decades of research, we know, as one recent overview of welfare-to-work strategies concludes, that *"Neither* job search–focused or adult education–focused programs have typically been successful in helping welfare recipients and other low income parents work steadily and access higher-paying jobs."[35]

In *The Memory of Earth*, award-winning science fiction author Orson Scott Card imagines a planet whose population is ruled by a thought-controlling satellite devoted to insuring that no one learns anything new; when inhabitants uncover some piece of forbidden knowledge, a psychological resistor is activated that causes them to immediately forget their discovery and reaffirm the society's existing beliefs.[36] In many ways, the recent turn back to an emphasis on skills training seems to follow the same pattern, as scholars whose own work demonstrates the failure of training nevertheless advocate expanded funding for these services. In the case of employment policy, however, the seeming absence of any learning curve is driven not by extraterrestrial thought rays but by the political constraints assumed to mark out the limits of possible policy options. Facing the problems of the past three decades—increasing inequality, stagnant or declining wages for the majority of nonsupervisory workers, and a persistently large population that is unable to work its way out of poverty—there are two primary directions employment policy can take. Either we set about to change something in workers, in order to make them more desirable for higher-paying employers, or we seek to change something about the quality of the jobs themselves, in an effort to convert low-wage jobs into something better. For the past thirty years, both policy makers and the army of scholars engaged in poverty research have largely treated this question as moot. The quality of jobs available is either assumed to be adequate or treated as an immutable fact of nature which cannot be changed by either employee activism or government intervention. Therefore, scholars have overwhelmingly framed their research by the unspoken assumption that, one way or another, the answers to poverty and unemployment must lie on the supply side of the labor market.

The return to an emphasis on training thus points to the limitations not only of federal employment policy but also of policy analysis as an enterprise. The industry of scholars devoted to evaluating training programs and commenting on employment policy has long accepted the convention that labor market problems must be solved on the supply side. In some cases, this conviction may reflect an unwillingness to buck corporate or government funders who are typically uninterested in championing unionization or social democracy. In other cases, scholars may be acting in the best tradition of policy analysis as the art of the politically possible, devoting themselves to developing proposals that are feasible within the current balance of political power. This is a legitimate, and sometimes even noble, undertaking. However, in the case of training, these assumptions have boxed policy analysts into a corner. Their own work demonstrates that training cannot succeed. However, when it becomes clear that the no-training approach of work-first is also a failure, these scholars have nothing to turn to, or fall back on, but the search for some new or slightly revised version of the human capital thesis.

Instead of seeking a ninth life for job training, the most productive direction employment policy can take is to abandon the search for supply-side solutions and concentrate instead on the demand side of the labor market: improving the quality of jobs available. It may be thought that this is an impossible task. However, recent history shows that, while there is no easy path to expanding the supply of decently paying jobs, there are clear steps that are promising for moving in that direction. This is true of the minimum wage increases of the past decade. It is even more true of unionization efforts undertaken under the new AFL-CIO leadership. In some ways, unionization is the elephant in the corner of employment policy debates, the looming option that most analysts choose to ignore. As shown in figure 7.1, the impact of unionization is dramatically greater than that of any training program—or work-first program—to date. Where the most successful training programs have produced earnings gains equivalent to less than 10% of the official poverty threshold, the impact of unionization is up to ten times as great. For cashiers, clerical workers, and janitors—exactly the type of entry-level service jobs that graduates of training programs might aspire to—the impact of unionization is the equivalent of between 41% and 66% of the poverty threshold.

This, finally, is the type of impact long sought by employment policy makers. While in some cases the union premium simply reflects the concentration of union members in the higher end of various occupations, in many cases union activities have directly impacted the quality of jobs in a given industry. In 2000, for instance, an industry-wide strike of janitors in downtown Los Angeles resulted in a contract that raises wages from $7.20 to $9.10 over a three-year period—an increase equivalent to 27% of the poverty line.[37] In such cases, unions have pursued a direction that is not generally contemplated in employment policy discussions: solving the problem of low-wage employment not by changing anything about the employees, but by changing the quality of jobs available. Certainly, such strategies may not be viable in every industry or labor market. Nor is unionization the only strategy for improving the quality of jobs available; public initiatives such as minimum wage increases, living wage ordinances, and progressive economic development policies may have similar positive impacts on upgrading the quality of jobs. What all these strategies have in common, however, is a commitment to improving the quality of jobs offered, and a willingness to face employer opposition in pursuit of this goal.

Is Conflict Anachronistic? The Question of Power

Both in its diversionary function and increasingly in the actual curricula of training programs, the ideology of job training at its heart is an argument about power. On the simplest level, the promotion of training as an alternative to

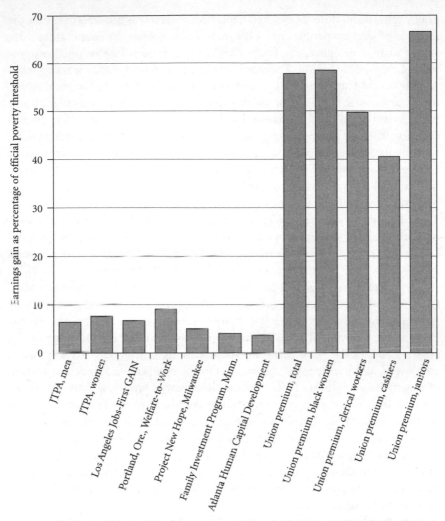

Y-axis: Earnings gain as percentage of official poverty threshold

X-axis labels:
JTPA, men
JTPA, women
Los Angeles Jobs-First GAIN
Portland, Ore., Welfare-to-Work
Project New Hope, Milwaukee
Family Investment Program, Minn.
Atlanta Human Capital Development
Union premium, total
Union premium, black women
Union premium, clerical workers
Union premium, cashiers
Union premium, janitors

Sources: Author's calculations based on Larry L. Orr et al., *The National JTPA Study: Impacts, Benefits and Costs of Title II Year-Round Programs: A Report to the U.S. Department of Labor* (Bethesda, Md.: Abt Associates, March 1994); Stephen Freedman, Jean Tansey Knab, Lisa Gennetian, and David Navarro, "The Los Angeles Jobs-First GAIN Evaluation: Final Report on a Work First Program in a Major Urban Center," Manpower Demonstration Research Corporation, New York, N.Y., 2000; Stephen Freedman, "The National Evaluation of Welfare-to-Work Strategies: Four-Year Impacts of Ten Programs on Employment Stability and Earnings Growth;" report prepared for U.S. Department of Health and Human Services and U.S. Department of Education, Office of Vocational and Adult Education, Manpower Demonstration Research Corporation, New York, N.Y., 2000; Dan Bloom and Charles Michalopoulos, *How Welfare and Work Policies Affect Employment and Income: A Synthesis of Research* (New York: Manpower Demonstration Research Corporation, 2001); U.S. Department of Labor. Bureau of Labor Statistics, "Union Members in 2000," January 2001; and Frank Parente, "The Future of Low Wage Employment," AFL-CIO Public Policy Department, Washington, D.C., 2000, http://www.aflcio.org.

Note: Figures show annual earnings gain as a percentage of family-of-three poverty thresholds.

Figure 7.1 Impact of Training Programs and Unionization on Wages

public jobs, plant-closing laws, and unionization rests on the assertion that the interests of working people and of the poor are best served by cooperating with, rather than challenging, the profit-maximizing strategies of private corporations. In this sense, political power is portrayed as irrelevant, as working-class Americans are assured that firms can be relied on to address their needs through the natural course of market behavior and that therefore there is no call for political activism or collective demands. Further, the logic of training policy suggests that if workers or unemployed people mobilize in opposition to management, they are likely to end up sabotaging their own best interests. In the intensified competition of the global marketplace, we are told, the imposition of legal or institutional constraints on companies is likely to backfire, rendering employers uncompetitive and thereby putting at risk the very jobs activists seek to protect. Thus the logic of job training policy suggests not only that the political power of workers and poor people is unnecessary but that it is often counterproductive. In the mantra of New Age management consultants, we must move beyond an us-versus-them mentality toward a philosophy of win-win.

The evidence presented in this book suggests that the assumptions underlying job training policy are fundamentally flawed. On close examination, it is simply not the case that low-income Americans can rely on the profit-maximizing behavior of private firms to serve their interests. On none of the central issues of the labor market is there a simple convergence of employers', employees', and poor people's interests. On the contrary, in the determination of wages, the institution of job security, the threat of layoffs, and the quality of working life, the interests of management and those of workers are largely in conflict. Similarly, in firms' hiring practices, location decisions, and staffing levels, the interests of corporate executives are in substantial opposition to those of local residents seeking to work their way out of poverty. Thus the implied promise of job training ideology—that workers can trust that when firms pursue their selfish interests they are also seeking the best interests of employees—appears unfounded.

More broadly, the suggestion that workers can do best by focusing our energy on education and training rather than more controversial demands appears untenable. It would be foolish to suggest that there are easy solutions to the economic dislocations of the past twenty years, or to project a simplistic optimism regarding the prospects of class-based mobilization. The globalization of production has significantly weakened the bargaining position of workers, and has limited the extent to which any national government can control its labor market. Even within these limitations, however, there are a range of policy directions which are likely to prove more promising than job training in improving the employment and earnings of low-income Americans.

First, the government could restore the minimum wage to its past value, which would immediately increase the earnings of 10% of the labor force. Second, the

Equal Employment Opportunity Commission could adopt a policy of much more aggressive prosecution of discrimination charges, thus improving the opportunities of women and minority workers and minimizing the extent to which gender and racial segmentation may be used to frustrate labor organizing. Third, those labor regulations which are on the books—including minimum wage, affirmative action, child labor, and health and safety standards —could be backed up by more serious enforcement. Fourth, the country might benefit significantly from legislation restricting the use of temporary workers to tasks which are indeed temporary, disallowing the practice of employing permanent "temporary" workers for years without vacations, health benefits, seniority, or any semblance of bargaining leverage. Fifth, legislation regulating plant closings might be strengthened, particularly in the case of companies that have received publicly funded economic development benefits. Sixth, the government could renegotiate the labor accords of the North American Free Trade Agreement and make labor standards a condition of participation in the Free Trade Area of the Americas and the World Trade Organization. Seventh, Congress could examine means for federalizing benefits such as welfare, unemployment insurance, and workers' compensation, in order to limit the practice of states and cities competing against each other to lower local benefit levels in the hope of attracting new business. Finally, perhaps the most important policy change might be to reform federal labor law—ban "right to work" statutes, mandate card-check elections and first-contract arbitration, and crack down on illegal firings of union supporters—in order to expand the number of workers who are able to negotiate with their employers on a more equal footing.

None of these proposals is original, and all of them have been attacked as unworkable by business advocates.[38] Yet I believe that this agenda is economically realistic. In some cases, available data indicate that progressive legislation can be enacted with little or no downside. For instance, much research on the minimum wage suggests that it could be raised significantly with little or no threat to employment levels.[39] In other cases, it is difficult to predict exactly what the tradeoffs will be, but it is clearly foolish to accept the declarations of business organizations at face value. Historically, every major piece of pro-labor legislation—including the institution of the eight-hour day and child labor laws—has been met by corporate predictions that the new regulations would drive firms out of business. Certainly, some forms of worker protection will drive some marginal firms out of business or out of the country. It is equally certain, however, that many industries are operating at sufficient profit margins to allow for improved wages and conditions without significantly threatening the job base. Globalization itself is largely a political phenomenon, which can be at least somewhat reshaped by legislative action. Moreover, the concentration of growth in the service industries means that an increasing proportion of firms have few options for relocating overseas and are thus more responsive both to the leverage of union representation and to public regulation. Thus I believe that much of the above agenda could be adopted without undermining the nation's economic health.

Yet while these proposals may be economically realistic, they are not politically realistic at the current time. The administration of George W. Bush is unlikely to support any of the above proposals, even if they are advocated by a Democratic Congress. More to the point, most of these proposals are unlikely to be passed even if a Democrat retakes the White House. Democrats as well as Republicans operate within the current realities of budget restrictions and political dependence on corporate contributions. The Clinton presidency itself provided an extended lesson in the limitations on economic policy that should be expected even under a Democratic administration. Even if some members of a liberal government might personally prefer a more progressive or institutional approach to poverty, the current balance of forces makes it impossible for elected officials to pursue policies that alienate their business constituency.

Thus the effort to alleviate unemployment and poverty remains less a question of policy than of politics. If there is a hope of moving in a more progressive direction, it lies not in winning the hearts and minds of those in power but in changing the political constraints under which they operate. In this case, the most important skill for working people to acquire is not the discipline demanded by employers but the solidarity required for collective mobilization.

APPENDIX A

Sources and Methodology for Comparison of Labor Supply and Demand

Defining "Decently Paying" Jobs

While the Original Orshansky poverty thresholds projected for 1984 through 1996 are well above the official federal thresholds, they are supported by a broad range of alternative methodologies for defining a minimally decent standard of living. Until 1981, the Bureau of Labor Statistics calculated a "lower living" budget designed to capture the basic needs of low-income families. In the last year these figures were published, the budget for a family of four was 165% of the official poverty line.[1] Schwarz reconstructed a version of this budget; his family-needs budget estimated a 1990 poverty line which was 155% of the official threshold for a family of four.[2] Renwick and Bergmann constructed a similar needs-based budget and calculated a 1989 poverty line for urban families which ranged between 146% and 183% of the official threshold.[3] Ruggles calculated thresholds based on the income and expenditure guidelines of the federal low-income housing program; for 1987 her threshold was 154% of the official line.[4] Weinberg and Lamas suggested a methodology using both updated family budget shares and regional data on minimal housing costs. For 1989, this methodology yielded regional poverty thresholds which ranged from 125% to 195% of the official line.[5]

Finally, Kleppner and Theodore used an updated version of this budget to calculate a definition of "living-wage" jobs that in 1997 was 202% of the official threshold.[6] In recent years, similar calculations have been used to support living-wage legislation around the country; as a rule, legislated living-wage levels have been significantly higher than the official poverty thresholds. Thus, while there is clearly room to argue with the assumptions underlying the Original Orshansky thresholds, they fall squarely within the range of options defined by scholars of alternative poverty measures.

Calculating the Number of Jobs Needed

All data on the number of jobs needed are from tapes of the March *Current Population Survey* supplement, in U.S. Department of Commerce, Census Bureau, *Current Population Survey: Annual Demographic File* (Washington, D.C., U.S. Department of Commerce, various years). I have calculated the number of families below the official poverty levels and below the Original Orshansky thresholds (for the official poverty thresholds, family numbers here are slightly higher than those published by the Census Bureau, since census tables exclude unrelated subfamilies, which I have included). I have then screened out all families with no working-age parent, including elderly single individuals.

I have made several simplifying assumptions regarding the number of jobs needed by each family, and at what wages. For families with only one working-age adult, I have assumed that this person needs one job which will pay the full threshold. I have ignored any job this adult may already hold, whether full-time or part-time, and assumed that he or she must leave this job in order to get a new, full-time, decently paying job. For families with two working-age adults, I have assumed that the primary earner will retain his or her current situation, whether full-time or part-time, with current earnings. The second adult is assumed to need one job which pays a salary sufficient to make up the difference between the primary earner's income and the threshold needed for their family size. This is my assumption for all families where both adults work full-time, both work part-time, one works full-time and the other part-time, or one works and the other does not.

In all these situations, I have calculated the average earnings of the primary earner (including earnings from self-employment) for each family size: I define "decently paying" for the second earner's job as the difference between this amount and the full family threshold. Thus each family is assumed to need only one more job to attain the poverty threshold. The one exception to this assumption is for families in which neither adult works at all; in this case, I have assumed that both adults will get jobs and that each of these jobs must pay half the needed threshold. For all families, the "primary earner" is the person who is working the most, whether this is the head of the household or his or her spouse. Where both adults have the same work status, the household head is designated as the primary earner.

This methodology was designed to maximize the extent to which poor families might earn their way out of poverty by combining more than one low-wage job. Yet there are a variety of possibilities which I have excluded. Specifically, I have not accounted for the possibility of families earning a living wage by cobbling together three or more part-time jobs. It would be ideal to have a method for testing all these possibilities, producing the best fit between the population and the job supply. But little data are available on average hours per week for part-time jobs, particularly at this level of family detail, or on the geographic and scheduling constraints on combining multiple jobs.

It is not clear how the results would be affected by altering these assumptions. The assumption that all families will have a maximum of two jobs discounts the usefulness of openings in low-wage jobs. At the same time, however, it also holds down the total number of "jobs needed." It is likely that the gap between supply of jobs and demand would be greater if one assumed families needed more jobs, even if we also allowed that these might be lower-wage jobs. In this sense, the assumptions used may be viewed as conservative guidelines.

Finally, I have deflated the number of jobs needed in each family size–work status cell by 4.2%, the figure that the 1990 census recorded as the share of all noninstitutionalized civilians aged sixteen to sixty-four who have a disability which prevents them from working.[7] Thus the final count of jobs needed is only for civilian, noninstitutionalized, and nondisabled heads of household or spouses, aged sixteen to sixty-four.

The detailed findings on the number of jobs needed for 1996 are presented in table A.1. Comparable figures using the official federal poverty thresholds are shown in table A.2.

Calculating Job Openings

The calculation of job openings in "decently paying" occupations draws on a combination of data sources for different types of workers. For full-time wage and salary workers, employment and wage data by detailed occupation for 1984 through 1996 are provided by the Bureau of Labor Statistics (BLS) in unpublished tabulations from the Current Population Survey (CPS).

For part-time wage and salary workers, employment data are also from BLS unpublished tabulations from the CPS. This information is available only by the broadest occupational categories. For self-employed workers, I have calculated annual employment totals based on data provided in *Employment and Earnings*. I then assumed that self-employment was distributed among broad occupational categories along the same lines as for all full-time workers. This method is obviously far from ideal, but it appears to be the most impartial means of estimating occupational employment among the self-employed. Since self-employed workers are a small share of the workforce, the potential distortions of this

Table A.I Jobs Needed for Impoverished Families with Working-Age Adults, 1996, Original Orshansky Thresholds (numbers of jobs in thousands)

Family work status	Family of one	Family of two	Family of three	Family of four	Family of five	Family of six	Family of seven	Family of eight	Family of nine+	Total
All families	16,504	6,262	3,790	3,198	1,924	927	367	153	147	33,272
Poverty threshold	$13,775	$17,631	$21,565	$27,630	$32,654	$36,853	$41,814	$46,675	$55,086	
No working-age parents	5,659	1,554	217	72	40	17	7	1	5	7,572
One working-age parent										
Jobs needed	10,390	3,255	2,358	1,300	516	212	111	38	33	18,213
Average wages needed	$13,775	$17,631	$21,565	$27,630	$32,654	$36,853	$41,814	$46,678	$55,086	
Two working-age parents										
Both full-time										
Jobs needed		107	123	297	243	122	49	12	11	965
Average wages needed		$10,956	$13,714	$15,611	$19,991	$22,773	$28,753	$34,411	$43,478	
One full-time, one part-time										
Jobs needed		110	113	243	188	96	22	18	14	805
Average wages needed		$10,596	$11,826	$15,454	$19,862	$21,644	$21,763	$25,159	$35,372	
One full-time, one not working										
Jobs needed		319	411	758	592	327	103	52	55	2,617
Average wages needed		$7,694	$9,738	$12,170	$15,441	$17,534	$22,914	$26,235	$36,920	
One part-time, one not working										
Jobs needed		128	109	108	72	34	15	6	7	479
Average wages needed		$12,616	$14,873	$20,164	$24,060	$26,165	$35,784	$33,838	$48,694	
Both part-time										
Jobs needed		36	34	34	20	5	2			131
Average wages needed		$12,960	$15,901	$17,974	$21,655	$26,977	$21,814			
Both not working										
Jobs needed		1,056	527	427	285	126	82	33	31	2,567
Average wages needed		$8,816	$10,753	$13,815	$16,327	$18,427	$20,907	$23,339	$27,543	

Source: Consumer Population Survey, Annual Supplement.

Table A.2 Jobs Needed for Impoverished Families with Working-Age Adults, 1996, Official Poverty Thresholds (numbers of jobs in thousands)

Family work status	Family of one	Family of two	Family of three	Family of four	Family of five	Family of six	Family of seven	Family of eight	Family of nine+	Total
All families										16,434
Poverty threshold	$7,995	$10,233	$12,516	$16,036	$18,952	$21,389	$24,268	$27,091	$31,971	
No working-age parents	2,146	366	78	42	15	8	1		4	2,660
One working-age parent										
Jobs needed	6,307	1,820	1,511	871	394	137	83	31	24	11,178
Average wages needed	$7,995	$10,233	$12,516	$16,036	$18,952	$21,389	$24,268	$27,091	$31,971	
Two working-age parents										
Both full-time										
Jobs needed		27	16	44	43	14	18	6	2	170
Average wages needed		$8,086	$7,595	$11,477	$10,952	$12,354	$16,631	$28,091	$28,369	
One full-time, one part-time										
Jobs needed		28	22	68	50	32	6	7	8	221
Average wages needed		$7,025	$6,657	$10,111	$11,272	$13,305	$12,907	$19,021	$20,688	
One full-time, one not working										
Jobs needed		108	134	253	209	141	44	25	33	947
Average wages needed		$5,472	$5,823	$7,005	$8,406	$9,431	$12,776	$15,319	$16,207	
One part-time, one not working										
Jobs needed		72	73	68	38	26	10	4	7	298
Average wages needed		$5,822	$7,496	$10,843	$12,946	$10,408	$18,328	$20,890	$25,579	
Both part-time										
Jobs needed		16	19	12	6	3				56
Average wages needed		$7,711	$9,392	$11,559	$16,554	$14,905				
Both not working										
Jobs needed		536	316	287	172	98	65	13	27	1,514
Average wages needed		$5,117	$6,258	$8,018	$9,476	$10,695	$12,134	$13,546	$15,986	

Source: Consumer Population Survey, Annual Supplement.

method should not have an appreciable effect on the overall comparison between labor supply and demand.

Wages for full-time wage and salary workers, by detailed occupation, are from BLS unpublished tabulations from the CPS for 1984–96. To calculate median annual salaries, I multiplied weekly salaries by the average number of weeks worked per year by full-time wage and salary workers, as reported in "Work Experience of the Population," BLS, various years. This is a simplifying assumption; although the average number of weeks worked per year obviously varies across occupations, this information was not available. For the 1984 to 1996 period, full-time wage and salary workers averaged either forty-five or forty-six weeks of work per year, including time off for paid vacation.

For part-time wage and salary workers, mean weekly earnings are reported for broad occupational categories by the BLS in unpublished tabulations from the CPS. As with full-time workers, I calculated annual salaries by multiplying the weekly earnings by the average number of weeks worked per year by all part-time wage and salary workers, as reported in "Work Experience of the Population," various years. For 1984 through 1996, this figure averaged thirty-three, thirty-four, or thirty-five weeks per year.

For self-employed workers, the best information available is the average annual income earned by all self-employed workers, reported by the Census Bureau in U.S. Department of Commerce, *Money Income of Households, Families and Persons*, various years. In order to estimate earnings for occupational categories, I have multiplied the average annual earnings for full-time wage and salary workers in each broad category by the overall ratio of full-time/self-employed total earnings.

Discouraged vacancies were estimated in two steps. First, for each year, I calculated the difference between actual employment growth and the level of growth which would have been needed for the job growth rate to reach its postwar high of 4.6%, realized in 1945–46. The total amount of excess demand—jobs that would have existed if workers had been available to fill them—was then distributed among full-time, part-time, and self-employed workers, and among occupations, according to their share of total employment.

The above methodology for calculating job openings was used for every year except 1990. A severe recession marked 1990–91, and employment declined both overall and in almost every occupation. Since overall employment declined, to assume that if the workers were available job openings would have increased by 4.6% results in a projection of excess demand of more than five million jobs. To imagine such great labor demand in a year of deep recession is untenable; instead, these results point to the limitations of the methodology. For this reason, I adopted a separate means of projecting discouraged vacancies for 1990. In 1984, the Bureau of Labor Statistics projected employment growth to 1995, using low-, moderate-, and high-growth assumptions.[8] These are the earliest employment projections following the 1981–82 recession, and nothing in the projections anticipates significant skill shortages later in the decade. I have taken this report's high-growth assumptions, calculated projected employment for 1990–91, and used this as a proxy for 1990 excess demand. This methodology projects an excess demand of 1.38 million jobs for 1990, well within the range of projections for other years using the 4.6% growth rate.

Finally, I have correlated these estimates of discouraged vacancies with occupational earnings data, in order to separate out those jobs with less than "decent" wages, and count only those openings in occupations which pay above this level.

APPENDIX B

Methodological Issues in the National JTPA Study

The National JTPA Study was beset by a series of methodological problems which shed doubt on its results. A number of the study's findings are counterintuitive: that male youth who enrolled in JTPA earned less than those who did not; that participating youth were more likely than nonparticipants to be arrested in the follow-up period; and that adult men in the study realized increased earnings but also increased public assistance payments. In each of these cases, the authors readily admit that they have no viable theory to account for the data. These findings and a myriad of methodological problems have made it difficult to draw clear conclusions from the report's data and have led one of the study's original architects to condemn the final report as "virtually useless to policy makers."[1]

The weaknesses in the National JTPA Study do not reflect incompetence on the part of the authors. On the contrary, at every point at which they confronted puzzling data, the authors made strenuous efforts to resolve contradictions or to determine which interpretation was most plausible. I believe the study's shortcomings largely reflect the inherent problems of conducting large-scale social science. The national study tracked 20,000 individuals, in sixteen different Service Delivery Areas (SDAs) and scores of separate programs, over a period of nearly five years. Throughout the course of the study, the authors were forced to adjust for problems in funding, uncooperative program operators, and missing data. Nearly every study of this size encounters inexplicable irregularities in the data which force researchers to use weaker proxy measures or to rely on best-guess estimates. The National JTPA Study is no different in this regard.

Whatever the source, a number of methodological problems affect the report's estimates of participant earnings and of the program's ultimate cost-benefit analysis. In each case, these issues have been resolved in ways which tend to accentuate the earnings gains achieved by those enrolled in JTPA. There is no reason to believe that these methodological decisions represent anything less than the honest best efforts of the report's authors. Nonetheless, if any one of these issues were resolved differently, the earnings attributed to JTPA participants would be less than those reported. Taken together, they might reduce the program's earnings impact and its net benefit to nearly zero.

Issues Affecting Earnings Estimates

Controls, Assignees, and Enrollees

The authors of the report initially set up a "treatment" group of people who were assigned to JTPA services and a "control" group which was to be denied services for the duration of the study. The study was thus designed as a comparison between "assignees" and "controls." However, as the study progressed, a sample study showed that a significant portion of those assigned to JTPA services were never actually enrolled in JTPA. The study was then redesigned as a comparison between "enrollees" and "controls." However, the sample study revealed that some of the unenrolled assignees *had* in fact participated in JTPA programs, even though they were never officially listed as enrolled. SDA staff often underreport enrollees. In order to maintain high placement rates, SDAs commonly wait to officially "enroll" someone in OJT (on-the-job training) or job clubs (after which they must be included in the program's performance statistics) until their first day on the job. Thus participants who fail to get jobs are never counted as part of the program, and operators are able to maintain inflated success rates.[2] To truly compare the earnings of JTPA participants with nonparticipants, the "treatment" group should include all those who took part in JTPA programs, whether or not they were officially enrolled by JTPA staff. However, the national study does not include this full population; its analysis of earnings focuses solely on those who were officially enrolled. In the same way that SDA staff screened out failures in order to inflate success rates, the exclusion of those who did not get jobs through JTPA produces an exaggerated sense of the program's impact.

The national study found that 36% of all assignees were never enrolled in training. Of these, slightly more than half did actually participate in JTPA programs—primarily OJT and job search assistance—without ever being placed into jobs or listed as officially enrolled by JTPA staff. Thus roughly 20% of all assignees (that is, 36% times 53.1%) participated in JTPA programs without

Table B.1 Earnings Gains for Title IIA Enrollees and Participants

Category	Earnings gain per enrollee	Earnings gain per participant
Women	$1,837	$1,438
Men	1,599	1,216
Female youth	210	165
Male youth non-arrestees	−868	−703

Source: Larry L. Orr et al., *The National JTPA Study: Impacts, Benefits and Costs of Title II Year-Round Programs: A Report to the U.S. Department of Labor* (Bethesda, Md.: Abt Associates, March 1994).

being enrolled. Since the excluded participants are those who did worse by the program, discounting them leads to an artificially high measure of the program's impact on earnings. As shown in table B.1, if earnings gains are calculated for all JTPA participants rather than for "enrollees" alone, the program's effects are significantly less than those reported in the national study.

Participants Lost to Second Follow-up

Data for the national study were collected when participants initially applied to JTPA and at two follow-up points, 18 months and 30 months after application. For the second round of follow-up interviews, the national study had insufficient funding to conduct personal interviews with all 20,000 people in the study sample. Therefore the authors constructed data for the 30-month follow-up using a combination of personal interviews and data from state unemployment insurance (UI) records. In most of the SDAs in the study, it was possible to combine interview and UI data to produce earnings estimates for the full study sample. However, in four of the study's sixteen SDAs, UI data were unavailable or incomplete. As a result, nearly 2,700 people from these SDAs, representing one-seventh of the original sample, were dropped from the national study.

The sixteen SDAs included in the national study were not selected at random, and their data are not necessarily representative of JTPA programs as a whole. Thus to drop certain of these SDAs does not change the sample's status from representative to nonrepresentative. Nevertheless, characteristics of the SDAs that were excluded may have biased the final results in a positive direction. The vast majority of those dropped from the study were located in Oakland, California, or Jersey City, New Jersey. These two sites are the two most densely populated urban areas in the study, with the highest poverty rates and most nonwhite populations. By largely excluding these cities from the study (three-quarters of the study subjects in these cities were dropped), it is possible that the authors inadvertently skewed the data in a direction which over-represents the experience of less depressed labor markets. It is impossible to estimate how the study's findings might differ if the full samples of Oakland and Jersey

City were included, but if we assume that training is most effective in tight labor markets, it is likely that earnings gains would be lower than those shown in the report.

Scaling of Survey and Unemployment Insurance Data

In those SDAs where UI data were available for the 30-month follow-up survey, the authors combined UI records with personal survey data. However, sample studies of those individuals for whom both survey and UI data were available showed that the two data sources did not agree. Earnings reported by UI were consistently lower than those reported in surveys. In order to make use of UI data for those individuals who could not be surveyed, the authors calculated an average ratio of UI earnings to survey earnings so that the two data sets could be reconciled. Having constructed this ratio, they were then faced with the choice of deflating the survey data to match the UI data or inflating the UI data to match the survey. The authors of the study had reason to believe that the UI data were slightly less reliable than those gathered from the survey and thus chose the latter approach. This is a choice for which both options are methodologically defensible.

Nevertheless, the choice has significant consequences for the earnings reported. The net benefits of earnings gains compared to program costs were $532 for women and $570 for men.[3] If the authors had deflated survey data to match UI instead of the reverse, these figures would drop to $225 and $207, respectively. While the choice of methods here is legitimate, it is worth noting that in this case as elsewhere the methodological dilemma was resolved by means which maximize the program's apparent impact.

Exclusion of Male Arrestees

In analyzing program impacts for different demographic groups, the study's authors originally found a large and statistically significant negative effect on male youth earnings. On closer examination, it turned out that over 80% of this negative effect was concentrated among the roughly 25% of male youth participants who had been arrested between their sixteenth birthday and application to JTPA. In response to this finding, Abt Associates separated out the arrestees and provided separate data for non-arrestees alone. In the report's final earnings analysis, only non-arrestees are counted.

I believe this exclusion is unwarranted. The study's authors offer no theory as to why previously arrested youth should be differentially affected by training programs and suggest no rationale for excluding them from the study. This decision is all the more puzzling given the authors' acknowledgment that the evaluation of JOBSTART, a similar youth training program, reported higher success among previously arrested youth than among those who had never been arrested. There is thus no convincing reason to exclude arrestees from the overall data. Taken as a separate group, previously arrested male youth suffered a loss of $6,804 as a result of JTPA participation.[4] If these youth were included in the overall totals for male youth, the data would show a statistically significant earnings loss for this group as a whole.

Gains Due to Women in "Other Services"

The single biggest earnings gain reported in the National JTPA Study is that for adult women who received "other services." There are several reasons to doubt the validity of these results. Data from the 18-month follow-up survey show much more modest impacts for women in "other services"—in line with the impacts for men listed in the final report. At 18 months, the study's authors reported, women receiving "other services" had statistically significant earnings gains in only one of six quarters; they concluded that the service "appears to have had only a short-lived effect on the earnings of adult women . . . possibly reflecting quicker placement in jobs that were similar to those the female assignees would have eventually found without access to JTPA."[5] But because of the switch from survey to UI data described above, the final report shows much higher impacts for the 30-month follow-up than at 18 months. What is more, the authors retroactively adjust the 18-month figures, reporting much higher earnings than those given in the actual 18-month follow-up surveys. The authors have been unable to reconcile these conflicting findings; they offer no theory to explain either the change in data for adult women or the resulting discrepancy between adult women and all other demographic groups regarding the impact of "other services." The study's director admits this is an "uncomfortable finding" but chose to publish the revised findings rather than go without 30-month data for this group.[6]

There are strong reasons to believe that the revised data are mistaken. Women who received "other services" started off as the least job-ready of the three service groups; the control group of comparable women had the lowest earnings of all control women. Furthermore, after enrolling in JTPA, those in "other services" received the least intensive services. By their nature, "other services" provide the least effective means for increasing earnings, offering neither the skills enhancement which comes with classroom training nor the subsidized job placement of OJT. Besides receiving the lowest quality of service, women in this group also received the lowest quantity of service, whether measured by hours, dollar value, or the percentage of participants receiving services.[7] Thus, if the report's data are true, the least capable women, who entered the program at the lowest earnings level, received the lowest quality and quantity of services and yet realized by far the greatest gain in earnings.

For all these reasons, the data reported for this group are unsupportable. The authors of the study may have been faced with a situation in which any choice of data was equally valid methodologically. Again, the authors chose to resolve this situation in a way that accentuates the positive. However, common sense strongly suggests that the data reported are unrealistic and that the true earnings gains of women in "other services" are probably significantly lower. I believe that by excluding the findings for this category of women, the report would have yielded more accurate estimates of JTPA impacts.

Taken together, the compounded effect of these methodological judgments is to significantly inflate the earnings reported for JTPA participants. If the study's authors had made what appear to be more appropriate judgments—had focused on participants rather than enrollees; included data on male arrestees; corrected the data for women in "other services"; retained complete data for Oakland and Jersey City; and reconciled UI and survey data by adjusting data to an average measure rather than the higher standard—the earnings gains of JTPA participants would be significantly lower than those reported in the National JTPA Study.

Issues Affecting Cost-Benefit Analysis

Each of the issues discussed above skews the final cost-benefit analysis toward overly optimistic conclusions. Several key methodological problems also affect this calculation.

The single biggest problem is that the report's analysis is restricted to incremental rather than total costs and benefits. The original intent of the national study was "to measure the total impact of JTPA training compared to receipt of no training."[8] However, in conducting follow-up surveys it became clear that many members of the control group had enrolled in non-JTPA training programs. The difference between participant and control group earnings thus reflects not the difference between JTPA and no training whatsoever but rather only the difference between JTPA and the more modest forms of non-JTPA training available to the control group. In order to accurately measure this relationship, the study's authors estimated the amount and cost of training received by the control group and then calculated the cost of providing the additional increment of training received by JTPA participants. The study's cost-benefit analysis takes "cost" to be the cost of this incremental training and "benefit" to be the difference between participant and control group earnings.

Thus the study never compares the total impact of JTPA with the impact of receiving no services at all. The cost-benefit analysis is confined to incremental costs and incremental benefits. It is difficult to know what to make of such an analysis. The purpose of a control group is to separate out the effects of the program from the earnings gains which participants would have realized on their own. By using a control group which itself received services, and by discounting the assumed cost of those services, the study implicitly assumes that the services received by the control group were instrumental in allowing them to earn the income they earned. But since we have no true control group (that is, no group which went without training altogether), it is impossible to know whether this assumption is warranted. It is quite possible, for instance, that the training services received by the control group were useless and that this group's earnings are very close to what they would have earned without any services. Many people become eligible for JTPA not through long-term poverty but due to a temporary "earnings dip" caused by layoffs or other sudden bad fortune. For many of these workers, there is a natural "bounce back" effect, as they find new jobs and regain income, all without the intervention of any governmental employment or training services. This suggests that the control group's earnings may not be very different from those of individuals who received no training services whatsoever. If this is true, it would be a mistake to discount that part of JTPA costs which match the cost of the control group's services, and a cost-benefit analysis which excluded these costs would project an unrealistically positive outcome.

To illustrate: for adult women who participated in JTPA, the full program costs per participant were approximately $2,600.[9] Adult women in the control group received training services whose cost was estimated at nearly $1,300. Thus the incremental training cost for adult women is approximately $1,300. Since program participants earned roughly $1,800 more than the control group over the 30-month follow-up period, the cost-benefit analysis compares this incremental gain in earnings with the incremental training costs and concludes that women in JTPA earned $500 more than the program cost. However, by discounting half of the actual JTPA program costs, the study implicitly assumes that the services represented by these costs were instrumental to the earnings of the control group. Since there is no way of knowing what the control group would have earned without any training services, it is impossible to know whether their $1,300 was well spent or wasted. By assuming that the control group's money was well spent, the authors by default assume that at least half of JTPA's money was well spent. Thus the study's methodology assumes away half the problem to be addressed.

Another problem is that the national study does not calculate margins of error for its final cost-benefit data. Virtually all of the measures calculated in the study resulted in large margins of error. For instance, for the earnings gains reported in chapter 3, three-quarters of the results are statistically insignificant, and even those which are significant have margins of error which often equal 50% or more of the point estimate. The calculation of cost-benefit analyses involves combining a series of measures—earnings gains, services received, cost of services—

which each have high margins of error. While it is impossible to determine exactly how these margins might interact, it is likely that the final outcome is subject to a very substantial margin of error. The report, however, presents its calculations with no error estimates whatsoever. The report's authors defend this practice by suggesting that point estimates are the best guess when margins of error are unknown. They insist that in determining whether JTPA represents money well spent, "the government must answer this question with a definite yes or no; it cannot simply say that the test was inconclusive."[10] Yet this last assertion is simply false. It is useful information—and quite likely true—to state that the benefits of JTPA are so modest as to be statistically insignificant. To avoid this truth does not help policy makers who are charged with setting national spending priorities.

NOTES

Introduction

1. U.S. Senate, *Job Training and Employment Legislation: Hearings before the Subcommittee on Employment, Manpower, and Poverty of the Committee on Labor and Public Welfare*, 93rd Congress, 1st session (Washington, D.C.: U.S. Government Printing Office, 1973), 127.

2. Speech to staff of the Southern Christian Leadership Conference, November 1967, quoted in Keith Jennings, "Understanding the Persisting Crisis of Black Youth Unemployment," in *Race, Politics, and Economic Development: Community Perspectives*, ed. James Jennings (New York: Verso, 1992), 160.

3. "The Rich Get Richer: And What to Do about It," *New York Times*, masthead editorial, April 19, 1992.

4. After thirty months, adult women enrolled in JTPA earned $5,631 and nonenrollees earned $4,896 on an annualized basis. In 1990, roughly the midpoint of the earnings period, the poverty threshold for a family of three was $10,419.

5. *Job Training and Basic Skills Act, S. 543*, Senate Labor Committee's proposed amendments to the *Job Training Partnership Act of 1989*, 16.

6. Burt Barnow, "Government Training as a Means of Reducing Unemployment," in *Rethinking Employment Policy*, ed. D. Lee Bawden and Felicity Skidmore (Washington, D.C.: Urban Institute Press, 1989); *Job Training and Basic Skills Act, S. 543*. For most of JTPA's history, trainees were followed up for only thirty days after graduation; later reforms extended this period to thirteen weeks.

7. *Workforce Investment Act of 1998*, U.S. Public Law 105–220, 105th Congress, 2nd session (August 7, 1998); Secretary of Labor Elaine Chao, "Remarks for Welcoming Ceremony," March 6, 2001, U.S. Department of Labor, http://www.dol.gov.

8. Tamara Lytle, "Laid-off P&W Workers to Get Training," *New Haven Register*, March 23, 1993, 1.

9. "Retrain for What?" *Nation* 257, no. 15 (November 8, 1993): 520.

10. Erin White, "Group Trains Welfare Recipients with Culinary Skills," *Yale Daily News*, January 23, 1996, 3.

11. Recorded in U.S. Congress, *Employment and Training Policy, 1982: Joint Hearings before the Subcommittee on Employment and Productivity of the Committee on Labor and Human Resources, United States Senate, and the Subcommittee on Employment Opportunities of the Committee on Education and Labor, House of Representatives, Part 1,* 97th Congress, 2nd session, March 15–16, 1982, 709. (Hereafter referred to as U.S. Congress, *Employment and Training Policy, 1982, Part 1.*)

12. Calvin Sims, "Corporate Vows to Aid Poor Produce Little in Los Angeles," *New York Times,* April 19, 1993, A1.

13. U.S. Congress, *Employment and Training Policy, 1982: Joint Hearings before the Subcommittee on Employment and Productivity of the Committee on Labor and Human Resources, United States Senate, and the Subcommittee on Employment Opportunities of the Committee on Education and Labor, United State House of Representatives, Part 2,* 97th Congress, 2nd session, March 17–18, 1982, 1016. (Hereafter referred to as U.S. Congress, *Employment and Training Policy, 1982, Part 2.*)

14. *Personal Responsibility and Work Opportunity Reconciliation Act of 1996,* U.S. Public Law 104–193, 104th Congress, 2nd session (August 22, 1996).

15. Myron Magnet, editor of the Manhattan Institute's *City Journal,* quoted in "Talk of the Nation: Welfare Reform in the U.S.," National Public Radio, May 7, 2001.

16. See Lawrence Mishel, Jared Bernstein, and John Schmitt, *The State of Working America, 2000/2001* (Ithaca: Cornell University Press, 2001) for the most comprehensive overview of labor market trends during this period.

17. Elizabeth Kolbert and Adam Clyber, "The Politics of Layoffs: In Search of a Message," *New York Times,* March 8, 1996, 1. In response to these concerns, 47% of respondents—and 63% of those already suffering from layoffs—thought that the government should step in to do something about the layoff problem.

18. One of the many popular statements of this thesis can be found in management consultant William Bridges's *Job Shift: How to Prosper in a Workplace without Jobs* (New York: Addison-Wesley, 1994). Bridges urges laid-off workers to realize that "it's not that the president or his critics don't care what happens to us. It's not that the organizations that once asked for our loyalty, and grew because of our efforts, have double-crossed us. The fault does not lie with that dreaded monster 'overseas competition'" (vii). Instead, Bridges advises that "your security will come first and foremost from . . . having the abilities and attitudes that an employer needs at the moment. . . . What you will need . . . is the ability to bend and not break, to let go readily of the outdated and learn the new . . . to live with high levels of uncertainty, and to find your security from within rather than from outside" (56).

Chapter One

1. *Weekly Compilation of Presidential Documents* 18 (October 4, 1982): 1250.

2. Remarks at the National Urban League Conference, *Weekly Compilation of Presidential Documents* 25 (August 8, 1989): 1222.

3. U.S. Department of Labor, Bureau of Labor Statistics, "Employment Status of the Civilian Noninstitutional Population, 1938 to Date," http://www.bls.gov; U.S. Department of Commerce, Census Bureau, "Poverty Status of Persons, by Family Relationship, Race and Hispanic Origin: 1959 to 1999," http://www.census.gov.

4. In the 1982 hearings leading to the adoption of the Job Training Partnership Act, when Assistant Secretary of Labor Albert Angrisani was asked how a recession economy could possibly absorb a large infusion of newly trained workers, he insisted that "the jobs are out there, and

it is a point of matching the people up with the skills in demand." U.S. Congress, *Employment and Training Policy, 1982, Part 1,* 33.

5. Sar Levitan, Frank Gallo, and Isaac Shapiro, *Working but Poor: America's Contradiction* (Baltimore: Johns Hopkins University Press, 1993), 94; Donald Baumer and Carl Van Horn, *The Politics of Unemployment* (Washington, D.C.: Congressional Quarterly Press, 1985), 19.

6. Remarks and Questions and Answers during a Teleconference with the U.S. Chamber of Commerce and the National Alliance of Business, *Weekly Compilation of Presidential Documents* 18 (December 19, 1982).

7. The most prominent of these arguments is in William Johnston and Arnold Packer, *Workforce 2000: Work and Workers for the 21st Century* (Indianapolis: Hudson Institute, 1987).

8. "A Maddening Labor Mismatch," *Time*, April 28, 1986, 48.

9. "The Miseries of Full Employment," *Economist*, August 27, 1988, 20.

10. Johnston and Packer, *Workforce 2000*, 116.

11. Gail DeGeorge, "Sign of the Times: Help Wanted," *Business Week*, November 10, 1997, 60–61.

12. Quoted in James Lardner, "Too Old to Write Code?" *U.S. News and World Report*, March 16, 1998, 39. The high-tech industry succeeded in increasing the number of visas provided for technology workers. However, there is reason to believe that there is no real shortage of programmers. Rather, employers appear to be eschewing older, more experienced, and more expensive software engineers in favor of foreign workers who can be paid lower salaries. The most comprehensive evidence on this issue is provided by Norman Matloff, "Debunking the Myth of a Desperate Software Labor Shortage," Testimony before the House Judiciary Committee, Subcommittee on Immigration, April 21, 1998. A complete version of this testimony can be found at http://heather.cs.ucdavis.edu/itaa.real.pdf.

13. Elaine Chao, Statement before the Senate Committee on Health, Education, Labor and Pensions, January 24, 2001. U.S. Department of Labor, http://labor.senate.gov/107hearings/jan2001/012401wt/chao.pdf.

14. Elaine Chao, Statement before the Senate Committee on Appropriations, Subcommittee on Labor, Health and Human Services, and Education, May 2, 2001, U.S. Department of Labor, http://www.dol.gov/_sec/media/congress/010502ec.htm; Chao, Statement before the Senate Committee, January 24, 2001.

15. Job growth from 1997 to 2000 averaged approximately 1.5% per year. U.S. Department of Labor, Bureau of Labor Statistics, "Employment Status of the Civilian Noninstitutional Population, 1938 to Date."

16. Katharine Abraham, "Structural/Frictional vs. Deficient Demand Unemployment: Some New Evidence," *American Economic Review* 73, no. 4 (September 1983): 708–24. Abraham plotted a best-fit regression equation drawing on the data from all six studies.

17. Harry Holzer, *Unemployment, Vacancies, and Local Labor Markets* (Kalamazoo, Mich.: W. E. Upjohn Institute for Employment Research, 1989). Holzer reports similarly low vacancy rates in his "Job Vacancy Rates in the Firm: An Empirical Analysis," *Economica* 61 (1994): 17–36.

18. U.S. Senate, *Senate Report 97-469: Report Accompanying S-2036, the Training for Jobs Act*, Committee on Labor and Human Resources, 97th Congress, 2nd session (June 9, 1982), 1.

19. *Personal Responsibility and Work Opportunity Reconciliation Act of 1996*, U.S. Public Law 104-193, 104th Congress, 1st session (August 22, 1996).

20. Paul Kleppner and Nikolas Theodore, "Work after Welfare: Is the Midwest's Booming Economy Creating Enough Jobs?" Midwest Job Gap Project, Chicago, Ill., 1997. The authors create their own basic budget to define a "livable wage"; in 1997, this budget was $25,907 for a family of three.

21. "Implementing Welfare Reform in America's Cities: A Survey, United States Conference of Mayors," Washington, D.C., November 1997, 3. The survey was sent to the thirty-four cities that make up the conference's Welfare-to-Work Task Force. Only thirteen of these cities were able to provide data on job supply; of these, twelve reported insufficient jobs.

22. On the economic status of those who left welfare for work in the late 1990s, see Jared Bernstein and Mark Greenberg, "Reforming Welfare Reform," *American Prospect* 12, no. 1 (January 2001), and chapter 6 of this book.

23. There are myriad statements by both policy analysts and elected officials disputing the notion of a job shortage. However, the evidence marshaled for these arguments is generally restricted to trends in the unemployment rate or anecdotes about employers' hiring experience. There is no statistical study of the labor market that purports to document the availability of decently paying jobs for all who need them. One of the clearest articulations of the argument asserting a sufficient supply of job openings is that of Lawrence Mead, in *The New Politics of Poverty: The Nonworking Poor in America* (New York: Basic Books, 1992). Mead presents no vacancy surveys, projections of labor demand, or any other direct statistical measure to substantiate his argument. One of his central claims is that the large number of undocumented immigrants who secure employment in the United States indicates that jobs are available for American citizens as well, if only they were willing to take "dirty work" at low wages. Apart from the fact that there is no obvious statistical correlation between the number of undocumented immigrants employed and the number of jobs needed for the nonimmigrant poor, undocumented workers often make ends meet through conditions which are either unavailable to American workers or prohibited for good reason. A large share of undocumented immigrants are single adults who come to the United States alone and (even if they send money home) are not burdened by the need to support a family at U.S. prices. Many live in hostels where rooms are shared by up to twenty workers rotating sleep shifts. Many earn subminimum wages, are cheated of overtime pay, and are subject to disciplinary and safety conditions prohibited by U.S. law. It is largely this superexploitability of immigrants which makes them attractive to employers. Indeed, rather than Americans' refusing to take the jobs performed by immigrants, it is often employers who institute a policy of hiring only undocumented workers, barring American applicants from consideration. For one such example see Alec Wilkinson, *Big Sugar: Seasons in the Cane Fields of Florida* (New York: Vintage, 1990). I have not reviewed Mead's or similar arguments in this book because, while his assertions may have considerable rhetorical sway, he does not present a body of relevant empirical evidence.

24. For the history of how the official poverty line was developed, see Gordon Fisher, "The Development and History of the Poverty Thresholds," *Social Security Bulletin* 55, no. 4 (winter 1992): 3–14.

25. The one-third ratio was derived from U.S. Department of Agriculture, Agricultural Research Service, *Household Food Consumption Survey 1955* (Washington, D.C.: U.S. Government Printing Office, 1956).

26. Fisher, "Development and History."

27. John Schwarz and Thomas Volgy, *The Forgotten Americans* (New York: Norton, 1992), 34.

28. Mollie Orshansky, "Counting the Poor: Another Look at the Poverty Profile," *Social Security Bulletin* 28, no. 1 (January 1965): 6.

29. Levitan, Gallo, and Shapiro, *Working but Poor*, 5.

30. Betty Peterkin and Faye Clark, "Money Value and Adequacy of Diets Compared with the USDA Food Plans," *Family Economics Review* (September 1969): 6–8.

31. Joseph Pechman, *Who Paid the Taxes, 1966–85?* (Washington, D.C.: Brookings Institution, 1985).

32. The 46% figure is for 1901, reported in Eva Jacobs and Stephanie Shipp, "How Family Spending Has Changed in the U.S.," *Monthly Labor Review* 113, no. 3 (March 1990): 21. The 1996 food share is from the U.S. Department of Labor, Bureau of Labor Statistics, *Consumer Price Index Detailed Report* (Washington, D.C.: U.S. Government Printing Office, January 1997), table 1.

33. Jacobs and Shipp, "How Family Spending Has Changed," 25, report that by 1986–87, the average family spent as much to operate and maintain a car as it did for food at home. In 1950, auto-related expenses were only 20% of the food bill.

34. Denton Vaughan, "Exploring the Use of the Public's Views to Set Income Poverty Thresholds and Adjust Them over Time," *Social Security Bulletin* 56, no. 2 (summer 1993).

35. The Thrifty Food Plan (formerly the Economy Food Plan) is the family budget used to determine eligibility for food stamps.

36. Mollie Orshansky and Carol Fendler, "Improving the Poverty Definition," in *1979 Proceedings of the Social Statistics Section of the American Statistical Association* (Washington, D.C.: American Statistical Association, 1980), 640–45. The one difference between Orshansky's original methodology and that used here is that Orshansky calculated the food share of average family budgets based on the Household Food Consumption Survey (HFCS), while I have used the Consumer Price Index (CPI). The two data sources differ slightly, but the CPI is updated annually and the HFCS only once a decade.

37. Schwarz and Volgy, *Forgotten Americans*, 43.

38. For a comprehensive survey of methodological shortfalls in the current poverty thresholds and alternative thresholds developed to compensate for these, see Patricia Ruggles's *Drawing the Line: Alternative Poverty Measures and Their Implications for Public Policy* (Washington, D.C.: Urban Institute Press, 1990) and Constance Citro and Robert Michael, eds., *Measuring Poverty: A New Approach* (Washington, D.C.: National Academy Press, 1995). The Citro and Michael study was commissioned by the U.S. Congress and performed by the National Research Council, and it represents the best chance to form an intellectual and political consensus in support of a new poverty measure. However, I do not believe the method proposed by the NRC is appropriate for the purposes of this discussion, for two reasons. First, the NRC includes public assistance in its measure of family incomes, so that people are not counted as poor if the provision of food stamps, heating assistance, or cash welfare raises them above the poverty threshold. This is a legitimate methodology, but it measures something different from what I am studying here: whether job training enables people to earn their way out of poverty through paid employment. For this purpose, it is important to know how many people are unable to support themselves through the labor market—*before* receiving any form of government support.

Second, the NRC's methodology removes several major categories of expenditure from the calculation of family needs—including health care, child care, and work-related transportation. All of these expenditures are instead accounted for by deducting the actual amount families spend on them from their total income. Instead of estimating how much income a family needs to obtain acceptable medical care, for instance, the NRC simply deducts their actual spending on health care from their income, treating this as a work-related expense. There are important pluses to this methodology—most important, it allows researchers and policy makers to identify the additional expenses faced by people who leave public assistance for work. However, the methodology has an obvious problem: by simply recording the amount that poor families actually do spend, it understates the amount they *should* be spending in order to obtain adequate care. The NRC recognizes this problem and calls for the creation of a separate index of "medical care risk" for those who cannot afford adequate health care. But this solution—essentially an off-the-books accounting which leaves poverty thresholds artificially low—does not change the fact that the NRC thresholds fail to capture the full range of family needs.

For these reasons, I have used the Original Orshansky method rather than the NRC thresholds. Still, while the NRC's thresholds are not directly comparable to those developed by more traditional methodologies, they point roughly in the same direction as earlier studies. The NRC estimates that its thresholds are slightly higher than those developed by Trudi Renwick and Barbara Bergmann, "A Budget-Based Definition of Poverty: With an Application to Single-Parent Families," *Journal of Human Resources* 28, no. 1 (1992): 1–24, and within the same range as those developed by Schwarz and Volgy, *Forgotten Americans*. The Original Orshansky thresholds are slightly but not dramatically higher than either of these. If the NRC threshold were revised so as to take full account of health care, child care, and transportation needs, it would identify a cutoff even closer to the thresholds presented here.

39. See appendix A for a more detailed description of this methodology.

40. Abraham, "Structural/Frictional," 713. John Schwarz, *Illusions of Opportunity: The American Dream in Question* (New York: Norton, 1997). Schwarz attempts to create a national vacancy statistic out of Abraham's report on the Florida and Texas pilot surveys. Unfortunately, it is simply impossible to extrapolate from such limited data. Schwarz is required to treat findings from two states in 1979–80 as representative of national trends over a twenty-year period. In addition, he is forced to provide estimates—based solely on his own imagination, with no supporting data whatsoever—for several of the key ingredients in his calculations, including the unemployment/vacancy ratio at various unemployment rates; the duration of discouraged vacancies; the share of discouraged vacancies that are full-time, year round jobs; the number of untapped opportunities for self-employment; and the success rate of newly self-employed entrepreneurs. Since several of these estimates are multiplied together in the process of his calculations, the uncertainty of the final result is compounded. Indeed, Schwarz's results appear to be eccentric: while regular employees account for nearly 90% of total U.S. employment, and self-employed workers only 11%, Schwarz projects that self-employment will account for fully five-sixths of all opportunities for living-wage jobs.

41. Abraham estimates that at unemployment rates of 5%, the unemployment/vacancy ratio ranges between 3:1 and 4:1, increasing as the unemployment rate rises. In 1996, the unemployment rate was 5.4%, and I have assumed an unemployment/vacancy ratio of 3.5:1. While Abraham's data focused on the average number of vacancies available at any one time, my calculation estimates the total number of vacancies over the course of the year. This assumes that the relationship between average and total vacancies is the same as that between average and total unemployment, an untested hypothesis. Thus this calculation yields a very rough approximation, but I believe it is useful as a ballpark estimate. In 1996, 16.8 million people were unemployed at some point during the year. Applying a ratio of 3.5, this yields 4.8 million vacancies for the year. Three percent of this figure is 144,000; six percent is 288,000. 288,000 is 1.1% of 25.9 million. If we consider only those people below the official poverty thresholds, 288,000 is 2% of the 14.4 million jobs needed. The number of people ever unemployed in the year is reported in "Work Experience of the Population in 1996," U.S. Department of Labor, Bureau of Labor Statistics, News Release USDOL 97-389, November 10, 1997.

42. *Employment and Earnings*, various issues. For 1997 to 2000 growth averaged 1.5% per year.

43. This methodology was used for every year except 1990–91, as explained in appendix A.

44. U.S. Department of Labor, Bureau of Labor Statistics, *Employment Projections 1996–2006* (Washington, D.C.: U.S. Department of Labor, Bureau of Labor Statistics, 1997), table 2: Employment by Major Industry Division, 1986, 1996, and projected 2006, http://www.bls.gov/emp/. The 1996 to 2006 growth rate represents a significant slowdown from the previous ten-year period, during which employment grew by 1.7% per year.

45. Johnston and Packer, *Workforce 2000*, xv–xvi. More recent projections are even less promising. In the Hudson Institute's updated study *Workforce 2020* (Indianapolis: Hudson Institute, 1997), 97, the most optimistic forecast projects 1995 to 2020 employment growth of only 1.3% per year.

46. Actual employment growth is subtracted from 4.6% to estimate the number of possible discouraged vacancies in any given year. This method yields a conservative upper boundary on excess demand for each individual year; however, it cannot be used for trend analysis. In years when actual employment growth is larger, the gap between this number and 4.6% is smaller, and therefore the estimate of potential discouraged vacancies is smaller. In this sense, reading the data as trends over time may yield counterintuitive results: for any given population in need, the number of discouraged vacancies will appear smaller, and the job gap larger, in years of high economic growth than in slow times. An analysis of historical trends in discouraged vacancies would require the type of firm-based data not yet available.

47. Abraham, "Structural/Frictional," 713.

48. This estimate remains considerably below that of Kleppner and Theodore, "Work after Welfare," who report that low-skill job seekers outnumber "living-wage," low-skill jobs by a ratio of 97:1.

49. Lawrence Mishel, Jared Bernstein, and John Schmitt, *The State of Working America, 1998–99* (Ithaca: Cornell University Press, 1999), 308, report that in 1996 there were roughly 2 million Americans whose wages were so low as to leave them below the official poverty line despite working full-time and year-round.

50. U.S. House of Representatives, *House Report 97-537: Report of the Committee on Education and Labor Accompanying HR 5320, the Job Training Partnership Act*, 97th Congress, 2nd session (May 17, 1982), 39.

51. U.S. Senate, *Senate Report 97-469*, 5, 31.

52. *The Job Training Parternership Act*, Public Law 97-300, 97th Congress, 2nd session (October 13, 1982). (Hereafter cited as Public Law 97-300.)

53. The Department of Labor has established "America's Job Bank," a feature on its web site which allows employers to post job openings and job seekers to post their résumés. However, use of the site is entirely voluntary; thus the jobs listed represent a small, random, and self-selected set of openings. There is no attempt to systematically match openings with workers, and information on the site is not used by DOL for statistical or planning purposes. Rick Clayton, Chief of the Division of Occupational and Administrative Statistics, Bureau of Labor Statistics, communication with the author, November 13, 1998.

54. Chao, Statement before the Senate Committee, January 24, 2001.

55. President's Committee to Appraise Employment and Unemployment Statistics, *Measuring Employment and Unemployment* (Washington, D.C.: U.S. Government Printing Office, 1962), 199, cited in Harry Frumerman, *Job Vacancy Statistics in the United States* (Washington, D.C.: National Commission on Employment and Unemployment Statistics, 1978), 4.

56. Richard Devens, *Employee Turnover and Job Openings Survey: Results of a Pilot Study on the Feasibility of Collecting Measures of Imbalances of Supply and Demand for Labor in an Establishment Survey* (Washington, D.C.: U.S. Department of Labor, Bureau of Labor Statistics, 1991).

57. Commissioner of Labor Statistics Katherine Abraham, communication with the author, November 17, 1998. The Job Openings and Labor Turnover Survey (JOLTS) was expected to produce its first data in 2001. The survey will produce a single vacancy statistic for the nation as a whole, with detail for several broad industrial groups and four geographic regions. Abraham reports that the Employment and Training Administration expressed interest in occupational vacancy data but did not press this interest as a legislative priority. The commissioner was not aware of any contact whatsoever from the Department of Health and Human Services officials overseeing the federal welfare program, Temporary Aid to Needy Families (TANF).

58. Gordon Fisher, "The Development of the Orshansky Poverty Thresholds and Their Subsequent History as the Official U.S. Poverty Measure," unpublished, 1992.

59. Michael Yates, *Longer Hours, Fewer Jobs: Employment and Unemployment in the United States* (New York: Monthly Review Press, 1994), 56–60.

60. The National Academy of Sciences estimated that 8.4 million Americans were missed by the 1990 census and recommended the use of sampling to correct for this undercount. Republican legislators mounted a vigorous campaign against this recommendation, including filing a federal lawsuit and mandating funding cuts designed to prevent the Census Bureau from staffing a sampling effort. Steven Holmes, "House Votes to Finance Census Work for 6 Months," *New York Times*, August 6, 1998, A16.

61. U.S. Congress, *Employment and Training Policy, 1982, Part 1*, 29.

62. Harrison Donnelly, "House Democrats Press $1 Billion Jobs Plan," *Congressional Quarterly Weekly Reporter* 40, no. 35 (August 28, 1982): 2125.

Chapter Two

1. From promotional comment on back cover of Ray Marshall and Marc Tucker, *Thinking for a Living: Education and the Wealth of Nations* (New York: Basic Books, 1992).

2. Secretary's Commission on Achieving Necessary Skills (SCANS), *What Work Requires of Schools* (Washington, D.C.: U.S. Department of Labor, 1991), v.

3. "Remarks by the President at Summit on the Twenty-first Century Workforce," June 20, 2001, news release, White House, Office of the Press Secretary, http://www.whitehouse.gov.

4. Lawrence Mishel, Jared Bernstein, and John Schmitt, *The State of Working America, 2000/2001* (Ithaca: Cornell University Press, 2001), table 2.4, 120. Real hourly average earnings for production and nonsupervisory workers, in constant 1999 dollars, fell from $13.91 to $13.24 from 1973 to 1999. Production and nonsupervisory workers account for more than 80% of all wage and salary employees.

5. Lawrence Mishel, Jared Bernstein, and John Schmitt, *State of Working America, 1998–99* (Ithaca: Cornell University Press, 1999), table 2.6, 124.

6. Mishel, Bernstein, and Schmitt, *State of Working America, 2000/2001*, 33–35, 95–107.

7. Ibid., 130.

8. National Priorities Project, *Working Hard, Earning Less: The Story of Job Growth in America* (Northampton, Mass., 1999), 2. The cutoff is $16,000 per year, slightly below the official federal poverty line for a family of four.

9. Average hourly wages in 1999 were $20.58 for those with college degrees and $11.83 for high school graduates. Mishel, Bernstein, and Schmitt, *State of Working America, 2000/2001*, table 2.18, 153.

10. "About 1 in 6 college graduates earns less than high school graduates," editor's commentary, *Monthly Labor Review* 121, no. 10 (October 1998).

11. Lawrence Mishel and Ruy A. Teixeira, *The Myth of the Coming Labor Shortage: Jobs, Skills, and Incomes of America's Workforce 2000* (Washington, D.C.: Economic Policy Institute, 1991); David Howell, Ellen Houston, and William Milberg, "Demand Shifts and Earnings Inequality: Wage and Hours Growth by Occupation in the U.S., 1970–97," CEPA Working Paper No. 6, Center for Economic Policy Analysis, New York, N.Y., 1999.

12. Gary Becker, *Human Capital: A Theoretical and Empirical Analysis, with Special Reference to Education*, 2nd ed. (New York: Columbia University Press, 1975).

13. For an analysis of the blind spots in neoclassical theory that have perpetuated the focus on education, see Richard Edwards, "Individual Traits and Organizational Incentives: What

Makes a 'Good' Worker?" *Journal of Human Resources* 11, no. 1 (1976): 51–68; and David Howell, Margaret Duncan, and Bennett Harrison, "Low Wages in the U.S. and High Unemployment in Europe: A Critical Assessment of the Conventional Wisdom," CEPA Working Paper No. 5, Center for Economic Policy Analysis, New York, N.Y., 1999.

14. Lynn Karoly, *The Trend in Inequality among Families, Individuals, and Workers in the United States: A Twenty-five Year Perspective* (Santa Monica: Rand Corporation, 1992); and "Anatomy of the U.S. Income Distribution: Two Decades of Change," *Oxford Review of Economic Policy* 12, no. 1 (1996): 77–96.

15. These results are consonant with the findings of several other studies. See Chinhui Juhn, Kevin Murphy, and Brooks Pierce, "Wage Inequality and the Rise in Returns to Skill," *Journal of Political Economy* 101, no. 3 (1993): 410–42; Frank Levy and Richard Murnane, "U.S. Earnings Levels and Earnings Inequality: A Review of Recent Trends and Proposed Explanations," *Journal of Economic Literature* 30 (September 1992): 1333–81; and Lawrence Katz and Kevin Murphy, "Changes in Relative Wages, 1963–87: Supply and Demand Factors," *Quarterly Journal of Economics* 107, no. 1 (February 1992): 35–78.

16. Karoly, *Trend in Inequality,* 1996. Mishel, Bernstein, and Schmitt, *State of Working America, 2000/2001,* 160–63, suggest that changes in within-group inequality account for slightly more than half the growth in overall income inequality between 1979 and 1999. This figure is lower than Karoly's in part because it defines similar groups not only by education and experience but also by race, ethnicity, marital status, and geographic region. Separating out these factors understates the amount of wage inequality among workers with similar education and experience.

17. See James Medoff and Katharine Abraham, "Are Those Paid More Really More Productive? The Case of Experience," *Journal of Human Resources* 16, no. 2 (1981): 186–216.

18. In the section that follows, I discuss a variety of sources, many of which predate Karoly or do not directly respond to her data. I do not intend to imply that the mismatch literature has either consciously or chronologically been written specifically as a response to Karoly. I believe it is conceptually useful, however, to analyze these sources as challenges to the seemingly decisive findings of Karoly's study.

19. For instance, this is the contention of the National Commission on Excellence in Education, *A Nation at Risk: The Imperative for Educational Reform: A Report to the Nation and the Secretary of Education* (Washington, D.C.: U.S. Department of Education, 1983).

20. For one review of the literature on alternative definitions of education and skill, see Levy and Murnane, "U.S. Earnings Levels."

21. National Commission on Excellence in Education, *A Nation at Risk,* 5.

22. Sandia Laboratories, "Perspectives on Education in America," *Journal of Educational Research* 86, no. 5 (1993): 259–310.

23. Kevin Murphy and Finis Welch, "Occupational Change and the Demand for Skill, 1940–1990," *American Economic Review* 38, no. 2 (1993): 122.

24. Sandia Laboratories, "Perspectives," 263.

25. Data for 1979 are from Gary Burtless, "Employment Prospects of Welfare Recipients," in *The Work Alternative: Welfare Reform and the Realities of the Job Market,* ed. Demetra Smith Nightingale and Robert Haveman (Washington, D.C.: Urban Institute Press, 1995). Gary Burtless, "Can the Labor Market Absorb Three Million Welfare Recipients?" *Focus* 19, no. 3 (summer–fall 1998), estimated a 60% rate in 1994. Pamela Loprest, "Families Who Left Welfare: Who Are They and How Are They Doing?" Urban Institute, Washington, D.C., 1999, estimated that 70% of recipients in 1995 through 1997 had a high school diploma or GED. U.S. General Accounting Office, *Welfare Reform: Moving Hard-to-Employ Recipients into the Workforce,* Report GAO-01-368 (Washington, D.C.: U.S. General Accounting Office, March 2001), 3, estimates that 55% to 70% of remaining TANF recipients in 1997 through 1999 had a high school diploma or GED.

26. Reading and math scores are reported in U.S. Department of Education, *Digest of Education Statistics 2000*, tables 113 and 123, http://nces.ed.gov. For trends over the 1970s and 1980s, see David Howell, "The Skills Myth," *American Prospect* 18 (summer 1994): 84. Sandia Laboratories, "Perspectives," 1993, reports that average SAT scores for the country as a whole fell by 5% between 1970 and 1990 but that this was strictly due to increased diversity in the pool of test-takers. Average scores for white, black, Asian American, Mexican American, American Indian, and Puerto Rican students all improved over the 1980s and 1990s. Gerald Bracey, *The Truth about America's Schools: The Bracey Reports, 1991–1997* (Bloomington: Phi Delta Kappan Educational Foundation, 1997), 216; U.S. Department of Education, *Digest of Education Statistics, 2000*, table 133.

A number of scholars have also looked beyond achievement tests to examine the trends in income inequality as they have affected different age groups. In general, a declining quality of education should lead to greater income inequality, since skilled workers become rarer and their wages are bid up more dramatically. Thus if school quality deteriorated in the past two decades, we would expect to see income inequality growing faster among workers educated in this period than among older workers. Every study to address this question has reached the same conclusion: inequality has risen equally among older workers and younger workers, and therefore no evidence exists for a deterioration in standards of worker education, however they are measured. See Juhn, Murphy, and Pierce, "Wage Inequality"; Gary Burtless, "The Payoff to Education in the Labor Market," in *Workers and Their Wages: Changing Patterns in the United States*, ed. Marvin Kosters (Washington, D.C.: American Enterprise Institute Press, 1991); and Frank Levy and Richard Murnane, "Skills, Demography, and the Economy: Is There a Mismatch?" in *Labor Markets, Employment Policy, and Job Creation*, ed. Lewis Solomon and Alec Levenson (Boulder: Westview, 1994).

27. Johnston and Packer, *Workforce 2000*, 95.

28. Briefly, the report's authors use an eccentric methodology for measuring "net" new entrants: they divide the population into gender, racial, and ethnic groups, measure the total number of each group which are either leaving or entering the labor force over the fifteen-year period, and then count the excess of entrants over leavers in each group as "net" entrants. Since white men are the largest single group of workers, and thus provide the greatest number of workers retiring in this period, a tremendous number of new white men must enter the labor market before the authors of *Workforce 2000* count a single "net" new entrant. By contrast, since women, blacks, and Latinos constitute a smaller share of the workforce and of retirees, even modest numbers of new workers will be counted as a significant influx of "net" entrants. This methodology leads to a dramatic distortion in the commonsense measure of labor force entrants. This analysis is provided in Mishel and Teixeira, *Myth*, 32.

29. Mishel and Teixeira, *Myth*, 32.

30. Richard Judy and Carol D'Amico, *Workforce 2020: Work and Workers in the 21st Century* (Indianapolis: Hudson Institute, 1997), 110, 87. The specter of a future labor force "dominated" by undereducated women and minorities was one of the most striking arguments of *Workforce 2000*, but it was not based in fact. The new report completely backtracks on this earlier suggestion and does its best to explain away the disavowal of what had earlier been a central claim: "Our emphasis on the gradual pace of workforce diversification may seem to contradict the widely reported finding of *Workforce 2000* that the proportion of women and minorities in the workforce would rise dramatically. In fact, there is no contradiction: those who thought that *Workforce 2000* predicted rapid diversification simply misunderstood its message."

31. U.S. Senate, Committee on Labor and Human Resources, *Senate Report 97–469: Report Accompanying S-2036, the Training for Jobs Act*, 97th Congress, 2nd session, June 9, 1982, 5, 31.

32. Carol J. Kososki, director, South Carolina Occupational Information Coordinating Committee, Testimony in U.S. Congress, *Employment and Training Policy, 1982, Part 1*, 713. Similarly, in U.S. Congress, *Employment and Training Policy, Part 2*, 568, Lloyd Hand, representing the

Business Roundtable, testified that "there is a large and growing shortage of sufficiently skilled workers in key technological occupations and professions."

33. Arlene Johnson and Fabian Linden, *Availability of a Quality Work Force* (New York: Conference Board, 1992).

34. Matloff, "Debunking the Myth of a Desperate Software Labor Shortage," Testimony before the House Judiciary Committee, Subcommittee on Immigration, April 21, 1998. A complete version of this testimony can be found at http://heather.cs.ucdavis.edu/itaa.real.pdf. Matloff, a professor of computer science at the University of California, Davis, reports that there is a 17% unemployment rate for programmers over age fifty and that only 19% of computer science graduates remain in the field twenty years after graduation, compared with 52% of civil engineers. He traces these problems to industry efforts to maintain a low-wage, high-burnout staff of recent college graduates and insecure foreign workers. See also James Lardner, "Too Old to Write Code?" *U.S. News and World Report*, March 16, 1998, 39–45.

35. Author's calculations based on data from Bureau of Labor Statistics, Occupational and Projections Data, 1986 edition, Bulletin 2251 (Washington, D.C.: U.S. Department of Labor, 1986), table B-1; and George Silvestri, "Occupational Employment Projections to 2006," *Monthly Labor Review* 120, no. 11 (November 1997): table 2. One of the primary claims put forward in *Workforce 2000* was that occupations with the highest educational requirements were also growing the fastest: "natural scientists and lawyers, for example, whose average skill requirements are the highest rated . . . are also the two fastest-growing occupations" (99). This argument involves a methodological sleight-of-hand, playing off a confusion between *fastest-growing* and *largest-growing* occupations. Occupations which are relatively small to begin with can grow by large percentages without adding a significant number of new workers to the labor force as a whole. While it was true that professional occupations were growing rapidly, the implication that these occupations dominated overall job growth was utterly false.

36. Alan Krueger, "How Computers Have Changed the Wage Structure: Evidence from Microdata, 1984–89," *Quarterly Journal of Economics* 108, no. 1 (1991): 33–60.

37. John DiNardo and Jorn-Steffen Pischke, "The Returns to Computer Use Revisited: Have Pencils Changed the Wage Structure Too?" Working Paper 5686, National Bureau of Economic Research, Cambridge, Mass., 1996.

38. Eli Berman, John Bound, and Zvi Griliches, "Changes in Demand for Skilled Labor within U.S. Manufacturing Industries: Evidence from the Annual Survey of Manufacturing," *Quarterly Journal of Economics* 109 (May 1994): 367–97; John Bound and George Johnson, "What Are the Causes of Rising Wage Inequality in the United States?" *Federal Reserve Bank of New York Economic Policy Review* 1 (January 1995): 9–17; Eli Berman, Stephen Machin, and John Bound, "Implications of Skill-Biased Technological Change: International Evidence," Working Paper 6166, National Bureau of Economic Research, Cambridge, Mass., 1996; George Johnson, "Changes in Earnings Inequality: The Role of Demand Shifts," *Journal of Economic Perspectives* 11, no. 2 (1997): 41–54.

39. Johnston and Packer, *Workforce 2000*, 103.

40. Jeffrey Keefe, "Numerically Controlled Machine Tools and Worker Skills," *Industrial and Labor Relations Review* 44, no. 3 (1991): 509–19.

41. Traer Sunley, assistant director of health and welfare for the State of California, Testimony on behalf of Governor Edmund G. Brown, Jr., in U.S. Congress, *Employment and Training Policy, 1982, Part 1*, 725.

42. Associate Professor Ray Shackelford, Department of Industrial Education and Technology, Ball State University, Muncie, Indiana, Testimony in ibid., 330.

43. Similarly, Senator Kennedy's testimony listed "data processing" along with computer programmers, medical technicians, lab technicians, and electricians as among the emerging high-tech occupations, in ibid., 14.

44. This segmentation was not entirely dictated by the inherent nature of computer technology, but rather was at least partly designed as a cost-containment strategy by large corporations. One hint of the motive is reported by Barbara Garson, *The Electronic Sweatshop: How Computers Are Transforming the Office of the Future into the Factory of the Past* (New York: Simon and Schuster, 1988), 166, who records the comments of a 1977 AT&T systems analyst: "the work must be carefully organized in the programming department so that the great bulk of it can be done by $3.00 an hour clerks with virtually no training." For a similar, more recent analysis, see Joan Greenbaum, *Windows on the Workplace: Computers, Jobs and the Organization of Office Work in the Late Twentieth Century* (New York: Monthly Review Press, 1995).

45. For instance, Bound and Johnson, "What Are the Causes," 13–14, concede that "the obvious problem with this view is that evidence in favor of it is largely circumstantial; it is very difficult to claim to have found a 'smoking gun' in what is essentially an argument involving residuals." For thorough critiques of the technologically based mismatch argument, see David Gordon, *Fat and Mean: The Corporate Squeeze of Working Americans and the Myth of Managerial "Downsizing"* (New York: Free Press, 1996), chapter 7; Howell, Duncan, and Harrison, "Low Wages"; and James Galbraith, *Created Unequal: The Crisis in American Pay* (New York: Free Press, 1998), chapter 2.

46. Beyond the problems of assuming causes that are not apparent in the evidence, there are two general difficulties in positing computer usage as the critical unmeasured skill. First, wage inequality began rising in 1970, while computer usage only became widespread in the mid-1980s. Second, while computer use is most common among women and highly educated workers, inequality has increased most among men and less-educated workers. For these reasons, while computer technology may have affected wages in some occupations, it seems unable to explain the dramatic changes in income distribution witnessed over the past twenty-five years.

47. Author's calculations based on Mishel, Bernstein, and Schmitt, *State of Working America, 2000/2001*, table 2.18, 153.

48. Kevin Murphy and Finis Welch, "Inequality and Relative Wages," *American Economic Review* 38, no. 2 (1993): 104–9; Arnold Packer and John Wirt, "Changing Skills in the U.S. Work Force: Trends of Supply and Demand," in *Urban Labor Markets and Job Opportunity*, ed. George Peterson and Wayne Vroman (Washington, D.C.: Urban Institute Press, 1992); Katz and Murphy, "Changes"; Marvin Kosters, foreword and "Wages and Demographics," in *Workers and Their Wages*, ed. Kosters; Gary Burtless, "Introduction and Summary," in *A Future of Lousy Jobs? The Changing Structure of U.S. Wages*, ed. Gary Burtless (Washington, D.C.: Brookings Institution, 1990); McKinley Blackburn, David Bloom, and Richard Freeman, "The Declining Economic Position of Less Skilled American Men," in *A Future of Lousy Jobs?*

49. Packer and Wirt, "Changing Skills," 31–33.

50. Thomas A. Stewart, *Intellectual Capital: The New Wealth of Organizations* (New York: Doubleday, 1997), 45–46.

51. Richard Murnane, John Willett, and Frank Levy, "The Growing Importance of Cognitive Skills in Wage Determination," paper presented to Seminar on Inner City Poverty, Institute for Social and Policy Studies, Yale University, March 1993; Sue Berryman and Thomas Bailey, *The Double Helix of Education and the Economy* (New York: Institute on Education and the Economy, 1992); Kosters, "Wages and Demographics"; Blackburn, Bloom, and Freeman, "Declining Economic Position"; Commission on the Skills of the American Workforce, *America's Choice: High Skills or Low Wages!* (Rochester, N.Y.: National Center for Education and the Economy, 1990).

52. Daniel E. Hecker, "Reconciling Conflicting Data on Jobs for College Graduates," *Monthly Labor Review* 115, no. 7 (July 1992): 5. Though the premium in the late 1980s and 1990s was higher than at any time in its recorded history, there has been no explosion in employer demand for education, and the present demand for skilled labor is not qualitatively different from that of the past. The most careful interpretation of the premium data suggests a modest, long-term

increase in the employer demand for education coupled with more dramatic fluctuations in the supply of college graduates. Katz and Murphy, "Changes."

53. Murphy and Welch, "Occupational Change"; Juhn, Murphy, and Pierce, "Wage Inequality"; Blackburn, Bloom, and Freeman, "Declining Economic Position."

54. Quote is from Juhn, Murphy, and Pierce, "Wage Inequality," 441.

55. Packer and Wirt, "Changing Skills," 31–33.

56. Hecker, "Reconciling," 9–10.

57. Mishel, Bernstein, and Schmitt, State of Working America, 2000/2001, table 2.18, 153.

58. Author's calculations based on ibid., table 2.19, 155. On this point see also Peter Gottschalk, "Inequality, Income Growth, and Mobility: The Basic Facts," Journal of Economic Perspectives 11, no. 2 (spring 1997): 21–40.

59. Data from 1979 are reported in Hecker, "Reconciling," 7; 1999 figure is from U.S. Department of Commerce, Census Bureau, "Educational Attainment in the United States, March 2000 Update," table 9.

60. Hecker, "Reconciling," table 1. Mismatch advocates have proposed two contradictory explanations for the relatively large numbers of college graduates in jobs that don't require a B.A. Frederic Pryor and David Schaffer, "Wages and the University Educated: A Paradox Revealed," Monthly Labor Review 120, no. 7 (July 1997): 3–14, suggest that the problem lies in the graduates themselves—those B.A.'s who end up in "high school jobs" actually have lower "functional literacy" than others and therefore are unable to land traditional college jobs. However, the difference they report in "functional literacy" scores between those B.A.'s in college jobs and those in high school jobs is quite marginal and seems incapable of explaining the significant earnings gap between these two groups. Richard Murnane and Frank Levy, Teaching the New Basic Skills: Principles for Educating Children to Thrive in a Changing Economy (New York: Free Press, 1996), 38, argue that there's no problem either with the B.A.'s or with their jobs; they suggest that college graduates in high school jobs are not in "true" high school jobs but rather in "upgraded high school jobs like a[n insurance company] customer service representative," which have come to require the level of skills previously attained only by college graduates. Hecker's data on occupational distribution of college graduates, however, suggest that many of these workers are in traditional, nonupgraded jobs that require neither the degree nor the substance of a college education.

61. Chad Fleetwood and Kristina Shelley, "The Outlook for College Graduates, 1998–2008: A Balancing Act," Occupational Outlook Quarterly 44, no. 3 (fall 2000): 3–9.

62. Hecker, "Reconciling," 11.

63. Johnston and Packer, Workforce 2000, xxvii.

64. This point was first brought to my attention by Dean Baker of the Economic Policy Institute, in a letter to the editor titled "Who Is Protected?" New York Times, August 4, 1993, A18. A complementary finding is reported by Medoff and Abraham, "Are Those Paid More Really More Productive?" who show that seniority raises for managerial and professional employees are unrelated to productivity.

65. Fleetwood and Shelley, "Outlook," report the Bureau of Labor Statistics' estimate that 21.3% of all jobs required a college degree in 1998; the number is projected to rise to 23.8% by 2008. The highest estimate of college demand is provided by the Commission on the Skills of the American Workforce, America's Choice, 3, which projected that nearly 30% of jobs would require a college degree by the year 2000.

66. Johnston and Packer, Workforce 2000, 99–100. Similarly, liberal economists Richard Freeman and Peter Gottschalk, eds., Generating Jobs: How to Increase Demand for Less-Skilled Workers (New York: Russell Sage Publications, 1998) assert that "where willing workers with little education once found ready employment at reasonable wages, our computerized, service-economy demands workers who can read and write, master technology, deal with customers,

and much else. Improved education and training will alleviate this problem" (inside jacket of hardcover edition).

67. Stewart, *Intellectual Capital*, 41.

68. David Howell and Edward Wolff, "Trends in the Growth and Distribution of Skills in the U.S. Workplace, 1960–85," *Industrial and Labor Relations Review* 44, no. 3 (1991): 486–502; Howell, Houston, and Milberg, "Demand Shifts."

69. Howell and Wolff, "Trends," 488. The skill indices are combined into three broad measures: "cognitive skills—the level of cognitive (analytical reasoning) and diagnostic (synthetic reasoning) skills required; interactive skills—the relative authority, autonomy, and degree of responsibility (for people and things) required on the job; and motor skills—the various physical and manipulative requirements of work." Cognitive skills are measured by two means: the "general educational development" measure of the DOT, which combines math, language, and reasoning skills; and "substantive complexity," "a composite measure of skills derived from a factor analytic test of DOT variables."

70. Over the entire 1960 to 1985 period, the share of total employment in occupations with the highest substantive complexity rose from 20% to 28%, while that for the lowest-skilled occupations fell from 20% to 15%. Ibid., 497.

71. Similarly, while demand for interactive skills increased by 0.2% per year for professionals and managers, it increased by only 0.03% for nonsupervisory workers.

72. Howell, Houston, and Milberg, "Demand Shifts," 8. Education was measured according to the percentage of employees in each occupation who had attained at least a high school diploma. Occupations with more than 80% high school graduates were deemed "high skill," those between 50% and 79% "moderate skill," and those under 50% "low skill." Cognitive skill was measured by the substantive complexity measure of the DOT. Howell and Wolff's previous work raised questions as to whether the DOT was an accurate measure of job content, since its skill indices were established in 1967 to 1974 and thus may not capture the contemporary content of occupations. The 1999 study reports that 1989 revisions to the DOT skill indices produced measures in keeping with the earlier rankings. Finally, the 1999 study also used a combined average of prose literacy, document literacy, and quantitative literacy, provided for detailed occupations in the National Center for Educational Statistics's 1992 National Adult Literacy Survey.

73. Since there has been a significant growth in part-time and part-year employment, I believe actual annual earnings provide a more accurate measure of the wage–skill relationship than either the average hourly wage or the earnings of full-time, year-round workers alone. Trends over time are similar by all three measures. Measuring the growth in annual earnings as a percentage of the growth in substantive complexity, table 2.8 indicates that wages rose 47.8% as fast as skill requirements in the 1960s, 43.5% as fast in the 1970s, and only 7.1% as fast in the early 1980s. Table 2.9 shows a similar trend through the 1990s of *declining* importance of skills or education as a determinant of wages.

74. Levy and Murnane, "Skills," 366. Francisco Rivera-Batiz, "Quantitative Literacy and the Likelihood of Employment among Young Adults in the United States," *Journal of Human Resources* 27, no. 2 (1992): 313–28, finds a significant relationship between math scores and the likelihood of securing full-time work. Since his data cover the entire workforce, however, it is impossible to know how much of this result reflects the experiences of college-educated professionals or how much math proficiency would help nonsupervisory workers. Murnane, Willett, and Levy find a relationship between math scores and wages ("Growing Importance of Cognitive Skills in Wage Determination"). This may reflect a true contribution to wage inequality, but it is difficult to draw firm conclusions from these findings: the data include college graduates; they find significantly different math–wage relationships for men and women, suggesting other forces at work; and they are unable to explain why even those workers with high math scores

had falling wages over this period. In their 1994 study, "Skills, Demography, and the Economy," Levy and Murnane found that the relationship between math scores and wages was stronger in the 1980s than the 1970s; they suggest that this helps explain both the college premium and the increase in income inequality. However, they concede that this relationship accounts for only a small share of the wage trends over the period.

75. Levy and Murnane, "Skills," 1367.

76. Philip Moss and Chris Tilly, "'Soft' Skills and Race: An Investigation of Black Men's Employment Problems," *Work and Occupations* 23, no. 3 (August 1996): 252–76.

77. Peter Capelli, "Challenge: To Acknowledge the Role of Work-Related Behavioral Skills and Attitudes as both a Cause of and Remedy for the Skills Gap," *EQW Issues* 9 (1995).

78. Quoted in Jennifer Salopek, "Train Your Brain," *Training and Development* 52, no. 10 (October 1998): 29.

79. Levy and Murnane, "Skills," 1336.

80. Howell and Wolff, "Trends."

81. Commission on the Skills of the American Workforce, *America's Choice*, 27.

82. Ibid., 3.

83. Johnson and Linden, *Availability*.

84. Ibid., 15–17.

85. One exception to this pattern is the annual survey conducted by *Training* magazine. Beginning in 1991, *Training* has consistently reported that roughly 20% of the firms in its survey offer remedial skills training to their employees, suggesting that many employers face a pressing need for job applicants with basic reading and math abilities. There are several reasons to doubt the accuracy of these findings. The survey draws from a list restricted to companies of 100 employees or more—a highly unrepresentative slice of the employer universe which Sandia Laboratories dismissed as accounting for under 2% of all U.S. companies. In addition, the survey response rate has been in the range of 15% for most years, much lower than comparable surveys. Finally, the wording of the question posed to employers is vague and open to broad interpretation. It is unsurprising, then, that while the magazine reports 20% of firms offering remedial training, only 2.2% of respondents identify this as a "critical training challenge" facing their company. In 1989, the magazine reported that those firms that did offer remedial training spent an average of $200 per person on such tutoring; thus even where firms identify a need for remedial skills upgrading, the need appears to be modest. For all these reasons, and because the magazine's statistics are so far out of line with those of more scientifically rigorous surveys (*Training* itself concedes that the American Management Association's poll of member firms found only 3% offering remedial training), I have not reported these findings in the body of the chapter. The Training Industry Report is published annually in the magazine's October issue. See also Chris Lee, "The Three R's," *Training* 26, no. 10 (1989): 67–76.

86. Commission on the Skills of the American Workforce, *America's Choice*, 3.

87. New York City Department of Employment, "New York City Employer Survey: Summary Report," 1994.

88. National Center on the Educational Quality of the Workforce, *First Findings from the EQW National Employer Survey* (Philadelphia: University of Pennsylvania, 1995). The Employer Survey was conducted in 1994 and 1997 and found very consistent results.

89. Ibid., 4.

90. Business Coalition for Education Reform, "Making Academics Count," reported at http://www.bcer.org. The U.S. Department of Commerce, Census Bureau, "Establishment Births, Deaths, Expansions and Contractions by Industrial Division from 1995 to 1996," reports that there were just under 6 million corporate employers in 1996. As of May 2001, the BCER website listed 3,140 companies on the "Honor Roll" of employers who have pledged to "Make Academics Count."

91. National Center on the Educational Quality of the Workforce, *First Findings*, 11.

92. Overview of maquiladora employment statistics is provided in *Mexican Labor News and Analysis* 4, no. 9 (May 16, 1999), http://www.ueinternational.org/vol4no9.html.

93. Reported in Thomas Palley, *Plenty of Nothing: The Downsizing of the American Dream and the Case for Structural Keynesianism* (Princeton: Princeton University Press, 1998), 169.

94. Quote is from materials distributed at GE's Supplier Migration Conference, reported in "Labor Page Special Report: Free Trade Area of the Americas," Jobs with Justice, Jamaica Plain, Mass., March 2001. GE stated that it was aggressively seeking 20% price cuts from its suppliers and threatened to stop doing business with suppliers that remained in the United States. On this topic see also Aaron Bernstein, "Welch's March to the South: As GE Pressures Suppliers to Shift to Mexico, Unions Dig In," *Business Week*, December 6, 1999.

95. Approximately 60% of maquiladora employees are women, and the majority of these are teenagers or women in their early twenties. Mexican law allows girls to work from the age of sixteen, but it is common for girls aged twelve to fifteen to be hired with forged papers. These workers generally drop out of school in order to work, and no educational standards are required as a criterion of hiring. *Mexican Labor News and Analysis* 4, nos. 4, 5, and 9 (March–May, 1999).

96. Alfredo Araujo, Coordinación Nacional, Frente Auténtico del Trabajo, interview with author, June 1999; *Mexican Labor News and Analysis* 4, no. 9 (May 1999).

97. Miranda Ewell, "Silicon Valley Home Piecework to Be Probed," *San Jose Mercury News*, July 1, 1999. For more extensive background on this phenomenon, see Miranda Ewell and K. Oanh Ha, "High Tech's Hidden Labor," *San Jose Mercury News*, June 28, 1999.

98. Murnane and Levy, *Teaching the New Basic Skills*.

99. Peter Capelli and Maria Iannozzi note that at the top of their list of concerns, employers "most often cite as essential criteria basic work attitudes such as showing up on time, following instructions, and taking pride in a job's outcome." "Challenge: To Acknowledge the Role of Work-related Behavioral Skills and Attitudes as both a Cause of and Remedy for the Skills Gap," *EQW Issues* 9 (1995): 3.

100. Capelli, "Challenge," 3–4.

101. Quoted in Moss and Tilly, "'Soft' Skills," 259.

102. Robert Zemsky, "What Employers Want: Employer Perspectives on Youth, the Youth Labor Market, and Prospects for a National System of Youth Apprenticeships," EQW Working Paper, National Center for the Educational Quality of the Workforce, University of Pennsylvania, 1994, 10. Similarly, Peter Capelli, "Is the Skills Gap Really about Attitudes?" EQW Working Paper, National Center for the Educational Quality of the Workforce, University of Pennsylvania, 1992, 9, cites military boot camp as producing appropriate work attitudes in most participants.

103. Zemsky, "What Employers Want," 11.

104. TWA, AT&T, Honda, Microsoft, and Starbucks are among the prominent companies that have turned to prison labor for a cheap, disciplined workforce. For descriptions of the range of companies now using prison labor, see Daniel Burton-Rose, ed., *The Celling of America: An Inside Look at the U.S. Prison Industry* (Monroe, Maine: Common Courage, 1998); Eric Schlosser, "The Prison-Industrial Complex," *Atlantic Monthly* (December 1998); and Christian Parenti, *Lockdown America: Police and Prisons in the Age of Crisis* (New York: Verso, 1999).

105. Walter Dickey, quoted in Steven Elbow, "Doing Time, 9 to 5," *Isthmus*, September 8, 1995, 10.

106. UNICOR Annual Report 2000, http://www.unicor.gov/about/annuals.htm.

107. Bob Tessler, owner of DPAS, quoted in Christian Parenti, "Inside Jobs," *New Statesman and Society* 8, no. 377 (November 3, 1995): 20.

108. George Sexton, *Work in American Prisons: Joint Ventures with the Private Sector*, National Institute of Justice, U.S. Department of Justice, Washington, D.C., November 1995, 7.

109. Moss and Tilly, " 'Soft' Skills," 268.

110. In a major survey of corporate employers, the Conference Board concluded that "underlying employers' complaints about inadequate education and skills shortage, the real problem is often that employees lack a good work ethic, appropriate social behavior, or a positive view of authority." Johnson and Linden, *Availability*, 16. Yet it is telling that despite their frustration with the quality of entry-level applicants, only 12% of the employers surveyed said they planned to raise wages if they were unable to recruit qualified workers. Ibid.

111. On this point see Paul Attewell, "What Is Skill?" *Work and Occupations* 17, no. 4 (November 1990): 422–48.

112. Freeman and Gottschalk, eds., *Generating Jobs*, inside jacket of hardcover edition.

113. Mishel, Bernstein, and Schmitt, *State of Working America, 2000/2001*, tables 2.5, 2.6, 124–25.

114. Ibid., table 2.18, 156.

115. Ibid., table 2.4, 120.

116. Mishel, Bernstein, and Schmitt, ibid., 181, calculate that the union premium in 1997 (based on hourly wages) was $3.31, or 23.2%. Adding in insurance and pension benefits yielded a total union compensation premium of $6.20, or 35.9%.

117. Ibid., table 2.35, 181.

118. Richard Freeman, "How Much Has De-unionization Contributed to the Rise in Male Earnings Inequality?" Working Paper No. 3826, National Bureau of Economic Research, Cambridge, Mass., 1991, 11. Mishel, Bernstein, and Schmitt, *State of Working America, 2000/2001*, table 2.37, 184, find that deunionization accounts for 22.5% of the increase in the college premium for male workers from 1978 to 1997. The 2000 unionization rate is reported in U.S. Department of Labor, Bureau of Labor Statistics, "Union Members in 2000," January 2001.

119. David Card and Richard Freeman, "Small Differences That Matter: Canada vs. the United States," in *Working under Different Rules*, ed. Richard Freeman (New York: Russell Sage Foundation, 1994), 189–222.

120. Card and Freeman, "Small Differences," 210. Similarly, the Inter-University Consortium for Political and Social Research reports that in 1988–91, 36% of respondents indicated that they would vote for a union if given an opportunity in a secret ballot election. http://www.icpsr.umich.edu/gss.

121. AFL-CIO, "Voice at Work: The Freedom to Choose a Union," Washington, D.C., 1999.

122. Paul Weiler, *Governing the Workplace* (Cambridge, Mass.: Harvard University Press, 1990); and National Labor Relations Board, *Fifty-fifth Annual Report of the National Labor Relations Board, for the Fiscal Year Ended September 30, 1990* (Washington, D.C.: U.S. Government Printing Office, 1990).

123. For comprehensive accounts of management tactics in union elections and the weakness of federal labor law, see Kate Bronfenbrenner, "We'll Close! Plant Closings, Plant-Closing Threats, Union Organizing and NAFTA," *Multinational Monitor* 18, no. 3 (March 1997): 8–14; and Palley, *Plenty of Nothing*, chapter 3.

124. See, for example, Peter Goodman, "Slavery Plain and Simple: Reebok, Nike, and Levi Strauss on the Prowl for Cheap Labor in Indonesia," *Progressive* 57, no. 6 (June 1993): 26–28; and "Human Rights Groups Slam U.S. Trade Decision on Guatemala," Campaign for Labor Rights *Action Alert*, August 1998, http://www.summersault.com/~agj/clr.

125. Goodman, "Slavery," 26; open letter to Nike CEO Phil Knight from U.S. Representatives Bernie Sanders, Marcy Kaptur, and fifty other members of the U.S. House of Representatives, November 1997, http://www.summersault.com/~agj.clr.

126. "Leslie Fay Maquila Workers Organize," *Labor Notes* 186 (September 1994): 5; "Update: Phillips-Van Heusen's Propaganda," *Dollars and Sense* 187 (June 1993): 5; "News Watch," *Labor Notes* 243 (June 1999): 4.

127. Gina Thornburgh, "On the Line: Leaning on Levi's," *Progressive* 62, no. 3 (March 1996): 16. Human rights groups have documented abuses at Levi's plants in Indonesia, the Philippines, Sri Lanka, Mauritius, and Mexico, all of which were set to benefit from the company's U.S. closures. "More Layoffs at Levi's," *Labor Notes* 241 (April 1999): 9.

128. The Bush administration's rejection of a 1990 AFL-CIO petition is reported in Richard Rothstein, "Why in the World Do We Tolerate Child Labor?" *San Francisco Examiner*, December 9, 1993, A23. The Child Labor Deterrence Act, introduced by Senator Tom Harkin and Representative George Brown, would have banned the import of goods produced by child labor and required the secretary of labor to certify that employers against whom complaints had been filed were in accord with international labor standards. The politics of international child labor under the Clinton administration and WTO are reported in Terry Collingsworth, "Child Labor in the Global Economy," *Foreign Policy in Focus* 2, no. 46 (October 1997).

129. Alec Wilkinson, *Big Sugar: Seasons in the Cane Fields of Florida* (New York: Vintage, 1990); Philip Shenon, "Saipan Sweatshops Are No American Dream," *New York Times*, July 18, 1993, A1; William Branigin, "Northern Marianas: Not a Workers' Paradise," *Washington Post*, October 14, 1997, 1. The Northern Marianas are a U S territory, which allows local manufacturers to declare their products "Made in the USA." However, the islands are exempt from minimum wage and labor laws; some contracts forbid workers to engage in political activity, request a raise, strike, or get married. House Republican leaders Tom DeLay and Dick Armey led the opposition to Democratic proposals which would have extended minimum wage laws to the Northern Marianas. "Making Delay Sweat," *Newsweek*, February 1, 1999, 16.

130. This point is made by Palley, *Plenty of Nothing*, 62.

131. Jared Bernstein, "Minimum Wages and Poverty," Testimony before the House Education and Workforce Committee, April 27, 1999, http://epinet.org/webfeatures/viewpoints/minwagetestimony.html. Numbers are for those earning within one dollar of the minimum wage.

132. Lawrence Mishel and Jared Bernstein, *The State of Working America, 1992–93* (Armonk, N.Y.: M. E. Sharpe, 1993), 195; Bernstein, "Minimum Wages"; U.S. Department of Commerce, Census Bureau, "Poverty 2000," January 29, 2001.

133. Bernstein, "Minimum Wages." Although the Clinton administration wanted to raise the minimum wage as soon as Clinton took office, it was only the combination of heightened voter anxiety about corporate downsizing and the approach of the 1996 elections that ultimately brought Congress to approve an increase, in the fourth year of the Clinton presidency. In 2001, the U.S. Chamber of Commerce and the National Federation of Independent Businesses maintained opposition to a minimum wage increase as one of their priority legislative goals, bragging of having defeated such a proposal in 2000, http://www.uschamber.com; http://www.nfib.com.

134. Employment by temporary agencies nearly tripled during the 1990s, increasing from 1.2 million to just over 3 million. Mishel, Bernstein, and Schmitt, *State of Working America, 2000/2001*, 253. Estimates of the share of new hires who are temporary employees were made independently by Labor Secretary Robert Reich and by the Bureau of Labor Statistics, reported in Peter Kilborn, "New Jobs Lack the Old Security in a Time of 'Disposable Workers,'" *New York Times*, March 15, 1993, A1. Virginia duRivage, Francoise Carré, and Chris Tilly, "Making Labor Law Work for Part-Time and Contingent Workers," in *Contingent Work: American Employment*

Relations in Transition, ed. Kathleen Barker and Kathleen Christensen (Ithaca: Cornell University Press, 1998), 263–80, estimate that part-timers, temporary employees, and other contingent workers make up 25% of the workforce as a whole. Mishel, Bernstein, and Schmitt, *State of Working America, 2000/2001*, table 3.14, 245, estimate that nonstandard workers accounted for 24.8% of the total workforce in 1999.

135. Mishel, Bernstein, and Schmitt, *State of Working America, 2000/2001*, 246–49; Chris Tilly, *Short Hours, Short Shrift: Causes and Consequences of Part-Time Work* (Washington, D.C.: Economic Policy Institute, 1990), 9–12.

136. On this point see duRivage, Carré, and Tilly, "Making Labor Law Work."

137. Gina Kolata, "More Children Are Employed, Often Perilously," *New York Times*, June 22, 1992, A1. Andrew Conte, "Teens in the Workforce: Sweatshops a U.S. Problem, Too," *Cincinnati Post*, March 14, 2000, reports that Rutgers University researcher Doug Ruse estimated that there were 148,000 children illegally employed in any given week in 1998.

138. Joan Lum, "Sweatshops Are Us," *Dollars and Sense* 213 (September–October 1997): 7; Joann Wypijewski, "Profits of Pain," *Nation* 258, no. 14 (April 11, 1994): 472; Carl Hartman, "Herman Wants Sweatshops Eliminated," Associated Press, April 21, 1998. A 2000 Department of Labor survey of urban garment industries found that 61% of cutting and sewing shops in Los Angeles, and 65% of those in New York, did not provide minimum wage or overtime. Robert Reich, "American Sweatshops," January 18, 2001, *American Prospect Online*, http://www.prospect.org.

139. Data for 1992 are from Kolata, "More Children," A1; 1999 numbers are from Child Labor Coalition, "Child Labor in the US," http://www.stopchildlabor.org. See also Martha Mendoza, "Toughest Labor Laws Not Enforced," Associated Press, December 18, 1997.

140. From 1981 to 1991, the number of discrimination cases settled annually by the Equal Employment Opportunity Commission fell by 58%, from 26,057 to 11,032, while the number of charges that were dismissed increased by 82%, from 21,097 to 38,369. *Nation* 257, no. 12 (October 18, 1993): 424.

141. Elaine Lan Chao, Statement before the Senate Committee on Health, Education, Labor and Pensions, January 24, 2001, http://labor.senate.gov/107hearings/jan2001/012401wt/chao.pdf.

142. Martin Carnoy and Richard Rothstein, *Hard Lessons in California: Minority Pay Gap Widens Despite More Schooling, Higher Scores*, Working Paper No. 116, Economic Policy Institute, Washington, D.C., 1996.

143. For the most comprehensive study, see Michael Fix and Raymond Struyk, eds., *Clear and Convincing Evidence: Measurement of Discrimination in America* (Washington, D.C.: Urban Institute Press, 1992). For an overview of the debate between skills and discrimination as an explanation for race-based wage differences, see also Harry Holzer, "Employer Hiring Decisions and Antidiscrimination Policy," in *Generating Jobs*, ed. Freeman and Gottschalk.

144. Howell and Wolff, "Trends," 495.

145. Reported in *Questions and Answers on Pay Equity*, National Committee on Pay Equity, http://www.feminist.com/fairpay/f_qape.htm.

146. Quoted in Robert Pollin, "Living Wage, Live Action," *Nation* 267, no. 17 (November 23, 1998): 20.

147. Traer Sunley, assistant director of Health and Welfare, California, testifying on behalf of Governor Edmund G. Brown, Jr., in U.S. Congress, *Employment and Training Policy 1982, Part 1*, 725.

148. Jerry Junkins, CEO of Texas Instruments, Inc., Statement before the Senate Labor and Human Resources Committee, 105th Congress, 1st session, January 11, 1995.

149. Quoted in Louis Uchitelle, "'Empowering' Labor Held Key to More Jobs," *New York Times*, July 27, 1993, C1.

150. Elaine Chao, Statement before the Senate Committee, January 24, 2001.

1. Remarks at the Tuskegee University commencement ceremony, *Weekly Compilation of Presidential Documents* 23 (May 10, 1987): 509.

2. Remarks at the National Urban League conference, *Weekly Compilation of Presidential Documents* 25 (August 8, 1989): 1222.

3. Remarks at the annual meeting of the American Political Science Association, Washington, D.C., August 1993.

4. *The Job Training Parternership Act*, Public Law 97-300, 97th Congress, 2nd session (October 13, 1982), sec. 106(a). The Workforce Investment Act has the same goals. *The Workforce Investment Act of 1998*, Public Law 105-220, 105th Congress, 1st session (August 7, 1998). (Hereafter cited as *Workforce Investment Act.*)

5. Figure refers to current dollar total for fiscal years 1984–2002. Figures for 1984–99 are reported in U.S. Department of Labor, Employment and Training Administration, "Employment Programs: Summary of Budget Authority, FY 1984 to Current, May 2001. Data for FY 2000–2002 are from U.S. Department of Labor, Employment and Training Administration, "Summary of Budget Authority, Fiscal Years 2000–2001" and "Summary of Budget Authority, Fiscal Years 2001–2002," April 6, 2001.

6. The transition from JTPA to WIA began in FY 2001, but it appears likely that it will take several years before the full WIA system is implemented as planned.

7. The Department of Labor will conduct a separate study of WIA effects but is not required to undertake the study until 2005.

8. Public Law 97-300, amended by *Job Training Reform Amendments of 1992*, Public Law 102-367, 102nd Congress, 1st session (September 7, 1992). The *Workforce Investment Act* largely provides the same kind of training to the same populations, with some changes in administrative procedures.

9. Title IIA programs accounted for nearly 40% of the total JTPA funding over the life of the program. The primary research on the effectiveness of JTPA was undertaken before youth trainees were split off into Title IIC. Therefore, while the analysis that follows refers only to Title IIA, it covers the full population of both adult and youth participants subsequently included in Titles IIA and IIC. U.S. Department of Labor, Employment and Training Administration, "Employment Programs: Summary of Budget Authority, FY 1984 to Current," May 2001.

10. National Commission for Employment Policy, *The Job Training Partnership Act: A Report* (Washington, D.C.: National Commission for Employment Policy, 1987), 53 n. 1. (Hereafter cited as NCEP, *JTPA.*)

11 NCEP, *JTPA*, 53. The 65% requirement was added in the 1992 JTPA Amendments. Fifty percent of youth participants must be high school dropouts, and welfare recipients must be included in proportion to their share of the local population. Ibid.; U.S. Department of Labor, *Implementation of the 1992 Job Training Partnership Act (JTPA) Amendments* (Washington, D.C.: U.S. Department of Labor, 1997).

12. Sar Levitan and Frank Gallo, *A Second Chance: Training for Jobs* (Kalamazoo, Mich.: W. E. Upjohn Institute for Employment Research, 1988), 19.

13. While the specific conditions of payment required of each training vendor are established by the local contracting authority, the U.S. Department of Labor has established general performance standards which must be met by each state in order to guarantee its own continued funding; in general, these same criteria are in turn applied to local authorities and training providers. For youth, participants who earn education credentials or improve or attain new skills are considered "positive terminations" even if they are not placed into jobs.

14. John Donahue, *Shortchanging the Workforce: The Job Training Partnership Act and the Overselling of Privatized Training* (Washington, D.C.: Economic Policy Institute, 1989), 5.

15. Private Industry Councils have been renamed "Workforce Investment Boards" (WIBs) under WIA.

16. U.S. Senate, *Senate Report 97-469: Report Accompanying S-2036, the Training for Jobs Act,* 97th Congress, 2nd session, June 9, 1982, 1–2.

17. Levitan and Gallo, *Second Chance,* 39, report that the average PIC has twenty-five members, including fourteen from the private sector, three from local educational institutions, two from community organizations, and two from labor unions.

18. The PIC/WIB and local government share equal responsibility for formulating an overall training plan for the area, establishing performance goals and other criteria for awarding contracts, and identifying procedures for recruiting participants. NCEP, *JTPA,* 39–40.

19. NCEP, *JTPA,* 65–66 for program year 1984, the first full year of JTPA's operation. Most recent data are for Project Year 1996, in Office of Policy and Research, Employment and Training Administration, *Job Training Partnership Act 1996 Program Statistics* (Washington, D.C.: U.S. Department of Labor, June 1998), table II-7.

20. U.S. Senate, *Senate Report 101-129 Accompanying the Job Training and Basic Skills Act,* 101st Congress, 1st session, September 14, 1989, 9. The 2% figure is supported by a number of other studies. NCEP, *JTPA,* 54, estimates that in the first year of JTPA, roughly 42 million people were eligible for Title IIA, and the program served 780,000, or 1.85% of the total. See also Donahue, *Shortchanging;* Burt Barnow, "Government Training as a Means of Reducing Unemployment," in *Rethinking Employment Policy,* ed. D. Lee Bawden and Felicity Skidmore (Washington, D.C.: Urban Institute Press, 1989).

21. The number of participants has remained roughly steady since 1999, with WIA serving 380,000 adults in FY 2001. Some categories of participants seem to be increased under WIA. However, these numbers cannot be directly compared with JTPA, since WIA includes more superficial "services" such as job counseling without substantive training or education. U.S. Department of Labor, Employment and Training Administration, *2001 Annual Performance Plan for Committee on Appropriation* (Washington, D.C.: U.S. Government Printing Office, March 2000).

22. Levitan and Gallo, *Second Chance,* 59, report that the transition from CETA to JTPA saw funding for support services cut from 59% to 11% of training funds.

23. For example, Gary Walker, *An Independent Sector Assessment of the Job Training Partnership Act* (New York: Grinker, Walker & Associates, 1985), cited in Barnow, "Government Training," 112, reported that "most SDAs did not pay any attention to the statute's broad mandate to serve those most in need of and able to benefit from its services." Under JTPA, each local government charged with operating job training was designated a Service Delivery Area, or SDA. U.S. Senate, *Senate Report 101-129,* 9, reported that while 38% of the JTPA-eligible population were high school dropouts, dropouts accounted for only 27% of program participants.

24. Levitan and Gallo, *Second Chance,* 69; Gary Orfield and Helene Slessarev, *Job Training under the New Federalism* (Chicago: University of Chicago Press, 1986), 198.

25. Orfield and Slessarev, *Job Training,* 176.

26. Ibid., 167.

27. Levitan and Gallo, *Second Chance,* 59.

28. For the simplest comparison of JTPA and WIA, see U.S. Department of Labor, Employment and Training Administration, *Key Features of the Workforce Investment Act as Compared to Current Law,* August 10, 1998, http://usworkforce.org.

29. See Barnow, "Government Training"; Donahue, *Shortchanging;* U.S. Senate, *Senate Report 101-129.*

30. U.S. Senate, *Senate Report 101-129,* 11. Emphasis in the original.

31. Office of Policy and Research, *Job Training,* tables II-8, II-1.

32. James Bovard, "The Failure of Federal Job Training," *Society* (May/June 1989): 63. Donahue, *Shortchanging*, 7, reports that as of 1986, over 90% of SDA programs in the country had met or exceeded job placement and cost-per-placement standards.

33. Orfield and Slessarev, *Job Training*, 3.

34. See Barnow, "Government Training"; Levitan and Gallo, *Second Chance*; Orfield and Slessarev, *Job Training*. On-the-job training (OJT) programs have increased participant earnings more than classroom training, but there is strong reason to believe that OJT functions primarily as a means of reserving job slots for participants rather than increasing their skills. Classroom training is the most effective means of increasing participants' hourly wages, which serves as the best available proxy for long-term employability.

35. Levitan and Gallo, *Second Chance*, 66.

36. Donahue, *Shortchanging*, 18–19.

37. Orfield and Slessarev, *Job Training*, 155.

38. Howard Bloom et al., *The National JTPA Study: Title II-A Impacts on Earnings and Employment at 18 Months* (Washington D.C.: U.S. Department of Labor, 1993), appendix F. (Hereafter cited as Bloom et al., *National JTPA Study at 18 Months*.) Levitan and Gallo, *Second Chance*, 101, report a more creative practice: a Michigan SDA placed training graduates in unpaid internships in order to count them as "placed in jobs," since JTPA regulations stipulate that graduates be placed in "unsubsidized jobs" but do not technically require that these "jobs" pay wages.

39. Levitan and Gallo, *Second Chance*, 27.

40. U.S. Department of Labor, *Semiannual Report of the Office of Inspector General, October 1, 1991–March 31, 1992* (Washington, D.C.: U.S. Department of Labor, 1992), 21.

41. U.S. General Accounting Office, *Job Training Partnership Act: Inadequate Oversight Leaves Program Vulnerable to Waste, Abuse, and Mismanagement* (Washington, D.C.: U.S. General Accounting Office, 1991), 26–27. See also U.S. Department of Labor, *Semiannual Report of Office of Inspector General*, various years; and U.S. General Accounting Office, *Major Management Challenges and Program Risks: Department of Labor*, GAO/OCG-99-11 (Washington, D.C.: General Accounting Office, January 1999).

42. Previous examples and audit information are from U.S. Department of Labor, *Semiannual Report of the Office of Inspector General, October 1, 1991–March 31, 1992*, 15. U.S. House of Representatives Committee on Ways and Means reports $1.7 billion in Title IIA outlays for Program Year 1992.

43. U.S. Department of Labor, *Semiannual Report of the Office of Inspector General, April 1, 1988–September 20, 1988*, 20.

44. Charles Masten, Testimony of the Inspector General, U.S. Department of Labor, before the Subcommittee on Postsecondary Education, Training, and Life-Long Learning, Committee on Education and the Workforce, U.S. House of Representatives, March 4, 1997, http://www.oig.dol.gov/public/media/testimony/19970304-2.html.

45. James Bovard, "Son of CETA: Job Training? No, Corporate Welfare," *New Republic* (April 14, 1986): 17; U.S. Department of Labor, *Semiannual Report, 1992*, 49. A slight variation on this scam, reported in Bovard, "Failure," 63, is the case of a Pittsburgh employer who hired his two sons as OJT trainees. This employer defended his practice with unusual candor: "Just because a businessman has an on-the-job training contract and his two sons are his only employees, where's the conflict of interest? Is it wrong to upgrade the skills of your children?"

46. Compaq's program is reported in James Bovard, "The Federal Job-Training Fiasco," *Reader's Digest*, March 1990, 139. The Pennsylvania case is from U.S. Department of Labor, *Semiannual Report of the Office of Inspector General, October 1, 1987–March 31, 1988*, 30. Similarly, U.S. Department of Labor, *Semiannual Report, 1992*, 19, reports that the single biggest OJT

provider in South Carolina had established agreements with 23 local firms to "screen" their existing employees for JTPA eligibility and then sign up the eligibles for OJT subsidies.

47. U.S. General Accounting Office, *Inadequate Oversight*, 24.

48. Examples are from ibid.

49. U.S. Department of Labor, *Semiannual Report of the Office of Inspector General, October 1, 1995–March 31, 1996*, 6.

50. U.S. General Accounting Office, *Inadequate Oversight*, 24.

51. U.S. Senate, *Senate Report 101-129*, 12.

52. Robin Leidner, *Fast Food, Fast Talk: Service Work and the Routinization of Everyday Life* (Berkeley: University of California Press, 1993) and Barbara Garson, *The Electronic Sweatshop: How Computers Are Transforming the Office of the Future into the Factory of the Past* (New York: Simon and Schuster, 1988), report that training for fast-food workers consists of less than four hours of actual instruction and that new hires are usually operating at adequate working speed by their second day on the job. For a description of the car wash program, see Susan Garland, "90 Days to Learn to Scrub? Sure, If Uncle Sam's Paying," *Business Week* (January 10, 1992): 70.

53. U.S. General Accounting Office, *Inadequate Oversight*, 3–4, 21.

54. In two such examples, Bovard, "Federal Job-Training Fiasco," 138–41, reports that the Toledo, Ohio, Private Industry Council provided OJT subsidies to a newly opening Radisson Hotel despite the absence of any special training program for participants. The hotel's Director of Human Resources explained that "we interviewed people, we found the ones we wanted—and then we checked their JTPA eligibility. If the person qualified for on-the-job training subsidies, it was just a bonus for us." Similarly, the state of Kentucky provided $6 million in JTPA subsidies for workers at a new Toyota plant, despite the company's explicit statement that "eligibility for JTPA subsidies in no way helped any person qualify for a job at Toyota." This was also the rationale for the farm worker program criticized in U.S. Department of Labor, *Semiannual Report of the Office of Inspector General, October 1, 1995–March 31, 1996*, 6.

55. U.S. Department of Labor, *Semiannual Report, 1998*, 4.

56. Ibid. suggests that up to 15% of IIA funds may have been appropriated for illegitimate expenses. U.S. Department of Labor, *Semiannual Report, 1992*, suggests that provider job placements are inflated by up to 25%; 60% of OJT contracts are for individuals who would have been hired anyway, and I have estimated that OJT represents roughly one-sixth of Title IIA expenditures. Larry L. Orr et al., *The National JTPA Study: Impacts, Benefits and Costs of Title II Year-Round Programs: A Report to the U.S. Department of Labor* (Bethesda, Md.: Abt Associates, March 1994) (hereafter referred to as Orr et al., *National JTPA Study Final Report*), shows 38.7% of adult participants referred to OJT; youth participation rates are much lower. Therefore 15% + 25% + (1/6 * 60%) = 50%.

57. The sites for the National JTPA Study were chosen, and initial implementation reports written, by the Manpower Demonstration Research Corporation, the country's foremost experts in evaluations of training programs. The study was designed and the results analyzed and summarized by Abt Associates, one of the most respected firms in the field of program evaluation. Since the national study is the first evaluation to use control groups, the report's authors note that it constitutes "the first valid and reliable evidence of the impacts of JTPA Title II-A programs." Bloom et al., *National JTPA Study at 18 Months*, 2. Participants in the national study were drawn from JTPA applicants in sixteen SDAs. The first step of the study was to classify all applicants according to the type of service they would have received if allowed to participate in JTPA: classroom training, OJT, or "other," more remedial services. Following this, individuals in each group were randomly assigned to either a "treatment" group which was enrolled in JTPA training or a "control" group which was barred from JTPA for the duration of the study. Since the treatment and control groups were randomly assigned, they were roughly matched by gender,

race, education, and work history; thus the study controlled for the effects of creaming or discrimination in the program.

58. The remaining twelve categories have margins of error of more than 100%, making their findings statistically meaningless.

59. The data for all male youth are much more negative than those shown here. If male youths with prior arrest records were included, the data would show a statistically significant earnings loss for this group as a whole. This problem is discussed in more detail in appendix B.

60. Bloom et al., *National JTPA Study at 18 Months*, 155. Emphasis in original.

61. Annual earnings are calculated by dividing 30-month earnings by 2.5. Poverty thresholds are for 1990, which is roughly the midpoint of participants' earnings stream.

62. In fact, Bloom et al., *National JTPA Study at 18 Months*, 101, 156, report that 46% of women and 47.2% of men who participated in the program reported that they had "previously received occupational training" before entering JTPA. There are no records regarding how many of these people may have been previously enrolled in JTPA itself.

63. Ibid., 181.

64. Ibid., 89. The authors note that these findings are open to conflicting interpretations: if increased employment is concentrated among the highest earners, the earnings gain as a whole may be illusory; on the other hand, if increased hours reflect the employment of participants who otherwise would have been unemployable, the increase in individual wages is greater than that reported here. Nevertheless, the data strongly suggest that a large share of JTPA earnings gains reflects increased employment rather than higher wages.

65. Ibid., 101, 133, report that 71.8% of adult women in the study had a GED or high school diploma upon applying to JTPA, 46% had previous occupational training, and 85% had previous work experience. Among men, 67% had a GED or high school diploma, 47.2% had previous training, and 90% had previous work experience.

66. Background profiles of participants are from ibid., 156.

67. Elaine Chao, Secretary Designate, Statement before the Senate Committee on Health, Education, Labor and Pensions, January 24, 2001, http://labor.senate.gov/107hearings/jan2001/012401wt/chao.pdf.

68. These problems are discussed in appendix B. To cite just one such concern, while the study's authors report unusually large margins of error regarding the earnings gains of program participants, they failed even to calculate a margin of error for the final cost-benefit analysis, making it impossible for the public to know whether the benefits reported are statistically significant.

69. U.S. General Accounting Office, *Job Training Partnership Act: Long-Term Earnings and Employment Outcomes*, GAO/HEHS-96-40 (Washington, D.C.: U.S. General Accounting Office, March 1996). Poverty calculations are based on 1993 thresholds for a family of three.

70. Barnow, "Government Training," 122–23.

71. Orr et al., *National JTPA Study Final Report*, 9. Laurie Bassi and Orley Ashenfelter, "The Effect of Direct Job Creation and Training Programs on Low-Skilled Workers," in *Fighting Poverty: What Works and What Doesn't*, ed. Sheldon Danziger and Daniel Weinberg (Cambridge, Mass.: Harvard University Press, 1986), 149, summarize their review of evaluations with the conclusion that "employment and training programs have been neither an overwhelming success nor a complete failure. . . . Our ability to improve the lot of any given participant and the collective economic well-being of the disadvantaged has been modest."

72. Bassi and Ashenfelter, "Effect of Direct Job Creation," 141.

73. James Heckman, "Is Job Training Oversold?" *Public Interest* (spring 1994): 91–115.

74. For FY 2002, the Department of Labor requested a budget of $900 million for just under 400,000 adult participants, or approximately $2,250 per person. U.S. Department of Labor,

Employment and Training Administration, "Building America's 21st Century Workforce: 2002 Annual Performance Plan for Committee on Appropriations," March 2001.

75. Orr et al., *National JTPA Study Final Report*, 180.

76. James Heckman, "Assessing Clinton's Program on Job Training, Workfare, and Education in the Workplace," Working Paper No. 4428, National Bureau of Economic Research, Cambridge, Mass., 1993, 11.

77. Orr et al., *National JTPA Study Final Report*, 180.

78. Peter Kilborn, "U.S. Study Says Job Retraining Is Not Effective," *New York Times*, October 15, 1993, A1.

79. Office of Policy and Research, *Job Training Partnership Act 1996 Program Statistics*, table V-9.

80. Duane Leigh, *Does Training Work for Displaced Workers? A Survey of Existing Evidence* (Kalamazoo, Mich.: W. E. Upjohn Institute for Employment Research, 1990), 109.

81. Judith Gueron, "Work and Welfare: Lessons on Employment Programs," *Journal of Economic Perspectives* 4, no. 1 (1990): 79–98.

82. Kathryn Porter, *Making JOBS Work: What the Research Says about Effective Programs for AFDC Recipients* (Washington, D.C.: Center on Budget and Policy Priorities, 1990), 25.

83. James Riccio and Daniel Friedlander, "GAIN and the Prospect of JOBS's Success: MDRC Reports Short-Term Positive Trends in California," *Public Welfare* 50, no. 3 (1992): 24.

84. Nathan Glazer, "Making Work Work: Welfare Reform in the 1990s," in *The Work Alternative: Welfare Reform and the Realities of the Job Market*, ed. Demetra Smith Nightingale and Robert Haveman (Washington, D.C.: Urban Institute Press, 1994), 29.

85. Stephen Freedman, "The National Evaluation of Welfare-to-Work Strategies: Four-Year Impacts of Ten Programs on Employment Stability and Earnings Growth," report prepared for U.S. Department of Health and Human Services and U.S. Department of Education, Office of Vocational and Adult Education (New York: Manpower Demonstration Research Corporation, 2000).

86. Stephen Freedman, Jean Tansey Knab, Lisa Gennetian, and David Navarro, "The Los Angeles Jobs-First GAIN Evaluation: Final Report on a Work First Program in a Major Urban Center" (New York: Manpower Demonstration Research Corporation, 2000).

87. Dan Bloom and Charles Michalopoulos, "How Welfare and Work Policies Affect Employment and Income: A Synthesis of Research" (New York: Manpower Demonstration and Research Corporation, 2001).

88. Table 3.10 provides author's calculations based on data in Gueron, "Work and Welfare" (for AFDC programs); Freedman et al., "GAIN: Final Report"; Freedman, "National Evaluation" for early 1990s programs; and Bloom and Michalopoulos, "How Welfare and Work Policies," for TANF programs other than GAIN. Earnings are taken from the final year of follow-up for each program and compared with poverty thresholds for a family of three. Poverty threshold is from 1984 for AFDC programs except San Diego SWIM, which is 1986; threshold is from 1994 for early 1990s programs, and from 1997 for TANF programs.

89. *Workforce Investment Act*, sec. 134.

90. U.S. Department of Labor, Employment and Training Administration, "Strategic Plan: Fiscal Years 1999–2004," September 2000.

91. U.S. Department of Labor, Employment and Training Administration, Office of Field Operations, "Summary Report on WIA Implementation," March 2001, 10, http://www.icesa.org/articles/template.cfm?results_art_filename=summaryrept.htm.

92. Ibid., 22.

93. Ibid., 9.

94. Indeed, WIA staff are encouraged to consider a participant's ability to land a well-paying job upon graduation as one of the criteria for awarding training vouchers. U.S. Department of

Labor, Employment and Training Administration, "Grants for Implementing Individual Training Account (ITA) Approaches through the ITA Experiment," September 2000, http://wdsc.doleta.gov/.

95. This is the explicit calculation of Heckman, "Is Job Training Oversold?" and Heckman, *Assessing Clinton's Program*, who assumes a 10% rate of return to training and calculates the total funding needed to restore 1979 earning levels.

96. For instance, the National JTPA Study explains that the report treats participants' increased earnings as "added output and therefore . . . not a cost to anyone else in society." Orr et al., *National JTPA Study Final Report*, 36.

97. Gueron, "Work and Welfare," 91 n. 13.

98. Freedman, "National Evaluation," provides the first controlled evaluation of the impacts of pure job search assistance. The "employment-focused" programs he studied provided no training but "encouraged rapid entry into the labor market." On average, the four such programs studied increased participant earnings by the equivalent of 5.1% of the poverty line. Since this is well within the normal range of impacts reported by JTPA and other programs, the results offer strong support to the notion that even the modest success of training programs actually represents simply a rearranging of the hiring queue.

99. See Kilborn, "U.S. Study," for example, on the Department of Labor's defense of the Trade Adjustment Assistance Act in the face of its Inspector General report condemning the program as largely ineffective.

100. With all JTPA's shortcomings, the one system that probably wastes more money and does less for its participants is the proprietary school system. For just one review of this problem see U.S. General Accounting Office, *Proprietary Schools: Millions Spent to Train Students for Over-supplied Occupations*, GAO/HEHS-97-104 (Washington, D.C.: U.S. General Accounting Office, June 1997).

101. Gertrude Stein, *Everybody's Autobiography* (New York: Random House, 1937), chap. 4.

102. Orr et al., *National JTPA Study Final Report*, 8.

103. Charles Betsey, Robinson Hollister, and Mary Papegerogiou, *Youth Employment and Training Programs: The YEDPA Years* (Washington, D.C.: National Academy Press, 1985), cited in Orr et al., *National JTPA Study Final Report*, 181.

104. U.S. General Accounting Office, *Long-Term Earnings*.

105. Orr et al., *National JTPA Study Final Report*, 17.

106. Ibid., 181–82.

107. The total number of women, men, female youth, and male nonarrestee youth who were officially enrolled in JTPA programs included in the national study is 6,786. This is the group for whom the report makes a cost-benefit analysis.

108. U.S. General Accounting Office, *Major Challenges and Program Risks: Department of Labor*, GAO/OCG-99-11 (Washington, D.C.: U.S. General Accounting Office, January 1999), 8.

109. Ibid.

110. Ibid.

111. U.S. General Accounting Office, *Department of Labor: Challenges in Ensuring Workforce Development and Worker Protection*, GAO/T-HEHS-97-85 (Washington, D.C.: U.S. General Accounting Office, 1997), 8.

112. U.S. Department of Labor, *Semiannual Report, 1996*.

113. U.S. General Accounting Office, *Multiple Employment Training Programs: Most Federal Agencies Do Not Know If Their Programs Are Working Effectively*, GAO/HEHS-94-88 (Washington, D.C.: U.S. General Accounting Office, March 1994). See also U.S. General Accounting Office, *Major Management Challenges*.

114. U.S. Department of Labor, Employment and Training Administration, "Job Training Partnership Act (JTPA) Title II and Title III Performance Standards for PYs 1998 and 1999," in

Training and Employment Guidance Letter No. 12-97 (Washington, D.C.: U.S. Department of Labor, June 30, 1998). Section 106 of the JTPA enabling legislation mandates the Secretary of Labor to establish biennial performance standards based on recent performance of contractors. Performance standards are generally set at a level equal to the 20th–35th percentile of past performance—i.e. at a level surpassed by 65%–80% of contracts in the past two years.

115. Ibid.

116. *Workforce Investment Act*, sec. 136.

117. This problem is described in U.S. Department of Labor, Employment and Training Administration, "Summary Report on WIA Implementation," 14.

118. U.S. Department of Labor, Employment and Training Administration, "A Brief Overview of JTPA Performance Standards," August 2001.

119. Unfortunately, those to whom it truly does matter—the poor and unemployed—have little or no say over policy. Indeed, if a majority of PIC members were required to themselves be training participants—or if all members of the Labor Committee were forced to live on the average salary of JTPA graduates—we might find the program's problems suddenly seem much more soluble.

Chapter Four

1. Doug Ross, "Enterprise Economics on the Front Lines: Empowering Firms and Workers to Win," in *Mandate for Change*, ed. Will Marshall and Martin Schram (New York: Berkeley Books, 1993), 53, 57.

2. Statement to the Senate Committee on Health, Education, Labor and Pensions, January 24, 2001, http://labor.senate.gov/107hearings/jan2001/012401wt/chao.pdf.

3. Michael Hammer and James Champy, *Reengineering the Corporation: A Manifesto for Business Revolution* (New York: HarperCollins, 1993), 53, 70.

4. Quoted in Barbara Garson, *The Electronic Sweatshop: How Computers Are Transforming the Office of the Future into the Factory of the Past* (New York: Simon and Schuster, 1988), 36.

5. Thus former Senator Quayle explained the rationale behind job training by noting, "For most of the unemployed, employment will come with the recovery of the economy; their unemployment will have been merely a painful interlude between periods of productive employment. But even with economic recovery, there are large groups among the unemployed who cannot look forward to employment without special help." U.S. Congress, *Employment and Training Policy, 1982, Part 1*, 2.

6. One of the earliest staples of "empowerment" rhetoric is the ubiquitous insistence on calling employees "associates," "team members," or anything but "employees." I believe this strategy reached its apogee at Coffee People, a retail chain in the Northwest, which refers to employees as "Human Beings"; a corporate fact sheet explains that "the people who *are* Coffee People *are* Human Beings," and insists that "owners will view current longtime Human Beings as an asset." "Coffee People Announces Franchise Opportunity," Coffee People fact sheet, 1998.

7. An early and insightful overview of "high performance" programs can be found in Mike Parker and Jane Slaughter, eds., *Working Smart: A Union Guide to Participation Programs and Reengineering* (East Lansing, Mich.: Labor Notes, 1994).

8. For a more thorough review of the variety of strategies which go under the rubric of these labels, see Eileen Appelbaum and Rosemary Batt, *The New American Workplace: Transforming Work Systems in the United States* (Ithaca: ILR Press, 1994); and Stephen Herzenberg, John Alic, and Howard Wial, *New Rules for a New Economy: Employment and Opportunity in Postindustrial America* (Ithaca: Cornell University Press, 1998).

9. In his *Locked in the Cabinet* (New York: Knopf, 1997), Robert Reich notes that this is one of the books President-elect Clinton had studied intensely prior to assuming office.

10. Robert Reich, *Work of Nations: Preparing Ourselves for 21st-Century Capitalism* (New York: Vintage, 1992), 82.

11. Ibid., 83.

12. Ibid., 90.

13. Ibid., 247.

14. W. Edwards Deming, *Out of the Crisis* (Cambridge, Mass.: MIT Press, 1982).

15. Secretary's Commission on Achieving Necessary Skills (SCANS), *What Work Requires of Schools* (Washington, D.C.: U.S. Department of Labor, 1991), xvi.

16. Arnold Packer and John Wirt, "Changing Skills in the U.S. Work Force: Trends of Supply and Demand," in *Urban Labor Markets and Job Opportunity*, ed. George Peterson and Wayne Vroman (Washington, D.C.: Urban Institute Press, 1992), 58–59.

17. Reich, *Work of Nations*, 183, 222.

18. Robert Howard, *Brave New Workplace* (New York: Viking, 1985), 3.

19. SCANS, *What Work Requires of Schools*, 4. Similarly, Michael Hammer and James Champy's best-selling *Reengineering the Corporation: A Manifesto for Business Revolution* (New York: HarperCollins, 1993), 2, declared that "America's largest corporations . . . must embrace and apply the principles of business reengineering, or they will be eclipsed by the greater success of those companies that do."

20. Phrases are from Steve Lohr writing in the *New York Times* and James Fallows writing in the *Atlantic Monthly*, cited in Howard, *Brave New Workplace*, 4.

21. Aaron Bernstein, "Why America Needs Unions: But Not the Kind It Has Now," *Business Week*, May 23, 1994, 82.

22. Samuel Bowles and Herbert Gintis, "Contested Exchange: New Microfoundations for the Political Economy of Capitalism," *Politics and Society* 18, no. 2 (1990).

23. Robin Leidner, *Fast Food, Fast Talk: Service Work and the Routinization of Everyday Life* (Berkeley: University of California Press, 1993), 46.

24. Except where noted, the following descriptions of McDonald's work are drawn from Leidner, *Fast Food* and Garson, *Electronic Sweatshop*.

25. Arlie Hochschild, *The Managed Heart: Commercialization of Human Feeling* (Berkeley: University of California Press, 1983) has termed this type of service work "emotional labor," in that the manufacture and projection of certain emotions is part of the job.

26. Similarly, Hochschild, *Managed Heart*, 149, describes a promotional campaign of the Winn-Dixie chain of stores, in which checkout clerks were required to wear a dollar bill pinned to their shirts. If they failed to perform any of the five "courtesy and service elements" advertised by the store, the dollar went to the customer; too many dollars lost would result in the worker being disciplined. The first and fifth of these elements were "sincere greeting when you are being checked out," and "sincere 'Thank You For Shopping Winn-Dixie.'" One wonders what happened if customers complained that these lines had been delivered, but in a formalistic style and without emotion. Did managers insist that workers must be more "sincere" in thanking customers for shopping at Winn-Dixie?

27. Leidner distinguishes between firms such as McDonald's, which aim only to control worker's outward behavior, and those such as the insurance firm she chronicles which seek to remake employees' internal psychology. My contention here is that even the former end up doing some of the latter, if not by direct intention. In theory, McDonald's doesn't care if employees are depressed as long as they act happy. In practice, however, most people are incapable of acting genuinely happy without this affecting the emotions they are actually feeling. The act spills over into internal life, and, as Hochschild notes, service employees often have trouble turning off their workplace personalities at the end of their shifts, and indeed get confused about what's "really"

them and what are their work personas. By asking workers to *act* genuinely happy, McDonald's ends up robbing them of the right or ability to *be* sullen.

28. Thus customer dissatisfaction that should be directed at management gets displaced onto workers. McDonald's staffing levels are set by a formula that projects the dollar volume of sales anticipated for each half hour of every day and then calculates the desired number of workers for each time period. The formulas are based on the assumption that workers will often be overworked and running to keep lines from overflowing. As a broader strategy, the pattern of managers simultaneously understaffing operations while conducting customer surveys that stress the company's commitment to providing the highest level of service serves to fragment potential class consciousness by turning customers and workers against each other.

29. Cited in Ester Reiter, *Making Fast Food: From the Frying Pan into the Fryer* (Montreal: McGill-Queen's University Press, 1991), 134.

30. Ibid., 131.

31. Ibid., 131.

32. Cited in ibid., 135.

33. Garson, *Electronic Sweatshop*, 41.

34. Except where otherwise noted, the description of reservations work is taken from ibid.

35. Charles Piller, "Bosses with X-Ray Eyes," *MacWorld* 10, no. 7 (July 1993): 118–23.

36. TWA has had much of its reservations work done by prisoners since the mid-1980s. This and other cases of prisoners used as a corporate workforce are described in Gordon Lafer, "Captive Labor: America's Prisoners as Corporate Workforce," *American Prospect* 46 (September–October 1999): 66–70.

37. Garson, *Electronic Sweatshop*, 66. The ability to plan "just in time" staffing levels through the new system is evident in Garson's report of a supervisor bragging that he had predicted the number of calls for a shift to within 6 of nearly 18,000 customers.

38. Roger Swardson, "Greetings From the Electronic Plantation," *City Pages*, October 21, 1992, excerpted in *Utne Reader* 56 (March/April 1993): 88–93.

39. Piller, "Bosses."

40. Garson, *Electronic Sweatshop*, 78–93.

41. Hochschild, *Managed Heart*, 111.

42. Leidner, *Fast Food*, 35.

43. Martha Gruelle, "Smile . . . Or Else! Clerks Say Safeway's Policy Leads to Sexual Harassment," *Labor Notes* 238 (January 1999): 16.

44. Linda Fuller and Vicki Smith, "Consumers' Reports: Management by Customers in a Changing Economy," *Work, Employment & Society* 5, no. 1 (March 1991): 2. Of the firms surveyed by Fuller and Smith, 86% used some form of customer feedback, including comment cards and toll-free telephone numbers. One manager referred to comment cards as "a report card on individual employees." The authors note that the use of undercover "shoppers" has grown so significantly that there are now specialized "shopping" firms that provide this service to firms unable to hire their own spies. They write, 11, "the knowledge that any interaction could flair into an antagonistic encounter, if the worker fails to provide service that satisfies the customer, may shape and reshape a worker's behavior. Organization power is a constant. . . . Much like the anonymous surveillance of the Panopticon [described in Foucault's *Discipline and Punish*] . . . service workers have no idea when an anonymous shopper will do business with them."

45. Garson, *Electronic Sweatshop*, 207.

46. Reuters, "U.S. Workplace Toilet Policy: Let Your Workers Go," April 9, 1998.

47. Herzenberg, Alic, and Wial, *New Rules*, 37–38.

48. Martin Jay Levitt, *Confessions of a Union Buster* (New York: Crown, 1993), 5.

49. Catherine Manegold, "Senate Republicans Deal a Major Defeat to Labor," *New York Times*, July 13, 1994, D18.

50. The U.S. Chamber of Commerce denounced the administration's proposal as "blacklisting." "U.S. Chamber of Commerce Vows to Fight Administration over 'Arbitrary' Blacklisting Regulations," News Release, U.S. Chamber of Commerce, Washington, D.C., July 8, 1999.

51. These policy positions are laid out on the U.S. Chamber of Commerce's web page, http://www.uschamber.com/_political+advocacy/issues+index.

52. Caroline Lund, "Union Beats 10-Hour Day at NUMMI," *Labor Notes* 186 (September 1994): 7. In August 1994, workers at the celebrated GM/Toyota NUMMI plant, often cited as an early high performance prototype, walked off the job in protest against management's attempt to introduce a 10-hour workday.

53. Associated Press, "Computer Workers May Not Get OT Pay," January 1, 1998.

54. Steven Holmes, "Some Workers Lose Right to File Suit for Bias at Work," *New York Times*, March 8, 1994, A1.

55. Peter Kilborn, "In a Growing Number of Stores, Hidden Security Microphones Are Listening," *New York Times*, May 28, 1994, 6.

56. Piller, "Bosses." Similarly, the American Management Association reports that 27% of companies surveyed stated that they read employees' e-mail. "NewsWatch," *Labor Notes* 243 (June 1999): 4.

57. Garson, *Electronic Sweatshop*, 210, reports that some workers have sought to protect themselves from this feature by sending out trivial memos to all-office mailing lists, thus creating "statistical static" which masks their true patterns of e-mail use.

58. Cheryl Buswell-Robinson, "Tracking Devices Anger Nurses," *Labor Notes* 242 (May 1999): 16. The manufacturer of these *Star Trek*–like devices reports that banks, warehouses, and prisons are among the prospective clients that have shown interest in the technology.

59. This story was reported in the *Times* (London) and cited in "NewsWatch," *Labor Notes* 244 (July 1999): 4.

60. "Electronic Monitoring," http://www.uschamber.com/_political+advocacy/issues+index. Quote is from Piller, "Bosses," 23.

61. "Capitol Matters: Assembly Will Vote on Anti-peeping Bill," *Los Angeles Times*, May 19, 1998.

62. Quoted in Dick Crofter, "Briggs & Stratton Boss Demands Concessions, Decries 'We-versus-Them Mentality,'" *Labor Notes* 181 (April 1994): 7.

63. Ellis Boal, "Activist Fired as Polaroid Disbands Company Union," *Labor Notes* 183 (June 1994): 4.

64. William Cronon, "Memorandum to Graduate Students and Faculty," Yale University, New Haven, Conn., February 11, 1992. The author served as an organizer with the Graduate Employees' and Students' Organization, as an elected representative to the Graduate School Executive Committee at Yale from 1990 to 1993, and as Research Director for the Federation of University Employees at Yale from 1995 to 1997. For one account of the 1995 strike, see Gordon Lafer, "Yale on Trial: Academic Life in the Age of Downsizing," *Dissent* (summer 1997): 78–84.

65. For an excellent summary of case studies in workplace redesign, see Appelbaum and Batt, *The New American Workplace*.

66. Richard Freeman and Joel Rogers, *What Workers Want* (Ithaca: Cornell University Press, 1999), chapter 5, report that workers who participate in Employee Involvement programs enjoy greater job satisfaction and increased input into workplace decisions.

67. Donald Wells, *Empty Promises: Quality of Working Life Programs and the Labor Movement* (New York: Monthly Review Press, 1987), 105.

68. Howard, *Brave New Workplace*, 113–14.

69. Union-buster Levitt, *Confessions*, 94, explained his strategy in unsubtle terms: "Most of the bosses I worked with felt the same: here they were, all primed for rape, and I come around and start talking seduction."

70. Quoted in Howard, *Brave New Workplace*, 127.

71. Jeff Keefe, "Hitching a Ride: Labor and the Perils of the Information Highway," *Dollars and Sense* 194 (July/August 1994): 14, reports that the company eliminated over 300,000 jobs between 1983 and 1993. Another 40,000 jobs were cut when AT&T split itself into three separate companies in the mid-1990s. Technology continues to be used to eliminate jobs, including 11,000 long-distance operator jobs (replaced by voice-recognition technology) in the 1993–98 period. On the more recent rounds of AT&T downsizing, see David Greising, "It's the Best of Times—Or Is It?" *Business Week*, January 12, 1998; and Doug Hoagland, "Out of Service: The Careers of Fresno Operators Get Disconnected by Technology," *Fresno Bee*, March 8, 1998.

72. Howard, *Brave New Workplace*, 20.

73. Steven Vallas, *Power in the Workplace: The Politics of Production at AT&T* (Albany: State University of New York Press, 1993), 127.

74. "NewsWatch," *Labor Notes* 172 (July 1993): 4.

75. Laurie Bassi and Mark Van Buren, "Sharpening the Leading Edge: The State of the Industry Report Reveals the Steps Companies Must Take to Ascend to the Top of the Training Field," *Training and Development* 53, no. 1 (January 1999): 30–32. There were 400,000 workers laid off at AT&T; 6,000 were laid off by Levi's decision to move production to the third world; Boeing laid off 12,000 people in 1998 despite booming business; Xerox laid off 9,000 despite growing profits and bonuses for the company's CEO; UPS forced a strike in 1997 over the desire to hire large numbers of low-wage part-timers; GM provoked a strike by shipping jobs to Mexico; and Sprint was found by the government to have violated labor laws by closing down a subsidiary rather than negotiate with its employees. On the 1998 strike at GM, see Jane Slaughter, "Labor on the Line: Too Little, Too Late for the UAW?" *Progressive* 62, no. 8 (August 1998): 20–21. On Boeing layoffs see Greising, "It's the Best of Times." On Xerox see "Xerox Chief Gets $6.5M Bonus," *CNN Financial News*, April 9, 1998.

76. Jay, "Coil Winder," in *Sabotage in the American Workplace: Anecdotes of Dissatisfaction, Mischief and Revenge*, ed. Martin Sprouse (San Francisco: Pressure Drop Press, 1992), 112–13.

77. Juliet Schor, *The Overworked American: The Unexpected Decline of Leisure* (New York: Basic Books, 1991). Lawrence Mishel, Jared Bernstein, and John Schmitt, *The State of Working America, 2000/2001* (Ithaca: Cornell University Press, 2001), 93–110, reports that work hours continued to grow during the 1990s but at a slower rate than the 1980s acceleration noted by Schor.

78. Dennis Hayes, *Behind the Silicon Curtain: The Seductions of Work in a Lonely Era* (Boston: South End Press, 1989), 31. The allure of this lifestyle seems to have run dry for many young programmers, at least the thousands who find themselves stuck in the world of permanent temps. Thousands of temporary programmers and systems analysts at Microsoft have organized the proto-union WashTech in an effort to improve wages, working conditions, and job security. Joe Brockert and Kevin Galvin, "Temporary Workers Seek Job Security, Benefits," Associated Press, June 22, 1998.

79. One of Levitt's central union-busting strategies was to have managers act contrite, admitting past mistakes and committing to be better in the future. He reports being repeatedly shocked at how many workers were willing to believe that these changes were heartfelt. Needless to say, the period of contrition lasted only until the union election. Lynn Chancer, *Sadomasochism in Everyday Life: The Dynamics of Power and Powerlessness* (New Brunswick, N.J.: Rutgers University Press, 1992), chapter 3, offers some insight into the psychosocial dynamics of work which make workers vulnerable to this sort of appeal.

80. Thomas Peters and Robert Waterman, *In Search of Excellence* (New York: Harper & Row, 1982), quoted in Howard, *Brave New Workplace*, 128–29.

81. Quoted in Howard, *Brave New Workplace*, 136.

82. Welch has eliminated more than 130,000 jobs during his tenure at GE. This count and following quotes are from Robert Slater, *Jack Welch and the GE Way: Management Insights and Leadership Secrets of the Legendary CEO* (New York: McGraw-Hill, 1999), 143, 147, 149, 154. For GE's role in leading a round of late-1990s layoffs, see Greising, "It's the Best of Times." The one example that may strain credulity even further than Welch is that of Weastec, a company that has used prison labor to produce auto parts but nevertheless declares in its mission statement that it is committed to "promote an environment of trust, understanding and communication" that "empower[s] all associates." The mission statement is published on the company's web site, at http://www.weastec.com. Weastec used prisoners to produce parts for Honda, as reported in Lafer, "Captive Labor."

83. Quote is from Edwin Booth, CEO of Job Boss Software, a company cited as a model of reengineering by *Job Shift* author William Bridges (*Job Shift: How to Prosper in a Workplace without Jobs* [New York: Addison-Wesley, 1994]). Cited in Caitlin Williams, "The End of the Job As We Know It: Author William Bridges Challenges Us to Train People Who Don't Have Job Descriptions," *Training and Development* 53, no. 1 (January 1999): 56. Similarly, Welch himself hints at the tensions inherent in this process, noting that Work-Out "doesn't mean abdication of decision-making authority by leadership. . . . We want everyone to have a say. We want ideas from everyone. But somebody's got to run the ship. . . . Empowerment doesn't mean anarchy. Involvement is less misleading . . . a say in the decision-making . . . a voice. And I'll tell you one thing: with voice comes responsibility" Slater, *Jack Welch*, 145.

84. Slater, *Jack Welch*, 148.

85. Mike Parker, "Election of Dissident Reveals Discontent at Model 'Team Concept' Plant," *Labor Notes* 184 (July 1994): 2.

86. Wells, *Empty Promises*, xiii.

87. Hayes, *Behind the Silicon Curtain*, 24 and elsewhere; Howard, *Brave New Workplace*, 155–57.

88. Howard, *Brave New Workplace*, 137.

89. Jane Slaughter, "'Partnership' Takes a Hit at Saturn," *Labor Notes* 241 (April 1999): 6; Robyn Meredith, "Many at Saturn Factory Find Less to Smile About," *New York Times*, March 6, 1998; Frank Swoboda, "Starting over at Saturn? 'Model' Labor-Management Pact May Be Coming Apart," *Washington Post*, March 8, 1998, H1.

90. "NewsWatch," *Labor Notes* 243 (June 1999): 4.

91. Hammer and Champy, *Reengineering*, 70.

92. Ali Zaidi, "In the Shadow of Kodak," *Dollars and Sense* 216 (March–April 1998): 9.

93. Howard, *Brave New Workplace*, 202–3.

94. Examples from academia are all drawn from David Noble, "Digital Diploma Mills: The Automation of Higher Education," *Monthly Review* 49, no. 9 (February 1998): 38–52.

95. Wells, *Empty Promises*, 114.

96. Ibid., 113, notes that the lack of solidarity is particularly noticeable in the treatment of workers who are burnt out: ". . . peer pressure at times bordered on vendettas against those who could not or would not cooperate in speedups and the like: workers who were physically or mentally weaker than their peers, those with emotional problems or drug dependencies, and, of course, those who were militant. (Since it was dehumanizing working conditions that contributed to the health problems of the workers, the bitter irony was that QWL not only left the dehumanization essentially intact—or even worsened it—but that it encouraged its victims to blame, and punish, each other.)"

97. Levitt, *Confessions*, 136.

98. Keefe, "Hitching a Ride," 16.

99. "NewsWatch," *Labor Notes* 187 (October 1994): 4, reports that the National Labor Relations Board found Sprint's closing of its La Conexion Familiar facility to constitute a violation

of federal law; the board directed the company to reopen the shop and reinstate its workers. The Labor Advisory Board under NAFTA also found Sprint to have violated its employees' rights but has not supported Mexican unions' request to block Sprint's access to the Mexican market on this basis. On the NAFTA complaint see Abby Scher, "Coming in from the Cold in the Struggle for Solidarity," *Dollars and Sense* 213 (September/October 1997): 26. The Sprint quality program is described in Communication Workers of America, *Wired for Justice: A Newsletter for Friends of Sprint Workers* 2, no. 1 (January 1994).

100. Lund, "Union Beats 10-Hour Day," 7.

101. Wells, *Empty Promises*, xiii.

Chapter Five

1. Quoted in Richard Fenno, *The Making of a Senator: Dan Quayle* (Washington, D.C.: Congressional Quarterly Press, 1989), 79.

2. Remarks on signing S. 2036 (JTPA) into law, *Weekly Compilation of Presidential Documents* 18 (October 13, 1982): 1304.

3. Ibid., 1303.

4. For a good description of the 1992 amendments, see Burt Barnow, "Thirty Years of Changing Federal, State and Local Relationships in Employment and Training Programs," *Publius* 23 (summer 1993): 75–94.

5. Quotes are from Susan Kellam, "Parties Hope Job Training Bill Will Spin Political Gold," *Congressional Quarterly Weekly Reporter* 50, no. 20 (May 16, 1992): 1341–45. Kennedy's remarks refer to the problems of fraud and creaming which had plagued JTPA in the past (see chapter 3). The 1992 amendments did indeed address these problems. The evidence that JTPA had had a negative effect on young participants' earnings was apparently not considered an equally serious problem.

6. Jon Weintraub, who in 1992 served on the staff of the House Education and Labor Committee, insists that passage of the 1992 amendments was not significantly affected by the Los Angeles riots (interview with the author, Washington, D.C., February 2, 1995). Rather, he suggests that after four years of negotiation and delay, members were committed to passing even a flawed package of amendments rather than risk missing the chance to pass anything at all. Even if the amendments were misguided regarding youth programs, according to Weintraub, they did address important problems of fraud and creaming in the operation of JTPA. This view is at odds with the comments of Kellam, who noted at the time that "the troubles in Los Angeles . . . only make the speedy passage of this bill more certain." Even if Weintraub's view is correct, however, this still indicates that the actual effectiveness of JTPA programs was not the foremost concern of the amendments' authors.

7. The 1980 Democratic platform is reprinted in *Congressional Quarterly Weekly Reporter* 38, no. 33 (August 16, 1980): 2390–420.

8. The 1980 Republican platform is reproduced in *Congressional Quarterly Weekly Reporter* 38, no. 29 (July 19, 1980): 2030–56. While the party supported training for minority youth, the platform suggested that youth unemployment could be substantially solved by instituting a sub-minimum wage for teenagers.

9. Speech to the American News Publishers Association, quoted in *Employment and Training Reporter* 36 (May 20, 1981).

10. This was the recommendation of the president-elect's Urban Task Force, chaired by then San Diego Mayor Pete Wilson. See David Rosenbaum, "Reagan Calls His Version 'Urban Enterprise Zones,'" *New York Times*, November 23, 1980, sec. 4, 2.

11. Business Roundtable, "Policies Proposed to Promote Growth in the Productivity of US Industry," Business Roundtable, Washington, D.C., August 1981.

12. The National Association of Manufacturers' Annual Report for 1980–81 outlines its Program to Revitalize American Industry in *Enterprise* 5, no. 1 (1980): 9–20.

13. Madeleine Hemming, interview with the author, Washington, D.C., February 3, 1995.

14. *Congressional Quarterly Weekly Reporter* 38, no. 32 (August 9, 1980): 2264. The labor plank of the 1980 Democratic platform, which was drafted with input from the AFL-CIO, included labor law reform, revising the Hatch Act, common situs picketing, improved workers' compensation and unemployment insurance, and repeal of right-to-work statutes. Training is not included in the labor plank. Jane Pines, interview with the author, Washington, D.C., February 2, 1995, Executive Assistant at the AFL-CIO's Human Resources Development Institute, confirmed that training was a low priority for the AFL-CIO in 1980 through 1982.

15. Fenno, *Making of a Senator*, 35.

16. Robert Guttman, interview with the author, Washington, D.C., February 2, 1995.

17. *Congressional Quarterly Weekly Reporter* 38, no. 29 (July 19, 1980): 2030–56; and 38, no. 33 (August 16, 1980): 2390–420.

18. Guttman, interview.

19. National Commission for Manpower Policy, *The Business Sector Role in Employment Policy: A Conference Report*, NCMP Special Report No. 31 (Washington, D.C.: National Commission for Manpower Policy, 1978), 34.

20. "As Layoffs Rise, So Do Skilled Job Openings," *Industry Week* 211, no. 6 (December 14, 1981): 32.

21. *Employment and Earnings* 41, no. 1 (January 1994): 182.

22. David Robinson, "The Attitudes of Employers and Business Professionals toward Government Manpower Programs," in National Commission for Manpower Policy, *Increasing Job Opportunities in the Private Sector: A Conference Report*, NCMP Special Report No. 29 (Washington, D.C.: National Commission for Manpower Policy, 1978), 156.

23. In 1981 Senate hearings, the Associated General Contractors of America summarized business views with the complaint that "CETA seems to have incorporated so many poverty-oriented prerequisites to participation that the program is almost useless as a training vehicle." *Employment and Training Reporter* 41 (June 24, 1981). Similarly, the same source quotes the Chamber of Commerce's testimony that "if the demand for skilled employees in new technologies is high . . . it is easier to retrain people who already have some skills and established work habits . . . than it is to teach the unskilled highly complicated jobs." So too the National Tooling and Machining Association called on the government to "focus some significant portion of its efforts on training qualified people for skilled occupations. . . . Although social uplift is commendable and needed, the United States cannot allow its skilled manpower base to deteriorate any further."

24. Lloyd Hand, quoted in Business Roundtable Report No. 82–3, Business Roundtable, Washington, D.C., April 1982.

25. The anti-business environment of the early and mid-1970s had caught corporate lobbyists by surprise, but it eventually led to a massive increase in corporate political strength. The Business Roundtable was formed in 1972 in response to the proliferation of new consumer, environmental, and workplace regulations. By 1979 its members included the top 10 corporations of the Fortune 500 and 113 of the top 200; together, they accounted for half the gross national product. (Sar Levitan and Martha Cooper, *Business Lobbies: The Public Good and the Bottom Line* [Baltimore: Johns Hopkins University Press, 1984], 34; Sidney Blumenthal, "Whose Side is Business On, Anyway?" *New York Times Magazine*, October 25, 1981.) The National Federation of Independent Business began with a few hundred members in 1970 and by the decade's end represented more than 500,000 firms. The U.S. Chamber of Commerce built a national network

of grassroots business activists; by 1980 it could generate 12,000 individual phone calls to Congress in a 24-hour period. Facing the challenge of a Democratic Congress working with a Democratic president in the late 1970s, businesses devoted an increasing share of their resources to political activity. By 1978, corporate lobbies were spending $900 million per year, and CEOs in the nation's top 1,000 manufacturing firms reported spending 40% of their work hours on "public issues," up from 20% only two years earlier. (Kim McQuaid, *Uneasy Partners: Big Business in American Politics 1945–1990* [Baltimore: Johns Hopkins University Press, 1994], 154.) The number of corporate political action committees grew nearly tenfold, from 89 in 1974 to 844 in early 1980 (John Perham, "The New Zest of the Corporate PACs," *Dun's Review* 115, no. 2 (February 1980): 51–52). The revitalization of corporate political power began bearing fruit in the late 1970s. In 1978, the defeat of labor law reform marked a critical turning point; as McQuaid, *Uneasy Partners*, notes, "if [business] could defeat a long-sought bill in a Democratic Congress during a Democratic presidential administration, big labor could go into political cold storage" (155).

26. The U.S. Chamber of Commerce, for instance, developed such effective relationships with the new administration that an increasing number of new firms clamored to join, and its membership more than doubled in the eighteen months following Reagan's election. Levitan and Cooper, *Business Lobbies*, 21.

27. David Vogel, *Fluctuating Fortunes: The Political Power of Business in America* (New York: Basic Books, 1989), 240. Levitan and Cooper, *Business Lobbies*, 51, report that the Chamber's 1980 recommendations for campaign contributions listed 100 pro-business congresspeople—all Republicans—and targeted a smaller number of enemies—all Democrats.

28. A number of national business lobbies banded together to form the Budget Control Working Group, which was widely considered the single most important group in insuring congressional approval of the president's 1981 program. The U.S. Chamber of Commerce characterized this campaign as its "biggest grass-roots saturation effort in history"; the chamber assigned fifty full-time staffers to lobby for the Reagan budget, compared with only four staffers devoted to its previously biggest crusade. William Miller, "Solid Support: Pulling out the Stops for Reagan Plan," *Industry Week* 209, no. 3 (May 4, 1981): 22–31. Also on this point, see John McClenahen, "Business Coalitions: More Clout in the Capital," *Industry Week* 211, no. 6 (December 14, 1981): 81–85.

29. Miller, "Solid Support."

30. McQuaid, *Uneasy Partners*, 180–83. The Reagan EEOC disallowed class action suits based on statistical evidence of discrimination and placed the burden of proof on plaintiffs to show specific individual intent to discriminate on the part of managers. The NLRB "began allowing employers to sack workers for complaining to state officials about unsafe working conditions or for swearing at nonstrikers from picket lines." Vogel, *Fluctuating Fortunes*, 249, reports that between 1980 and 1982 the number of OSHA inspectors was cut by 400, inspections fell by 15%, citations for serious hazards were cut in half, and fines decreased by two-thirds. In the first few months after Reagan appointees became a majority of the NLRB, eight major legal precedents were reversed, affecting nearly 40% of the decisions made since the mid-1970s, and the share of representation decisions won by business leapt from 46% in 1979–80 to 72% in 1983–84. The share of all NLRB appeals won by unions had been two-thirds in the Ford administration and one-half in the Carter administration, but fell to only 25% in the first Reagan administration (ibid., 270). McQuaid, *Uneasy Partners*, 183, reports that the anti-labor NLRB had a direct impact on collective bargaining outcomes. Vogel, *Fluctuating Fortunes*, 256, notes that there were fewer work stoppages in 1982 than at any previous point in the postwar era. While labor costs had increased by 8.3% per year from 1973 to 1981, they rose only 2.5% in 1983. Wage increases for union workers remained low even after the recession of the early 1980s. After fifteen years of steady increases, major collective bargaining agreements signed in 1983 contained an average wage decrease of 1.4%.

31. McQuaid, *Uneasy Partners*, 183, reports that "courts allowed firms to evade unions by contracting out work to nonunion subcontractors, to void union contracts by moving corporate facilities, to create two-tier union contracts . . . and even (temporarily) to void union contracts by pro forma bankruptcy proceedings."

32. Guttman reports that in crafting training legislation, both the Senate Republicans and the administration consulted primarily with the business lobbies and the governors.

33. Margaret Weir, *Politics and Jobs: The Boundaries of Employment Policy in the United States* (Princeton: Princeton University Press, 1992), 118–19.

34. Donald Baumer and Carl Van Horn, *The Politics of Unemployment* (Washington, D.C.: Congressional Quarterly Press, 1985), 119.

35. The PSE share of CETA funding is reported in Harrison Donnelly, "The CETA Roller Coaster," *Congressional Quarterly Weekly Reporter* 40, no. 10 (March 6, 1982): 519. The PSE budget and staffing levels for 1981 are recorded in John Palmer and Isabel Sawhill, eds., *The Reagan Record: An Assessment of America's Changing Domestic Priorities* (Washington, D.C.: Urban Institute Press, 1984), appendix C, p. 366.

36. On business views of Reagan economic policy, including the 1981 tax cut, see Levitan and Cooper, *Business Lobbies*; Vogel, *Fluctuating Fortunes*; and Blumenthal, "Whose Side," 29.

37. The text of Stockman's November 20, 1980, memorandum to the president elect is excerpted in David Stockman, "How to Avoid an Economic Dunkirk," *Challenge* 24, no. 1 (March–April 1981): 17–21.

38. David Stockman, *The Triumph of Politics: Why the Reagan Revolution Failed* (New York: Harper & Row, 1986), 89.

39. George Gilder, *Wealth and Poverty* (New York: Basic Books, 1981), 162. The account of Reagan's distributing this book to his cabinet is reported in Vogel, *Fluctuating Fortunes*, 227. Similarly, conservative ideologue Charles Murray held that training programs were useless, since the primary problem of low-income workers was that they had "never been socialized into the discipline of the workplace"; Murray suggested that the solution to structural unemployment lay in attitude adjustment, noting that "the Marine Corps can instill exemplary work habits in recruits who come to the Corps no more 'job-ready' than the recruits to the job-training program." Charles Murray, *Losing Ground: American Social Policy 1950–1980* (New York: Basic Books, 1984), 214–16.

40. *Employment and Training Reporter* 24 (February 25, 1981).

41. *Employment and Training Reporter* 30 (April 8, 1981).

42. This phrase was coined by *Conservative Digest* publisher Richard Viguerie. A statement of his argument can be found in Richard Viguerie, "Defund the Left," *New York Times*, August 11, 1982, A23.

43. On May 18, 1981, Stockman was awarded a citation by the Conservative Caucus, whose president lauded him as the man without whom "the prospect for defunding the left simply wouldn't be here." Adam Clymer, "Conservatives Gather in Umbrella Council for a National Policy," *New York Times*, May 20, 1981, A17.

44. When Reagan entered office in 1980, two-thirds of the public revenues raised in the country were federal; over the 1981 to 1983 period, this ratio was reversed, with state and local revenues accounting for two-thirds of public money. George Peterson, "Federalism and the States: An Experiment in Decentralization," in *Reagan Record*, ed. Palmer and Sawhill, 246. The administration developed a variety of strategies for more directly undermining the capacity for liberal-minded mayors to enact progressive economic policies. For example, the Reagan transition team's Urban Task Force proposed that the administration withhold federal funding from all cities with rent-control laws. David Rosenbaum, "Reagan Aides Urge Rent-Control Cities Lose All U.S. Grants," *New York Times*, November 21, 1980, A1.

45. On elimination of the Community Services Agency, see Lester Salamon, "Nonprofit Organizations: The Lost Opportunity," in *Reagan Record*, ed. Palmer and Sawhill, 274–75.

On the plight of the Legal Services Corporation, see United Press International, "Legal Services: Reagan's Attack," *Boston Globe*, December 1, 1983.

46. Timothy Saasta, "Tying Charity's Hands," *New York Times*, August 2, 1983, A19. A notable exemption was provided for businesses receiving government contracts.

47. "Defunding the Left," *National Journal* 14, no. 22 (May 29, 1982): 943.

48. Howard Wolman and Fred Teitelbaum, "Interest Groups and the Reagan Presidency," in *The Reagan Presidency and the Governing of America*, ed. Lester Salamon and Michael Lund (Washington, D.C.: Urban Institute Press, 1985), 315. While a wide range of nonprofit groups lost funding in the early 1980s, the administration's cuts fell most heavily on advocacy organizations and on groups which originated in 1960s political activity, as shown in Salamon, "Nonprofit Organizations," 280.

49. Demetra Smith Nightingale and Carolyn O'Brien, *Community Based Organizations in the Job Training Partnership System* (Washington, D.C.: Urban Institute Press, 1984), 21.

50. Pines, interview.

51. Palmer and Sawhill, eds., *Reagan Record*, appendix C, 366.

52. For overviews of the general legislative goals of business lobbies during this period, see Levitan and Cooper, *Business Lobbies*; Vogel, *Fluctuating Fortunes*; McQuaid, *Uneasy Partners*.

53. Robinson, "Attitude of Employers," 153, reports on the results of a joint U.S. Chamber of Commerce/Gallup Poll done in May–July, 1978. Of the top six concerns respondents voiced regarding federal training programs, four were related to worker attitudes.

54. Robinson, "Attitude of Employers," 154. The responses which the survey cites as representative include the following:

> We have not been successful in hiring the disadvantaged because most do not want or need to work. . . . they cannot afford to work for us because they have less expenses and no taxes when they get their income from the government. . . . [G]overnment handout programs . . . destroy the incentive or the will to find meaningful work. . . . Place more restrictions on unemployment insurance, and you will have more people to work.

55. National Commission for Manpower Policy, *Business Sector Role*, 96.

56. Mark Bernardo, quoted in Harrison Donnelly, "Youth Subminimum Pay Fate Tied to Adult Wage Floor," *Congressional Quarterly Weekly Reporter* 39, no. 10 (March 7, 1981): 420.

57. "Business vs. Labor—A New Test of Muscle," *Industry Week* 201, no. 6 (June 11, 1979): 24.

58. National Commission for Manpower Policy, *Business Sector Role*, 98. The popularity of military discipline for minority youth dates back at least to the Moynihan Report (U.S. Department of Labor, Office of Planning and Research, *The Negro Family: The Case for National Action* [Washington, D.C.: U.S. Government Printing Office, 1965]) which, as the Vietnam War was escalating, suggested that the social problems of African American male youths might be addressed by encouraging more of them to enroll in the armed forces.

59. Martha Del, "New Congress, New Life for Labor Issues," *Nation's Business* 71 (February 1983): 36.

60. Richard Nathan, "The Reagan Presidency in Domestic Affairs," in *The Reagan Presidency: An Early Assessment*, ed. Fred Greenstein (Baltimore: Johns Hopkins University Press, 1983).

61. James Singer, "Labor Department: It's in Business's Hands Now," *National Journal* 13, no. 17 (April 25, 1981): 726; Del, "New Congress," 36.

62. *Employment and Training Reporter* 34 (May 6, 1981). *Enterprise* 5, no. 12 (December 1981/January 1982), records the National Association of Manufacturers' approving comment on the cuts, noting that "there was no incentive to go back to work under that program."

63. Levitan and Cooper, *Business Lobbies*, 110–11. The authors note that "the Omnibus Reconciliation Act of 1981 represented the most sweeping implementation of employer priorities in the history of the UI program." Isabel Sawhill and Charles Stone, "The Economy: The Key to Success," in *Reagan Record*, ed. Palmer and Sawhill, 82, report that this "suitable work" provision was rejected in Congress despite enthusiastic business support; however, a wide range of additional restrictions was approved. As a result, total UI benefits in the 1982 recession were $8 billion below the level they would have been in the absence of these changes. Due to restricted eligibility rules, only 45% of the unemployed received benefits in any month of 1982, compared with 75% in the recession of 1973–75.

64. *Enterprise* 5, no. 12 (December 1981/January 1982); *Enterprise* 5, no. 4 (April 1981).

65. Gary Orfield and Helene Slessarev, *Job Training under the New Federalism* (Chicago: University of Chicago Press, 1986), 49.

66. *Employment and Training Reporter* 47 (August 5, 1981).

67. Demetra Smith Nightingale, *Federal Employment and Training Policy Changes during the Reagan Administration: State and Local Responses* (Washington, D.C.: Urban Institute Press, 1985), ix.

68. It may be argued that CWEP participants were working for their welfare check and not for free. Nevertheless, it remains true that the sole distinction between the old public service jobs and CWEP positions is that the former provided a living wage and the latter did not.

69. Gary Mucciaroni, *The Political Failure of Employment Policy, 1945–1982* (Pittsburgh: University of Pittsburgh Press, 1990), 178–79.

70. On the use of PSE jobs to substitute for civil service cuts in fiscally strapped cities, see Baumer and Van Horn, *Politics of Unemployment*, 93, 111.

71. *Employment and Training Reporter* 11 (November 19, 1980).

72. *Employment and Training Reporter* 30 (April 8, 1981).

73. Quoted in Lester Salamon and Alan Abramson, "Governance: The Politics of Retrenchment," in *Reagan Record*, ed. Palmer and Sawhill, 52.

74. Vogel, *Fluctuating Fortunes*, 245.

75. Salamon and Abramson, "Governance," 52.

76. For a good description of the uniqueness of the 1981 budget process, see Wolman and Teitelbaum, "Interest Groups," 297–329.

77. *Employment and Training Reporter* 24 (February 25, 1981).

78. Ralph Kinney Bennett, "CETA: $11 Billion Boondoggle," *Reader's Digest*, August 1978, 72–76. Bennett's descriptions of the first two programs are cited in Baumer and Van Horn, *Politics of Unemployment*, 130; the last description is cited in Mucciaroni, "Political Failure," 177. The right's view of PSE as the last refuge of 1960s leftism is further illustrated by Gilder's portrayal of "CETA money . . . financing the efforts of radical filmmakers in Chicago, artists' collectives in Cambridge, and a modern-dance troupe in the Berkshires. Frazzled 'community organizers' clambered aboard, along with gay-movement militants, protest mobilizers against nuclear plants . . . actors in deserted community theaters . . . pot-farming 'foresters' in state parks, laid-back paralegals and rape-crisis emergency aides . . . courtroom attendants dallying with the public defender, haze-headed workers in youth drug clinics" (*Wealth and Poverty*, 159).

79. It is telling that JTPA has retained such a clean reputation in comparison to CETA. There are no data with which to directly compare levels of fraud and abuse in the two programs, but the evidence discussed in chapter 3 suggests that JTPA fraud is probably at least as high as CETA fraud following the 1978 amendments. Since the fraud in JTPA is largely committed by private employers rather than poor people, however, it has not attracted anything approaching the criticism leveled at CETA. Patricia McNeill suggests that "private sector participation . . . has shielded local officials from concerns about possible liability for fraud and abuse" ("The Job Training Partnership Act: A Chronology of Its Development with Recommendations for the

Future," prepared for the U.S. House of Representatives, Committee on Education and Labor, 1986, 37). To the extent that CETA's image embodied the absence of hard-headed discipline, the fact that JTPA activities are overseen by a private sector body may be presumed to guarantee that this problem has been taken care of.

80. Quoted in Baumer and Van Horn, *Politics of Unemployment*, 130.

81. Ibid., 62, 128, 132, 149.

82. On this point, see Weir, *Politics and Jobs*, 127. Baumer and Van Horn, *Politics of Unemployment*, 136, note that following the 1978 amendments, many cities removed CETA administration from the mayor's office and transferred more responsibility to community organizations.

83. John Mollenkopf, *The Contested City* (Princeton: Princeton University Press, 1983).

84. *Employment and Training Reporter* 35 (May 13, 1981).

85. *Employment and Training Reporter* 41 (June 24, 1981). Any hopes of the liberal Democrats resisting the Reagan budget agenda were definitively dashed in the early summer of 1981, when the first budget resolution was sent back to Congress with the administration demanding an additional $20 billion in spending reductions. The House leadership sought to defeat this bill on procedural grounds but lost a crucial vote 210–207. At this point the Democratic leadership functionally lost control of the House it nominally commanded. The *Employment and Training Reporter* 43 (July 8, 1981) wrote at the time that "the impact of the Reagan victory in the House June 26 appears difficult to exaggerate, as a demonstration of the power of the Administration, of the support within Congress for the President's determination to drastically reduce social spending." The staff director for the House Subcommittee on Employment Opportunities is quoted calling the second budget bill "the most sweeping, traumatic, historic measure in my 11 years on the Hill. A single piece of legislation rewrote hundreds of programs. . . . our members hated it; they were cutting programs they had spent their careers creating. . . . [The administration] made eunuchs of these strong old men."

86. In September 1980, the newly organized National Alliance of Community Based Organizations staged a Washington rally calling for the protection of public service jobs, and in early 1981, a Budget Coalition of 150 labor and community organizations, including the U.S. Conference of Mayors, assembled to denounce the Reagan budget plan and to call for PSE's continuation. *Employment and Training Reporter* 4 (October 1, 1980); 25 (March 4, 1981).

87. Baumer and Van Horn, *Politics of Unemployment*, 127; Steven Weisman, "President to Seek Deferrals in Rises for Eight Key Benefits," *New York Times*, September 18, 1981, A1; Frank Gresock, "Phase-out of Revenue Sharing May Be One of New Budget Cuts," *Bond Buyer*, September 18, 1981, 1.

88. Harrison Donnelly and Dale Tate, "Reagan Seeks Halt in CETA Public Service Employment; Asks Jobless Benefits Cuts," *Congressional Quarterly Weekly Reporter* 39, no. 11 (March 14, 1981): 457–58.

89. The National League of Cities agreed to the elimination of the remaining PSE jobs, which contained no income eligibility restrictions, but argued for retention of those slots reserved for the economically disadvantaged. The U.S. Conference of Mayors concentrated much of its lobbying on the issue of whether federal or local officials would be responsible for funding unemployment benefits for those laid off from PSE, and on whether future funding would be controlled by local or state authorities. In April, the National Urban League came out in favor of enterprise zones, which were being promoted by the administration as a substitute for PSE, presumably in the hope that urban tax waivers would fuel the expansion of minority-owned businesses. *Employment and Training Reporter* 21 (February 4, 1981); 25 (March 4, 1981); 30 (April 8, 1981); and 34 (May 6, 1981). In 1982 Rev. Leon Sullivan's OIC similarly voiced its support for enterprise zones. U.S. Congress, *Employment and Training Policy, 1982, Part 2*, 144.

90. *Employment and Training Reporter* 36 (May 20, 1981).

91. *Employment and Training Reporter* 44 (July 15, 1981).

92. Senator Quayle opened the March 1982 joint hearings on JTPA by stating that the committees' goal was to "produce a training and employment bill that, in fact, will be signed by the President." U.S. Congress, *Employment and Training Policy, 1982, Part 1*, 1.

93. Quoted in Harrison Donnelly, "House Passes Scaled-Down Job Training Measure, 356–52," *Congressional Quarterly Weekly Reporter* 40, no. 32 (August 7, 1982): 1895.

94. U.S. Senate, *Senate Report 97–469: Report Accompanying S 2036, the Training for Jobs Act*, 97th Congress, 2nd session, June 9, 1982, 84.

95. McNeill, "Job Training Partnership Act," 17.

96. U.S. House of Representatives, Committee on Education and Labor, *Report No. 97–537 Accompanying HR 5320, the Job Training Partnership Act*, 97th Congress, 2nd session, May 17, 1982.

97. Mucciaroni, *Political Failure*, 165.

98. U.S. House of Representatives, *Report No. 97–537*, 36. Even the Democrats' arguments on behalf of wages for trainees were often couched in the rhetoric of Reagan defederalism, insisting that local governments knew best what would work in their economies and should not have their hands tied by Washington. U.S. Senate, *Senate Report 97–469*, 84–85.

99. U.S. House of Representatives, *Report No. 97–537*, 66. Elsewhere, Weiss was an outspoken supporter of PSE and characterized Reagan economic initiatives as a series of "pathetic policy failures."

100. U.S. Congress, *Employment and Training Policy, 1982, Part 1*, 14.

101. U.S. Congress, *Employment and Training Policy, 1982, Part 2*, 121.

102. Ibid., 150, records the National Urban League's support for targeting.

103. Ibid., 675.

104. Quote is from the testimony of Jobs for Youth, ibid., 935.

105. *Congressional Quarterly Weekly Reporter* 38, no. 29 (July 19, 1980): 2030–56.

106. U.S. Senate, *U.S. Senate Report No. 97–649*, 4.

107. U.S. Congress, *Employment and Training Policy, 1982, Part 1*, 2.

108. Baumer and Van Horn, *Politics of Unemployment*, 158–68.

109. *Employment and Training Reporter* 23 (February 17, 1982).

110. Fenno, *Making of a Senator*, 35–55. For the freshman Senator, JTPA appeared as an unexpected plum opportunity to establish a reputation as a skilled legislator. Quayle had no particular policy expertise nor longstanding interest in employment issues. However, he had won his seat in an upset election against veteran Democrat Birch Bayh by repeatedly emphasizing the Democrats' failure to alleviate soaring unemployment among Indiana auto workers. As unemployment rose through his first term, Quayle championed the need for Republicans to fashion some response. He insisted from the first on crafting a bill which would win the backing of the Labor Committee's ranking Democrat, Senator Ted Kennedy. In part, Quayle's bipartisanship reflected strategic concerns: his subcommittee's nominal Republican majority could easily be defeated by the defection of either of two northern liberal Republicans, and he would have greater authority in shaping the final conference compromise if he could speak from a position of consensus. In addition, a widely supported bill would allow him to negotiate administration demands from a position of strength rather than simply serving as the president's mouthpiece.

111. The administration sought a total ban on wages and stipends, opposed the public jobs in the Summer Youth Employment Program, and rejected the requirement that PICs share planning authority with local elected officials.

112. Fenno, *Making of a Senator*, 115.

113. "Republicans' New Budget Road Looks a Bit Rocky," *New York Times*, December 24, 1981, A16.

114. Ibid. Indeed, the 1982 elections brought widespread losses for the Republicans, cutting their representation in the House by nearly 30 seats and returning functional control to the liberal House leadership; Baumer and Van Horn, *Politics of Unemployment*, 167.

115. Guttman, interview.

116. In 1981, PSIP was funded at $283 million, out of a total CETA budget of $7.8 billion. William Lanouette, "Life after Death—CETA's Demise Won't Mean the End of Manpower Training," *National Journal* 14, no. 6 (February 6, 1982): 241.

117. Vogel, *Fluctuating Fortunes*, 54–57, discusses the late-1960s attacks on corporate facilities and business's concern that the country's elite youth were being steered away from business careers and toward anti-business activism.

118. Ibid., 59–70.

119. Ibid., 69–70. Among others, Common Cause, Friends of the Earth, the Natural Resources Defense Council, Public Citizen, Environmental Action, the Consumer Federation of America, and the Center for Law and Social Policy were all established in 1969 or 1970.

120. Ibid., 115–21. In 1973, the Watergate special prosecutor filed charges against American Airlines, Goodyear, and Minnesota Mining and Manufacturing for illegal campaign contributions. Illegally gathered funds from the milk producers' lobby were used for the break-in of Daniel Ellsberg's psychiatrist's office. Ultimately, twenty-one companies pleaded guilty to violating federal campaign laws. Lockheed was convicted in 1976 of spending $24 million on foreign bribes. Later that year, Northrop's president was forced to resign over charges that the company had paid $30 million in foreign bribes.

121. Ibid., 126. In 1975 two bills were introduced calling for the break-up of the oil companies; both were eventually defeated by close votes, but the government did institute a special windfall profits tax targeted at the major oil companies.

122. Ibid., 54, 114.

123. Ibid., 137.

124. Ibid., 143. Citicorp chair Walter Wriston charged at the time that the economic planning initiative was a first step toward an "economic police state."

125. The fight against labor law reform was a breakthrough in establishing a unified front of small and big business. It also represented an innovation in business lobbying techniques. Rather than rely on major corporate CEOs, who might provoke negative public reaction, the campaign was framed as a battle between "big labor" and "small business." To this end, the CEOs of the Business Roundtable lent their corporate jets to be used ferrying small businessmen to the capital. One Senate aide noted, "I can't remember a time when we last experienced a lobby effort like this. I don't think they missed a single possible opponent of the bill in our state." McQuaid, *Uneasy Partners*, 155.

126. Under pressure from Republican and business opposition, the bill was amended multiple times from 1976 to 1978. By the time it was passed in 1978, the bill's central tenets had been gutted: the new language omitted the legal right to a job and the requirement of government planning for full employment; it added the goals of zero inflation and a balanced budget, to be achieved by 1983. For a history of the Humphrey-Hawkins bill, including business opposition, see Helen Ginsburg, *Full Employment and Public Policy: The United States and Sweden* (Lexington, Mass.: Lexington Books), 63–80. For an analysis of business opposition to the bill, see Weir, *Politics and Jobs*, chapter 5.

127. National Commission for Manpower Policy, *The Business Sector Role*, 34.

128. Ibid., 53. Quote is from National Alliance of Business President Lloyd Hand.

129. Ibid., 53. Training programs had long been considered a logical vehicle for corporate expressions of public concern. Levitan and Cooper, *Business Lobbies*, 15, report that in the early 1970s, the National Association of Manufacturers "attempted to reverse its public image as a naysayer to all government social welfare interventions and to create a more positive image. The efforts included a manpower training project for minorities."

130. Jim O'Connell, interview with the author, Washington, D.C., February 3, 1995. In 1978 O'Connell was a staffer for Senator Jacob Javits, the ranking Republican on the Labor

Committee. In 1995 he served on the Business Roundtable's Employment Task Force. National Commission for Manpower Policy, *The Business Sector Role*, 56, quotes NAB President Hand as warning that "the President is under considerable political pressure to add billions to the subsidized public jobs program," and suggesting the need to prove that "the private enterprise system is capable of meeting this challenge."

131. On the business embrace of PSIP, see Margaret Price, "Can CETA Overcome Business' Resistance?" *Industry Week* 203, no. 4 (November 12, 1979): 34–38; "Business Gets a Shot at Slicing Unemployment," *Business Week*, August 13, 1979, 78.

132. Quoted in Stanley Modic, "Excellence in Management Awards: Profile of a Winner," *Industry Week* 211, no. 2 (October 19, 1981): 61–63.

133. Vogel, *Fluctuating Fortunes*, 252. Multiple press accounts of "Greed Electric" helped lead to the elimination of "safe harbor leasing" in the 1982 tax law.

134. Ibid., 256.

135. Russell Milliken, Mead Corporation, quoted in Timothy Clark, "Business behind Closed Doors," *National Journal* 14, no. 14 (April 3, 1982): 597. Similarly, Vogel, *Fluctuating Fortunes*, 256, reports that in March 1982, the Business Roundtable agreed to support the elimination of several tax loopholes.

136. James Burke, "Corporations Can Do Something about Unemployment through Job Training Partnership," Business Roundtable Report No. 82–6, Business Roundtable, Washington, D.C., June 1983. In 1983, Burke was chair of the Roundtable's Employment Policy Task Force.

137. Martin Lefkowitz, U.S. Chamber of Commerce economist, interview with the author, Washington, D.C., February 3, 1995. Lefkowitz's comment was offered in a discussion of the chamber's support for JTPA in 1982. The chamber's chief lobbyist on JTPA similarly reported that businesspeople saw training as an alternative to industrial policy, which enjoyed relatively wide support in the early 1980s. Hemming, interview.

138. Vogel, *Fluctuating Fortunes*, 256. In 1984, a survey found that a majority of business executives thought the recession had been good for the country.

139. Hemming, interview.

140. *Employment and Training Reporter* 3 (September 23, 1981); Weisman, "President to Seek Deferrals"; Helen Dewar and Martin Schram, "New Budget Cuts Reportedly Target 75,000 US Jobs," *Washington Post*, September 18, 1981, A1; Gresock, "Phase-out"; George Church, "Blood, Sweat and Tears: Preparing for More Bone-Tiring Battles over the Budget," *Time*, September 28, 1981, 18; Daniel Cook, "Reagan's Axe is Falling on Job Training," *Industry Week* 211, no. 4 (November 16, 1981): 19–20.

141. Renee Berger, "Private-Sector Initiatives in the Reagan Era: New Actors Rework an Old Theme," in *Reagan Presidency*, ed. Salamon and Lund, 185. Berger was on the task force's staff.

142. Commerce Secretary Malcolm Baldrige, addressing the National Alliance of Business, quoted in *Employment and Training Reporter* 7 (October 21, 1981).

143. Testimony of Assistant Secretary Albert Angrisani, *Employment and Training Reporter* 8 (October 28, 1981).

144. Carlton Spitzer, "Lobbying, Ethics and Common Sense," *Public Relations Journal* 38, no. 2 (February 1982): 34–36.

145. Statement of the Corporate Responsibility Task Force, in Business Roundtable Report No. 81–8, Business Roundtable, Washington, D.C., September 1981. Similarly, Leo Northart, "Private Sector Initiative," *Public Relations Journal* 38, no. 4 (April 1982): 6, quotes NAM President Alexander Trowbridge worrying that "The American public will seek an improvement in the quality of life, and if it doesn't see business as a contributor to that effort, then our political strength will ebb and the pendulum can swing back to the onerous levels of past adversary relationships."

146. Quoted in Del, "New Congress," 36. Similarly, Assistant Secretary of Labor for Employment and Training Albert Angrisani suggested that the private sector could eventually take over responsibility for all training services, cited in *Employment and Training Reporter* 8 (October 28, 1981).

147. Business Roundtable, Business Roundtable Report No. 81–6, Business Roundtable, Washington, D.C., July 1981. For similar statements by the U.S. Chamber of Commerce, see *Employment and Training Reporter* 20 (January 27, 1982).

148. Baumer and Van Horn, *Politics of Unemployment*, 179.

149. Blumenthal, "Whose Side," 29.

150. In September 1981, Budget Director Stockman told the White House policy group that a number of social programs including job training "are going to have to be eliminated entirely in next year's budget." Stockman, *Triumph of Politics*, 323.

151. Cited in Laurence Barrett, *Gambling with History: Reagan in the White House* (New York: Doubleday, 1983), 402.

152. *Employment and Training Reporter* 4 (September 30, 1981).

153. Richard Wirthlin, memorandum of February 2, 1982, cited in Barrett, *Gambling*, 338.

154. Barrett, *Gambling*, 414.

155. Cited in ibid., 391.

156. Steven Weisman, "Reagan Tiptoes around Some Economic Liabilities," *New York Times*, September 26, 1982, A1.

157. Stockman's views are characterized by Guttman, who participated in several last-minute White House meetings convincing the president to endorse JTPA.

158. In its final form, JTPA embodied several key compromises on the issues of greatest contention. Funding was set at $3.8 billion, in keeping with the Quayle compromise and in contrast with the House's proposal of $4.5 billion and the administration's $2.4 billion. The new bill marked a sharp break from the CETA delivery system for distributing these funds. Under JTPA, resources would go to the governors rather than the mayors. Although the Democrats won pass-through language establishing formulas for the intra-state distribution of funds—thus relieving local officials of the need to appeal to the discretion of governors—the formula was cast in terms which served to underfund urban areas. Two-thirds of the funds for JTPA were distributed according to an area's unemployment rate and one-third according to its poverty rate. Since large cities typically contain many poor people who are out of the labor market—and therefore not officially unemployed—a formula which gave primary consideration to unemployment rates inevitably steered money away from the concentrations of nonworking poor people in urban centers. At the local level, authority for planning programs and establishing criteria for awarding contracts was to be shared jointly by local elected officials and the Private Industry Council. Finally, the bill contained a complete ban on public service jobs and a near-total prohibition on paying wages or stipends to trainees.

159. Meeting with Editors and Publishers of Trade Magazines, *Weekly Compilation of Presidential Documents* 18 (September 24, 1982): 1205.

160. U.S. Senate, *Senate Report 97–469*, 38.

161. U.S. Congress, *Employment and Training Policy, 1982, Part 2*, 581.

162. McNeill, *Job Training Partnership Act*, 15.

163. U.S. Congress, *Employment and Training Policy, 1982, Part 2*, 569. For similar expressions by the National Alliance of Business, U.S. Chamber of Commerce, National Association of Manufacturers, Committee on Economic Development, and National Tooling and Machining Association, see ibid., 536, 562, 652; and *Employment and Training Reporter* 22 (February 10, 1982).

164. In explaining the administration's position, Assistant Secretary of Labor Angrisani suggested that "because there are no wages or allowances [in JTPA] . . . the person who gets into the program is really going to want to be trained to improve him- or herself. What wages

and allowances do is ruin the motivational aspects of the program." *Employment and Training Reporter* 31 (April 14, 1982).

165. Fenno, *Making of a Senator*, 130.

Chapter Six

1. Linda McMahon, quoted in Paul Street, "The Poverty of Workfare: Dubious Claims, Dark Clouds, and a Silver Lining," *Dissent* (fall 1998): 59.

2. The Clinton welfare proposal was based primarily on David Ellwood, *Poor Support: Poverty in the American Family* (New York: Basic Books, 1988).

3. David Ellwood, "Welfare Reform as I Knew It: When Bad Things Happen to Good Policies," *American Prospect* 26 (May–June 1996): 22–30.

4. See for example Sheldon Danziger and Jeffrey Lehman, "How Will Welfare Recipients Fare in the Labor Market?" *Challenge* 39, no. 2 (March–April 1996); Gary Burtless, "Employment Prospects of Welfare Recipients," in *The Work Alternative: Welfare Reform and the Realities of the Job Market*, ed. Demetra Smith Nightingale and Robert Haveman (Washington, D.C.: Urban Institute Press, 1995); Paul Kleppner and Nikolas Theodore, *Work after Welfare: Is the Midwest's Booming Economy Creating Enough Jobs?* (Chicago: Midwest Job Gap Project, 1997); National Association of Business Economists, *NABE Outlook and Policy Survey* (Washington, D.C., 1996). In July 1996 the Congressional Budget Office issued a report finding that a majority of states would be unable to satisfy TANF's numerical goals for getting welfare recipients into jobs. Robert Pear, "Budget Agency Says Welfare Bill Would Cut Rolls by Millions," *New York Times*, July 16, 1996, A12.

5. Robert Reich, *Locked in the Cabinet* (New York: Knopf, 1997), 178.

6. Alan Finder, "Welfare Clients Outnumber Jobs They Might Fill," *New York Times*, August 25, 1996, A1. Finder reports that even the conservative Cato Institute admitted that New York and other big cities couldn't provide jobs for everyone due to come off welfare; Cato suggested that the urban poor simply needed to move to faster-growing parts of the country.

7. The best research available at the time of the PRWORA debates was a three-year evaluation of California's GAIN program, which followed 33,000 recipients in six counties. Even in the single most successful county, the evaluation reported very modest differences between those who went through the GAIN program and those who did not. James Riccio et al., *GAIN: Benefits, Costs and Three-Year Impacts of a Welfare-to-Work Program* (New York: Manpower Demonstration and Research Corporation, 1994).

8. Jeffrey Katz, "Major Aspects of Welfare Bill Approved by Subcommittee," *Congressional Quarterly Weekly Reporter* (February 18, 1995), 525–29.

9. Children's Defense Fund, "CDF Condemns Plan That Makes 1.2 Million More Children Poor to Fund Giveaways for the Rich," Associated Press, November 10, 1995.

10. Dick Morris, *Behind the Oval Office: Getting Reelected against All Odds* (Los Angeles: Renaissance Books, 1999), 93. Similarly, Reich, *Locked in the Cabinet*, 329, reports that, one week before the 1996 elections, Morris lieutenant Mark Penn briefed the cabinet on how the president had bounced back from the 1994 debacle:

> We did this by co-opting the Republicans on all their issues—getting tough on welfare, tough on crime, balancing the budget and cracking down on illegal immigration. . . . The suburban swing are busy at their jobs and worry about the values their kids are picking up. These aren't the sorts of things a president can do much about, of course. But it was important to show the president was concerned. So we emphasized teen smoking, school uniforms, nighttime curfews, drug testing at school, and sex and violence on television. All these polled very well.

11. Morris, *Behind the Oval Office*, 298.

12. Quoted in Elizabeth Drew, *Whatever It Takes: The Real Struggle for Political Power in America* (New York: Penguin Books, 1997), 130.

13. Drew, *Whatever It Takes*, 133.

14. Morris, *Behind the Oval Office*, 300. In addition, at least some Clinton advisors saw their interests directly threatened by the prospect of a broader party victory. Drew, *Whatever It Takes*, 135, reports that domestic policy advisor and Democratic Leadership Council member Bruce Reed warned Clinton that he should sign PRWORA because if the Democrats retook Congress, liberal committee chairmen might block any consensus bill from passing, thereby denying the president the opportunity to make good on his best-known campaign pledge.

15. Reported in Reich, *Locked in the Cabinet*, 320, and Drew, *Whatever It Takes*, 132–34.

16. Drew, *Whatever It Takes*, 135; Morris, *Behind the Oval Office*, 301.

17. Sheila Zedlewski, Sandra Clark, Eric Meier, and Keith Watson, "Potential Effects of Congressional Welfare Reform Legislation on Family Incomes," (Urban Institute, Washington, D.C., July 26, 1996).

18. Peter Edelman, acting assistant secretary for planning and evaluation, and Mary Jo Bane, assistant secretary for children and families, resigned on September 11, 1996, with Edelman explaining, "I have devoted the last 20-plus years to doing whatever I could to help in reducing poverty in America. I believe the recently enacted welfare bill goes in the opposite direction." Wendell Primus, deputy assistant secretary for policy and evaluation, resigned in August 1996. David Ellwood, who had been assistant secretary for planning and evaluation, had resigned in September 1995, already disillusioned with the direction of the president's evolving welfare policy. Barbara Vobejda and Judith Havemann, "2 HHS Officials Quit over Welfare Changes; Protest by Clinton Friend, Influential Academic Shows Split in Administration," *Washington Post*, September 12, 1996, A1.

19. Quoted in Drew, *Whatever It Takes*, 149.

20. *Personal Responsibility and Work Opportunity Reconciliation Act.* Up to 20% of recipients in each state may be exempted from the five-year limit if they face special needs. The share of current recipients that must be engaged in work activities escalated, under the legislation's formula, from 25% in 1997 to 50% in 2002. For one useful summary of the TANF work provisions, see U.S. General Accounting Office, *Welfare Reform: States' Experiences in Providing Employment Assistance to TANF Clients*, GAO/HEHS-99-22, Washington, D.C., February 1999.

21. Julie Strawn, Mark Greenberg, and Steve Savner, "Improving Employment Outcomes under TANF," Center for Law and Social Policy, Washington, D.C., January 2001, 5.

22. Irwin Stelzer, "Lessons of the U.S. Job Machine," American Enterprise Institute, Washington, D.C., May 1997.

23. "Why Is LA GAIN So Successful?" Los Angeles County GAIN web page, http://dpss.co.la.ca.us/gain/default_gain.cfm.

24. The Department of Labor explained that one of the "basic goals" of the 1992 amendments was "to focus JTPA on providing more training and less stand-alone job placement." Quote is from the preamble to the amendments' Final Rule. Federal Register, *20 CFR Part 626, et al.: Job Training Partnership Act; Final Rule*, vol. 59, no. 170, September 2, 1994, 45805. Cited in U.S. Department of Labor, *Implementation of the 1992 Job Training Partnership Act (JTPA) Amendments* (Washington, D.C.: U.S. Department of Labor, 1997), 3–13. For the employment and earnings of welfare recipients receiving various types of JTPA services, see U.S. Department of Labor, Office of the Inspector General, *Profiling JTPA's AFDC Participants*, Report No. 06-98-002-03-340, U.S. Department of Labor, May 7, 1998.

25. U.S. General Accounting Office, *Welfare Reform: States' Experiences in Providing Employment Assistance to TANF Clients*, GAO/HEHS-99-22 (Washington, D.C.: U.S. General Accounting Office, 1999), 2–3. The same report, 13, cites the example of Ohio's program, where the share

of clients receiving either job skills training or education fell from one-third in the pre-TANF era to one-tenth under the current regime.

26. Joel Handler and Yeheskel Hasenfeld, *We the Poor People: Work, Poverty, and Welfare* (New Haven: Yale University Press, 1997), 62–64, 77.

27. U.S. General Accounting Office, *Welfare Reform: Moving Hard-to-Employ Recipients into the Workforce*, Report GAO-01-368, March 2001, 3.

28. Quoted in Laura Meckler, "GOP Celebrates Welfare Success," Associated Press, May 27, 1999.

29. On the impact of the late-1990s expansion on job opportunities for welfare recipients, see Jared Bernstein and Mark Greenberg, "Reforming Welfare Reform," *American Prospect* 12, no. 1 (January 1–15, 2001).

30. Pamela Loprest, "Families Who Left Welfare: Who Are They and How Are They Doing?" Urban Institute, Washington, D.C., 1999, shows that the type of jobs held and level of wages earned by recent welfare leavers are nearly identical to those of other low-income women.

31. The TANF funding formula treats all reductions in a state's welfare caseload as if they represent recipients placed in jobs. Thus states that cut their rolls through any means whatsoever—including tighter eligibility criteria, shorter time limits, or discouraging applicants from signing up in the first place—are deemed to have satisfied the employment quotas, even if they produce no evidence that former recipients have found work. TANF establishes a formula for "caseload reduction credits." For example, if a state's caseload falls by 10 percent, its employment quota for that year is reduced by 10 points. On this point, see Handler and Hasenfel, *We the Poor People*, 210. In 1999, the Senate reaffirmed its lack of interest in the fate of welfare recipients when it rejected a proposal that would have required the Department of Health and Human Services to report annually on the employment status of former TANF recipients. Paul Wellstone, "America's Disappeared," *Nation* 269, no. 2 (July 12, 1999): 5–6.

32. Mark Greenberg, "Welfare Reauthorization: An Early Guide to the Issues," Center for Law and Social Policy, 2000, 6, http://www.clasp.org.

33. Loprest, "Families Who Left Welfare," 12. Similar results from a six-state study are reported by Randy Albelda, "What Welfare Reform Has Wrought," *Dollars and Sense* 221 (January–February 1999); Chris Tilly, "Beyond Patching the Safety Net: A Welfare and Work Survival Strategy," *Dollars and Sense* 221 (January–February 1999); and Strawn, Greenberg, and Savner, "Improving Employment."

34. Loprest, "Families Who Left Welfare," table 2; Washington state study is reported in Center for Law and Social Policy, *CLASP Update: A CLASP Report on Welfare Reform Developments*, January 2001, 11, http://www.clasp.org.

35. Loprest, "Families Who Left Welfare," 12. On this point, see also Robert Reich, "American Sweatshops," *American Prospect Online*, http://www.prospect.org.

36. Loprest, "Families Who Left Welfare," 20–21.

37. Center for Community Change, "Policy Alert: Monitoring the Impact of Welfare Reform," http://www.communitychange.org; Children's Defense Fund, "Families Struggling to Make It in the Workforce: A Post-Welfare Report," 2000, http://www.cdf.org.

38. Loprest, "Families Who Left Welfare," 5.

39. Frances Fox Piven, "Thompson's Easy Ride," *Nation* (February 26, 2001), http://www.thenation.com; National Campaign for Jobs and Income Support, "Credit Where Blame Is Due: Governor Thompson's Record on Low-Income Programs and Policy," January 16, 2001, http://www.cbp.org.

40. Loprest, "Families Who Left Welfare," tables 1, 3.

41. Congressman Phil English, *Congressional Record* 1995, H3362, cited in Stephanie Burkhalter, *The Poor Are Not Like the Rest of Us: The Social Construction of Welfare Mothers in Congressional Policy Discourse*, M.S. thesis, University of Oregon, 1996, 124.

42. Kathryn Edin and Laura Lein, *Making Ends Meet: How Single Mothers Survive Welfare and Low-Wage Work* (New York: Russell Sage, 1997), 63, report that welfare recipients in their sample had an average of 5.6 years' work experience before enrolling in AFDC. They cite a 1993 finding by the U.S. House of Representatives that 60% of AFDC recipients had worked in the previous two years. Similarly, the U.S. Department of Labor found that 59% of AFDC recipients enrolled in JTPA programs had worked within the past three years. Office of the Inspector General, *Profiling JTPA's AFDC Participants*. On this point see also Sandra Morgen and Jill Weigt, "Poor Women, Fair Work, and Welfare-to-Work That Works," unpublished manuscript, 1998; and Virginia Schein, *Working from the Margins: Voices of Mothers in Poverty* (Ithaca: Cornell University Press, 1995).

43. Edin and Lein, *Making Ends Meet*, 64. Indeed, many single mothers end up on public assistance because their jobs prevent them from guaranteeing even emergency care for their children. Schein, *Working from the Margins*, 83, describes three such examples: a woman who applied for public assistance after being told she'd be fired if she took off early one winter night at 10:00 P.M. when her child was sick; another who went on welfare after being fired for missing a day of work to care for a sick child; and a third whose starting time was switched from 7:00 to 6:00 A.M., forcing her to get her kids up at 4:30 each morning to drive them across town to their grandmother before reporting to work.

44. Christopher Cook, "Plucking Workers: Tyson Foods Looks to the Welfare Rolls for a Captive Labor Force," *Progressive* 62 no. 8 (August 1998): 28–31. Quote is from Tyson Foods spokeswoman Jennifer Cave.

45. Steven Greenhouse, "Many Participants in Workfare Take the Place of City Workers," *New York Times*, April 13, 1998, A1.

46. Juan Gonzalez, "Read These Ballots and WEP," *New York Daily News*, October 21, 1997, 12.

47. Sal Albanese, "How I'd Make Workfare Work," *New York Daily News*, July 9, 1997.

48. "Pierre," quoted in Kimberly Freeman, *Welfare Reform As We Know It: First-Hand Accounts from the Frontlines* (Washington, D.C.: Jobs with Justice, 1997), 7.

49. "Robert," quoted in ibid., 2.

50. Lynette Holloway, "Plurality of Workfare Recipients Said to Vote in Favor of a Union," *New York Times*, October 24, 1997, B1.

51. Public works, park maintenance, protective services, and health services were among the most common occupations of CETA workers. Richard Nathan, Robert Cook, and V. Lane Rawlins, *Public Service Employment: A Field Evaluation* (Washington, D.C.: Brookings Institution, 1981).

52. Until 1978, CETA legislation required that workers be paid the prevailing wage for their occupations.

53. On this point, see Morgen and Weigt, "Poor Women," 25.

54. "Celucci Ousts Advisers," *Boston Globe*, August 14, 1994.

55. Piven, "Thompson's Easy Ride"; Milwaukee Deputy Mayor David Riemer, quoted in Margo Huston, "W-2 Work or Else: W-2 Cash for Training Called a 'Step Back,'" *Milwaukee Journal Sentinel*, September 17, 1998, 1.

56. In 1996 alone, 8,000 recipients were forced to leave the City University system in order to perform workfare assignments. Eleanor Bader, "Unfair Workfare," *Dollars and Sense* 213 (September–October 1997): 31.

57. U.S. Department of Labor, Employment and Training Administration, *Fact Sheet: Welfare-to-Work Grants*, http://wtw.doleta.gov/resources/fact-grants.htm.

58. Lorraine McDonnell and Gail Zellman, *Education and Training for Work in the Fifty States: A Compendium of State Policies* (Santa Monica: Rand Corporation, 1993), table 4.1. Figure is for "customized training" programs.

59. Stephen Freedman, Jean Tansey Knab, Lisa Gennetia, and David Navarro, "The Los Angeles Jobs-First GAIN Evaluation: Final Report on a Work First Program in a Major Urban Center," Manpower Demonstration Research Corporation, New York, N.Y., 2000, 9.

60. Strawn, Greenberg, and Savner, "Improving Employment Outcomes," 6.

61. Freedman et al., "GAIN: Final Report," figure 1.

62. U.S. General Accounting Office, *Welfare to Work: Current AFDC Program Not Sufficiently Focused on Employment* (Washington, D.C.: U.S. General Accounting Office, 1994), 10.

63. McDonnell and Zellman, *Education and Training*, table 5.1. Somewhat less misleading is Illinois's Project Chance. Nevertheless, this is still quite a way from a truly frank welfare program, which would have to be named Project Not Very Likely.

64. Judith Gueron, "Work and Welfare: Lessons on Employment Programs," *Journal of Economic Perspectives* 4, no. 1 (1990): 89.

65. Ruth Conniff, "Big Bad Welfare: Welfare Reform Politics and Children," *Progressive* 58, no. 8 (August 1994): 18–21.

66. Freedman et al., "GAIN: Final Report," 5–6, 10.

67. Freedman et al., "GAIN: Final Report," 6.

68. Los Angeles County GAIN web page. An even more romantic view is that of Jason Turner, the chief architect of welfare to work programs in both Wisconsin and New York City. Explaining the importance of workfare, Turner insists, "Work is one's gift to others, and when you sever that relationship with your fellow man, you're doing more than just harm to yourself econom ically. You're doing spiritual harm." Quoted in Jason DeParle, "Committed to a Moral Motive for Work: The Designer of Wisconsin's Welfare System Comes to New York," *New York Times*, January 20, 1998, C11.

69. Edin and Lein, *Making Ends Meet*, 73, report that overwhelmingly, "women who had been through [welfare to work programs] believed the jobs that the caseworkers recommended were not a realistic alternative to welfare."

70. Quoted in Freedman et al., "GAIN: Final Report," 3.

71. Quoted in Edin and Lein, *Making Ends Meet*, 74.

72. See, for example, National Center on the Educational Quality of the Workforce, *First Findings from the EQW National Employer Survey* (Philadelphia: University of Pennsylvania, 1995).

73. Masha Regenstein and Jack Meyer, *Job Prospects for Welfare Recipients: Employers Speak Out* (Washington, D.C.: Urban Institute, 1998), 25; Bill Leonard, "Welfare to Work: Filling a Tall Order," *HR Magazine* 43, no. 6 (May 1998): 84.

74. Virginia O'Leary, "The Hawthorne Effect in Reverse: Trainer Orientation for the Hard-Core Unemployed Women," *Journal of Applied Psychology* 56, no. 6 (1972): 491–94.

75. U.S. General Accounting Office, *Welfare Reform*, 24.

76. Kay Hymowitz, "Job Training That Works," *Wall Street Journal*, February 13, 1997.

77. Ira Shor, "Working Hands and Critical Minds: A Paulo Freire Model for Job Training," *Journal of Education* 170, no. 2 (1988): 113–15.

78. Ibid.

79. On managers' input into the curricula of school-to-work transition programs, see Hanah Roditi, "Youth Apprenticeship: High Schools for Docile Workers," *Nation* 254, no. 10 (March 16, 1992): 340–43.

Chapter Seven

1. Quoted on *All Things Considered*: "In the Aftermath of the Shooting Death of a Young Black Man by Police, Community Leaders Say Attempts to Bridge the Gap between Police and Minorities in Cincinnati Have Fallen Short," National Public Radio, April 23, 2001.

2. The administration's 1982 job training proposal (S. 2184) called for a temporary program authorized for five years only. "Administration Draft CETA Replacement Bill Targets Disadvantaged, Increases State Role," *Daily Labor Report* 34 February 19, 1982, A7.

3. Official poverty rates fell significantly in the late 1990s; however, given the failure to update the government's threshold, as described in chapter 1 and appendix A, part of this gain had to do with the definition of the poverty threshold rather than being substantive. Even using the government threshold, the number of people in poverty remained stubbornly high.

4. Representative Bill Gooding, quoted in James Bennett, "Clinton to Seek $1 Billion for 'Skills Gap': Appeal Is Bipartisan, but He Does Not Cite a Source for Financing," *New York Times*, January 29, 1999, A10.

5. Bill Clinton and Al Gore, *Putting People First: How We Can All Change America* (New York: Times Books, 1992), 126–27.

6. Only eight months after taking office, Labor Secretary Reich told the Conference on the Future of the American Workplace that "the jury is still out on whether the traditional union is necessary for the new workplace." Louis Uchitelle, "Labor Leaders Fight for a Place in the President's Workplace of the Future," *New York Times*, August 8, 1993, 32.

7. In its initial legislative agenda, the Republican Congress proposed cutting, but not eliminating, federal job training efforts.

8. George W. Bush, "Remarks by the President in Commencement Address," University of Notre Dame, May 21, 2001, http://www.whitehouse.gov.

9. Elizabeth Kolbert and Adam Clyber, "The Politics of Layoffs: In Search of a Message," *New York Times*, March 8, 1996, A1. In his 1998 State of the Union address, President Clinton stressed his commitment to "offer help and hope to those Americans temporarily left behind by the global marketplace or by the march of technology. . . . That's why we have more than doubled funding for training dislocated workers . . . and if my new budget is adopted, we will triple funding." "Transcript of the State of the Union Message from President Clinton," *New York Times*, January 28, 1998, A19.

10. U.S. Department of Labor, Employment and Training Administration, *Employment Programs: Summary of Budget Authority, FY 1984 to Current.*

11. U.S. Department of Labor, Employment and Training Administration, "2002 Annual Performance Plan for Committee on Appropriations," March 2001.

12. Robert Guttman, interview with the author, February 2, 1995, Washington, D.C.

13. Paula Collins, spokesperson for the Business Roundtable, telephone interview with the author, January 27, 1995.

14. Jeff Keefe, "Hitching a Ride: Labor and the Perils of the Information Highway," *Dollars and Sense* 194 (July/August 1994): 16. Similarly, Laurie Dougherty, "Looking for Work in a Buyer's Market," *Dollars and Sense* 194 (July/August 1994): 12, reports that in 1994 NYNEX announced its intention to cut 16,000 jobs, while simultaneously touting a plan to donate twenty voice-mail boxes to a Boston homeless shelter to help residents apply for jobs.

15. Laurie Udesky, "The 'Social Responsibility' Gap: Sweatshops behind the Labels," *Nation* 258, no. 19 (May 26, 1994): 666.

16. Annette Reeping, quoted in William Wagel, "New Beginnings for Displaced Workers: Outplacement at GE," *Personnel* (December 1988): 18.

17. Quoted in Dawn Gunsch, "Laid-off Workers Hone Job Skills," *Personnel Journal* (March 1993): 46.

18. Elaine Chao, Statement before the Senate Committee on Appropriations, Subcommittee on Labor, Health and Human Services, and Education, May 2, 2001, U.S. Department of Labor, http://www.dol.gov/_sec/media/congress/010502ec.htm.

19. A 1991 survey of local chambers of commerce found that, while 62% had had members serve on the PIC board, only 16% had firms which hired JTPA graduates. U.S. Chamber of Com-

merce, "Assessing Chamber of Commerce Involvement in the Delivery of Job Training Partnership Act Services," 1991. This accords with McNeill, who found that "most PIC members do not use JTPA to meet their hiring needs" (37). Patricia McNeill, "The Job Training Partnership Act: A Chronology of Its Development with Recommendations for the Future," prepared for the U.S. House of Representatives, Committee on Education and Labor, 1986.

20. Jim O'Connell, interview with the author, Washington, D.C., February 3, 1995.

21. U.S. Department of Labor, Bureau of Labor Statistics, Labor Force Statistics from the Current Population Survey, table 8, "Total Displaced Workers by Selected Characteristics and Employment Status in February 2000."

22. "NAFTA Job Retraining Program out of Money," *Northwest Labor Press* 102, no. 8 (April 20, 2001): 1. The NAFTA/Trade Adjustment Assistance program provided up to $12,000 per employee for training assistance, much more than is available in even the most intensive of WIA services.

23. Julie Conelly, "As Industrial Jobs Decline, Training Programs Grow," *New York Times*, January 30, 2001, A6. Even in well-funded programs with generous benefits, it is unclear what careers participants can retrain for. Conelly's account highlights two individual success stories of steelworkers. One went back to school to get a degree in labor studies (laudable but of limited market value), and the other found a job as a job training specialist.

24. "Demand Drops for Tech Workers," *Eugene Register-Guard*, April 2, 2001, 2A. Mary Anne Ostrom, "Labor Chief Wants to Review Visa Program for Skilled Workers," *San Jose Mercury-News*, April 15, 2001.

25. Chao, "Statement before the Subcommittee," May 2, 2001; "Jobless Rate at 4.3 Percent; Payrolls Plunge around the Nation," *San Francisco Examiner*, April 9, 2001, A13.

26. Quoted in U.S. Department of Labor, Office of Public Affairs, press release, "Statement of Labor Secretary Elaine L. Chao regarding the Unemployment Situation," April 6, 2001.

27. *All Things Considered*, April 23, 2001.

28. United States Conference of Mayors, press release, "Conference Initiative Addresses Skills Gap in the Workforce," March 20, 2001, http://www.uscm.org.

29. Laura Meckler, "Drop in Welfare Rolls Appears Bottomed Out," *Eugene Register-Guard*, April 4, 2001, 1A.

30. In part, public administrators began speculating that the most employable welfare recipients had already left the rolls, and those left might need more intensive services before they could enter the workforce. As President Bush explained, "The easy cases have already left the welfare rolls. The hardest problems remain—people with far fewer skills and greater barriers to work." George W. Bush, "Remarks by the President in Commencement Address, University of Notre Dame." In fact, it is not clear that those receiving welfare in 2001—or those likely to return to the rolls in the face of recession—are particularly in need of skills training. However, if a work-first strategy fails to find jobs for welfare recipients in a weak economy, elected officials may face a choice: either openly force poor people to go without any means of subsistence, or concede that the only thing these people lack is the money to support their families, and take responsibility for providing public jobs or higher benefit levels for them. In this context, the return to a more training-based policy, together with the designation of those remaining on the rolls as "hard to employ," may provide officials with a legitimate means of limiting both benefits and real jobs programs for the poor.

31. Ralph Ranalli, "Swift Wants New Rules on Welfare: Would Change Requirements on Work, School," *Boston Globe*, April 30, 2001, A1.

32. U.S. General Accounting Office, *Welfare Reform: Moving Hard-to-Employ Recipients into the Workforce*, Report GAO-01-368 (Washington, D.C.: U.S. General Accounting Office, 2001), 18–19.

33. Stephen Freedman, "The National Evaluation of Welfare-to-Work Strategies: Four-Year Impacts of Ten Programs on Employment Stability and Earnings Growth," report prepared for U.S. Department of Health and Human Services and U.S. Department of Education, Office of Vocational and Adult Education, Manpower Demonstration Research Corporation, New York, N.Y., 2000, 4.

34. See, for instance, Julie Strawn and Karin Martinson, *Steady Work and Better Jobs: How to Help Low-Income Parents Sustain Employment and Advance in the Workforce* (New York: Manpower Demonstration Research Corporation, 2000), 4. The authors offer eight proposals for "promoting access to better jobs"; six of these relate to education and training, stressing that "for the majority of low-income parents, the ability to move into better jobs will depend on access to effective skill upgrading services."

35. Julie Strawn, Mark Greenberg, and Steve Savner, "Improving Employment Outcomes under TANF," Center for Law and Social Policy, Washington, D.C., January 2001, 8. Emphasis added.

36. Orson Scott Card, *The Memory of Earth* (New York: Tor Books, 1992).

37. Nancy Cleeland, "L.A. Janitors OK Contract in Landmark Vote," *Los Angeles Times*, April 25, 2000, A1; Service Employees International Union, "Justice for Janitors 2000: Nationwide Campaign Produces Year of Life-Changing Victories," http://www.justiceforjanitors.org.

38. For discussion of a similar set of economic prescriptions, see Edward N. Wolff, "The Rich Get Richer . . . and Why the Poor Don't," *American Prospect* 12 (February 12, 2001): 3.

39. David Card and Alan B. Krueger, *Myth and Measurement: The New Economics of the Minimum Wage* (Princeton: Princeton University Press, 1995).

Appendix A

1. Patricia Ruggles, *Drawing the Line: Alternative Poverty Measures and Their Implications for Public Policy* (Washington, D.C.: Urban Institute Press, 1990), 49.

2. John Schwarz and Thomas Volgy, *The Forgotten Americans* (New York: Norton, 1992), 42.

3. Trudi Renwick and Barbara Bergmann, "A Budget-Based Definition of Poverty: With an Application to Single-Parent Families," *Journal of Human Resources* 28, no. 1 (1992): table 2.

4. Ruggles, *Drawing the Line*, 43.

5. Daniel Weinberg and Enrique Lamas, "Some Experimental Results on Alternate Poverty Measures," in *Proceedings of the Social Statistics Section, 1993* (Washington, D.C.: American Statistical Association, 1994), 549–55. The figures cited here are slightly higher than those published by Weinberg and Lamas. Their calculations are based on a food share of "roughly 20 percent," despite the fact that their citation records a food share of 17%. I have recalculated their methodology using the 17% figure. In conversation with Weinberg, he agreed that these figures were more accurate, the original figures having been presented as a general estimate.

6. Paul Kleppner and Nikolas Theodore, *Work after Welfare: Is the Midwest's Booming Economy Creating Enough Jobs?* (Chicago: Midwest Job Gap Project, 1997), 9, specify a "livable wage" budget of $25,907 for a family of three. The official 1997 threshold for a family of three was $12,802.

7. U.S. Department of Commerce, Census Bureau, *1990 Census of Population and Housing: Summary Social, Economic, and Housing Characteristics, United States* (Washington, D.C.: U.S. Government Printing Office, 1992), table 4, 185.

8. U.S. Department of Labor, Bureau of Labor Statistics, *Occupational Projections and Training Data 1984* (Washington, D.C.: U.S. Government Printing Office, 1984), table B-1.

Appendix B

1. Fred Romero, "The JTPA National Study: Lessons Not Learned," memorandum of April 11, 1993, 1. Romero represented the Department of Labor in designing the National JTPA Study in 1985–86.

2. Howard Bloom et al., *The National JTPA Study: Title II-A Impacts on Earnings and Employment at 18 Months* (Washington D.C.: U.S. Department of Labor, 1993), appendix F.

3. Larry L. Orr et al., *The National JTPA Study: Impacts, Benefits and Costs of Title II Year-Round Programs: A Report to the U.S. Department of Labor* (Bethesda, Md.: Abt Associates, March 1994), exhibit 6.9. (Hereafter cited as Orr et al., *National JTPA Study Final Report.*)

4. Ibid., exhibit 4.17.

5. Bloom et al., *National JTPA Study at 18 Months*, xliv.

6. Larry Orr, telephone interview with the author, April 11, 1994.

7. Orr et al., *National JTPA Study Final Report*, exhibits 5.1, 5.3.

8. Romero, "Lessons Not Learned," 3. Larry Orr, director of the national study, explains that the receipt of other services by control group members is an unavoidable reality, and therefore that those overseeing the study both at Abt Associates and at the Labor Department assumed from the outset that the report would focus on the incremental impact of JTPA compared to control group services. I believe that Romero's characterization more accurately captures congressional intent in mandating a study to measure JTPA's effects on the employment, earnings, and welfare dependency of participants.

9. Orr et al., *National JTPA Study Final Report*, exhibit 4.2.

10. Ibid., 161.

INDEX

and race and gender discrimination, 95–96
structure compared to CETA, 89, 117
training services offered, 89–90, 93
JOBSTART, 109, 235
Johnson and Johnson, 71
Johnston, William, 55
Jones, Reginald, 182
Judy, Richard, 249 n. 30

Karoly, Lynn, 49–50
Kennedy, Edward, 158, 168, 175, 279 n. 110
King, Martin Luther, Jr., 1
Kleppner, Paul, 225
Kodak, 150–151
Krueger, Alan, 54–55

Labor law reform, 80, 223, 280 n. 125
Lamas, Enrique, 225
Leidner, Robin, 262 n. 52, 267 n. 27
Lein, Laura, 286 nns. 42–43, 287 n. 69
Leslie Fay, 80
Levi Strauss, 80, 145, 214
Levitan, Sar, 28
Levitt, Martin Jay, 153, 269 n. 69, 270 n. 79
Levy, Frank, 65–66, 72, 252 n. 60
Los Angeles Jobs-First GAIN, 112, 196, 204, 206–207
Los Angeles riots (1992), 12, 158

Manpower Demonstration Research Corporation, 112, 218, 262 n. 57
Maquiladoras, 71, 80–81, 255 nns. 94–95
Matloff, Norman, 242 n. 12, 250 n. 34
McDonald's, 132–136
McNeill, Patricia, 277 n. 79
McQuaid, Kim, 274 nns. 25, 30, 275 n. 31
Mead, Lawrence, 243 n. 23
Medoff, James, 252 n. 64
Michael, Robert, 244 n. 38
Microsoft, 140, 255 n. 104, 270 n. 78
Milberg, William, 253 n. 72
Military, as model for job training, 73, 167, 255 n. 102, 276 n. 58
Minimum wage
and business lobbies, 167, 257 n. 133
real value of, 81–82
violations, 71, 258 n. 138
Mishel, Lawrence, 249 n. 28
Mollenkopf, John, 171
Morris, Dick, 193, 283 n. 10
Moss, Philip, 66, 74
Mucciaroni, Gary, 174
Murnane, Richard, 65–66, 72, 252 n. 60
Murray, Charles, 275 n. 39

A Nation at Risk, 51
National Alliance of Business, 70, 160, 180, 281 n. 130

National Association of Manufacturers, 116, 162
employment policy, 141, 167, 276 n. 62, 280 n. 129, 281 n. 145
history, 180, 182
National Center for the Educational Quality of the Workforce, 66, 70, 72
National Federation of Independent Businesses, 257 n. 133, 273 n. 25
National JTPA Study, 101–102, 118, 158, 262 n. 57
National Labor Relations Board, 80, 162, 274 n. 30
National League of Cities, 165, 278 n. 89
National Tooling and Machining Association, 160, 273 n. 23
National Urban League, 165, 278 n. 89
Nike, 80
Nixon, Richard M., 17, 174, 180
North American Free Trade Agreement (NAFTA), 213, 217, 256 n. 123, 289 n. 22
Northwest Airlines, 150
NYNEX, 288 n. 14

Occupational Safety and Health Administration (OSHA), 172, 179
bathroom policy, 139
and Reagan appointees, 162, 274 n. 30
O'Neill, Tip, 169
On the-job training, and fraud, 99–101, 262 n. 54
Opportunities Industrialization Centers, 165, 278 n. 89
Orfield, Gary, 96
Orr, Larry, 234
Orshansky, Mollie, 27–29

Packer, Arnold, 55
Panetta, Leon, 194
Perkins, Carl, 168
Personal Responsibility and Work Opportunity Reconciliation Act (PRWORA)
and Clinton, 192–195
and job training, 190–191, 196, 204
Phillips-Van Heusen, 80
Polaroid, 141–142
Poverty line, 27–31
Pratt & Whitney, 12
Primus, Wendell, 284 n. 18
Prison labor
corporations using, 255 n. 104, 268 n. 36
and work ethic, 73–74, 271 n. 82
Private Industry Councils
authority under JTPA, 89, 93, 282 n. 158
business support for, 179–184, 288 n. 19
community organizations in, 176
Private Sector Initiative Program, 160, 179–181, 280 n. 116
Project STRIVE, 208

Pryor, Frederic, 252 n. 50
Public service employment
  elimination of, 162–172, 278 nn. 86, 89
Punctuality
  employer demand for, 68–69
  as skill, 75–76

Quayle, Dan, 156–158, 177–178, 189, 266 n. 5,
  279 nn. 92, 110, 282 n. 158

Race discrimination, 83–84, 162, 258 n. 140,
  274 n. 30
Radisson Hotels, 262 n. 54
Reagan, Ronald W.
  and CETA, 156, 164
  and defederalism, 91, 187, 275 n. 44, 279 n. 98
  and employment policy, 159, 167, 174
  and National Labor Relations Board, 80, 162,
    274 n. 30
  and race discrimination, 83, 162, 258 n. 140,
    274 n. 30
  and support for JTPA, 94, 156, 187
  and welfare, 167, 173
Reed, Bruce, 284 n. 14
Reengineering the Corporation, 124, 150, 267 n.
  19
Reich, Robert, 128–130, 192, 194, 212, 267 n. 9,
  288 n. 6
Renwick, Trudi, 225
Rivera-Batiz, Francisco, 253 n. 74
Rubin, Robert, 194
Ruggles, Patricia, 225

Schaffer, David, 252 n. 60
Schein, Virginia, 286 n. 43
Schwarz, John, 28, 225, 245 n. 40
Secretary of Labor's Commission on Achieving
  Necessary Skills (SCANS), 45, 129
Self-esteem, 208
Shalala, Donna, 194
Shaw, Clay, 198
Shor, Ira, 208
Simon, Paul, 174
Skill shortages
  in congressional JTPA testimony, 41, 53, 55,
    86
  in employer surveys, 67–69, 256 n. 110, 273 n.
    23
  in high-tech industries, 41, 53–55, 242 n. 12,
    250 n. 34, 251 nn. 44–46
Slessarev, Helene, 96
Smith, Vicki, 268 n. 44
Soft skills, 66, 72–73, 267 n. 26–27
Sprint, 145, 153, 271 n. 99
Starbucks, 255 n. 104
Stephanopoulos, George, 194
Stewart, Thomas, 57, 62

Stockman, David, 164–165, 186, 282 n. 150
Sullivan, Leon, 165, 278 n. 89
Summer Training and Education Program
  (STEP), 109
Sun Microsystems, 71
Swift, Jane, 218

Teamwork
  and prison labor, 74, 271 n. 82
  and union busting, 152–154
Teixeira, Ruy, 249 n. 28
Temporary Assistance to Needy Families
  (TANF)
  and discipline, 208–209
  and job training, 196, 289 n. 30
  and welfare rolls, 198, 217, 285 n. 31
  and workfare, 190, 192, 196
  and work-first, 200, 216–217
Temporary workers, 82
Theodore, Nikolas, 225
Thompson, Tommy, 198–199, 202, 204
Tilly, Chris, 66, 74
Total Quality Management, 7, 125–129
Toyota, 262 n. 54
Trade Adjustment Assistance, 109, 167, 172,
  289 n. 22
Training, 254 n. 85
Turner, Jason, 287 n. 68
TWA, 255 n. 104, 268 n. 36
Tyson Foods, 201

Unemployment insurance, 167, 276 n. 54
  and business lobbies, 276 n. 62, 277 n. 63
Union busting, 80, 139, 153–154, 269 n. 69,
  270 n. 79
Unions, labor, 17, 79–80, 139, 256 n. 123, 257 n.
  128, 274 n. 30
  impact on wages, 77–79, 220–222, 256 n.
    118
  unorganized workers' desire for, 79, 256 n.
    120
  and workfare workers, 203
United Parcel Service, 145
University of California at Los Angeles, 151
Urban Institute, 194
U.S. Chamber of Commerce, 70, 116
  and 1980 elections, 162, 274 nn. 26–28
  and employer demand for skills, 166, 273 n.
    23
  and employment policy, 141, 160, 182–183,
    257 n. 133, 276 n. 54
  history of, 180, 273 n. 25
U.S. Conference of Mayors
  and employment policy, 25, 158
  and public service employment, 165, 171,
    278 nn. 86, 89
  and welfare reform, 199

U.S. Department of Labor
  fragmentation of training authority, 119
  JTPA oversight, 98

Volgy, Thomas, 28

Weastec, 271 n. 82
Weinberg, Daniel, 225
Weintraub, Jon, 272 n. 6
Weiss, Ted, 175, 279 n. 99
Welch, Jack, 149–150, 271 nn. 82–83
Welfare-to-work programs, 14–15
  and discipline, 206–209
  impact of training, 110–112, 265 n. 98
Wells, Donald, 143, 271 n. 96
Westinghouse, 71
Willett, John, 253 n. 74
Wilson, Pete, 197
Winn-Dixie, 267 n. 26
Wolff, Edward, 84, 253 n. 72

Work ethic
  employer demand for, 256 n. 110, 276 n. 54
  impact on wages, 74
Workfare
  compared to public service jobs, 168, 286 n. 51
  Reagan policy, 167, 173
  and TANF, 190–192, 286 n. 56
Workforce 2000 report, 22, 34, 52–53, 61–62, 249 nn. 28–30, 250 n. 35
Workforce Investment Act (WIA), 121, 217
  population served, 96, 114, 213
  training services offered, 89, 113, 119
World Trade Organization, 80

Xerox, 145, 148

Yale University, 12, 142, 269 n. 64
York University, 152
Young, Kenneth, 1